The Unhappy Divorce of Sociology and Psychoanalysis

CW00954310

Studies in the Psychosocial

Edited by **Peter Redman,** The Open University, UK Stephen Frosh, Centre for Psychosocial Studies, Birkbeck College, University of London, UK and Wendy Hollway, The Open University, UK

Titles include:

Lynn Chancer and John Andrews (*editors*)
THE UNHAPPY DIVORCE OF SOCIOLOGY AND PSYCHOANALYSIS
Diverse Perspectives on the Psychosocial

Stephen Frosh
HAUNTINGS: PSYCHOANALYSIS AND GHOSTLY TRANSMISSIONS

Uri Hadar
PSYCHOANALYSIS AND SOCIAL INVOLVEMENT
Interpretation and Action

James S. Ormrod
FANTASY AND SOCIAL MOVEMENTS

Margarita Palacios
RADICAL SOCIALITY
On Disobedience, Violence and Belonging

Derek Hook
(POST) APARTHEID CONDITIONS
Psychoanalysis and Social Formation

Gath Stevens, Norman Duncan and Derek Hook (*editors*)
RACE, MEMORY AND THE APARTHEID ARCHIVE
Towards a Transformative Psychosocial Praxis

Irene Bruna Seu
PASSIVITY GENERATION
Human Rights and Everyday Morality

Kate Kenny and Marianna Fotaki (*editors*)
THE PSYCHOSOCIAL AND ORGANIZATION STUDIES
Affect at Work

Studies in the Psychosocial Series
Series Standing Order ISBN 978–0–230–30858–9 (hardback)
978–0–230–30859–6 (paperback)
(outside North America only)

You can receive future titles in this series as they are published by placing a standing order. Please contact your bookseller or, in case of difficulty, write to us at the address below with your name and address, the title of the series and the ISBNs quoted above.

Customer Services Department, Macmillan Distribution Ltd, Houndmills, Basingstoke, Hampshire RG21 6XS, England

---

The Unhappy Divorce of Sociology and Psychoanalysis

Diverse Perspectives on the Psychosocial

Edited by

Lynn Chancer and John Andrews
Hunter College and the Graduate Center of the City University of New York, USA

Selection, introduction and editorial matter © Lynn Chancer and John Andrews 2014

Individual chapters © Respective authors 2014

Foreword © Craig Calhoun 2014

Preface © Jeffrey Alexander 2014

All rights reserved. No reproduction, copy or transmission of this publication may be made without written permission.

No portion of this publication may be reproduced, copied or transmitted save with written permission or in accordance with the provisions of the Copyright, Designs and Patents Act 1988, or under the terms of any licence permitting limited copying issued by the Copyright Licensing Agency, Saffron House, 6–10 Kirby Street, London EC1N 8TS.

Any person who does any unauthorized act in relation to this publication may be liable to criminal prosecution and civil claims for damages.

The authors have asserted their rights to be identified as the authors of this work in accordance with the Copyright, Designs and Patents Act 1988.

First published 2014 by
PALGRAVE MACMILLAN

Palgrave Macmillan in the UK is an imprint of Macmillan Publishers Limited, registered in England, company number 785998, of Houndmills, Basingstoke, Hampshire RG21 6XS.

Palgrave Macmillan in the US is a division of St Martin's Press LLC, 175 Fifth Avenue, New York, NY 10010.

Palgrave Macmillan is the global academic imprint of the above companies and has companies and representatives throughout the world.

Palgrave® and Macmillan® are registered trademarks in the United States, the United Kingdom, Europe and other countries.

ISBN 978–1–137–30456–8 hardback
ISBN 978–1–137–30457–5 paperback

This book is printed on paper suitable for recycling and made from fully managed and sustained forest sources. Logging, pulping and manufacturing processes are expected to conform to the environmental regulations of the country of origin.

A catalogue record for this book is available from the British Library.

A catalog record for this book is available from the Library of Congress.

Typeset by MPS Limited, Chennai, India.

Contents

List of Figures and Tables

Figures

Table

Foreword

Psychoanalysis and sociology took shape about the same time. Both were influenced by an extraordinary late nineteenth and early twentieth century combination of intellectual ferment and consolidation of disciplines as well as by the Enlightenment and Romanticism, moral philosophy and modern science, German idealism, and much more materialistic thought. Both understood themselves as transforming previous intellectual approaches through systematic empirical inquiry.

Surely, there were also differences. Sociology developed from roots in social movements and broad, largely extra-academic intellectual currents like the intersection of evolutionary thought and progressive reform. It moved into universities during the 1890s and gained relative stability as a discipline alongside others in social science. Psychoanalysis developed in quasi-academic medical circles, with roots in a long history of clinics and hospitals for the insane as well as private treatment. But it remained mostly outside universities, maintaining its separate training and intellectual circles in autonomous institutes even after the rest of medical education was absorbed more fully into universities.

Psychoanalysis had a more individual and temporally compact origin in the work of Freud and the intellectual milieu of fin-de-siècle Vienna. Sociologists should be careful, though, not to exaggerate the myth of heroic individual invention. From Charcot and Bleuler through the range of participants in early psychoanalysis who fell outside efforts to maintain orthodoxy—Adler, Jung, and Reich—we should recognize the contributions of the wider range of thinkers, researchers, and therapists. This is not simply a matter of fairness but of grasping that powerful as was the heritage of Freud, psychoanalysis had many innovators and very quickly established roots in different settings.

Sociology had no singular inventor even if Comte coined the word. Arguably the main traditions were German, French, and American, with heroic founder figures in Weber, Durkheim, and the Chicago School. But within each national school, variations and arguments were and have remained as sharp as in psychoanalysis: Tarde against Durkheim in France; the conventional sociology of the German Sociological Association against Weber's call for value-neutrality in Germany; and Parsonian functionalism against the Chicago School in the US. And cutting across these was the Marxist tradition that influenced a variety of schools of sociological thought, not all explicitly Marxist though. Indeed, psychoanalysis and sociology were both shaped by tensions between engagement in social change and sometimes movements and projects of establishing scientific autonomy.

Most dramatically, psychoanalysis pursued the depths of individual personality and character. Sociology commonly set itself against individualism and indeed against psychology. The contrast is real, and it is one of the reasons why the present volume is a useful effort in building bridges. But of course the disjuncture should not be overstated. Psychoanalysis examined social relations, especially in the family, as sources of individual psychology, and Freud and others extended psychoanalytic thinking to explore broad social questions. Sociology contributed to interdisciplinary social psychology and, in a few cases, tried to understand individuals not just oppose individualism. There have also been advocates for methodological individualism but this is not a matter of following leads from psychoanalysis.

Most methodological individualism in fact takes individuals to be rather simple and unitary, decision-making bundles of interests and preferences. The theorists in question do not necessarily say individuals *are* quite so simple. Rather, some acknowledge that simplifying assumptions are merely required to make the models work. But the issue is an important one for sociology more generally, well beyond methodological individualism. In its repeated efforts to demonstrate the power and quasi-autonomy of the social, sociology risks neglecting the complexity of individuals. This can take the form of what Dennis Wrong called, in the era of functionalism, an "oversocialized concept of man." It can take the form of imagining that individual action is shaped by consistent interests rather than contradictory desires. It can take the form of forgetting that nodes in seemingly stable networks are in fact highly volatile shapers of relationships.

Psychoanalysis offers sociology one path for grasping the interior space and complexity of individuals. This is partly a matter of attending to exceptionally influential and intense social life that helps to shape individual persons in families and other close relationships. Psychoanalysis is not only an exploration of individual sources—of a purely interior life. It addresses the interaction of the internal and external in experience, affect, memory, and learning. Psychoanalytic approaches vary in their attention to the social shaping of the person—and some emphasize innate predispositions and the very earliest experiences more than others. Still ego-analysis, object-relations, and the interpersonal analysis of Harry Stack Sullivan and Karen Horney are centrally focused on social persons; for all its differences, Lacanian approaches also stress a self forged in relation to an external world of symbols and language as well as experience—that is, a self that is not purely innate.

Still, for most of the psychoanalysts, the social world is rather simpler than for sociologists. That psychoanalytic research is so tied to individual depth-psychological therapy is one reason. Even if external sources are identified, the focus remains on intra-psychic phenomena. Psychoanalysis explores the family in enormous detail though largely through emotionally charged (or repressed) memory rather than other sorts of evidence. But society beyond the family tends to appear somewhat schematically. There is often a leap from the microsocial to culture at large. Even the important theme of how families, and thus the experience and formation of persons, are shaped by class, community, or cross-cultural variation is commonly in the background of attention. The very historical and social specificity of the notion of individual is at best unevenly taken up.

Nonetheless, if the emphases of sociology and psychoanalysis seem poles apart, fruitful connections and integrations have occurred. Early analytic approaches to "character" shaped a whole field of research on personality and socialization that grew in an era when social psychology was a stronger bridge between the disciplines of sociology and psychology than at present. This bridging produced work that not only influenced each academic field but fed back into psychoanalytic thinking. The same can be said about work on culture and personality though anthropologists were more at the center than sociologists. Studies of small groups were another area of strong and fruitful interaction, though again somewhat faded from the center of sociological attention today. Some of this work was linked to London's Tavistock Institute that became a center not only for the object-relations approach to psychoanalysis but for new and partially analytically inspired approaches to bureaucracy and organizations from Elliot Jacques to Eric Miller and A.K. Rice. Critical theorists drew not only on psychoanalysis but also contributed studies like *The Authoritarian Personality*. Talcott Parsons published in *Psychiatry*, the journal of the William Alonson White Institute that was at the center of the "interpersonal" movement in psychoanalysis. The influence of Lacan on poststructuralism was enormous. And feminist theory became a central zone where psychoanalysis and sociology influenced each other and new thought influenced both in diverse perspectives from Luce Irigaray to Nancy Chodorow to Juliet Mitchell.

Still, as the editors of the present book suggest, there is something of an unfulfilled promise in the relationship—a much greater potential than actually realized one. The book brings together accounts of the relationship, each finding a different balance among past success and underexplored possibilities. It also contains helpful discussions of directions the relationship might take now—in life-history research, for example, or the study of violence. It explores topics that demand attention to both social and personal levels of complexity from social movements to race and racism and the affective issues of immigration politics. It is appropriate and helpful that chapters explore their authors' personal experience of engaging in both sociology and psychoanalysis. This is all the more interesting where contributors are both sociologists and analysts (since, to paraphrase Gardner Lindzey, some of the best interdisciplinary relationships are formed in individual minds). But, of course, Lindzey also encouraged interdisciplinary teams and collaborations, and it would be nice to see more of each.

Some of the authors in this book are more optimistic about future relations between psychoanalysis and sociology than others; some see a renewal underway. If this is so, it may be ironically because psychoanalysis has moved more into universities (often into humanities fields) at the same time that it has seen its influence in psychiatry and psychotherapy decline in much of the world. To be really optimistic perhaps we should look to settings like Argentina where psychoanalysis has not only thrived but became woven into the very fabric of public life and culture as did both social science and psychiatry. But as this volume makes clear, we can also look to some impressive historical precedents, and some very interesting contemporary examples. Psychoanalysis and sociology made sharply distinct claims on the modern sensibility but they take up common interests nevertheless, offering each other sources of new insight and inspiration.

Craig Calhoun
Professor, London School of Economics

Preface

This volume explores the marginalization of psychoanalytic thinking in contemporary sociology, a problem well known but badly understood and deeply incongruous. Sigmund Freud was one of the most original and compelling social thinkers of the twentieth century. He opened up the emotional dynamics and cultural strains of modern life as brilliantly as Max Weber, explored symbolism and solidarity as ingeniously as Emile Durkheim, and in his capacity for conceptual elaboration and theoretical complexity surpassed them. No modern social thinker has created theory at once as systematic or as dynamic as Freud.

For contemporary sociology to have marginalized such work of genius, not to mention the century of psychoanalytic theorizing that followed in its wake, represents a grievous mistake. Some essays in this volume represent felicitous efforts at remediation. Others provide explanations of why this intellectual impoverishment has occurred.

Sociology understands itself as an aggregative science, moving downward from collective social fact to individual explanation. Psychoanalysis is disaggregating, moving upward from individual motives to collective action. Efforts from either tradition to gain access to the fruits of the other have often been reductive, sociologists awkwardly professing to explain individual motives via social structures, psychoanalysts interpreting social forces via individual emotions and drives.

To provide conceptual integration across this great divide would require a second Freud or another Weber, following up on the pioneering initial steps Parsons took half a century ago. The best efforts to cross the chasm, exemplified in many of the following contributions, have built bridges in more modest and piecemeal ways. Placing this part of the psychoanalytic edifice with that piece of sociological architecture, many deeply original and counter-intuitive sociological insights have emerged. Eric Fromm, Theodor Adorno, Eric Erickson, Neil Smelser, and Nancy Chodorow (and Parsons in his empirical model)—each of these psychoanalytic-cum-sociological thinkers produced problem-oriented investigations and theories that proved highly persuasive to contemporary colleagues.

Such brilliant chasm crossings have been the exception not the rule. The reason is that sociologists have tended to conflate supra-individual, collective patterning with objective and impersonal social force. To correct this mistake, sociology needs to recognize not only the social in the individual but the individual in the social. Patterns and structures can be collective, deeply emotional, and subjectively meaningful all at the same time.

Culture is patterned emotion. Emotion is culture experienced. Sociology examines emotions writ large. Psychoanalysis studies societies writ small. If the social is subjective, then a meaning-centered sociologist must learn to speak with the listening voice of the psychoanalyst, to employ the same hermeneutic method of deep interpretation, and to read structures of social feeling as imaginatively as psychotherapists read individual-feeling texts.

Jeffrey C. Alexander
Professor, Yale University

Acknowledgments

Not unlike its subject matter, this book has a long and varied genealogy. It emerges from and gives concretized form to the workings of a small reading group started over 20 years ago by Catherine Silver and Lynn Chancer, and is still "in business." The purpose of "our little group," as we have fondly referred to it, has been to bring together people interested in, and doing research on, both the social/sociological and psychic/psychoanalytic dimensions of diverse topics. In common, we gave each other intellectual and emotional support since the larger field we value in many important respects (sociology) has for decades not encouraged, but tended to marginalize, explicitly psychosocial endeavors. Although the people in our psychosocial reading group changed and evolved over the years, it has fulfilled this purpose admirably, amply, for and beyond its "core" participants. Years ago, we met at the West Village apartment of Columbia-trained sociologist and psychoanalyst Suzanne Schad-Somers, whose hospitality before she sadly and prematurely passed away has continued on the Upper West Side in George Cavalletto's apartment. For people who attend regularly, and even for those who drop in and out, George's generous provision of food and his fantastic ("renowned," at least for us) cappuccinos have contributed to memorable afternoons and evenings of readings and excellent conversation, laughter, and a more open-minded, genuinely wide-ranging sense of intellectuality and theoretical sophistication than many of us were encountering elsewhere. Without Catherine's and George's inspiring intelligence and warmth—key "psychosocial" elements of the group's longevity—this book would not be possible.

And, thus, we dedicate *The Unhappy Divorce of Sociology and Psychoanalysis* not only to George and Catherine but to "our little group" as a whole. For whether long-time members or one-time "guests" (including a few clinicians, Catherine among them, and now Patricia Clough in-training), this meeting place has consistently provided a meaningful forum for exchange and debate traversing disciplinary boundaries. We apologize in advance for anyone this brief list omits to mention, but collective credit for this volume's existence simultaneously belongs with both usual and "dropping in" scholars too: with Arlene Stein, Tom DeGloma, Joshua Klein, Dena Smith, Micki McGee, Vikash Singh, Alan Roland, Ilgin Yorukoglu, Tony Jefferson (sometimes, when in from the UK), Doyle McCarthy (when in from Fordham), Stanley Aronowitz and Christina Nadler, among others. Members of our group have also assisted in organizing and participating in one-day mini-conferences on Psychoanalysis and Sociology now approaching quasi-institutionalized status themselves: 2014 marks the fifth pre-ASA mini-conference on this theme. Organized by Lynn Chancer and Lauren Langman, the mini-conferences provide a wider, national space for sociologists to discuss the social-and-psychic character of culture in and outside the US. To Lauren, too, special and sincere thanks for his major intellectual and organizational help in making these at once intellectual, political, and sociological mini-conferences happen and grow. Thanks, too, to ongoing participants in the mini-conferences including Harried Fraad, David Smith, Neil McLaughlin, Fred Alford, sometimes Gary Alan Fine—among many others not named whose participation is nonetheless greatly valued—for bringing these mini-conferences alive with their psychosocial passions and interesting contributions.

Others merit equally grateful acknowledging. Hardly can we leave out the sociologists and analysts from a range of subfields—from graduate students to senior professors—whose essays in this collection make the volume, we believe, a unique contribution. Enormous thanks to the series editors, Wendy Hollway, Peter Redman, and Stephen Frosh, for putting together a psychosocial book series and for your interest in including a volume primarily (though not exclusively) US-oriented. Your comments and support have been invaluable. To Sasha Roseneil, thank you for your role, along with Wendy and Peter, in building intellectual and institutional support in the UK about the significance and persuasiveness of psychosocial endeavors (as we have been trying, analogously, to do in the US). At Palgrave Macmillan, Libby Forrest and Nicola Jones have been wonderfully patient, intelligent, and helpful—both efficient, and enjoyable—to work with throughout the book's evolution into print. Hardly least, many thanks also to Graduate Center research assistant extraordinaire Kevin Moran. Kevin's careful and extremely smart editorial and administrative assistance have been invaluable in the last stages of this book's completion (and through the psychosocial ASA mini-conferences as well), as has been his willingness to work long hours and committedly stick with the many ups-and-downs of keeping track of over twenty varied contributions at all stages of the production process. He has assisted with the book intellectually as well, and we are very grateful for his support and clear understanding of this volume's underlying motivations.

For, when all is said and done, the purpose of this volume—and the superb group of original essays it contains—is to have an effect, to legitimize diverse modes and applications of psychosocial analyses both theoretically and methodologically, and to nudge the US field into giving multi-dimensionality the consideration it, too, deserves. If we succeed in getting sociology to give psychoanalysis another look, and a better chance, we will feel the effort to have been worthwhile indeed.

Notes on Contributors

Jeffrey Alexander is the Lillian Chavenson Saden Professor of Sociology and Co-Director of the Center for Cultural Sociology at Yale University, USA. Among his recent books are *Performance and Power* (2011), *Trauma: A Social Theory* (2012), *The Dark Side of Modernity* (2013), and *Obama Power* (with Bernadette Jaworsky, 2014).

John Andrews teaches sociology at Hunter College and Fordham University in New York City, USA. He has published most recently in the journals *Women and Performance* and *Social Text*, and is currently completing a book manuscript exploring the confluence of collective moods and the economy in American culture and politics.

George Cavalletto is an adjunct professor at Brooklyn and Hunter Colleges, City University of New York, USA. His particular interests include the intellectual history of social theory. He is the author of *Crossing the Psycho-Social Divide: Freud, Weber, Adorno, and Elias* (2007).

Lynn Chancer is Professor of Sociology at Hunter College and the Graduate Center of the City University of New York, USA. She has written four books and many articles on a variety of topics related to social theory, gender, crime, and deviance including *Sadomasochism in Everyday Life: Dynamics of Power and Powerlessness* (1992), *Reconcilable Differences: Confronting Beauty, Pornography and the Future of Feminism* (1998), and *High Profile Crimes: When Legal Cases Become Social Causes* (2005).

Nancy J. Chodorow is Professor Emerita of Sociology at the University of California, Berkeley; Lecturer on Psychiatry, Harvard Medical School, Cambridge Health Alliance; and a Training and Supervising Analyst at the Boston Psychoanalytic Society and Institute. Her books include *The Reproduction of Mothering* (1978; 2nd ed., 1999); *Feminism and Psychoanalytic Theory* (1989); *Femininities, Masculinities, Sexualities: Freud and Beyond* (1994); *The Power of Feelings: Personal Meaning in Psychoanalysis, Gender, and Culture* (1999); and *Individualizing Gender and Sexuality: Theory and Practice* (2012). She has authored many articles on comparative psychoanalytic theory and technique, Loewald, and the Loewaldian tradition. Nancy Chodorow is in private practice in Cambridge, MA.

Thomas DeGloma is Assistant Professor of Sociology at Hunter College, City University of New York, USA, where he specializes in the areas of culture, cognition, memory, symbolic interaction, and sociological theory. His forthcoming book is titled *Seeing the Light: On the Social Logic of Personal Discovery*. DeGloma has published articles in *Social Psychology Quarterly*, *Symbolic Interaction*, and *Sociological Forum* and is an associate editor of the journal *Symbolic Interaction*.

Anthony Elliott is Director of the Hawke Research Institute and Research Professor of Sociology at the University of South Australia. He has authored numerous books including *Reinvention* (2013), *On Society* (with Bryan Turner, 2012), *Mobile Lives* (with John Urry, 2010), *Deadly Worlds: The Emotional Costs of Globalization* (with Charles Lemert, 2006), *Social Theory since Freud* (2004), and *Concepts of the Self* (2001).

Tony Jefferson is Emeritus Professor of Criminology at Keele University, UK. He has also held visiting professorships in Sweden, Denmark, Australia, and the US. He has researched and published widely on topics including youth subculture, the media, policing, race and crime, masculinity, fear of crime and, most recently, racial violence. His published works include *Doing Qualitative Research Differently* 2nd ed. (with Wendy Hollway, 2013), *Policing the Crisis* 2nd ed. (with Stuart Hall et al., 2013), *Psychosocial Criminology* (with Dave Gadd, 2007), and *Resistance through Rituals* 2nd ed. (edited with Stuart Hall, 2006). Between 1999 and 2002, he was the British Editor of the journal *Theoretical Criminology*.

Philip Manning is Professor and Chair in the Department of Sociology and Criminology at Cleveland State University, USA. He has published two books: *Erving Goffman and Modern Sociology* (1992) and *Freud and American Sociology* (2005). His most recent paper is "Three Models of Ethnography" published in *Theory and Psychology* (2009).

Neil McLaughlin teaches sociological theory at McMasters University, Canada, and writes on critical theory, public intellectuals, and the sociology of ideas. He has written case studies on the Frankfurt School, Erich Fromm, David Riesman, George Orwell, Edward Said, and George Soros and is presently writing about sociology as well as about public intellectuals in Canada.

Siamak Movahedi is Professor of Sociology at the University of Massachusetts, Boston, USA. He is Training and Supervisory Analyst and the Director of the Institute for the Study of Psychoanalysis & Culture at the Boston Graduate School of Psychoanalysis. He has authored numerous works in major books and journals in Sociology, Psychology, and Psychoanalysis such as *American Sociological Review*, *American Imago*, *American Psychologist*, *Canadian Journal of Psychoanalysis*, *Comparative*

Studies in Society and History, Contemporary Psychoanalysis, Journal of the American Psychoanalytical Association, and the *International Journal of Psychoanalysis.*

Jeffrey Prager is Professor of Sociology at University of California, Los Angeles, USA, and Senior Faculty Member and Co-Dean of the New Center for Psychoanalysis, Los Angeles, USA. Prager is also in private practice in Beverly Hills. He has published widely in psychoanalytic sociology including his award-winning *Presenting the Past: Psychoanalysis and the Sociology of Misremembering* (1998) and several articles on trauma and social redress.

Catherine B. Silver is Emerita Professor of Sociology at Brooklyn College and at the City University of New York Graduate Center, USA. She has written books and articles on issues concerning the sociology of knowledge, women's careers, social identity, and ageing. Silver works from a cross-cultural and cross-disciplinary perspective. For years she taught a course on Psychoanalytic Sociology at the Graduate Center. She is now a psychoanalyst in private practice in Manhattan, a senior faculty member and a training analyst at the National Psychological Association for Psychoanalysis (NPAP). She has been teaching a course on Psychoanalysis and Culture. She wrote articles on paranoia among early sociologists and on womb envy. She is on the editorial board of *Psychoanalytic Review* and *The International Journal of Psychoanalysis.*

Vikash Singh was a PhD student at Rutgers University and from Fall 2014 he is Assistant Professor at Montclair State University, New Jersey. His research interests include religion, embodiment, everyday violence, social theory and phenomenology, caste and race, ethics, popular culture and aesthetics, and collective action. He has also worked on a number of projects on urban and rural poverty, homeless children, entitlements, and social movements in India. He has previously published in *Ethnography, Culture and Religion, Sociological Forum,* and *The International Journal of Zizek Studies.*

Neil J. Smelser has spent most of his academic career (1958–1994) in Sociology at the University of California, Berkeley. Between 1994 and 2001, he was Director of the Center for Advanced Study in the Behavioral Sciences at Stanford. His major works include *Economy and Society* (1956), *Social Change in the Industrial Revolution* (1959), *Theory of Collective Behavior* (1962), *Comparative Methods in the Social Sciences* (1976), *Social Paralysis and Social Change* (1991), *The Social Edges of Psychoanalysis* (1998), *The Social Faces of Terrorism* (2008), and *The*

Odyssey Experience (2008). In 2001 he co-edited, with Paul B. Baltes, the 26-volume *International Encyclopedia of the Social and Behavioral Sciences*. He has been recognized by election into the American Academy of Arts and Sciences, the American Philosophical Association, and the National Academy of Sciences. During 1996–1997, he served as President of the American Sociological Association, and in 2002 he received the first Mattei Dogan Award for a distinguished career in sociology from the International Sociological Association.

Arlene Stein is Professor of Sociology and serves on the graduate faculty of the Women and Gender Studies program at Rutgers University, USA. Her research interests include sexual politics, social movements, political culture, trauma, and collective memory. She is the author of three books: *Sex and Sensibility: Stories of a Lesbian Generation* (1997), *The Stranger Next Door* (2001), and *Shameless: Sexual Dissidence in American Culture* (2006). She is also the editor of two collections of essays, and received the Simon and Gagnon Award, from the American Sociological Association, for career contributions to the study of sexualities. Her book *Reluctant Witnesses: Telling Holocaust Stories in America* is forthcoming.

George Steinmetz is Professor of Sociology and German Studies at the University of Michigan, USA. He has written widely in the areas of historical sociology and culture. His work includes *Sociology and Empire: Colonial Studies and the Imperial Entanglements of a Discipline* (2011), and *The Devil's Handwriting: Precoloniality and the German Colonial State in Qingdao, Samoa and Southwest Africa* (2007). He has also written several articles relevant to this volume including "Bourdieu's Disavowal of Lacan: Psychoanalytic Theory and the Concepts of 'Habitus' and 'Symbolic Capital'" (in *Constellations*, 2006) and "'Toward Socioanalysis: On Psychoanalysis and Neo-Bourdieusian Theory" (in Phillip Gorski, ed. *Bourdieusian Theory and Historical Analysis*, 2011).

Ilgin Yorukoglu has an MA in Cultural Studies and a PhD in sociology from the Graduate Center, City University of New York, USA, and teaches sociology at the City College as well as at Fordham University, USA. Her current research investigates the relationship between coherence, belonging and the meaning of citizenship for an individual holding multiple identifications which seemingly conflict with each other.

Gilda Zwerman is Professor of Sociology at State University of New York, Old Westbury, USA. Her research interests include social movements, clandestine organizations, political violence, and African–American protest history. Her writings on these subjects have been published in *Protest Cultures, Mobilization, Qualitative Sociology, Feminist Review, International Social Movement Research, Feminist Review, Crime and Social Justice,* and *the Encyclopedia of Activism.* She is also the author of the *Biography of Martina Navratilova* (1995).

Introduction: The Unhappy Divorce: From Marginalization to Revitalization

Lynn Chancer and John Andrews

It seems fair to say that, in the mainstream of American sociology, psychoanalysis is often seen as outside the field's primary concerns. In 2014, many if not most contemporary scholars in the field are inclined to view the Freudian tradition suspiciously, and as beyond the purview of the "bread and butter" issues—including class, race and gender inequalities—that concern and frame the field in the US. The realms of the psychic and the psychoanalytic are perceived as too intent on prioritizing the individual and the individualized, the subjective and the sui generis, to be properly sociological; then, too, psychoanalytic methods and those of social scientific research tend to be seen as having little or nothing in common. As a result, in this second decade of the twenty-first century, graduate students and senior professors/advisers may hesitate before employing or encouraging the use of psychoanalytic concepts and tools in sociological research. Will this make one's work unacceptable or not sufficiently sociological by common standards? Then too, practically speaking, highlighting this strain of thought may make it harder—in a time period permeated with anxieties and scarcities—to find academic jobs on which people's livelihoods and fulfillment depend.

The purpose of this volume is to contend, though, that this marginalization of social/psychic approaches, especially those psychoanalytically oriented, is foolhardy: it bespeaks a premature jettisoning of the intellectual "baby with the bathwater." Instead, we argue that while some reasons for skepticism have been merited, perspectives that draw selectively on several major ideas emphasized in the psychoanalytic tradition—notably the individual and social unconscious, sexuality, emotions from anxiety to guilt, defense mechanisms of both individual and collective kinds, and recent developments in the study of

1

psychosocial affect (or 'the affective turn')—can offer fresh insights into stubborn, and worsening, psychosocial problems. Moreover in other places, like the UK, signs of renewed interest in the "psychosocial," including psychoanalysis, have led to the formation of a new psychosocial section (or "stream") within the British Sociological Association. At the very least, then, the relevance of psychoanalytic ideas to sociological theory is a line of inquiry meriting further exploration. The field limits its explanatory power by foreclosing concepts and tools from this tradition; rather, especially at this historical moment, willingness to explore psycho-social dimensions of understanding could contribute to creative thinking, even a paradigm shift, that future scholars may wonder at not having supported sooner.

Have we recently hit a wall though, arguably, regarding in-depth illumination of staple sociological concerns? Take class inequalities, steadily worsening for decades in the US and world-wide, even as neoliberal capitalism—beset again by chronic crises and protests—continues to find its own innovative ways to deflect attention from its shortcomings. The channeling by conservative elites of emotions like anger and anxiety suggests the use of unconscious social processes in system maintenance during the very same decades when, ironically enough, sociologists have shied away from notions and methods that might better grasp deeply social-psychological appeals. Racial disparities, too, remain rigidly in place: for instance, in 2013, unemployment rates for Black Americans remained approximately twice (6.6% for whites, 12.6% blacks) that of whites (Pew Research Center, August 21, 2013), and disparities in incarceration rates remain horrifyingly asymmetric. Moreover in the US, as well as throughout Western Europe, impassioned debates over immigration manifest a thoroughly symbiotic enmeshment of emotionality and discriminatory cultural discourses. And, while immigration, race, and ethnicity are aptly deemed timely sociological subfields, do we comprehend *why* prejudicial anti-immigrant sentiment runs high—let alone what to do about it? Regarding gender, feminist gains have been notable on the one hand; on the other, sexism is alive and well in many places. Hardly have economic and political equalities trickled down across classes and races of women as democratically as social movement activists (and feminist sociologists) of the 60s and 70s initially hoped.

While such ongoing inequities have been empirically well-documented in sociology, they have not been nearly so well-elucidated analytically. Questions like what happened to vital social movements of the 1960s, and how it came to pass that people who experience multi-faceted forms of injustice(s) do not necessarily rebel against them, comprise "why" questions that continue to stymie time-honored but possibly calcified approaches to the discipline. But what justifies looking to approaches that merge psycho- and socio-analyses, and which draw open-mindedly and liberally on Freudian-influenced notions and methods, to provide inspiration and assistance?

Perhaps one reason, among the many given by authors in ensuing chapters, reaches across this volume's otherwise diverse perspectives. This is the observation that on the whole, and perhaps (collectively) unconsciously, American sociology does not routinely base its analyses on a sufficiently multi-dimensional view of human beings and their/our social interactions. This is so despite many individual sociologists' professing to eschew "rational choice theory" approaches. Unwitting over-simplifications, though, are rather remarkable given that social actors are so obviously endowed of logic at the same time filled with emotional and sexual feelings about which we/they may, or may not, be aware. By contrast, however, the Freudian tradition is incomprehensible unless one starts from the premise that people are at once rational and angry/sad/anxious/defended; they/we act at once or alternately with determination and/or ambivalence, with consistency as well as contradictoriness, and consciously but sometimes with little clue as to our actions' underlying motivations and effects. Thus turning back to Freudian ideas in this volume is meant to serve, in part, as a corrective to the American sociological field's comparative reluctance—thus far—to accord human complexity its due (see also Chancer, 2013).

But, more specifically, how do the essays in this volume make a case for the necessity of psycho-social (including Freudian) ideas and methods to more thoroughly grasp both group and individual life? Before and in the course of explaining this volume's contents, a few preliminary caveats need stating. One concerns the historical record—thoroughly documented in the essay by sociologist George Cavalletto and sociologist/psychoanalyst Catherine Silver that opens the volume's Part I—that psychoanalysis was not always at the margins rather than the center of US sociology. Rather, during the heyday of the Columbia University Department of Sociology in the 1940s and 1950s when names like Robert Merton and C. Wright Mills dominated the discipline, so too did the work of Talcott Parsons—himself not only a major sociologist but a trained psychoanalyst—find academic recognition. At that time the number of articles about psychoanalysis and sociology appearing in major journals, many of which were influenced by Parsons' work, was surprisingly high from our present vantage point. Parsons conceived sociology and psychoanalysis as having different points of departure though he also sought to bring them together through his "theory of the personality." As Parsons declared, "In the broadest sense, the contribution of psychoanalysis to the social sciences has consisted of an enormous deepening and enrichment of our understanding of human motivation." (1964, p. 17).

Then, too, psychoanalytic approaches to understanding the social have marked European and especially German intellectual contexts: specifically, social philosophers of the Frankfurt School drew on psychoanalytic theories of unconscious processes to explain the rise of fascism. As Theodor Adorno remarked in his introductory lectures on sociology, "We of the Frankfurt School found ourselves incorporating so-called 'psychological' considerations in the so-called 'objective' theory of society at a relatively early stage. We did it. . . . for the simple and tangible reason that without exact knowledge of the projection of society inside individuals, it would not be comprehensible that countless individuals. . . . constantly act even now in a manner contrary to their own rational interests . . ." (Adorno, 2001, p. 116). In an essay here on the Frankfurt School's influence, Canadian sociologist Neil McLaughlin discusses the work of Erich Fromm as exemplary even if—and maybe for this very reason—Fromm became a "forgotten intellectual," as McLaughlin suggests, after fleeing to the US where the Frankfurt School was less influential.

But sociologists and philosophers of the Frankfurt School of Social Research used Freudian psychoanalytic ideas to address a broad range of topics from work and consumerism through sexual repression and class consciousness. One of the School's most well-known treatments of Freud was developed in *Eros and Civilization* (1955), wherein Marcuse held that capitalist society imposes surplus repression on the individual while drawing ever-increasing surpluses from labor. Marcuse's thought in *Eros* and in other works had a strong influence on the New Left and on feminist, queer, youth, and anti-racist movements in the US. In the French context, Lacanian psychoanalysis propelled much of feminist social theory in the 1970s and 1980s as well as Louis Althusser's analyses of ideology and interpellation (Althusser, 2001).

Thus it is predominantly only over the last forty years or so, and then primarily within the American sociological field, that psychoanalytic ideas—if acknowledged at all—have been perceived as though a relic of the past. On the other hand, as Lynn Chancer contends in her essay on C. Wright Mills' social psychology, it seems equally clear that symbolic interactionism has attained greater hegemony as the most influential theory of individual agency in the discipline. Scholars in subfields including the sociology of gender and sexuality, the study of mental health and addiction, and the sociology of emotions may take up psychoanalytic concepts—usually doing so in tandem with other socio-logical theories and methods—but Freudian ideas tend to be accorded only brief mention. By contrast, symbolic interactionism is an estab-lished and regularly discussed perspective within sociology. It should be noted, though, that psychoanalytic thought has enjoyed a much more sustained influence in other areas including literary and film criticism, American studies, performance studies, and other humanities-oriented and interdisciplinary fields.

What happened to psychoanalytic ideas in the "mainstream" of sociology, though, from the time of the Frankfurt School in Europe and Talcott Parsons' sway in America through these last seemingly "post-Freudian" decades of the twenty-first century? Other essays in Parts I and II explore major factors that contributed to the slow but steady marginalization of psychoanalytic perspectives, especially from the 1980s onward. The first factor is at once historical and theoretical: with the emergence of 1960s and 70s social movements, the Freudian psychoanalytic tradition started to seem "politically incorrect"; it became stigmatized by association with biological and universalistic modes of thought. For these earlier decades gave birth to social con-structionism and its obvious, and continuing, relevance for sociology as a field. These were the years of Goffmanian anti-institutionalism when sociology vibrated sympathetically with counter-cultural currents critical of prisons, mental hospitals, and other "total institutions," and when Foucault and others decried the "totalizing" dictates of modernist ideas. Hardly was biology believed any more to be destiny as feminists, too, thankfully rebelled from essentialism, and as leftists in France like Foucault advocated specific and provisional rather than grand theo-retical approaches to history and politics. Amidst these developments, Parsons and Freud seemed not liberating but conservative—the "wrong side" of history, certainly, with which progressive sociologists would want to be aligned. An essay in Part I by Thomas DeGloma fills out this period, showing how two social movements—regarding child sexual abuse and recovered memory, respectively—emerged from understand-able concerns with the "conservative" aspects of Freud, especially in reference to feminist concerns, as they debated opposing arguments about the workings of the unconscious.

A second reason for marginalization is as methodological as the previ-ous was intellectual: through the 80s and 90s, a time period correlated with the Reagan–Bush years of unremitting rightward drift, so did what could be called an empirical or positivist bias become more firmly entrenched and funded. The field increasingly justified its existence as a social science by insisting that theory should develop from empirical research, not the other way around. Sociology was influenced by Newtonian scientific orientations, not nearly so much by later developments in quantum physics that embraced Einstein's turn toward relativity as more aptly descriptive of the world. Quantitative as well as qualitative sociological researchers have held onto earlier scientific terminology, emphasizing a particular definition of science within their/our survey methods, regression analyses, and ethnographies. The empirical became (nearly) the entirety of the sociological and, given desires for scientific status and recognition, Freudian ideas appeared by contrast "anti" sociological virtually by definition. And whereas conventional scientific methods treasured falsifiability, key Freudian tenets—sexual energy, the unconscious, defense mechanisms—could hardly be observed, measured, or proved by positivistic criteria even though Freud himself, and the different schools he bequeathed, looked to empirical traces and manifestations to confirm the existence of unconscious processes through case studies.

Paradoxically enough, classical sociological theory is replete with references to collective energies of which groups are unaware; pivotal ideas that have been at the core of the discipline's development assume, even though they cannot decisively prove, unconscious *collective* motivations coloring social actions and reactions. For example, in *The Rules of Sociological Method* (Durkheim, 1982), Durkheim's contentions about crime and the "collective conscience" of society are impossible to understand without presuming the persistence of unconscious social processes; then, too, Marx's notion of ideology depends on the postulating of collective unconsciousness. And how is it possible to understand the famous anxious Protestant of Weber's sociological imagination short of holding that these early capitalists were—as a group—unconscious about what drove them?

Why, then, contemporary sociological resistance? Given what could be considered a peculiar omission or (sociologically unconscious) overlooking, it is interesting to reflect on Catherine Silver's argument in this same section. Silver taps paranoia—that is, she discusses paranoid fears and thinking—to better understand marginalization and the institutional controls and reprisals early sociologists faced if employing psychoanalytic ideas. Also drawing on reviews and articles in AJS and ASR between the mid-1940s and the mid-1960s, Silver shows how the marginalization of the psychoanalytic took many forms including attacks on individuals, dismissal of ideas, lack of institutional recognition, and the internalization of what she calls, drawing on the work of George Steinmetz, a positivistic "epistemological unconscious." Through her analyses of these sociological journals, she finds that the expression of paranoid fears and paranoid thinking emerges in the context of struggles for legitimacy and the recognition of sociology as a science. Trained as a sociologist as well as a psychoanalyst, Silver concludes her essay by illustrating these ideas vis-à-vis insights from her own struggles to integrate the two disciplines.

Like Silver, the three authors of articles in Part II are dually trained as sociologists and psychoanalysts—indeed, who better to reflect on the compatibility, or lack thereof, between the two fields? Thus the first two articles of Part II present in effect a debate—a fascinating and provocative one—about the extent to which sociological and psychoanalytical approaches can, or cannot, be integrated. For even if once closely aligned in the 40s and 50s, are sociology and psychoanalysis now divorced (albeit, perhaps, unhappily?) for good reasons, or are they more like kindred cousins with more in common than usually acknowledged? As former president of the American Sociological Association Neil Smelser argues, ongoing disciplinary separation stems from dissimilar premises, methods, and assumptions; at the same time, pragmatically, he allows that psychoanalytic ideas can sometimes be useful to sociologists when studying specific empirical problems.

This is quite different from the perspective presented in Siamak Mohavedi's passionate essay "The Narcissism of Minor Differences." Mohavedi holds that, quite to the contrary, structural arguments in sociology and psychoanalysis have decidedly related premises and that contemporary theorists—not just classical ones—have used ideas similar in meaning to psychoanalytic ones. He even cites Goffman, a sociologist known to have openly disdained Freudian psychoanalysis, as a case in point of potential theoretical compatibility. But whereas Silver discusses sociologists' reactions through the Freudian concept of paranoia, Mohavedi uses narcissism—and Freud's insights about narcissism of a particular kind—to better understand sociologists' resistances to incorporating psychoanalytic concepts within their disciplinary territory. While Nancy Chodorow does not speak about resistances, she does provide a well-articulated discussion of her experiences—especially the difficulties—she encountered as a feminist who was also at one and the same time an academic sociologist and a psychoanalyst. In a previously unpublished talk re-edited for the purposes of this volume, Chodorow makes clear not that sociology and psychoanalysis are incompatible—quite the contrary—but that, in some professional contexts at least, the two were treated as such. Yet, as Chodorow vividly illustrates, the psychoanalytic tradition offers much to sociology with its rich attention to subjectivity—even if this potential has been misunderstood, or misrecognized, as somehow "anti" or "a" sociological.

Whereas Part II focuses on whether psychosocial syntheses are possible, Part III turns to three well-known social theorists—Erich Fromm (known predominantly as a psychoanalyst but also trained as a sociologist), C. Wright Mills, and Pierre Bourdieu—who may or may not have explicitly drawn on psychoanalytic concepts. Of course, the entire opus of Fromm's work was concerned with both the social and the individual/psychoanalytic. On the other hand, while renowned sociologists like Mills and Bourdieu were drawn to character structure analysis (Mills) or defiance of binary divides between the subjective and objective (Bourdieu), both nevertheless avoided explicit use of psychoanalytic concepts in their writings. Might such avoidance of psychosocial connections have influenced not just their own work but the unfolding of sociology in and outside the US—and if so, how?

Commencing Part III, Neil McLaughlin's essay on Fromm, "Escapes from Freedom: Political Extremism, Conspiracy Theories and the Sociology of Emotions," picks up almost exactly on the closing note of pragmatic caution where Smelser's essay left off: namely, can sociology use psychoanalysis at least for delimited empirical investigations? Simultaneously, McLaughlin's contribution supports Mohavedi's more optimistic stress on compatibility by asserting that—while the Frankfurt School may be (relatively) overlooked in contemporary sociological theory—Erich Fromm's work has more potential for fruitful empirical application than any other theorist in this tradition. McLaughlin develops his case by elaborating, as Smelser recommends, on the applicability of Fromm for studying three broad cultural tendencies: authoritarianism in contemporary movements (like the Tea Party); destructiveness among genocidal leaders and unaffiliated terrorists in the West; and automaton conformity as gleaned through a proliferation of conspiracy theories in North America. Concrete investigation of these subjects, according to McLaughlin, must tap both historical understandings *and* psychoanalytic knowledge to understand why some individuals, not others, commit crimes or become involved with extremist groups.

Continuing Part III, Chancer discusses C. Wright Mills' 1950s' interest in character structure, elaborating on ramifications for the development of American sociology of Mills having largely (but not entirely) excluded Freudian ideas from his own psychosocial theorizations. Mills' collaboration with Hans Gerth (1953) provided a multi-dimensional understanding of human beings but was also more in sync with symbolic interactionism's evolution than some of Freud's more radical ideas about the unconscious, anxieties and fears, defense mechanisms and sexuality. Had Mills been attuned to the liberatory promise of some of Freud's ideas, though, he might have legitimized Frankfurt School-like studies of the US in American sociology from the 60s through the present—rather than, as actually happened, Fromm and other Frankfurt School thinkers becoming relatively more marginal.

In a related vein, George Steinmetz considers whether the work of Pierre Bourdieu, a huge force in both European and US sociology from the 70s through the present, would have benefited from attention to, and recognition of, the power of psychoanalytic ideas. But whereas the McLaughlin and Chancer essays stress theorists' connection (or, in Mills' case, lack of connection) with Freud, Steinmetz analyses the extent to which Lacanian concepts in particular would have been helpful for Bourdieu's own "socio-analytic" observations—even if Bourdieu failed to explicitly recognize such utility. Indeed Goffman, Mills, Bourdieu. . . . each of these well-known sociological theorists have in common, in different ways, stopping short of grounding their work self-reflexively, and co-relatively, to themselves. However concerned about false antimonies including that between subjectivity and objectivity, then, Bourdieu nonetheless maintained a boundary, a conventional distance, between the psycho- and the socio-analytic. Had Bourdieu lived longer though, Steinmetz implies (Steinmetz, 2006), he might have become more appreciative of psychoanalysis—a surmise partly borne out in some of Bourdieu's later and more autobiographical writings, for example, his *Pascalian Meditations*.

Last but not least in Part III, Philip Manning discusses the writing of a variety of contemporary ethnographers including Elijah Anderson, Mitchell Duneier, and Loic Wacquant, whose work might also have benefited from more explicit attention to psychoanalytic connections. Manning discusses how issues like transference and counter-transference tend to be left out of well-known ethnographers' descriptions, thereafter possibly affecting and diminishing their powers of multi-dimensional interpretation. Perhaps such an omission of (self)reflexivity—even in the work of sociologists interested in such understandings—stems from sociologists' long-standing associations of Freudian and other psychological traditions with emphases on only individual rather than social causality (the latter distinguishing our collective enterprise from that of psychologists and analysts).

For Freudian and other psychosocial approaches do tend to turn one's analytic gaze inward—and in this respect, yes, individualistically—even if thereafter turning outward, back to relations with others. But to start investigations with oneself, precisely as Freud did when using his own dreams as "data" in *The Interpretation of Dreams* (Freud, 2010), is the opposite of how sociologists typically proceed. Instead, from Durkheim to Bourdieu, most start with the outer world—at least explicitly—never necessarily circling back to socio-psycho-analysis of the relativity, the relationship, between their/our external and internal dynamics. But looking inward as well as outward, and probing the "personally" indi- vidual as well as the "politically" social, was also the orientation of femi- nist theories—especially radical feminist theories—of the 60s and 70s.

Thus, it is not surprising that both psychoanalytic and feminist ideas have been marginalized at different times in the history of the American social sciences, including but not limited to the history of sociology. This coincidence between feminism and psychoanalysis is the starting point of Part IV's section on not just theory but "practices." Essays in this section tackle social issues from diverse perspectives, focusing on challenges that arise *not* from sociologists avoiding psychoanalysis but when sociologists try—quite explicitly—to meld the two in different ways. Thus, following Manning, Part IV begins with an essay provoca- tively entitled *Personae* (after Ingmar Bergman's film of the same name) in which social movements scholar and feminist Gilda Zwerman indeed reflects on her own social and psychic background, using this "data" to examine her choice of subject matter as well as a deeply inter-subjective connection that developed between herself and another woman. In Zwerman's words "inter-subjective relationships that are established between the researcher and the respondent are often repressed." By con- trast, her creative narrative explores psychoanalytic and social reasons behind the connection she forged with Judy Clark, who is serving a life sentence for participating in acts of political violence in association with the Black Liberation Army. According to Zwerman, this connection began with a fantasy and involved a relationship of "doubling" between the researcher and her "subject" that, little by little, profoundly affected them both.

Associations with essentialism, the hegemony of positivism, proclivi- ties to investigate outside rather than within: if these factors illuminate the persistence of psychoanalysis' marginalization by sociology, the time may have come to move beyond an outdated prejudice. Old inclinations against psychoanalytic perspectives that seem to have thrown the "baby out with the bathwater" may be detrimental to an otherwise open-minded sociological sensibility in the second decade of the twenty-first century. For, just as Marcuse titled his best-known monograph *One Dimensional Man*, so sociological scholars may be stuck—unwittingly, and even curiously—in one-dimensional sociological frameworks.

By way of corrective, after Zwerman, Part IV continues by showcasing actual research that co-considers—rather than marginalizing or divorcing—social-and-psychic dimensions of specific issues and subfields. A first group of essays uses psychoanalytic or psychosocial ideas to grapple with ongoing or recent problems in contemporary American society and culture. A second incorporates Freudian concepts to enrich scholarship about concrete sociological subfields from religion, neo-racism, and media through the study of racism, immigration, and citizenship. Within the first group, John Andrews' essay "Foreclosure from Freud to Fannie Mae" probes the 2007 mortgage crisis in the US by viewing it through a simultaneously psychoanalytic and social lens. Whereas Silver tapped the Freudian idea of paranoia and Mohavedi narcissism, Andrews draws on the psychoanalytic concept of foreclosure to investigate the entanglement of homeowners' inner rage and collapsing housing markets as both emerged in the US from the 2007 economic crisis through the present.

From psychosocial appropriation of Freud's idea of foreclosure, Part IV moves to an equally innovative psychosocial interpretation of melancholia. In "Racial Melancholia and a Devitalized America: The Enduring Effect of Racism," sociologist and (again) trained psychoanalyst Jeffrey Prager brilliantly (re)presents the ongoing effects of racism's horrors on the structure and culture of American society. He suggests that Freud's notion of melancholia—which, unlike mourning, involves a loss continuing to haunt the present—helps explain both the stubborn persistence of discrimination and the impoverishment (even psychosocial deathliness) virulent racism wreaks overall on American life.

Also engaged with complex cultural strains, Australian sociologist Anthony Elliott's essay grapples with discourses of individualism, and the intense emotional and bodily effects bequeathed by the dramatic economic and technological transformations associated with globalization. Whereas theorists like Giddens, Beck, and Baumann have honed in on the structural and cognitive consequences of globalization, Elliott demonstrates how psychoanalytic approaches lend key insights into what he calls the "new individualism." For him, contemporary individualism is characterized by a radical flexibility and willingness for instant self-reinvention, so much so that melancholia—a fundamental loss of self to grief—has come to define the practice of everyday life. This is followed by Arlene Stein's psychosocial discussion of trauma's individual as well as collective effects. For Stein, drawing on her own research into intergenerational transmission of Holocaust victims' experiences, such at once social-and-personal trauma cannot be deeply grasped short of psychosocial tools. Specifically, she shows that the emphasis on guilt that dominated chronicles of survivors coming to the US post-World War II has not adequately captured what Stein finds, namely, that shame and stigma are longer-term problems echoing into the present and needing to be recognized and redressed for children of survivors in the twenty-first century.

Similarly noteworthy in this section is an essay by sociologist Vikash Singh that turns, and indeed self-reflexively, to why and how he was drawn to psychoanalytic ideas over the course of researching three distinctive aspects of contemporary Indian culture. Whether participating in the Kanwar religious pilgrimage, or studying neo-caste (and neo-racist) ideologies, or probing the appeal of several extraordinarily popular television series in India going back to the 80s (one of which he remembers watching himself), Singh became convinced sociological perspectives alone were insufficient to explain "subjective" dimensions of the phenomena he hoped to illuminate. Rather, to illuminate each of these cases—corresponding with the sociology of religion, race (and caste), and media, respectively—Singh brings to bear distinctive theoretical analyses that draw on sociological as well as psychoanalytic perspectives from Freud to Kristeva and Lacan.

Concerns about sociological literature's inadequacy likewise motivate a theoretically and politically nuanced essay by Tony Jefferson arguing for the importance of distinguishing studies of racial prejudice from that of racial hatred. Jefferson uses the highly profiled British case of the murder of Stephen Lawrence to develop a case for this distinction. He contends that in dominant sociological interpretations, these two kinds of racism—prejudice and hatred—have been conflated, a "psychosocial" problem which not only interferes with precision of analysis but, in the UK, has sometimes led to ironic social injustices.

In another creative rendering that concludes Part IV, Ilgin Yorukoglu mobilizes a psychosocial perspective to criticize limitations in the literature on immigration that typically emphasizes group difference and assimilation. Building on her ethnographic work among Turkish women living in Berlin, Yorukoglu contends that migrants develop unique "acts of belonging" in order to traverse cultural contradiction and to assuage deep-rooted psychic anxiety. In particular, she looks at how her gay subjects negotiate the Western imperative to "come out" as a way of articulating Turkish identity and group bonds. Once again, the conventional literature on immigration emerges—in Yorukoglu's eyes—as inadequate for grasping the complexities of both subjective experiences and objective barriers encountered when analyzing this (actually more multi-dimensional) sociological subfield.

Last but not least, and as co-editors of this array of fine articles on the past, present, and future of psychoanalytic sociology, Chancer and Andrews would be sorely remiss not to acknowledge the huge influence of the New York City study group to which we have belonged for many years (and which Chancer and Silver started over twenty years ago—see Acknowledgements). This volume, too, has been at once a social and individual, a psychological as well as collective, multi-dimensional endeavor. For without the inspiration of "our little group," as we have often referred to it—of George Cavalletto, Patricia Clough, Thomas DeGloma, Joshua Klein, Tony Jefferson, Catherine Silver, Dena Smith, Arlene Stein, among many others including, more recently, contributions from Christina Nadler and Kevin Moran from the Graduate Center of the City University of New York—we would not have felt a need to try officially, and in writing, to legitimize an area of sociology that stays marginalized only to the risk of the field as a whole.

Our intention is that this volume will encourage other scholars' ongoing multi-dimensional work by transforming the relationship between sociology and psychoanalysis from one too easily overlooked to a more synergistic—and mutually respectful—recognition of distinctive insights developed from within both approaches. Bringing sociology and psychoanalysis back together—into a happy relationship, if not necessarily a marriage—provides sociology one more tool, one more avenue for analyzing mechanisms, defenses and feelings sometimes social, sometimes psychic, often both. Given the complex character of our inner and outer worlds, and the dynamic web of individual/social relations affecting and interconnecting us all for worse—and frequently (too) for the better—every tool we have deserves inclusion, not marginalization.

References

Adorno, T. (2001) *Introduction to Sociology* (Palo Alto: Stanford University Press).
Althusser. L. (2001) *Lenin and Philosophy and Other Essays* (New York: Monthly Review Press).
Chancer, L. (2013) 'Sociology, Psychoanalysis, and Marginalization: Unconscious Defenses and Disciplinary Interests', *Sociological Forum*, 28 (3), 452–468.

Durkheim, E. (1982) *The Rules of Sociological Method* (New York: Free Press).

Freud, S. (2010) 'The Interpretation of Dreams' in J. Strachey (ed.) *The Standard Edition Of the Complete Psychological Works of Sigmund Freud* (New York: Basic Books).

Gerth, H. and C. W. Mills (1953) *Character and Social Structure* (New York: Harcourt, Brace & Co.).

Parsons, T. (1964) *Social Structure and Personality* (New York: Free Press).

Steinmetz, G. (2006) 'Bourdieu's Disavowal of Lacan: Psychoanalytic Theory and the Concepts of 'Habitus' and 'Symbolic Capital'', *Constellations*, 13 (4), 445–464.

Part I
The History of Sociology and Psychoanalysis in the United States: Diverse Perspectives on a Longstanding Relationship

1
Opening/Closing the Sociological Mind to Psychoanalysis

George Cavalletto and Catherine Silver

For sociologists interested in integrating psychoanalytic ideas and concepts in their work, important lessons, both positive and negative, can be gleaned from the past history of the relationship between the social sciences and psychoanalysis. Specifically, regarding US sociology, one period is arguably of particular interest: the period following World War II, from the late 1940s through the 1950s.

Evidence from these years suggests that the influence of psychoanalytic ideas was extraordinarily widespread among American intellectuals. Reflecting on the period, Peter Berger reports that psychoanalytic ideas about the unconscious, repression, and the centrality of sexuality and childhood played a significant role in the "world-taken-for-granted" of college-educated Americans (Berger, 1965, pp. 26, 28). American sociologists of the period, the evidence suggests, shared in this attachment to psychoanalytic ideas. According to a survey of the major fields of sociology written in conjunction with the American Sociological Society's 1954 annual meeting, "the theories of Sigmund Freud have become pervasive in American thought-ways in the mid-twentieth century and in contemporary American sociology. Many sociologists are using adaptations of psychoanalytic methods, segments of its theories, and . . . selected and varied concepts" (Hinkle, 1957, p. 574). Contained in the reflections of another sociologist writing during the period, we find stated that "an awareness of psychoanalysis has tended to become a normal quality in an American social scientist" (Madge, 1962, p. 565). And Howard Kaye, in an astute overview of the period, retrospectively came to a similar conclusion: "In the 1950s and 1960s, Freudian theory was deemed to be a vital part of the sociological tradition. . . . Freud was very much an object of admiration and discipleship in Western academic and cultural circles" (1991, p. 87).

This essay examines several aspects of this "opening" of the sociological mind to psychoanalysis. First, we present statistical evidence
to support the reportorial and anecdotal accounts above. We continue
with a detailed analysis of various articles and book reviews dealing
with psychoanalysis published in the late 1940s and the 1950s in the
professional journals considered at mid-century to be dominant in the
field: the *American Journal of Sociology (AJS)* and *American Sociological
Review (ASR)* (Parsons and Barber, 1948, p. 250; Kinloch, 1988, p. 181).
The main findings of these examinations will then be placed within
the historical record of major institutional and ideological changes that
affected academic sociology in the period, with the goal of providing
not only evidence of an upsurge of a positive interest in psychoanalytic
ideas but also an explanation of why there arose a sociological backlash
against the use of these ideas and why it proved so effective. For as we
shall see, this backlash was of such ferocity that by the end of the 1950s
the newly "opened" sociological mind had become for the most part
"closed."

Preliminary data

Figure 1.1 covers the period 1900–2005 and indicates graphically the
percentage of articles and book reviews using terms that refer to psychoanalysis, first in all sociological journals (the dotted line) and secondly
in *AJS* and *ASR* (the thin line, and the line made up of dashes). The
percentage figures reflect the proportion of all articles and book reviews
published in each year that contain one or more terms from a list of
terms related to psychoanalysis. As the graph makes clear, beginning
in the mid-1910s, the percentage of articles and book reviews that contained one or more of these terms rose decade by decade and peaked in
the mid-1950s, only to decline at first gradually and then, by the mid-
1960s, precipitously, eventually falling by 2005 to a level comparable to
that of 1920. Most notably, the graph makes evident that with regard
to *AJS* and *ASR*, the proportion of articles and book reviews referencing psychoanalysis in the early 1950s exceeded 10 per cent while the
proportion in the earliest and most recent decades hovered during most
years around 2 per cent.

Readers will notice that several abrupt upsurges occurred in the years
before and after the 1950s, the most significant one being in the late
1930s. The abruptness of this earlier rise reflects, in part, a response to
the death of Sigmund Freud in 1939 and it had a quite different character than the one that peaked in the 1950s—for one thing, almost all

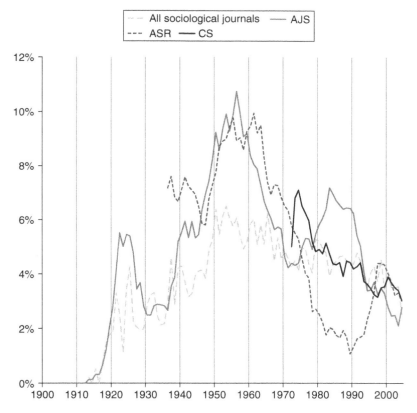

Figure 1.1 Sociological journal articles and book reviews with references to psychoanalysis, 1900–2004

Source: Data compiled from Sandbox, a beta search program of JSTOR. Lines represent percentages of items (articles, reviews) out of total items of each year that contain one or more of the following terms: Freud, Freudian, psychoanalysis, psychoanalytic, Horney, Lacan.

of the authors of the articles published in the earlier period were non-sociologists (Jones, 1974, p. 32), whereas (as we shall see in the next section) all but two of the articles of the 1950s were written by sociologists. Readers will also notice that Figure 1.1 indicates several instances of sharp declines in psychoanalytic references, most conspicuously *ASR's* abrupt and deep drop-off in the early 1970s. This particular decline was the direct result of the journal's elimination of its book review section and the launching in its place of a new publication devoted solely to book reviews, *Contemporary Sociology* (*CS*). That such a steep decline in references resulted not from changes in the journal's article section but rather from the elimination of its book review section and—equally important—that the percentage figures of the new book review journal were immediately higher than those of *ASR*, both strongly suggest what the analysis below confirms: in the years preceding its elimination, *ASR*'s book review section accounted for a majority of this journal's items referencing psychoanalysis, a finding also repeated in the case of *AJS*.

Figure 1.2 focuses on a narrower time period than Figure 1.1: the period 1948–1960, and indicates the number of articles and book reviews with *a significant focus on psychoanalysis*. These numbers are

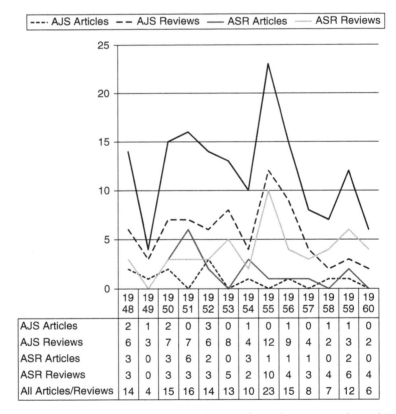

	19 48	19 49	19 50	19 51	19 52	19 53	19 54	19 55	19 56	19 57	19 58	19 59	19 60
AJS Articles	2	1	2	0	3	0	1	0	1	0	1	1	0
AJS Reviews	6	3	7	7	6	8	4	12	9	4	2	3	2
ASR Articles	3	0	3	6	2	0	3	1	1	1	0	2	0
ASR Reviews	3	0	3	3	3	5	2	10	4	3	4	6	4
All Articles/Reviews	14	4	15	16	14	13	10	23	15	8	7	12	6

Figure 1.2   Articles and book reviews with a significant focus on psychoanalysis, *American Sociological Review* and *American Journal of Sociology*, 1948–1960

considerably smaller than those represented in percentage terms in Figure 1.1. The smaller numbers reflect the fact that when all the articles and book reviews pinpointed by the computerized search that yielded the figures of Figure 1.1 were directly examined, more than half of them did not include any significant discussion of psychoanalysis.

Also, Figure 1.2 confirms as a general principle what Figure 1.1 presented as a consequence of *ASR*'s elimination of book reviews in 1972: both journals' book review sections were more open to a discussion of psychoanalytic ideas than were their article sections (that is, book reviews constituted 87 per cent of all items dealing significantly with psychoanalysis in *AJS* and 68 per cent of such pieces in *ASR*). Other types of variations are also revealed by the table and graph of Figure 1.2: for one thing, more articles and book reviews with a significant focus on psychoanalysis were published in the first six years of the period 1948–1960 than in the last six years (this was especially true of articles, with 72 per cent of all such articles appearing in the first six years). Moreover, Figure 1.2 reveals major differences between the two journals' article and book review sections: in particular, the Figure's table shows that *AJS* published significantly fewer psychoanalytically focused articles than *ASR* (*AJS*: twelve articles; *ASR*: twenty-two articles), while at the same time *AJS* published significantly more psychoanalytically focused book reviews than *ASR* (*AJS*: seventy-three book reviews; *ASR*: forty-nine book reviews).

This in turn suggests that to gain a better understanding of the quality and range of these journals' opening to psychoanalysis, their writings' actual contents need to be examined. From this examination, we should be able to uncover reasons behind differences in the writings of the first and last years of the period, and between the two journals' handling of psychoanalytic issues; we should also be able to gain general insight into differences between those who favored and those who opposed the opening to psychoanalysis.

Analysis of articles and book reviews

The article sections of *AJS* and *ASR*

Articles positively disposed toward psychoanalysis

Several basic facts emerge from an overview of the articles from 1948–1960 in *AJS* and *ASR* that contain a significant focus on psychoanalysis. Overall, thirty-four articles with this focus appear in the two journals, a much higher proportion (65 per cent) in *ASR* than in *AJS*. Of all the articles published during the period, twenty-three (68 per cent) were deemed positively disposed toward psychoanalysis and the use of psychoanalytic ideas in sociology. Of articles positively disposed to psychoanalysis versus ones judged negatively disposed, the records of *AJS* and *ASR* are diametrically opposed: the 1948–1960 issues of *AJS* contained only four positive articles (out of the journal's twelve psychoanalytically focused articles); on the other hand, *ASR* contained 19 positive articles (out of twenty-two in total).

When the positive and negative articles from both journals are considered together, one discovers another distinction dividing them into two groups. Each group is characterized by a distinct style of sociological journal writing. One group is written in an *essayist style*, a broad category that includes observational description and the refinement of interpretation, the review of alternative ideas and an engagement in general theorizing. A second group of articles is written in a *scientistic style*, a narrower category that includes a concern with hypothesis formation, the operationalization of concepts and statistical analysis of data. In some ways, this stylistic difference points to factors involved in the methodological distinction between qualitative and quantitative research methods, although "essayist" clearly refers to a broader category than "qualitative," while "scientistic" is quite close to "quantitative." (Moreover, beyond its reference to a specific regard for quantitative methods, "scientistic" also brings with it an allusion to the various ways that its adherents often make manifest a conviction that quantitative methods constitute the only source of genuine factual knowledge, whether that be of nature or of human society, thereby, along with restricting "science" to quantitative methods, idealizing it as well (Habermas, 1971, pp. 4–5). When considered in terms of the articles that were positively disposed toward psychoanalysis, this divide has a distinctly chronological aspect: of the articles favoring the use of psychoanalytic ideas, all those of an essayist style were published before 1953; although several of a scientistic style were also published before 1953, only those of this style were published after 1953.

The most significant articles of the essayist type—two essays of general theorizing—appear at the beginning of the period: both by Talcott Parsons. In the first, published in the January 1948 issue of *AJS*, Parsons begins by expressing concern about the insecure academic status of sociology and in particular the discipline's perceived inferiority in comparison with the more mature and theoretically integrated social science of economics. It is in this context that Parsons announces his championship of "a new synthesis" that would allow sociology to reach "full maturity." Explicitly modeling his ideas here on the integration of disciplines that he had institutionally achieved at Harvard with the setting up of the Department of Social Relations in 1946, Parsons posits as sociology's goal the creation of a master general theory that would combine concepts of sociology, anthropology and a Freudian-influenced social psychology. This unified theory, Parsons asserts, would draw much from Freud, who should be placed alongside Durkheim and Weber at the head of the sociological canon. Sociologists, Parsons adds, need also to examine the ideas of the neo-Freudians, for along with Freudian theory, "their work is a major contribution toward the synthesis which must develop if sociology is to come to full maturity" (Parsons and Barber, 1948, pp. 247, 252, 253).

In his second article, published in *ASR* in 1950 (and a transcript of his presidential address at the 1949 annual meeting of the American Sociological Society), Parsons vigorously reiterates his belief in the importance of creating for the social sciences "a general system of theory." By this, he meant a theory that would serve these sciences in the way that theoretical physics serves varied scientific investigations of the properties of matter and energy. Foreshadowing ideas that would shortly appear in *Toward a General Theory of Action* (1951), Parsons calls for a theoretical "synthesis of sociology with parts of psychology and anthropology" and he devotes particular attention to what he sees as a breakthrough in establishing a theoretical common ground by which to connect theories of "the personality structure on the psychological level with the sociological analysis of social structure" (1950, pp. 8, 9). With the understanding that the psychology of which he speaks incorporates psychoanalysis, Parsons advances the claim that in the work of connecting psychological and sociological theories,

> great progress has been made. The kind of impasse where 'psychology is psychology' and 'sociology is sociology' and 'never the twain shall meet,' which was a far from uncommon feeling in the early stages of my career, has almost evaporated. There is a rapidly increasing and broadening area of mutual supplementation. (p. 9)

Echoes of Parsons' espousal of a sociological opening to psychoanalysis can be found in journal articles published in the early years of the period though most frequently this is advanced from a perspective of a specialized sociological subfield rather than that of cross-disciplinary theory formation. Typical in this regard are articles by Ernest and Harriet Mowrer who, beginning in the 1920s, associated themselves with a notable group of social workers, psychiatrists, and sociologists to create a psychoanalytically informed subfield of family studies (LaRossa and Wolf, 1985, p. 534; Hinkle, 1957, p. 593). In a 1951 *ASR* article, the Mowrers devote much of their attention to a discussion of the various ways that their sociological subfield is grounded on the reconfiguration of the Freudian "sex instinct" into "a more complex series of socially derived motivational units" (p. 28), thereby allowing "the family social psychologist [to] utilize a number of the theories and concepts of psychoanalysis, but structured by a cultural context and implemented by role analysis in the dynamics of marriage interaction" (p. 33). Thus, drawing on ideas from Eric Fromm and Karen Horney, the Oedipus complex is reconceptualized by the Mowrers as originating not from instinctual incestuous desires but rather from parental enactments of cultural heterosexual patterns. Also, drawing ideas from George Herbert Mead, they reconceptualize Freud's ego and superego as the interaction of the "I" and "me" and as originating in the context of role-taking interactions within the family (pp. 29, 30).

The work of another advocate of pro-psychoanalytic sociology, George Simpson, presents an intriguing variant of these efforts in the period 1948–1960. That Simpson was an outspoken champion of the sociological incorporation of psychoanalytic ideas is made clear in a number of his writings. In one 1950 *ASR* article, Simpson displays an impressive degree of passion (at least when measured against the journal's usually dispassionate tenor). He argues that, especially given its longstanding interest in the subject, sociology has failed to adequately confront "the tragedy of humanity" represented by suicide and that it is restrained from doing so by its own "prudery and squeamishness" as well as by its (value–neutral) refusal to "give answers" (p. 663). It is in this context that he calls for the inclusion in sociological research of a Freudian-based "psychoanalytic psychiatry" which, he asserts, would bring to these endeavors "the key" to the "Pandora's box" of human irrationality, adding that with respect to the causes of suicide, "it is high time we have some answers" (p. 663). Other than its rhetorical flourishes, Simpson's article is written in the standard journal essayist format. However, the editors of *ASR* placed it not in the journal's article section but rather in a section entitled "Notes on Research and Teaching," thereby assigning it the diminished status that adheres to articles that have not been approved by peer review. Furthermore, the other psychoanalytically oriented articles written by Simpson in the 1950s appear in less prestigious journals (including the only full-fledged critique of William Sewell's highly influential anti-psychoanalytic work, discussed here in the next section [Simpson, 1957]). When Simpson's name appears at the end of the 1950s in one journal, it is in a caustically dismissive review of his book *Sociologist Abroad*; the reviewer calls the book "an embarrassingly bad book," the "primitive" nature of its content indicated by the absurdity of its main thesis, that is, "that sociologists should be psychoanalysts" (Bierstedt, 1960, p. 194).

Each in their own way, the articles by the Mowrers and Simpson exemplify approaches aimed at integrating psychoanalytic ideas into sociology. Another approach, though, envisioned the clinical and theoretical fusion of psychoanalysis and sociology. The clearest example of this is a 1952 *ASR* article by Bingham Dai, whose self-defined "sociopsychiatric approach" drew equally on sociological concepts ("primary group," "role taking") and psychodynamic concepts ("primary self," "self-concepts"). Dai, whose graduate school mentors were Herbert Blumer and Harry Stack Sullivan (Blowers, 2004), incorporates some ideas from Freud while explicitly arguing for a rejection of Freud's theory of libidinal development. In its place, he offers a mix of ideas based on the clinically oriented conceptual union of neo-Freudian notions of "self" and the sociological concept of "role" (p. 47).

So far, articles discussed advance approaches that deem psychoanalytic ideas of central concern. In another type of article, the author adds—as a kind of afterthought—relatively short discussions of psychoanalytic ideas to an article that otherwise deals solely with sociological materials. For instance, a 1948 *ASR* overview of family studies by Leonard Cottrell contains several brief passages that assert the usefulness of psychoanalytic concepts (for example, "there can be no question of the tremendous amount of insight and understanding" that family studies has gained from "Freudian psychoanalysts"). Cottrell uniformly places these passages within a more elaborated non-psychoanalytic discussion of sociological concepts, the latter providing the basic substance of his presentation (p. 126). Similarly, in a 1950 *AJS* article, Herbert Goldhamer advances a six-page discussion of various sociological approaches to issues dealing with the relationship between public opinion and personality formation and then briefly settles on an insightful discussion of the possible usefulness to opinion research of the psychodynamic concept of displacement.

With the partial exception of Dai's text (Dai identifies his approach as that of both "a lay-analyst and a sociologist" [p. 44]), the articles under examination in this paper maintain a distinctly sociological viewpoint. In part this is a result of the fact that, in a break with practices of the 1930s and early 1940s, *AJS* and *ASR* in the period 1948–1960 each published just one psychoanalytically relevant article authored by a non-sociologist, both articles (by social psychologists) being nonetheless focused on issues of sociological concern (Allen, 1954; Gold, 1958). But what is more important than the fact that all the psychoanalytically oriented articles of 1948–1960 are formulated within frames of reference consistent with sociological concerns is that the overall character of these frames of reference changes in a consistent and generalizable way through the period.

One crucial indicator of this change is the shift in the articles' dominant writing style from essayist to scientistic, a change evidenced by the stylistic changes of the pro-psychoanalytic articles appearing in *AJS* and *ASR*: as stated earlier, all the pro-psychoanalytical essayist style articles appeared before 1953; almost all of the pro-psychoanalytic scientistic style articles appeared after 1953. While reflective of a broader reorientation that affected the journals' article sections in general (one study of the publishing record of *ASR* finding that "survey research" became the most popular sociological journal format starting in 1952, having replaced "general theory," which had previously held that position [Wilner, 1985, pp. 8, 19]), this change in style may be viewed as epitomizing a major transformation of the whole academic setting in which sociological work occurred, a transformation (as we will show in a later section) propelled by pressures both ideological and institutional toward limiting sociological knowledge to that associated with the statistically oriented constrained empiricism that came to dominate much of mainstream American sociology in the mid-1950s.

A review of articles published at different points between 1948 and 1960 by two relatively prominent sociologists of the era, Robert Winch and Warren Dunham, vividly illustrates the emergence of scientistic pressures as reflected in the works of sociologists interested in psychoanalysis. In Winch's 1951 *ASR* article "Further Data and Observations on the Oedipus Hypothesis: The Consequence of an Inadequate Hypothesis," the author reports on an ongoing project that had as its aim to recast psychoanalytic theory into a set of testable hypotheses—that is, into hypotheses concerning the validity of Freud's theory of the Oedipus complex. Winch's notion of how this would validate Freudian ideas involved efforts to create a series of hypotheses written in a form such that Freud's theory could be tested by the statistically attuned measurement of responses to questionnaires. Beginning with findings from earlier published studies (Winch, 1943, 1946, 1949), Winch reports that in the case of males his central hypothesis supporting Freud's Oedipus theory—that is, that the nature of the relationship with the parent of the opposite sex accounts for differences in courtship outcomes—was validated by a statistical analysis of survey results from a thousand male students. These results revealed a correlation between a reported preference for mothers over fathers and failure in courtship (p. 795). Winch then contrasts these findings with female students' responses to the same survey questions, the result revealing here an inadequacy in the hypothesis and, by inference, in Freud's theory itself. In contrast to the corresponding male case, no correlation was found to exist between female preference of fathers over mothers and courtship failure. This leads Winch to conclude that, regarding women, the central Oedipus hypothesis (and implicitly Freud's theory) needed reformulation by incorporating more sociologically framed postulates about patriarchal cultural norms (p. 795).

As if to acknowledge the methodological difficulties involved in attempting to operationalize Freud, two later *ASR* articles by Winch (Winch, Ktsanes and Ktsanes, 1954; Winch, 1955) deal principally with the mechanics involved in the proper formation of testable hypotheses; the only explicit mention of Freud's theories is a reference to them as a "general belief system" from which various testable hypotheses might be drawn (1955, p. 53). However, issues of psychoanalysis reemerge in an *AJS* article that Winch coauthored with Douglas More in 1956; this seeks to counter arguments of unnamed academic antagonists who are characterized as insisting "personality could not be reduced to holes in an IBM card" (p. 445). Winch and More's counterargument relies on demonstrating what statistical approaches can do, namely, quantitatively scoring interviews dealing with categories derived from Henry Murray's need schema; the authors explain that they have come to prefer this schema over the alternative psychoanalytic model since Freud's "system does not provide clearly defined unidimensional variables" and is thus difficult to make "operational" (pp. 445, 446).

Writings published in *AJS* and *ASR* at different points over the period by Warren Dunham provide another set of indicators of the difficulty faced by those who came to feel that a crucial condition for the sociological use of psychoanalytic ideas involved a statistically attuned recasting of those ideas. Early in this period, a 1948 *ASR* article by Dunham entitled "Social Psychiatry" casts a positively framed prognostication—that is, "psychoanalysis . . . must mesh eventually with a dynamic sociology of inter-personal and cultural relationships" (p. 186)—within a relatively subtle analysis of the history of the sociological involvement with psychoanalysis. In particular, Dunham argued that the emergent sociological field of social psychiatry drew many of its ideas from psychoanalysis, both in its "orthodox" version (Freud) and in those more coterminous with "social psychology" (in particular, Harry Stack Sullivan), including, somewhat problematically, from the culture and personality school. Central within Dunham's article is his optimistic forecast of a "coming together of certain psychoanalysts, psychiatrists, anthropologists, psychologists and sociologists" (p. 196); barely mentioned are concerns with hypothesis formation and statistical testing. But two reviews by Dunham published in the next several years (*AJS* in 1949 and *ASR* in 1951) indicate a growing concern with what he was coming to see as the methodological sloppiness of others committed to psychoanalysis. As a consequence, as the first of these reviews asserts, there was a need to "design experimental situations which will serve as adequate and valid tests of the various elements of [psychoanalytic] theory" (p. 561), a position Dunham strengthened in a later 1954 *AJS* review insisting that all efforts to integrate psychoanalysis must be ruled by the scientistic imperative of "constantly testing psychoanalytic hypotheses" (p. 104). And in a 1956 *ASR* article that Dunham co-authored, he casts psychoanalysis as now beyond the bounds of effective application; in this particular study, a statistical analysis of clinical outcomes serves to validate the article's anti-psychoanalytic hypothesis ("that psychotherapeutic treatment of juvenile delinquents . . . does not serve to prevent them from becoming adult offenders"); his earlier, more open embrace of psychoanalysis has clearly been supplanted by questions about lack of scientific grounding (Adamson and Dunham, 1956, pp. 313, 314, 320).

An examination of the trajectory of Winch's and Dunham's changing attitudes toward the use of psychoanalysis suggests two related patterns. In the case of Winch, the dream of operationalizing psychoanalysis turns from an easy enthusiasm to disillusionment and disavowal; in the case of Dunham, a relatively comfortable embrace of wide-ranging psycho-social approaches turns insistently scientistic and then openly skeptical. In both cases, a rigorously methodological commitment to operationalizing Freudian concepts brings in its wake disaffection not with the use of operational methods but from Freudian concepts themselves. One might have expected that at least some would have objected to the narrowed approach this work represented, but at least at the discursive level of *ASR* and *AJS* publishing, no objections were raised.

Rather the fact that before 1953, of all the pro-psychoanalytic writings published in *AJS* and *ASR*, only Winch's and Dunham's writings (if we consider also the latter's reviews) actively advocated an approach of hypothesis formation and statistical testing, whereas after 1953, every one of the pro-psychoanalytic writings published in *AJS* and *ASR* adhered to this same approach, leads us to another surmise. For Winch's and Dunham's disenchantment seems reflective of the wider movement within sociological circles mentioned above toward a scientistic frame of reference. This frame included both the conviction that in the social sciences the only legitimate ideas are those scientistically derived, and that there were difficulties inherent in any attempt to operationalize psychoanalytic ideas (that is, such ideas were particularly illegitimate scientifically and thus useless to sociology).

Nonetheless, it is clear from the published record that Winch's and Dunham's disenchantment was not shared universally by sociologists interested in psychoanalysis. Pro-psychoanalytic articles continued to appear in the journals after 1953, although few in number (7 pro-psychoanalytic articles were published in the journals in the seven-year period 1953–1960, a significant falling off from the 16 articles that appeared in the five-year period 1948–1952). Every one of these post-1953 articles is intended to be scientistic; each can be seen an exercise in transforming hypotheses into statistically backed conclusions. Moreover, each repeats the same model that orders argument and directs the presentation of thought vis-à-vis the same sequencing of purpose: *hypotheses, data collection, statistical analysis, findings.*

Consider one example of how articles published after 1954 adhered to this standardized structure. This example, a 1956 *ASR* article by Russell Dynes, Alfred Clarke and Simon Dinitz, begins with the authors' rendering of an idea found in "much of the psychoanalytic literature" in the form of a hypothesized proposition: "unsatisfactory interpersonal relations in early childhood" lead in adults to "neurotic striving for power, recognition and success" (p. 212). To test this proposition's validity, the authors concoct a two-part questionnaire: an aspiration scale, with questions measuring "the willingness to forego certain satisfactions in order to achieve occupational advancement" and an index of parent–child interaction (querying, for example, "how frequently have you felt that you were not wanted by your father?"). The questionnaire was administered to 350 college students, and analyzed answers led in turn to the authors' findings: a statistically significant correlation between high occupational aspiration and unsatisfactory interpersonal family relations (p. 213).

Articles negatively disposed toward psychoanalysis

We now examine articles appearing between 1948 and 1960 in *AJS* and *ASR* which, while containing a significant focus on psychoanalytic ideas, aim to discredit these ideas and their use in sociology. These articles, for the most part, appear in *AJS* rather than *ASR*—a reversal of the previously noted predominance of positive articles in *ASR* (negative articles in *AJS*, eight; negative articles in *ASR*, three). Of the negative articles that appear in the early part of the period (1948–1952), more than half adopt an essayist style of journal writing while almost all the articles of the later part of the period (1954–1960) adopt a scientistic style.

Found in many of these negative articles is the complaint that using psychoanalysis leads to a reductive transformation of social behaviors into psychodynamic machinations. Reductionism here connotes a misguided privileging of psychic realities and an unjustified downgrading of determinant powers of social realities. For example, an *AJS* article published in 1950 by Thelma Herman McCormack appraising myriad approaches to understanding the motivation of political radicals finds the "Freudian approach" to be reductively grounded on twin assumptions: political predispositions originate in "infantile needs" and radicalism stems from "the child's rebellion against parental authority" (p. 21). The examination of the attitudes of radicals is thus reduced to considerations of basic personality disturbances—for example, socialist advocacy emerges as an expression of "latent homosexuality" (pp. 20–21). Castigating psychoanalytically influenced social scientists who view "public attitudes [as] . . . projections of private need," McCormack asserts that instead such examinations should be embedded in appraising the wider social-historical context and considered sociologically in their connection to the formation of social movements and social change (p. 21).

Also common to a number of the negative articles is the structuring of the argument through the drawing of a contrast between (inadequate) psychoanalytic and (more satisfactory) sociological approaches. Such a comparison is at the heart of a 1950 *ASR* article by Mirra Komarovsky about stresses on marriages caused by the "over-attachment" of the wife to her family of orientation. Komarovsky's study exhibits a nuanced psychological (albeit anti-Freudian) understanding, her target being sociologists of the family whose patriarchal biases are said to draw support from psychoanalysis. The problem of female over-attachment, she asserts, has been overlooked by sociologists of the family who view in-law problems (and, by inference, many other aspects of kinship relations) in terms of male predisposition to become a "mother love victim." According to Komarovsky, this view ultimately reflects a "theoretical bias" traceable to the Freudian prominence given to the Oedipus, rather than the Electra, complex (p. 515). Further, she asserts that the "psychiatric literature" and Freud's view that "anatomy is [the female's] fate" inspired this skewed view. For the sociologist of the family, the female's "life history" is thus seen not as an expression of personal development and achievement, as is the male's life, but reductively in terms of her "biologically determined sexual characteristics, i.e., penis envy or masochism" (p. 508).

Komarovsky's alternative to such views is sociological—she does not propose an alternative feminist psychoanalytic theory—and it is shaped by scientistic methods in ways similar to many of the other articles examined here. First, Komarovsky offers an elaboration of empirically derived mechanisms of sex-role training which favor the emotional emancipation and independence of the boy (not the girl); then she statistically derives empirical indicators (including Winch's compilations of female college students' attitudes discussed above); and, finally, she sums up by stating a to-be-empirically-tested hypothesis, that is, greater sheltering of a girl has a "latent dysfunction" for women and marriage in general (p. 512).

In the articles by McCormack and Komarovsky, the dismissal of psychoanalysis—and, in particular, *Freudian* psychoanalysis—plays something of a secondary role within broader presentations of sociological ideas. This is not the case with another category of negative articles in both *AJS* and *ASR* wherein the central thrust aims straightforwardly at delegitimizing sociological efforts to integrate psychoanalysis. For example, in a 1950 article published in *ASR*, Alfred Lindesmith and Anselm Straus—co-authors of the classic symbolic interactionist textbook *Social Psychology* (1949)—issued an across-the-board attack on the culture and personality school, focusing their criticisms on varied efforts by the school's proponents to make psychoanalytic concepts and methods relevant to social science. Spicing their attack with overt sarcasm—for instance, they mockingly congratulate one anthropologist for his "excess of enthusiasm [that] carries the *post hoc* method to an all-time high" (p. 598)—the authors bundle together Benedict, Mead, Kluckhohn, Erikson, Kardiner, and Fromm, accusing them all of myriad methodological sins. These include confusing facts with interpretation; circular reasoning that deduces psychic entities from observed behaviors that are then conceptually reified and used to explain the same behaviors; relying on suppositions of fanciful constructs of "unconscious" factors when confronted with contradictory empirical evidence; offering non-empirically based theories of psychic essentialism and what the authors call "infantile determination" (pp. 591, 597).

In an even broader critique, Reinhard Bendix in a 1952 *AJS* article advances a rigorously argued and tightly reasoned assault on the use of psychoanalytic concepts in sociological work. Given the radically different levels of abstraction between the objects of social and psychic analysis—in the former, normative behavioral and cultural patterns common to social groups; in the latter, unique emotional meanings particular to an individual—Bendix argued that a total disconnect exists between the two realms. Bendix cleverly reconfigures elements from the conceptual schemas of Erik Erikson and Norbert Elias in a way that undermines these two authors' attempts to link the psyche and the social, and he sets up and then dismisses a series of claims advancing notions of a correspondence between these two realms—claims embodied in such concepts as "national character," "public personality," "basic personality type," and "social character." In particular, he caustically dismisses the writings of Oscar Lewis and Erich Fromm (asserting with regard to the latter that his concept of "'Social character' is a science fiction" [300]). Bendix also takes to task studies premised on the claim of major socially caused historical variations in psychic formations; social formations, he asserts, radically change over the course of history but the range of possible personality types do not. Consequently, he pronounced, there is absolutely no way to overcome the "incongruity between institutions and psychological habitus" since quite distinctive psychic states—for example, conviction, apathy, greed, fear—can lead to the same social behaviors (p. 301).

With the exception of a major section of Komarovsky's article, none of negative articles so far discussed contains a focus on hypotheses formation, statistical testing, or the operationalization of concepts. Although Bendix's critique in particular drew some degree of attention (and was republished in the era's most notable collection of psychosocial articles [Smelser and Smelser, 1963]), its impact may have been muted by not being framed within the emerging scientistic parameters of 1950s mainstream sociology. (Indeed, George Steinmetz locates Bendix among the era's small circle of "sociological critics of methodological positivism," adding that "all of these critics lost some of their scientific authority in relation to the purveyors of the new dominant paradigm" [2005c, p. 308]). But a very different reception met a series of articles by William H. Sewell, who in the 1950s was instrumental in building, in his son's words, "the powerful and notoriously positivist sociology department" at the University of Wisconsin (Sewell Jr., 2005, p. 174). Sewell's statistically based articles attracted widespread notice, one article in particular (1952) being reprinted in more than half a dozen social science collections (Alwin, 2001). Notice even reached beyond academia; Sewell reports that he received "letters from all over Europe" thanking him for freeing the letter writers from the oppression of Freudian ideas (Maraniss, 2004, p. 126).

The thrust of Sewell's arguments focused on data gleaned from a 1940s' rural field study of 162 farm children of "old American stock," research first presented in a 1949 *ASR* article in which Sewell laboriously describes interview techniques he devised to induce country-shy farm mothers to reveal how they had nursed, weaned, and toilet-trained their children. In the project's summary article, published in 1952 in *AJS*, Sewell characterizes the goal of his overall project as offering empirical tests of which psychoanalytic theory was in great need given the latter's "lack of attention to . . . adequate statistical and experimental techniques" (p. 149). At stake, Sewell insists, is more than the question of scientific adequacy: "Even more serious, many pediatricians, clinical psychologists, family counselors, and other practitioners have accepted psychoanalytic theory on faith" (p. 150). Sewell's scientistic corrective consists of the construction of a series of hypotheses serving to format his field data for statistical testing so as to compare two separate sets of codes punched into IBM cards: binary scores derived from mothers' interviews concerning their early child care practices (bottle fed/breast fed, early/late bowel training, and so on) and binary scores (favorable/ unfavorable) derived from standard personality tests administered to the children (Sewell acknowledges the crudeness involved in his binary scoring of personality attributes [p. 154]). After a detailed methodological discussion of hypothesis formation and data preparation, Sewell reports that his statistical output validates his central hypothesis stated in its null form: no more of a statistical relationship exists between the two sets of data concerning child training practices and personality attributes than would be expected by chance alone. Whatever differences the children exhibited in social adjustment cannot be linked to prior differences in infant training. On this basis, Sewell asserts, "this study cast serious doubts on the validity of the psychoanalytic claims regarding the importance of infant disciplines" (pp. 158–159).

Overlooked in later discussions of Sewell's 1952 *AJS* article is that it concludes with a caveat: perhaps what affects children's personality adjustment is not training practices per se but rather "the attitudes and behavior of the mother. This aspect of the mother–child relationship was purposefully excluded [from the original study]" (p. 159). To this comment Sewell adds in a footnote that psychoanalysts, including Erich Fromm, have suggested that it is in such maternal relationships that childhood practices have their real effect: the problem with such ideas though, he adds, is that "no scientific study" has been undertaken that might substantiate them.

Three years later Sewell, serving as the lead author of an *ASR* article, offered just such a "scientific study" (Sewell, Mussen and Harris, 1955). Reconfiguring the data gathered almost a decade before from the interviews with rural mothers, he creates a matrix of possible correlations between thirty-eight distinct indicators of infant training practices. Sewell's premise is that if significant correlations emerged, they would indicate "a single, pervasive, underlying general attitude, such as acceptance or rejection or maternal dominance or indulgence" (p. 140). However, Sewell finds that the factor analysis used to isolate just such correlations turns up none, thus leading to the conclusion that "this study throw[s] into serious question . . . the belief that specific practices reflect some general attitude toward the child"; underlying maternal attitudes, which would appear across several childrearing practices, simply do not exist (p. 148).

In all his work dealing with psychoanalysis, Sewell appears to have maintained an outward demeanor of scientific detachment (albeit one based on narrowly positivistic convictions). Nonetheless, his articles generally and his 1952 article in particular seem to have achieved among various sociological circles the status of an irrefutable scientific refutation of psychoanalysis. Critics and supporters of psychoanalysis alike used and repeated the term "devastating" in interpreting Sewell's work. For instance, for Robert Faris, a long-time critic, the 1952 article was a "devastating research study" that made plain "the shallowness of [the] presumptions" of Freudian followers (1953, p. 439); for Gerald Platt, a student of Parsons and a champion of psychoanalytic sociology, the work's overall impact was "devastating for psychoanalytic theory" (1976, p. 350). Moreover, such a view seems to have been shared by Sewell himself who privately, according to colleagues, "delighted in the distressed reactions [his articles caused] diehard Freudians" (Hauser and Camic, 2006, p. 202).

However, Sewell's branding of psychoanalytic ideas as non-scientific did not on its own vanquish these ideas. His work succeeded because it was but a part of the larger transformation that, as previously mentioned, was taking hold of mainstream sociology in the early 1950s. Nonetheless, the publication records do suggest that Sewell's summary article came at a propitious moment. As already discussed in reference to pro-psychoanalytic articles, within a year of the appearance of Sewell's article, the overall configuration of both positive and negative psychoanalytic articles appearing in *ASR* and *AJS* radically changed: before 1953, almost all of the published positive articles and more than half of the negative articles were of the essayist type; after 1953, all the positive articles and all but one of the negative ones are concerned with hypothesis formation and statistical testing.

Thus 1953 is a turning point: the weight of science descends upon all who discuss psychoanalysis in the article sections of *AJS* and *ASR*. And concurrently with the triumph of scientism, other changes follow. Starting at this point and continuing into the 1960s, the ambition and scope of articles dealing with psychoanalysis, both positively and negatively, correspondingly declines. In the case of negative critiques, a scattering of articles appears over the next eight years, their targets limited and their overall focus non-psychoanalytic. Consider as an example an *ASR* article published in 1959 in which John Kitsuse and David Dietrick offer a closely argued, almost nitpicking critique of Albert Cohen's theory of delinquent subculture. While mostly not touching on psychoanalysis, a crucial aspect of the authors' critique does center on Cohen's use of the psychoanalytic concept of "reaction formation," which the authors term "speculative," "untestable," and "incapable of generating hypotheses"—that is, inapplicable to the purely sociological alternative Kitsuse and Dietrick champion (pp. 211, 214).

The book review sections of *AJS* and *ASR*

Turning to examine the journals' book reviews published between 1948 and 1960, we discover that the two journals exhibited quite distinct tendencies toward books dealing with psychoanalytic subjects. *AJS* published far more reviews dealing with books touching on psychoanalysis than did *ASR* (73 book reviews in *AJS*, 50 book reviews in *ASR*), and *AJS*'s high figures exist in spite of the fact that it devoted fewer pages overall to reviews and published significantly fewer reviews (the total number of book reviews between 1948 and 1960 in *AJS* is 1,960; in *ASR* 2,448). Also the journals differ starkly over which of its sections (book reviews or articles) was more or less open to psychoanalytically oriented subjects. Whereas *AJS* published far fewer psychoanalytically focused articles than *ASR*, it published far more psychoanalytically focused book reviews; the opposite applies to *ASR*, which published far more psychoanalytically focused articles than *AJS* and far fewer such book reviews. Relatedly, too, *AJS*'s book reviews dealing with psychoanalysis are far more favorably disposed than *ASR*'s (*AJS*'s reviews are 82 per cent positive; *ASR*'s reviews 58 per cent positive) in contrast to the journals' article sections where *AJS*'s articles are mostly negative and *ASR*'s articles mostly favorable. These differences suggest that we are dealing with distinct sets of orientations that distinguish not only the book review section of *AJS* from that of *ASR* but, within each journal, its book review section from its article section as well.

How can we explain not only the high number of book reviews in *AJS* that deal with psychoanalytic issues but also the journal's very high percentage of reviews that treat psychoanalysis in a positive manner? And on the contrary, how can we explain not only the low number of book reviews in *ASR* that deal with psychoanalytic issues but also the journal's relatively low percentage of reviews treating psychoanalysis favorably? A series of especially stark contrasts emerges from analyzing the first five years. Between 1948 and 1953, *AJS* ran 37 reviews touching on psychoanalytic ideas; 33 of them contain a favorable appraisal of these ideas (89 per cent positive). Over the same period, *ASR* published only 16 reviews touching on psychoanalytic ideas; 11 of them contain a negative appraisal of these ideas (65 per cent negative).

To probe deeper, let us look at two examples of favorable *AJS* book reviews published this early period. The first is a 1952 *AJS* review by Buford H. Junker, an independent-minded sociologist and anthropologist (Junker Papers, 2011), recommending to sociologists a book written for psychoanalysts: *Principles of Intensive Psychotherapy*, written by the psychoanalyst Frieda Fromm-Reichmann. Junker very favorably on the general usefulness of psychoanalysis to sociologists says: "the psychoanalytic perspective can be of considerable value to the sociologist who works directly with the people who provide the data of sociological interest," adding that such a perspective will help the sociologist "sharpen his awareness of the covert psychodynamics of any given social role" and increase his awareness of the "interpersonal phenomena" of "transference" and "countertransference" (p. 414).

The second example is a 1953 AJS review of a book authored by the Psychoanalyst Saul Scheidlinger for psychoanalytically attuned practitioners of group therapy. While criticizing the book's failure to deal with methodological issues involving "the interpretation of evidence" and for its disregard of the dictates of "the canons . . . of research," G. S. Swanson—a champion throughout the 1950s of an empirically based sociological use of psychoanalytic ideas—ties the book's subject matter to what he favorably calls the "surge of interest in social phenomena by psychoanalytically oriented scholars." This is a "surge," he indicates, that originated with the exploration of unconscious group processes that began with Freud's 1922 book *Group Psychology and the Analysis of the Ego* and that is also reflected in "the present state of all this ferment" generated by contemporary psycho-social thinkers, among whom he lists Horney, Fromm, Kardiner, Sullivan, and Erikson—all well-known figures whom, Swanson adds, "should be paired with the many sociologists and anthropologists who have looked to psychoanalysis for new ideas" (p. 618).

With the example of these two reviews, note the elements of disconnection with what is usually considered the province of sociology. Neither of the reviewed books, for instance, is addressed to sociologists. In fact, an overview of all of the reviewed books focusing on psychoanalysis published by *AJS* during the period reveals that a vast majority of these books is not addressed to sociologists. Relatedly, neither of the books discussed in the review examples above is the work of a sociologist. While not true of all of the books reviewed in *AJS* between 1948 and 1960, most of the authors of these books are academic psychologists, psychiatrists and, especially, psychoanalysts. Among these names, we find (often repeatedly) 16 well-known psychoanalysts and psychoanalytically inclined psychiatrists and psychologists, including Marie Bonaparte, Sigmund Freud, Erik Erikson, Rollo May, Bruno Bettelheim, Frieda Fromm-Reichmann, Theodor Reik, Harry Stack Sullivan, Alfred Adler, and Erich Fromm.

Although not true of the two example reviews above, the disconnection of *AJS*'s reviews from sociology often extends to the journal's choice of reviewers. Between 1948 and 1957—and as distinct from authors of the journal's psychoanalytically oriented *articles* being, with one exception, all sociologists—slightly less than 1/3 of *AJS* reviewers of books touching on psychoanalysis were written by non-sociologists; that is, they were written for the most part by psychiatrists, academic psychologists, and psychoanalysts. The case of the psychoanalyst Bruno Bettelheim is an extreme example of this situation, having published during the period eleven reviews in *AJS*, almost all on books by fellow psychoanalysts and all expressive of favorable views toward psychoanalysis.

But why were *AJS*'s practices when it came to book reviews so different than those used for its article section? Part of the answer pertains to the low academic status of book reviews ("book reviews are the second-class citizens of scientific literature," conclude two separate studies of academic book reviews [Riley and Spreitzer, 1970, p. 361; Champion and Morris 1973, p. 1257]). That 31 per cent of *AJS*'s reviewers of psychoanalytically oriented books were not sociologists may be seen as an effect of the low status of book reviews (and editorial work associated with them) in the world of sociology (especially when compared to journal articles). At *AJS*, this low status was manifested institutionally by a failure to appoint an acknowledged book review editor. Prior to 1958, the journal's title page did not list any position that could be construed as responsible for book reviews, and a computerized search through all previous issues of the journal fails to turn up any mention of a book review editor.

This suggests that *AJS*'s actual process of selecting books and reviews was until then rather haphazard, a matter delegated to assistants outside the primary lines of editorial control who understood their task as tracking down and gathering an adequate number of reviews for each issue. It appears that their overriding priority was finding reviewers (whether they were or were not sociologists does not seem to have mattered much) who were knowledgeable about psychoanalysis and in many such instances this also meant reviewers who were favorably disposed to psychoanalysis; this was extremely so in the case of the non-sociological authors—twenty-one or of the twenty-two reviews written by non-sociologists over the period favored psychoanalysis (in contrast to the reviews written by sociologists, although even with these, three-quarters were also favorable). Seeming to confirm this conjecture, an immediate effect of *AJS*'s official appointment in 1958 of an acknowledged book editor—James A. Davis—was that, from that date onward, *AJS* did not publish another review of a psychoanalytic book written by a non-sociologist.

ASR's book review section shows a starkly different picture from that of *AJS*. First of all, *ASR* reviewed different books than did *AJS*: only seven of the two journals' combined total of 54 psychoanalytically focused reviews were of books reviewed by both journals. The review sections of the two journals also exhibited quite different patterns of reviewer selection, each apparently guided by a different set of standards. With regard to psychoanalysis, this meant a major divide in the journals' respective approaches: while *AJS*'s book review section was open to the advocates of psychoanalysis, for the most part *ASR*'s book review section was not. Moreover, *ASR* appears to have actively sought reviewers known to be hostile to psychoanalytic ideas.

Let us look now, by way of contrast, at two examples of *ASR* book reviews published in the early years of our period. The first, a 1948 review by the sociologist Richard LaPiere, manifests an outright animus toward psychoanalysis that would become even more vitriolic in a later work, *The Freudian Ethic* (1959). (Lewis Coser, offended by its caustic mixture of anti-Freudianism and phobic anti-liberalism, characterized this book as "an ill-tempered and ill-informed pamphleteering broadside" exemplified by its central thesis, which Coser quotes: "the Freudian theory of man . . . insidiously destroys the fabric of American society" both by undermining the Protestant "ethic of enterprise" and by promoting in its place "such [working] class qualities as irresponsibility, lack of enterprise, and lack of personal self-reliance" [1960, p. 212; also see Silver in this volume].) In his 1948 *ASR* book review, LaPiere's ostensible subject is three books that, taken together, argue for the usefulness of psychoanalysis to social scientists: a collection of minor Freud essays on the effects of war edited by the Holocaust scholar Sander Katz, a book subtitled *The Relationship Between Psychoanalysis and Sociology* written by the German sociologist-philosopher Walter Hollitscher, and the first volume of what became the well-established series *Psychoanalysis and the Social Sciences* edited by the anthropologist Géza Góheim.

In reviewing these three books, LaPiere places center stage a metaphoric-laden tale of sociological catastrophe. When "the alien gospel of Freud" first infiltrated America following World War I, as LaPiere starts his review, "a large segment of the sociological fraternity came to accept it and thereby was forced to give up hope for the future of mankind. For the new gospel held that the instincts of man that they had previously believed were the basis of social life [are] actually bestial, pre-social drives." Now in the aftermath of World War II, LaPiere adds, American sociology faces a renewed onslaught of "psychoanalytic proselytizing" from an "increasing flood of books on psychoanalysis" as represented by the three books under review (p. 346). "The danger of the current vogue of introducing psychoanalytic theorizing into sociology," LaPiere writes, "is . . . that it leads to a distortion of the facts of social life," for "psychoanalysis is not a science" but rather is "contra-scientific"; at heart it is "a system of magic," a set of practices based upon "the mysteries of the cult" (p. 347). "The chief danger to sociology in the current psychoanalytic vogue," concludes LaPiere, is that "sociological nonsense . . . results when any attempt is made to use psychoanalytic concepts as scientific tools" (p. 348).

The second example, a 1953 *ASR* review by Robert E. L. Faris of the book *Psychoanalysis as Science* by an academic psychologist and two psychiatrists, had a notable impact, becoming a point of discussion in several books dealing with the question of whether psychoanalysis was sufficiently scientific (Mack, 1955; Richfield, 1954, 1956). Faris structures his review as a list of the failings of psychoanalysis— its "ten major shortcomings of scientific spirit and method"—derived in part from the book's own "clear presentation" of the ways "general Freudian theory does not rest on a rigorously scientific basis." According to Faris, this is a situation that the book's authors themselves seek to remedy by enlisting "objective research studies" and "improvement in research methods in this field" (p. 437). Foremost among Faris' list of psychoanalysis's "shortcomings" is the usual scientistically conceived culprit: the failure to advance testable propositions that allow for the possibility of falsification. At times, the specificity of Faris' list exhibits a certain non-scientistic acuity: for instance, with regard to the followers of Freud, he points to their overreliance on characterizations of personality traits in terms of bodily functions and anatomical differences (the "label[ling of] all orderliness as 'anal' . . . and [of] status complaints by women as 'penis envy'") and to their indiscriminate use of reifications of psychic processes (the "anthropomorphizing [of] . . . abstractions of the whole personality [id, ego, and superego], endowing each with a spurious independent existence . . . [and engaging in] allegorical imagery and figures of speech about strife between them" [p. 437]). But Faris' guiding judgment finds its most overt statement in the review's conclusion: he suggests that "the distinctive Freudian theory [will not] survive" for "closed minds can hold to erroneous ideas for an indefinite time." This theme ("closed minds") is the subject of the last third of the review, which focuses on a series of instances in which followers of psychoanalysis continue to hold onto ideas science has shown erroneous. Among the dubious examples offered are the continued utilization of ideas from Adorno et al.'s *The Authoritarian Personality* even though the book has been "contradicted by other studies . . . and therefore [is no longer] reliable as evidence of a scientific character" (none of the book's various scientistic critiques are cited), and the continued adherence to the psychoanalytic belief in "the importance of early childhood" even though "Sewell's recent devastating research reveals the shallowness of presumptions of this type" (Sewell, 1952, as above).

As is true of the above two examples, the psychoanalytically oriented books that *ASR* chose almost always contain elements of some sociological interest, in contrast to many of the reviews of such books published in *AJS*. Of the books covered by these two *ASR* reviews, both reviews briefly describe their connections to sociology: in one case, an argument calling for the sociological use of Freudian ideas; in the other, an exploration of making psychoanalysis more scientific and compatible with the social sciences. In seeking to explain *ASR*'s success in keeping its review section relevant to sociology, it is important to note that the journal was—and remains— a publication of the national professional organization of American sociologists, the American Sociological

Society (as it was known at the time). It makes perfect sense, then, to conjecture that this organizational tie impressed upon the *ASR* editors a commitment to sociological relevance. In turn, this led to a commitment to the journal adopting, however informally, selective criteria including the principle that reviews and books reviewed should pertain to at least some sector of the journal's sociological readership.

An observation needs to be added here concerning the journals' selection of reviewers to deal with psychoanalytically oriented books. Over the period, *ASR*'s reviewers were almost exclusively sociologists (90 per cent) and, in the few cases when they were not, they were academic practitioners of closely related social sciences (two anthropologists, two academic psychologists, and one professor of social work). Thus *ASR*'s adherence to a policy of recruiting sociologists to cover the needs of its book review section, and *AJS*'s reliance on non-sociologists to do a significant portion of this work, may well be related to the fact that *ASR* had—whereas *AJS* did not have—direct organizational connections to the ASS membership, including specialists of diverse subfields, leaders of regional affiliations, and leading figures working within the subject-area sections organized in conjunction with the association's annual meetings. It may also be conjectured that *ASR*'s record of publishing such a high proportion of book reviews critical of psychoanalytic ideas is, in part, a reflection of the journal's closer (and more 'organic') relationship to ASS's membership. In other words, the high proportion of reviews hostile to psychoanalysis reflected—and, of course, assisted—an emergent hostility increasingly shared by prominent sectors of the organization's membership to the sociological incorporation of psychoanalysis.

As we saw in our discussion of the two journals' article sections, beginning in the late 1940s these sections both began to register and respond to pressures associated with the profound changes of the era in the institutional surround, academic culture, and fundamental frames of references associated with the practices of sociology. Hence, just at the time when a wave of excitement over newly conceived sociological uses of psychoanalysis spread through some sociological circles—perhaps best symbolized by Parsons' 1949 ASS presidential address (discussed at the beginning of the last section)—a rage for scientific rigor arose to challenge what Swanson (referring to various manifestations of the sociological opening to psychoanalysis) would call "the present state of all this [psycho-social] ferment." At the beginning of our period (1948 to 1953), the two journals' book review sections played very different roles in this battle, as evidenced by the fact that in those crucial years, while a majority of *AJS*'s reviews of books on psychoanalytic issues registered an approval of these ideas, a majority of *ASR*'s reviews registered disapproval. But even this alignment was short lived; in the later years of the 1950s, as the swell of this psycho-social ferment dissolved, the differences between the journals with regard to psychoanalysis dissolved as well. By the time *AJS* had appointed an official book-review editor, the journal ceased the practices that had differentiated it: no longer did the tone of its reviews of psychoanalytically oriented books differ notably from that of *ASR*'s; no longer did it haphazardly select non-sociological authors to review these books; and no longer did it publish reviews of books on psychoanalytical issues that seemingly were irrelevant to sociology. If anything, the journal seemed no longer interested in the types of psycho-social books that previously it had so readily reviewed—indeed, in the last years of the decade *AJS* published so few reviews of psychoanalytically influenced books that their number was but a quarter of what it had been earlier and a mere half of what *ASR* published at the time.

Institutional context

It is evident that a shift occurred from 1948 to 1960 in how psychoanalysis was represented in *AJS* and *ASR*, a shift especially notable when viewed in terms of the increasingly scientistic types of argumentation (for and against psychoanalysis) granted a hearing in their pages. This shift took place within a larger historical movement that altered both the ideological and institutional environment in which sociological practices occurred, an alteration that can be conceptualized schematically as a transformation of American sociology from a splintered institutional field in the pre-1950 period (in which the principal actors did not share a set of criteria that defined scientific capital) to a more settled field of the 1950s (in which the principal actors did share such a definition) (Steinmetz, 2005b, pp. 121–123; Bourdieu, 1975, p. 21).

Reflecting sociology's fragmented field in the earlier period, the article sections in *AJS* and *ASR* during the 1930s and 1940s offered an assortment of epistemological viewpoints, their most prevalent orientation being an essayist approach to general theorizing that included a broad range of authorial voices, methodological approaches, and topics (Wilner, 1985, pp. 7–10). In particular, sociology's lack of 'fieldness' in the decades preceding the 1950s is epitomized by the journals' early openness to psychoanalysis. This was evident in *ASR*'s first volumes (publication began in 1936) which contained numerous articles sympathetic to psychoanalysis, including separate papers by the psychoanalyst Karen Horney and the ethnographer and psychoanalyst George Devereux, and in two special issues in *AJS* in 1939—a March issue devoted to "The Individual and the Group" (with separate articles by the psychoanalyst Thomas French and by the Marxist clinical psychologist J. F. Brown) and, shortly following Freud's death, a November special issue entirely devoted to his ideas.

All eleven of the articles in this latter *AJS* issue presented favorable views of Freud's work and championed various aspects of that work as pertinent to the social sciences. But, remarkably, only one of these eleven articles was written by a sociologist—Ernest Burgess, who was also the editor-in-chief of *AJS* at the time—while six were by prominent psychoanalysts, each of whom had played important roles in promoting psychoanalysis in the United States. An obituary published in the same issue eulogized Freud for "uncovering the role of the unconscious and the non-rational elements in action," calling him "one of the great pioneers and molders of the modern sciences of personality and culture" ("Sigmund Freud 1939," p. 453).

The articles that appeared in *AJS* and *ASR* in the 1950s reflect a very different sociology than that of the 1930s. In the 1950s, the discipline can be seen as undergoing a major transformation: the number of students studying sociology and of professors teaching it massively grew; one indicator of this growth is that the membership in the American Sociological Society registered a six-fold increase from 1,034 in 1940 to 6,436 in 1959 (Rhoades, 1981, pp. 33, 42). Equally noteworthy was an unprecedented influx of foundation and government money; one indicator here is an astonishing increase in the proportion of *AJS* articles acknowledging outside financial support, reaching 52 per cent by the beginning of the 1960s whereas prewar figures were under 2 per cent (McCartney, 1971, pp. 387–388). Along with these changes, as George Steinmetz in particular has argued, the prevailing intellectual tenor of sociology underwent a major change; central to sociology becoming a settled institutional field was the emergent dominance in the production of sociological knowledge of a cluster of methodological positions that combined empiricist ontology, positivist epistemology, and scientistic naturalism. "Methodological positivism," as Steinmetz has labeled this cluster of positions, came to prevail ideologically among the personnel of most of the leading sociology departments and funding agencies and, it can be conjectured in a very specific manner, among many of the academic heavyweights who served as editors and peer reviewers of *AJS* and *ASR* (Steinmetz, 2005a, p. 117, 2005c, p. 292).

Changes in the format and tone of *AJS* and *ASR* serve as expressions of this major reorganization of American sociology. According to one study, a comparison of the number of qualitative and quantitative articles published each year in *ASR* found that for each of the years 1936–1951 there existed a fairly constant ratio of seven qualitative to three quantitative articles. In 1952, however, this balance was abruptly overturned with the ratio becoming three quantitative to one qualitative article—a ratio that then held firm through the rest of the 1950s (Wilner, 1985, pp. 9, 19). Another related confirmation that 1952 was an important turning point in the rise of new scientistic norms is that, in this year, the number of articles in *ASR* using survey research leapt from seven articles (the average number for each of the years 1936–1951) to twenty-six (with similar figures for the years following) (Wilner, 1985, p. 19). Studies of *AJS*'s record indicate that the 1950s in general, and the early 1950s specifically, was a time of major reorganization of sociological norms. The new norms were predicated on the scientistic foundation of the operationalization of concepts and the utilization of quantitative measures, leading to a situation in which almost all of the articles published by *AJS* and *ASR* contained some aspect of quantitative sociology (by the 1970s, this figure had become 87 per cent) (Platt, 1996, pp. 191, 272; Gigerenzer, 2001, p. 3687).

Steinmetz points to the very layout of the pages of *ASR* and *AJS* as registering the emergent hegemony of "methodological positivism": the 1930s' essayist flow of full-page text was replaced by pages of two tightly packed columns and, increasingly, by the display of tabular statistical table, a change meant to mirror contemporary "hard science" journals. Concomitant with these stylistic changes was the marginalization of interpretative, introspective and other qualitative and essayist methods—all stylistic approaches that implicitly reference the personhood of the writer. As Steinmetz puts it, "The distrust of [the] authorial voice as subjective was initially linked to the distinction between facts and values, but the voiceless style soon became established in sociology . . . without reference to its original philosophical political motives" (2005b, p. 119). The authorial voice of positivist epistemology—a voiceless voice, without subjective overtones—might fruitfully be seen as an institutional reworking of the personality trait of *anti-intraception* (which is to be severely discomforted by subjective experiences) as analyzed by one of the outstanding psycho-social works of the 1950s (Adorno et al., 1950, p. 235). The need to defend sociology from the truly human authorial voice, indeed the urge to banish the effects of the personal altogether, could also be seen as sharing common roots not only with efforts of the period to blatantly refute psychoanalytic ideas but, more broadly, with related undertakings driven by the imperative to recast any phenomena that touches upon matters of the psyche into quantifiable, testable propositions.

Conclusion

From our examination of the articles and reviews dealing with psychoanalytical ideas in *AJS* and *ASR* during the years 1948–1960, there emerges a complex pattern of crosscurrents of approval and disapproval of the sociological use of these ideas. A majority of *AJS*'s articles rejected strongly the sociological use of these ideas, almost always in an extremely harsh manner. Most of *ASR*'s articles advanced arguments in support of the sociological incorporation of psychoanalytic ideas, at times in a highly positive manner. In a reversal of this pattern, a substantial majority of *AJS*'s reviews favored psychoanalysis, sometimes in quite glowing terms, while nearly half of the reviews in *ASR* contain unfavorable evaluations, some of which are quite harsh.

A chronological divide contributes to the complexity of this pattern, with 1953 serving as the pivotal year: two-thirds of the articles regarding the sociological use of psychoanalytic ideas and, more importantly, almost all of the more significant articles and reviews appeared in the first half of our period. After 1953, as already noted, the articles in particular evidence a noticeable drop in ambition and scope. Moreover, the very written structures that organized thought on the issue changed: before the end of 1953, almost all of the articles favoring psychoanalysis and more than half of the articles hostile to it were written in an essayist style; after 1953, all the favorable articles and all but one of the critical articles were written in a scientistic style, with a focus on hypothesis formation and statistical testing.

This shift from essayist to scientistic style in writing about the sociological use of psychoanalysis makes evident how "style" affects the very thought process by which the issues involved were conceptualized. For instance, consider the interpretative and intuitive aspects of Komarovsky's essayist critique of the way the patriarchal biases of family sociology drew support from Freudianism, with the latter's predisposition to conceive issues of childhood as male-centered (the Oedipus rather than the Electra complex) and its biologically reductive notions of the female child (her alternatives being "penis envy or masochism"). Then compare Komarovsky's approach with Sewell's scientistic (and, in real terms, hollow) finding that neither differences in infant maternal practices nor differences in underlying maternal attitudes have any influence on young children's personality development.

In spite of this overlay of contrariness—between one journal and the other, between reviews and articles within the same journal, and between articles and reviews of the early and late years of the period—we have unearthed from our examination two rather simple tales. The first tale is specific to efforts to create a psychoanalytic sociology in the period 1948–1960. It begins with an upsurge in excitement concerning what was perceived to be an opening of new ways to incorporate psychoanalytic ideas into mainstream sociology. This upsurge is followed closely by the emergence of a strong backlash which succeeded, first, in restraining acceptance of these efforts by narrowing the available frames of reference to those consistent with the dictates of methodological positivism, and then, finally, in the almost total elimination of even such constrained efforts from mainstream sociology.

The second tale has a longer time frame and concerns the larger world of American mainstream sociology in general. It begins in the pre–World War II period when sociology was open to a diversity of approaches (the most popular journal style being an essayist approach to general theorizing). This situation is then overturned in the post–World War II period by an institutional and ideological transformation that brought with it a positivistic ideology and that together transformed an unsettled fragmented field of diverse sociological practices into a settled institutional field of greatly constricted practices (the dominant journal style now being "scientistic"). The first and second tale come together in the beginning of the 1950s, when the second tale of the institutional transformation and emergent ideological hegemony provided the driving force leading the first tale's proponents of psychoanalysis to give way to a double capitulation—first to scientism and second to the dismissal of psychoanalysis as unscientific.

Several qualifications need to be added to this depiction of institutional and ideological transformation. While the attempt to create a mainstream psychoanalytic sociology was largely thwarted in the 1950s, interesting work in this field, though marginalized in various ways, continued to be done. Most significantly in this regard, we have the case of Talcott Parsons. The inclusion of cultural anthropology and academic and psychoanalytic psychology within Parsons' Department of Human Relations seems to have shielded scholars at Harvard from some of the pressures associated with the rising dominance of the narrow empiricist requirements of methodological positivism. Recall Parsons' promise of a theoretical breakthrough proclaimed in the January 1948 issue of *AJS* and in his presidential address before the ASS Annual Meeting in 1949 (published in *ASR* in 1950). Following these early pronouncements, Parsons continued throughout the 1950s to expand upon his effort to create the theoretical bases by which to connect "the personality structure on the psychological level with the sociological analysis of social structure" (as he defined one of his goals in his ASS address). In this endeavor, besides material contained in three books (Parsons and Shils, 1951; Parsons, Bales, and Shils, 1953; Parsons and Bales, 1955), he also published seven major articles over the next ten years.

These seven articles constitute a significant part of Parson's contribution to psychoanalytic sociology. All were explicitly written from a sociological perspective and all sought to find in psychoanalysis a set of concepts by which to expand the theoretical grounds of sociology. Most importantly, the seven articles were all written for sociologists, not psychologists, something that is apparent even from their titles; for instance, "the Superego and the Theory of Social Systems" (1952) and "Social Structure and the Development of Personality," Psychiatry (1958). And it is in this latter article that Parsons famously asserted, "Had Freud lived long enough . . . he would inevitably have become in part, a sociologist" (p. 107). But here is the point: although written for sociologists, none of Parsons' articles were published in *AJS* or *ASR* or in any other American sociology journal. Instead, most were published in psychoanalytic or psychiatric journals and were first delivered as talks at psychoanalytic or psychiatric conferences. An understanding seems to have been reached: American mainstream sociology, as represented by *AJS* and *ASR*, was closed to the expansive presentation of psychoanalytic sociology as found in Parsons' articles. Indeed, when compared to the pro-psychoanalytic articles written by others that were published in the two journals in the 1950s, one is struck by an obvious evaluation: none of these articles have anything near the scholarly breadth and theoretical weight evident in Parsons' articles. Such a comparison also presents us with the thought of how odd and out of place any of these articles would have been if by chance *AJS* or *ASR* had chosen to publish it.

It is helpful to note that a few other prominent sociologists of the period escaped the dominance of scientistic approaches writing works that incorporated, often in a rather disguised manner, psychoanalytic ideas (David Riesman, 1953; Hans Gerth and C. Wright Mills, 1953; Philip Rieff, 1959). The presence of such work suggests there was room at least in some sociological circles for iconoclasts and non-conformists (Calhoun and VanAntwerpen, 2007). Clearly young academics like

G. E. Swanson, who was hired at the University of Michigan in 1949 as a counterweight to the scientistic faction that already dominated the sociology department there in the late 1940s (Steinmetz, 2007, p. 346), continued throughout the decade of the 1950s and beyond to do interesting work in the area of psychoanalytic sociology. On the other hand, it should be noted that all but one of the enduring psycho-social books of the decade were published before 1956; this might suggest to us that the effects of the backlash had for the most part been successful by the second half of the decade. Even looking at Parsons' later psychoanalytic writings suggests a noticeable decline of output beginning in the late 1950s and, even more significantly, in the 1960s a seeming abandonment of his earlier psychoanalytically inclined interests and a shift toward a more purely sociological orientation when dealing with issues like the institutional treatment of mental illness (Parsons, 1964).

In the late 1970s, Donald Levine (1978) looked back at the various recorded manifestations of the opening of the sociological mind to psychoanalysis during the late 1940s and 1950s. Despite the spread of psychoanalytic ideas in the American cultural psyche, this sociological opening—for all the excitement and labor involved—had been, he concluded, tenuous and momentary, "something of a mirage" (p. 176).

References

Adamson, L. and H. W. Dunham (1956) "Clinical Treatment of Male Delinquents: A Case Study in Effort and Result," *American Sociological Review*, 21 (3), 312–320.

Adorno, T. W., E. Frenkel-Brunswik, D. J. Levinson, and R. Nevitt Sanford (1950) *The Authoritarian Personality* (New York: Harper and Brothers).

Allen, D. A. (1954) "Antifeminity in Men," *American Sociological Review*, 19 (5), 591–593.

Alwin, D. F. (2001) "Colleagues Remember William Sewell," *Footnotes* July/August, http://www.asanet.org/footnotes/julyaugust01/fn5.html.

Bendix, R. (1952) "Compliant Behavior and Individual Personality," *The American Journal of Sociology*, 58 (3), 292–303.

Berger, P. (1965) "Toward a Sociological Understanding of Psychoanalysis," *Social Research*, 32 (1), 26–41.

Bierstedt, R. (1960) "Review of *Sociologist Abroad* by George Simpson," *The American Journal of Sociology*, 66 (2), 194.

Blowers, G. (2004) "Bingham Dai, Adolf Storfer, and the Tentative Beginnings of Psychoanalytic Culture in China: 1935–1941," *Psychoanalysis and History*, 6 (1), 93–105.

Bourdieu, P. (1975) "The Specificity of the Scientific Field and the Social Conditions of the Progress of Reason," *Social Science Information*, 14 (6), 19–47.

Calhoun, C. and J. VanAntwerpen (2007) "Orthodoxy, Heterodoxy, and Hierarchy: "Mainstream" Sociology and Its Challengers," in C. Calhoun (ed.) *Sociology in America: A History* (Chicago: University of Chicago Press).

Champion, D. J. and M. F. Morris (1973) "A Content Analysis of Book Reviews in the *AJS*, *ASR*, and *Social Forces*," *American Journal of Sociology*, 78 (35), 1256–1265.

Coser, L. A. (1960) "Review of *the Freudian Ethic* by Richard LaPiere," *Annals of the American Academy of Political and Social Science*, 328 (Mar), 211–212.

Cottrell, L. S., Jr. (1948) "The Present Status and Future Orientation of Research on the Family," *American Sociological Review*, 13 (2), 123–136.

Dai, B. (1952) "A Socio-Psychiatric Approach to Personality Organization," *American Sociological Review*, 17 (1), 44–49.

Dunham, W. H. (1948) "Social Psychiatry," *American Sociological Review*, 13 (2), 183–197.

Dunham, W. H. (1949) "Review of *the Psycho-analytic Approach to Juvenile Delinquency*, by Kate Friedlander," *American Journal of Sociology*, 54 (6), 560–561.

Dunham, W. H. (1951) "Review of *the Mark of Oppression*, by Abram Kardiner and Lionel Ovesey," *American Sociological Review*, 16 (5), 730–732.

Dunham, W. H. (1954) "Review of *Twenty Years of Psychoanalysis*, eds. Franz Alexander and Helen Ross," *American Journal of Sociology*, 60 (5), 730–732.

Dynes, R. R., A. C. Clarke and S. Dinitz (1956) "Levels of Occupational Aspiration: Some Aspects of Family Experience As a Variable," *American Sociological Review*, 21 (2), 212–215.

Faris, R. E. L. (1953) "Review of *Psychoanalysis as Science: The Hixon Lectures on the Scientific Status of Psychoanalysis* by E. Pumpian-Mindlin," *American Sociological Review*, 18 (4), 437–439.

Gerth, H. and C.W. Mills (1953) *Character and Social Structure: The Psychology of Social Institutions* (New York: Harcourt, Brace & Co.).

Gigerenzer, G. (2001) "Digital Computer: Impact on the Social Sciences," *International Encyclopedia of the Social and Behavioral Sciences*, 6, 3684–3688.

Gold, M. (1958) "Suicide, Homicide, and the Socialization of Aggression," *American Journal of Sociology*, 63 (6), 651–661.

Goldhamer, H. (1950) "Public Opinion and Personality," *American Journal of Sociology*, 55 (4), 346–354.

Habermas, J. (1971) *Knowledge and Human Interests*. Boson: Beacon Press.

Hauser, R. M. and C. Camic (2006) "Biographical Memoirs: William Hamilton Sewell," *Proceedings of the American Philosophical Society*, 150 (1), 201–204.

Hinkle, G. J. (1957) "Sociology and Psychoanalysis," in H. Becker and A. Boskoff (eds) *Modern Sociological Theory in Continuity and Change* (New York: Dryden Press).

Junker Papers (2011) *Guide to the Buford Junker Papers: 1930–1975* (Chicago: University of Chicago Library).

Junker, B. H. (1952) "Review of *Principles of Intensive Psychotherapy* by Frieda Fromm-Reichmann," *American Journal of Sociology*, 57 (4), 413–414.

Jones, R. A. (1974) "Freud and American Sociology, 1909–1949," *Journal of the History of Behavioral Sciences*, 10 (1), 21–39.

Kaye, H. L. (1991) "A False Convergence: Freud and the Hobbesian Problem of Order," *Sociological Theory*, 9 (1), 87–105.

Kinloch, G. (1988) "American Sociology's Changing Interests As Reflected in Two Leading Journals," *The American Sociologist*, 19 (2), 181–194.

Kitsuse, J. I. and D. C. Dietrick (1959) "Delinquent Boys: A Critique," *American Sociological Review*, 24 (2), 208–215.

Komarovsky, M. (1950) "Functional Analysis and Sex Roles," *American Sociological Review*, 15 (4), 508–516.

LaPiere, R. T. (1948) "Review of *Freud: On War, Sex and Neurosis* by Sander Katz; *Sigmund Freud: An Introduction* by Walter Hollitscher"; "*Psychoanalysis and the Social Sciences* by Géza Góheim," *American Sociological Review*, 13 (3), 346–348.

LaPiere, R. T. (1959) *The Freudian Ethic* (New York: Duell, Sloan and Pearce).

LaRossa, R. and J. H. Wolf (1985) "On Qualitative Family Research," *Journal of Marriage and Family*, 47 (3), 531–541.

Lawrence, R. J. (1981) *A History of the American Sociological Association 1905–1980* (Washington DC: American Sociological Association).

Levine, D. N. (1978) "Psychoanalysis and Sociology," *Ethos*, 6 (3), 175–185.

Lindesmith, A. R. and A. L. Strauss (1940) *Social Psychology* (New York: Dryden Press).

Lindesmith, A. R. and A. L. Strauss (1949) "A Critique of Culture-Personality Writings," *American Sociological Review*, 15 (5), 587–600.

Mack, R. W. (1955) "The Scientific Status of the Social Sciences," *ETC: A Review of General Semantics*, 12 (3), 201–213.

Madge, J. (1962) *The Origins of Scientific Sociology* (New York: The Free Press).

Maraniss, D. (2004) *They Marched into Sunlight: War and Peace, Vietnam and America October 1967* (New York: Simon & Schuster).

McCartney, J. L. (1971) "The Financing of Sociological Research: Trends and Consequences," in E. A. Tiryakian (ed.) *The Phenomenon of Sociology* (New York: Appleton Century-Crofts).

McCormack, T. H. (1950) "The Motivation of Radicals," *American Journal of Sociology*, 56 (1), 17–24.

Mowrer, E. R. and H. Mowrer (1951) "The Social Psychology of Marriage," *American Sociological Review*, 16 (1), 27–36.

Parsons, T. (1950) "The Prospects of Sociological Theory," *American Sociological Review*, 15 (1), 3–16.

Parsons, T. (1952) "The Superego and the Theory of Social Systems," *Psychiatry*, 15, 15–25. A paper presented before the Psychoanalytic section of the American Psychiatric Association (Cincinnati, May). Reprinted in T. Parsons (1964) *Social Structure and Personality* (New York: The Free Press).

Parsons, T. (1958) Social Structure and the Development of Personality: Freud's Contribution to the Integration of Psychology and Sociology," *Psychiatry*, 21, 321–340. Reprinted in Talcott Parsons, *Social Structure and Personality* (New York: The Free Press).

Parsons, T. (1964) *Social Structure and Personality* (New York: The Free Press).

Parsons, T. and R. F. Bales (1955) *Family, Socialization and Interaction Process* (New York: The Free Press).

Parsons, T., and B. Barber (1948) "Sociology, 1941–46," *American Journal of Sociology*, 53 (4), 245–257.

Parsons, T. and E. A. Shils (eds) (1951) *Toward a General Theory of Action* (Cambridge: Harvard University Press).

Parsons, T., R. F. Bales and E. A. Shils (1953) *Working Papers in the Theory of Action* (New York: The Free Press).

Platt, J. (1996) *A History of Sociological Research Methods in America: 1920–1960* (Cambridge: Cambridge University Press).

Platt, G. M. (1976) "The Sociological Endeavor and Psychoanalytic Thought," *American Quarterly*, 28 (3), 343–359.

Richfield, J. (1954) "The Validation of Scientific Theories," *Scientific Monthly* (Sept), 79, 306–309.

Richfield, J. (1956) *The Validation of Scientific Theories* (New York: Collier).

Rieff, P. (1959) *Freud: The Mind of the Moralist* (Chicago: The University of Chicago Press).

Riesman, D., N. Glazer, and R. Denney (1953) *The Lonely Crowd: A Study of the Changing American Character* (New Haven: Yale University Press).

Riley, L. E. and E. A. Spreitzer (1970) "Book Reviewing in the Social Sciences," *The American Sociologist*, 5 (November), 358–363.

Sewell, W. H. (1949) "Field Techniques in Social Psychological Study in a Rural Community," *American Sociological Review*, 14 (6), 718–726.

Sewell, W. H. (1952) "Infant Training and the Personality of the Child," *American Journal of Sociology*, 58 (2), 150–159.

Sewell, W. H., P. H. Mussen, and C. W. Harris (1955) "Relationships Among Child Training Practices," *American Sociological Review*, 20 (2), 137–148.

Sigmund Freud: 1856–1939 (1939) "Obituary," *American Journal of Sociology*, 45 (3), 453.

Simpson, G. (1950) "Methodological Problems in Determining the Etiology of Suicide," *American Sociological Review*, 15 (5), 658–663.

Simpson, G. (1957) "Empiricism and Psychoanalysis in the Sociology of the Family," *Marriage and Family Living*, 19 (4), 382–385.

Smelser, N. J. and W. T. Smelser (eds) (1963) *Personality and Social Systems* (New York: John Wiley and Sons).

Steinmetz, G. (2005a) "The Genealogy of a Positivist Haunting: Comparing Prewar and Postwar U.S. Sociology," *boundary 2*, 32 (2), 109–135.

Steinmetz, G. (2005b) "The Epistemological Unconscious of U.S. Sociology and the Transition to Post-Fordism: The Case of Historical Sociology," in J. Adams et al. (eds) *Remaking Modernity: Politics, History, and Sociology* (Durham: Duke University Press).

Steinmetz, G. (2005c) "Scientific Authority and the Transition to Post-Fordism: The Plausibility of Positivism in U.S. Sociology since 1945," in G Steinmetz (ed.) *The Politics of Method in The Human Science: Positivism and Its Epistemological Others* (Durham: Duke University Press).

Steinmetz, G. (2007) "American Sociology before and after World War II: The (temporary) Setting of a Disciplinary Field," in C. Calhoun (ed.) *Sociology in America: A History* (Chicago: University of Chicago Press).

Swanson, G. E. (1953) "Review of *Psychoanalysis and Group Behavior* by Saul Scheidlinger," *American Journal of Sociology*, 58 (6), 618–619.

William, S. Jr. (2005) "The Political Unconscious of Social and Cultural History, or, Confessions of a Former quantitative Historian," in George Steinmetz (ed.) *The Politics of Method in the Human Sciences: Positivism and Its Epistemological Others* (Durham, NC: Duke University Press).

Wilner, P. (1985) "The Main Drift of Sociology between 1936 and 1984," *History of Sociology*, 5 (2), 1–20.

Winch, R. F. (1943) "The Relation between Courtship Behavior and Attitudes toward Parents among College Men," *American Sociological Review*, 8 (2), 164–174.

Winch, R. F. (1946) "Interrelations between Certain Social Background and Parent–Son Factors in a Study of Courtship among College Men," *American Sociological Review*, 11 (3), 333–341.

Winch, R. F. (1949) "Courtship in College Women," *American Journal of Sociology*, 55 (3), 269–278.

Winch, R. F. (1951) "Further Data and Observations on the Oedipus Hypothesis: The Consequences of an Inadequate Hypothesis," *American Sociological Review*, 16 (6), 784–795.

Winch, R. F. (1955) "The Theory of Complementary Needs in Mate-Selection: A Test of One Kind of Complementariness," *American Sociological Review*, 20 (1), 52–56.

Winch, R. F., T. V. Ktsanes and V. Ktsanes (1954) "The Theory of Complementary Needs in Mate-Selection: An Analytic and Descriptive Study," *American Sociological Review*, 19 (3), 241–249.

Winch, R. F. and D. M. More (1956) "Quantitative Analysis of Qualitative Data in the Assessment of Motivation: Reliability, Congruence, and Validity," *American Journal of Sociology*, 61 (5), 445–452.

2
Paranoid and Institutional Responses to Psychoanalysis among Early Sociologists: A Socio-Psychoanalytic Interpretation

Catherine B. Silver

Introduction

In this essay, I analyze the paranoid and institutional responses of early American sociologists to the use of psychoanalytic ideas. Such responses began to be expressed mainly after World War II as sociology was constituted as a separate social science discipline in academia. My interest in paranoid responses began while I was working on a paper on the misalliance between sociology and psychoanalysis. Despite periods of acceptance and creative integration from the turn of the century until the mid-1950s, general trends since then suggest the gradual retreat, dilution, dismissal, and finally disappearance of psychoanalytic ideas from mainstream sociological discourse. How could this have happened?

In my work with George Cavalletto (see this volume's previous essay), we found that a significant number of articles and reviews in two mainstream sociological journals (the *American Journal of Sociology* and the *American Sociological Review*) were clearly hostile and antagonistic to psychoanalytic ideas. As a sociologist and analyst, I felt personally attacked, dismissed, and confused by the negativity and paranoid feelings expressed. In some ways, I clearly identified with pioneer sociologists who had unsuccessfully tried, as I had, to bring sociology and psychoanalysis together. By analyzing the publications of early sociologists through a socio-psychoanalytic lens, I am trying to make sense of my own struggles, frustration, and ambivalence in combining my dual training as sociologist and psychoanalyst. I wanted to understand the broader struggles between the disciplines that ultimately led to a decline of psychoanalytic ideas in sociology.

The challenges faced by American sociologists in the 1940s, 1950s, and early 1960s to create and sustain a "scientific" professional identity occurred within a competitive and crowded academic milieu and at a time when disciplines like economics, anthropology, and psychology were enjoying greater recognition (Jones, 1974). In this context, and using a psychoanalytic framework, I argue that the struggle to position sociology as a science inflicted narcissistic injuries at both the individual and collective levels. The fears of marginalization and the desire to create a distinctive professional identity initiated defenses such as phantasies of omnipotence, linear thinking, and splitting between cognition and affect. Defenses have a double function: (1) to create boundaries and a false sense of security, and (2) to force others to submit to and comply with normative expectations. In addition, the expression of negative affects and their diffusion among members of a group or organization elicits a need to control social action and regulate knowledge formation, thus providing coherent/rational, unitary, and universal theoretical discourse.

I distinguish *paranoid anxiety/fears* from *paranoid thinking* in order to differentiate between individual and social defenses and their mutually reinforcing impact. Paranoid anxieties stem from early (pre-verbal) childhood fears of loss, abandonment, and annihilation (Bion, 1984) that shape personality styles of functioning and a sense of identity (Shapiro, 1965; Klein, 1937).

Paranoid thinking, though, has to do with the use of cognitive language patterns expressed around narrow, rigid, and formulaic modes of discourse (Elliott, 2002; Sedgwick, 2003, pp. 124–151). It belongs to a system of anticipation and suspiciousness that suggests the suppression of affects, the selective scanning of ideas, and the repression of aggressive tendencies. As a social defense, paranoid thinking often frames political, economic, and social ideas concomitant with the emergence of modernity. Political discourse and administrative structure can be used to normalize the "childlike" expression of individual fears and anxieties that are experienced in settings where authority, dependency, and subordination dominate. Paranoid thinking, with its focus on narrow cognitive definitions, its vigilance, and its fixed boundary maintenance, can help reduce individual anxieties by channeling individual fears into formal institutional regulations and professional culture. In this paper I illustrate, within a specific socio-historical context, the reciprocal and mutually re-enforcing mechanisms linking paranoid anxieties and paranoid thinking as they were expressed in early sociologists' writings aimed at elaborating a professional identity.

Earlier in the 1920s and 1930s, the recognition of the role and usefulness of psychoanalysis in the social sciences was relatively widespread, exemplified by a special 1939 issue of the *American Journal of Sociology* on Freud's contributions to the social sciences. Sociologists in a variety of different fields commonly used psychoanalysis as a way to link individual and collective action. Ernest Burgess, a sociologist, in 1939 expressed his optimism and enthusiasm for the use of psychoanalysis in the following way:

> Many sociologists have utilized psychoanalytic concepts for their illuminating social processes in the behavior of the person and the group. . . . Social conflict between classes, nations, and races seemed to take new meaning in the context of the Freudian significance of mental conflict in the individual. . . . To the degree that this procedure enriched the conceptual system of sociology and rendered it more adequate for its tasks, it unquestionably was advantageous. (Burgess, 1939, p. 368)

However, the post–World War II era saw an increased distance and hostility to psychoanalysis despite the contributions of important social theorists like Adorno, Benjamin, Fromm, Riesman, Rieff, Parsons, Miller and Swanson, and Smelser. Partly to blame were the crudely psychoanalytic character studies hastily produced in support of the allied effort in World War II. However, the more fundamental causes were postwar transformations of the social sciences, fueled and funded by government grants and corporate support; the use of social engineering to rebuild societies; a growing enthusiasm, even obsession, for "scientific" methods and empiricism; and the peculiar set of intellectual views prompted to some degree by the American Cold War rhetoric and paranoid policies of the 1950s (including rhetoric that characterized psychoanalysis as a "foreign" influence promoting socialistic, antireligious, and antisocial views of society). These sociopolitical transformations carried with them the ideological hegemony of practical-minded scientific presuppositions that allowed little room for alternative, less "scientific" approaches (Cavalletto, 2007, 2010; Steinmetz, 2005, 2007).

Burgess's optimism about psychoanalysis was qualified, though, by the emerging distrust and suspicion expressed, for example, by Read Bain in an article assessing the importance of Freud's ideas for sociologists:

> Psychoanalysis exhibits many traits similar to those of a religious cult. There are numerous bitter feuds and fanatic factions within the

fold; symbolism, ritualism, and logical confusion abound; it flourishes upon dogmatic denial of the ordinary postulated and methods
of natural sciences. . . . The fundamental Freudian assumption is that
the human personality is a more or less abnormal or subservient by-
product of non-social, or even anti-social instinctual tendencies. It
fails to envisage the human personality as a culture-product as well
as a culture producer. (Bain, 1936, p. 203)

This quote encapsulates what became major themes of attack on
the use of psychoanalytic ideas including the unconscious, instinctual
forces, and intra-psychic conflict as well as on training institutes that
were characterized as promoting a cult-like practice outside the controls
of academia. The quote also suggests paranoid fears based on a narrow,
limited knowledge and biased view of Freud's work. The embrace of
positivism in the social sciences and the rejection of psychoanalytic
concepts were already expressed by Gregory Zilboorg who, in 1939,
predicted a trend toward "megalomanic scientism." Looking back, it
seems clear that social-scientific explorations, filtered through the new
positivistic lens, created a strong condemnation of Freudian and post-
Freudian ideas and made the overlap of anthropology, history, social
theory, and psychoanalytically inclined psychology appear unscientific,
anti-social, and even suspiciously foreign (Levine, 1978).

This article concretely applies socio-psychoanalytic concepts to analyze negative responses of some early sociologists to the introduction of
psychoanalytic theories and concepts into sociological discourse during
a time of professional uncertainty and struggles for power and recognition. In consideration of articles and reviews employing psychoanalytic
ideas in the *American Journal of Sociology* and the *American Sociological
Review* in the 1940s, 1950s, and early 1960s, I focus on articles and
reviews with negative content to understand how they shaped attitudes
toward psychoanalysis at a time when sociology was struggling to create
a distinct professional identity amidst the increasingly bureaucratized,
science-oriented, and paranoid anti-Communist political mood of post–
World War II America.[1]

Theoretical overview of paranoid constructs in psychoanalysis

Paranoid responses to losses, real or imagined, have a long history in
psychoanalysis starting with Freud's (1911a) study of Dr. Schreber's
diaries and continuing with Melanie Klein and Joan Riviere's (1964)

discussion of the paranoid-depressive position and Lacan's (1993) conceptualization of a pre-paranoid self. Lacan bases his analysis of a self-generating and self-reinforcing pre-paranoid self on negative affects that threaten one's identity in the form of misrecognition (1977). This pre-paranoiac self identifies with the desire of an "Other" through language and symbolization.

Freud (1911b) stressed that paranoia is organized around a complex array of affects, ranging from grandiosity, delusional jealousy, and homosexual fears through to a compulsive mindset and repressed aggression (Laplanche and Pontalis, 1988). Melanie Klein (1937) located paranoia at a preverbal level in the first years of life involving fear of loss and annihilation. Through a process of projective identification, the infant experiences and phantasizes aggression coming from both outside (the poisoned mother's breast) and inside (the infant's own body). As a defense, the child splits the threatening object and projects the unacceptable part into an "Other." Concretely, splitting and projective identification are mechanisms that separate the "good breast" from the "bad breast," that is, negative from positive affects; isolate different levels of consciousness; and de-link emotions from cognition, all signaling the loss of emotional power (Lear, 1998; Layton, 2006). Psychoanalytic theories suggest then that the mechanism of splitting controls and assuages paranoid anxiety and fears. Within modernity, the multiplicity of splits based on class, gender, geographical location, race, ethnicity, religion, and sexual orientation creates unstable and often incommunicable mental states within overlapping emotional spaces (Eigen, 1999). This multiplicity of psychic splits makes individuals feel helpless, confused, and vulnerable, providing a fertile ground for manipulation and control.

In adults, paranoid fears are responses to actual or anticipated losses of autonomy, safety, prestige, well-being, professional identity, money, and, above all, life. These paranoid fears reawaken childhood psychic wounds and the need for protection and dependency. When these needs stay unfulfilled, individuals retreat into narcissistic rage and/or cynicism over the dashed hopes of being rescued. The feeling of psychic vulnerability and the wish for protection bring about defenses such as megalomania, phantasies of grandeur, and paranoid thinking.

Freud has been described as one of the great practitioners of the "hermeneutics of suspicion" which is Ricoeur's (1970) term for the critical deconstruction of how certain categories in social and political discourse impose morality to our conscious understanding and experiences of desire. Drawing on Ricoeur, Sedgwick (2003, p. 124) suggests that the emergence of many social theories, including psychoanalysis, were based to some extent on paranoid thinking in attempt at cultural dominance. Paranoid thinking is found in all theoretical constructs that advocate the unifying power of closed systems in which linear and causal links prevail (Roustang, 1996). The rise of positivism around the use of scientific tools, mathematics, and statistics illustrates this process, namely, the creation of a discourse that assumes a universalistic function and synthesizing unity.

Paranoid thinking can provide a false sense of emotional security, one grounded in an epistemological certainty that covers up aggressive impulses and closes off avenues for doubt, ambivalence, and novel experiences. Teresa Brennan (2000) suggests that the objectification and rationalization of knowledge in modernity fosters paranoid thinking by turning everything into commodities, ones framed by mechanisms of envy, jealousy, and suspiciousness. In her framework, these negative feelings are used as "emotional capital" to sustain a consumer economy; this re-enforces the existing power structure through psychic co-option and compliance. In such an "affect economy," negative emotions and paranoid fears are generated while simultaneously sustaining mechanisms of self-regulation and control that further the commodification of the economy and uphold dominant power structures (Clough, 2007; Andrews, 2009). Could it be that similar dynamics occurred in the context of a struggle for recognition and legitimacy in the academic marketplace of ideas in the 1940s and 1950s as a new form of knowledge—psychoanalysis, in this sense like a commodity—gave rise to envy, jealousy, suspicion, and a need to control its spread and usage?

A socio-psychoanalytic interpretation of the misalliance of sociology and psychoanalysis

As the discipline of sociology consolidated in the 1940 and 1950s, sociologists separated themselves from neighboring disciplines such as economics, philosophy, psychology, and social anthropology in order to establish a unique professional identity. The tendency to reject psychoanalytic ideas and the monopolization of a certain kind of "scientific" knowledge can be understood by looking at the articles and book reviews with psychoanalytic content that were published in the leading sociological journals—the *American Journal of Sociology* and the *American Sociological Review*—between 1920 and the mid-1960s. After a modest but steady increase in the number of articles and reviews from the 1920s to the mid-1950s, a precipitous drop followed. The proportion of articles and reviews in sociology journals with any psychoanalytic content fell from an average of 8 per cent in the 1950s to 6 per cent in the 1960s and to 1.5 per cent in the 1980s (see, again, Cavalletto and Silver in this volume).

It is worth comparing sociology with social anthropology during the 1940s and 1950s to understand the increasing isolation of sociology from psychoanalytic approaches. Unlike sociologists, social anthropologists remained open to psychoanalytic ideas and to the use of reflexivity as part of their research methods (Kirkpatrick, 1939). For instance, Devereux (1939) saw no contradiction between scientific attitudes and the use of psychotherapeutic techniques in field research, stressing the mutual influence of the researcher and interviewees on the type of data collected and interpretations given. For him, an understanding of psychoanalytic methods would provide researchers with more precise tools for studying the unconscious workings of the mind as expressed through language, myth, and cultural artifacts essential to the study of social institutions. Among sociologists there was a gradual disengagement from social anthropology and increasing separation in major universities between sociology and anthropology departments. In this process of intellectual detachment sociologists lost a connection to the theoretical and methodological possibilities of using psychoanalysis in their work. More broadly, by distancing themselves from social anthropology, mainstream sociologists actively rejected an intellectual paradigm that put the self and the unconscious at the center of theory and research.

From a psychodynamic perspective, this need to separate and create distance in search of a professional identity reveals fault lines that touch upon unconscious childhood fears of loss and annihilation, fears that open up narcissistic injuries and prompting paranoid thinking. Such negative psychic states triggered defense mechanisms—splitting, projection, rationalization, and intellectualization[2]—that were expressed in some sociologists' work as aggressive verbal attacks, rational and measured argumentation, and/or the internalization of a positivistic unconscious.

The view of psychoanalysis as *"unscientific," "myth-oriented,"* and *"mystical"* became widespread among early sociologists (Pumpian-Mindlin, 1952). The mainstream critiques of psychoanalytic concepts focused primarily on the role of the unconscious and of the repression of sexual instincts/desires, both seen as nonbehavioral, nonobservable, and thus inappropriate objects of research. However, the rejection of psychoanalysis went beyond the rejection of specific concepts: it was directed to the field as a whole and was expressed through feelings of anger, fear, mistrust, and danger.

Allow me to illustrate the expression of paranoid fears using some quotations from articles and reviews in *ASR* and *AJS* between the mid-1940s and the mid-1960s. Psychoanalysts see language as revealing emotional states and unconscious wishes, and indeed early sociologists revealed paranoid fears through the type of language used in their writings. I am not undertaking here a systematic content analysis of negative terms; rather, I want to illustrate the destructive power of negative affects. Let me start with the following quote:

> One of the more persistent weeds in the social science garden is Freudianism. It is an adaptable plant thriving without factual nourishment that returns, season after season, in one or another of its apparently infinite variations. Many have tried to hoe it out, many have tried to smother it with the preponderance of contrary evidence, and some have endeavored to kill it with poisonous words. But so far the species has survived and at the moment it is again flourishing at the expense of more useful and productive constructs. (LaPiere, 1948a, p. 231)

For LaPiere, "Psychoanalysis is *poisoning*[3] the field of sociology" and needs to be killed; "psychoanalytic ideas are *endangering* the scientific development of the discipline"(1948b, p. 346). LaPiere (1960) later described the *danger* of a psychoanalytic ethics that could *destroy* the fabric of American society and its Protestant entrepreneurial spirit by letting loose uncontrollable urges. For Robert E. Faris (1953, p. 437), "psychoanalysis is *polluting* social psychology and sociology," and "there is a danger of *entrapment* by inefficient concepts." Even C. Wright Mills (1940, p. 911) labeled psychoanalysis as "*systematic motives-mongering.*" The use of words such as "*poisoning*," "*endangering*," "*polluting*," "*killing*," "*entrapment*," "*destroying*", and "*systematic motive-mongering*" taps into aggressive tendencies and unconscious paranoid anxieties of loss (Bion, 1984; Eigen, 2001). These words illustrate negative emotional states widespread at the time which made intellectual and academic discourse (especially with psychoanalysis) difficult if not impossible to sustain (Coser, 1950).

From a psychoanalytic perspective, these words illustrate mechanisms of splitting between "us" and "them," and the projection of hostility onto an Other as a means of protection from professional vulnerability. As a symbolic expression of unconscious feelings, such language recalls Melanie Klein's description of how children's paranoid fears of catastrophic annihilation result in sadistic attacks and expression of negative affects through projection and projective identification. The quotations cited above, along with many others, were pronounced in the name of *"protecting"* and *"safe-guarding"* sociological knowledge as a science from contamination from an impure and dangerous source: psychoanalysis.

Paranoid fears of contamination from toxic ideas also played a central role in colonial domination by supporting a philosophy of racial and cultural purity. Political paranoia was a tool for enforcing the colonization of foreign lands, a cornerstone in the establishment of modern capitalism (Brennan, 2000). In the ex-colonies, the politics of paranoia was used to regulate and control fears experienced by colonizers and colonized alike (Fanon, 1963). Among the colonizers, paranoid policy provided a sense of legitimacy and loyalty while dependency was encouraged among the colonized (Roland and Silver, 2010). Internalizing paranoid thinking insured conformity with the normative social order and colonial discourses. The politics of paranoia promoted an ideology that empowered the dominant group in the name of modernization, science, and rationality.

I am not drawing a strict parallel between the politics of paranoia under colonialism and the relationship between sociology and psychoanalysis during the formative years of sociology. However, I am suggesting that the processes of intellectual domination and the colonizing of the mind under the aegis of modernization and science have some similarities. Under the name of science, positivism, and rationality, mainstream sociologists came to dominate and control ways of knowing by keeping at bay psychoanalytic formulations for being *"mystical,"* *"primitive,"* *"immature,"* and above all *"unscientific,"* not unlike the premodern mind that colonizers sought to control and manage.

The verbal attacks on psychoanalytic ideas continued for decades. However, the more crude and direct expressions of paranoid fear were gradually supplanted by scientific arguments that continue to express the fear of loss under the guise of rational discourse (Sewell, 1952; Sewell, Mussen, and Harris, 1955; Bendix, 1952; Kohn and Clausen, 1955; Hyman and Sheatsley, 1954; Glaser, 1956). For example, Cameron and McCormick (1954, p. 556) in a book review wrote: "The characteristic tone [of psychoanalytic work and clinical literature] is *normative* and *propagandistic* rather than scientific, and there has been *no rigorous testing* of hypotheses as yet. The usefulness of the *subjective concept for any scientific purposes* remains to be demonstrated." While the style of discourse has shifted, the content of the argument stayed the same: psychoanalytic theory is incompatible with sociological thinking because psychoanalysis is ideological and concepts cannot be tested empirically.

When sociologist William Sewell attempted to test psychoanalytic ideas around childrearing and personality attributes, the results of the statistical analysis were interpreted as demonstrating a total failure of psychoanalytic conceptualization. It is ironic that among empirically sophisticated researchers, little thought was given to the limitations of the type of sample (162 rural children and their mothers in the 1940s), data collection (interviews with frightened traditional mothers and standardized tests given to rural children), coding procedures (binary), or sociological formulations that left out many important variables, such as the quality of mother–child interaction. Sewell, even after refining his model, stated unambiguously and with great certainty that childrearing practices have no impact on personality attributes.[4] The tone and conclusions of his research were clear: psychoanalysis does not belong within sociology; it is a waste of resources. His conclusions later influenced the selection of articles and book reviews published in *AJS*'s section on "Personality and Social Structure."[5] Because of his stature in the field, Sewell's position on psychoanalysis had a devastating effect on those sociologists trying to combine the two disciplines (Platt, 1976). Within our psychoanalytic framework, such research and discourse exemplifies paranoid thinking by presenting ideas with absolute certainty, lack of reflexivity, omnipotence, and above an *a priori* rejection and hostility toward studying psychic phenomena. Behind the positivistic arguments was a full attack on Freudianism.

Other major criticisms of psychoanalysis as summarized by Robert E. Faris (1953) accused psychoanalysis of "Biological determinism; incautious reliance on the obvious; a lack of generalizability; a lack of hypothesis testing and objectivity; pathologizing social behavior; equating primitive, child, and psychotic behavior; dogmatic thinking; and double talk; and unwarranted claims of confirmation of theory by successful therapy." These widely expressed methodological critiques, especially the lack of hypothesis testing, comprised a recurrent theme that excluded any substantive intellectual discussion of Freudian and post-Freudian psychoanalytic models. Methodological critiques became a way to support a dominant sociological discourse in the name of science while discrediting the legitimacy of a different and/or competing intellectual paradigm, as was clearly illustrated by the critiques of Adorno et al.'s *The Authoritarian Personality* (1950). Sophisticated critiques of *The Authoritarian Personality* (Jehoda and Christie (eds), 1954) recognize the difficulty in creating innovative ways—as in the construction of the "F" scale—to operationalize affects, emotional states, and psychic conflicts (Steward and Hoult, 1959). With the exception of Else

Frankel-Brunswik's positive response, no intellectually serious dialogue took place in an attempt to integrate the two disciplines. These examples point to a totalizing certainty that leaves no room for reflexivity, ambivalence, or ambiguity. From a psychoanalytic perspective, they illustrate a disassociation between cognition, on the one hand, and affects, on the other, which is characteristic of paranoid thinking (Lear, 1998). Early sociologists' dismissive attitudes and feelings toward psychoanalysis became normalized as part of a legitimate, *scientific* critique. This rational and coldly wishful scientific approach was far more detrimental in effects than the cruder expression of paranoid fears in earlier years. Intellectual and institutional support for a scientific and rational framework provided a sense of emotional security—however illusory—and professional legitimacy. Paranoid thinking, with its totalizing, narrow, and rigid way of knowing, created an emotionally safe and supposedly neutral intellectual space within clear disciplinary boundaries.

The diffusion of paranoid thinking took the form of institutional controls and regulations over the creation of intellectual knowledge. For example, in the 1940s and 1950s, the concept of character structure, first introduced by Freud (1916), had been one of the most fruitful areas in the integration of psychoanalytic and sociological ideas (Fromm, 1951; Fromm and Maccoby, 1970; Mills, 1940; Lindersmith and Strauss, 1950; Mowrer and Mowrer, 1951). By the late 1950s, "character structure" had disappeared from sociological discourse, engineered in part through a change in the American Sociological Society's (ASS) section on "Personality." The section changed its name from "Culture and Social Personality" to "Social Structure and Personality" to focus away from the role of culture and social context as they shaped personality toward measurable personality traits. By the mid-1960s, "character structure" was no longer part of the sociological vocabulary. The field of "social personality"—once open to a variety of approaches especially psychoanalytic ones—had morphed, emphasizing a narrow cognitive definition of personality that could be measured and tested empirically (Dunham, 1948; Goldhamer 1948). Furthermore, a shift in the 1959 membership of the American Sociological Society section "Social Structure and Personality" showed a clear theoretical shift from supporting psychodynamic frameworks to promoting cognitive approaches. While the remnants of psychoanalytic formulations remained in applied fields such as family, criminology, social work, and mental illness with lower academic status and little visibility, sociologists interested in analyzing the impact of personality on social behavior allied themselves with methodological positivism and cognitive Psychology (Dunham, 1954).

By the early 1960s and after the organizational restructuring of the ASS into the ASA, the use of scientific formulations had become part and parcel of a widely accepted consensus in mainstream sociology, one firmly situated in institutional structures that supported mechanisms like gate keeping, access to funding, segmentation, and the marginalization of subfields. In major universities, especially Midwestern ones, the spread of "positivism" meant that quantitative approaches within functionalist frameworks became the privileged research strategies and the ones most likely to be funded by large private foundations and governmental agencies (Manning, 2005).

A positivistic and statistical orientation based on universalistic assumptions became a normalizing process that worked to contain more disruptive and uncontrollable—but potentially more creative— paranoid fears about the use of psychoanalysis in sociology. The normalization of positivistic thinking across sociology took the form of what Steinmetz (2006, p. 111) called an "epistemological unconscious." By this he means the creation of knowledge around three components: (1) the consolidation of methodological positivism around assumptions about the nature of the social order (ontological concern), (2) the support of specific ways of knowing social reality through direct observation (epistemological concern), and (3) the scientific-naturalistic belief in the unity of the social order and the natural sciences. The spread of an epistemological unconscious contributed to the gradual dilution of psychoanalytic ideas in mainstream sociology and limited the burgeoning discipline's access to other ways of knowing through philosophy, literature, art, or poetry. Gradually but surely, sociology underwent a transformation through which "scientific correctness," even among psychoanalytically oriented sociologists, became the norm (Smelser, 1998, p. 184). The focus on narrow methodological critiques impeded serious intellectual engagement with psychoanalysis; as already noted, an intellectual connection with psychoanalytic ideas was feared insofar as contaminating and poisoning sociological thinking. Open discussions of psychoanalytic ideas in ASA meetings were minimal (Cavalletto and Silver) or coded as intellectually inferior, non-academic, foreign, and above all unscientific.

Somewhat surprisingly, a distancing from psychoanalysis also occurred among symbolic-interaction theorists including Blumer (1954), Goffman (1955, 1956), and Becker (1953). Their rejection or distancing from psychoanalytic ideas included Freudian as well as post-Freudian theoretical orientations with broader social concerns like those of Karen Horney, Erich Fromm, and Harry Stack Sullivan. While not directly hostile, symbolic interactionists perceived psychoanalytic ideas as irrelevant to their behavioral models of social interaction. Given the sophisticated ideas of Herbert Mead and Charles Horton Cooley about the role of the psyche and the self in the analysis of social action, the dismissal of psychoanalytic ideas among their followers was striking. Compared to the quantitative sociologists, though, interactionists monitored their expression of open hostility and dismissal. For example, while Blumer was clearly averse to using psychoanalysis in sociology, he did not attack or criticize Freud's ideas directly in his writings. Interactionists developed what Philip Manning (2005, p. 70) calls a strong "silent opposition" to psychoanalytic ideas in their views of psychoanalysis as dogma.

Although social interactionists' focus on subjectivity, language, culture, and self-identity could has provided a bridge with psychoanalysis, it remained quietly dismissive. Social interactionists argued that concepts such as the unconscious, repression, projection, defenses, and narcissism added nothing to their theoretical understanding of human action but rather distracted from an analysis of social interaction *per se* by imputing hidden motivations that were not observable and thus not analyzable. They argued that the inclusion of intra-psychic mechanisms like inner conflicts would blur the basis of social action and the role of normative structures in shaping human interaction, which they defined as their key theoretical project. It is puzzling that social interactionists did not discuss transference and counter-transference phenomena as part of their understanding of social action the way social anthropologists did in their fieldwork (Sapir, 1939; Dollard, 1936). Transference and counter-transference are key factors in the dynamics of treatment; they shape and give meaning to the clinical encounter.[6] These interpsychic mechanisms also shape face-to-face interaction outside the clinical setting. They influence the way an interaction takes place as well as the mutual meaning that develops between a researcher and its subject. Arrestingly, the argument for social interactionists is that interpsychic mechanisms would threaten neutrality and objectivity in the research process, making it too personal! Although the style of the argumentation differs, interactionists like quantitative sociologists both express negative affects as a means of promoting a unifying theory about the nature of the social order, a theory not open to the inclusion of subjective factors. Further, social interactionists may have experienced threats to their professional identity—not only from other disciplines but more crucially from within the sociological community itself. Their avoidance of psychoanalysis became a badge of loyalty to structural-functionalist approaches. Despite different methodologies, interactionists shared basic theoretical assumptions with their more quantitatively oriented colleagues about the nature of the social order. By ignoring psychoanalysis, they may have been protecting themselves from delegitimization in the context of what Patricia Clough calls "the ideological hegemony of empiricism and empirical positivism" (Clough, 1992, p. 12).

Positivistic controls and regulations spread to include ethnography and narrativity. Clough argues that the "realist" narratives were used to hide the workings of the unconscious: "Ethnography provides a sociological discourse with a realistic narrative that elicits a certain scenario of unconscious desire in order to disavow the production of the unconscious all together" (Clough, 1992, p. 9). Thus with few important exceptions, such as Dai, Parsons, and Smelser, early sociologists, whether using statistical analyses, survey research, interactional analysis, or ethnography, found no room for the unconscious or other psychoanalytic concepts in their work. This general trend suggests the near ubiquity of the discipline's paranoid thinking which crystallized around a deterministic theory of social action and the phantasy of a unified and controllable subject identity. Psychoanalysis became a scapegoat, a way to unify sociologists against paranoid fears of being marginalized by forces coming both from outside and inside the sociological community. This intellectual distancing entailed mechanisms of splitting and projective identification which rationalized any consideration of psychic forces, especially ones involving the expression of sexual and aggressive desires in oneself and in the Other. Such theoretical exclusions were made under the name of an opposition to biological determinism, yet they hint at an underlying puritanical streak in sociological thinking and a paranoid fear of psychoanalysis's power to unleash sexual and aggressive desires that could threaten the normative social order.

By the mid-1960s, the positivist outlook defined sociology. Even when sociologists used psychoanalytic concepts in their work, it was within a functional-structural theoretical vein, one in which concepts like superego or personality structure became variables used to explain an outcome, such as educational attainment or occupational choice, rather than being the object of study themselves. Sociologists studying the ways normative structures shaped individuals' actions and emotions selected aspects of Freudian theory that fit sociological models of socialization and social control (Glaser, 1956; Gold, 1958; Parsons, 1950a). For example, the superego as an agent of normative control was given a special place in highlighting the role of socializing agents, especially the family. By being primarily concerned with controlling aggressive and libidinal drives, this view brought about that Dennis Wrong (1961) called and "oversocialized conception of man." The selective appropriation of Freudian psychoanalysis for use within Hobbesian and evolutionary sociological models obscured Freud's cultural and inter-subjective paradigms, which stressed the mutually reinforcing dynamics between individual, culture, and society (Kaye, 1991).

Another way in which sociologists distanced themselves from psychoanalysis was in their use of reflexivity. The use of the personal and the idiosyncratic in research had not always been seen as detrimental to sociological research. Early on, Ogburn (1925) had argued that a researcher's ability to use therapeutic techniques in research would ensure more objectivity, by minimizing personal biases. However, with the spread of positivism, introspection came to be viewed as overly-biased and was thus rejected as a legitimate way of accessing social knowledge. The use of reflexivity and self-knowledge in research became defined as a form of personal "confession" that had no place in sociology. Linking personal observations to academic research transgressed fundamental, some would say sacred, rules of sociological methods (Durkheim, 1895). The fear of potential contamination of academic research through self-knowledge and self-disclosure created anxiety that had to be contained by using splitting mechanisms, and creating strict boundaries between the personal and the academic.

Thus an *n* of 1 in sociological research was clearly unacceptable, not only because of the nature of sociological concerns about objectivity and the need to generalize but more fundamentally because it opened up the possibilities of relying upon and revealing deep psychic issues that (necessarily) trouble the limits of empiricism, positivism, and narrativity. For Freud, linking the personal and the theoretical opened a creative space, an in-between that sustained theoretical breakthroughs and groundbreaking paradigm shifts. Seen in this light, Freud's *Interpretation of Dreams* (1900) was an exceptionally daring work: it acknowledged a powerful link between self-knowledge, self-disclosure, and theoretical formulation undertaken for the sake of science. Yet, Freud had the strength to recognize that the use of the self in theory building was double edged: it provided him with theoretical insights and clinical breakthroughs but also led him to question the arbitrariness of his own theoretical formulations. For example, he wondered whether Schreber's paranoid delusions might not be just as trustworthy as his own theoretical formulations, suggesting a delusional and paranoid component to his own theoretical thinking: "It remains for the future to decide whether there is more delusion in my theory than I should like to admit, or whether there is more truth in Schreber's delusion than other people are as yet prepared to believe" (Freud, 1911a, p. 182). Such public acknowledgment of potential danger of interpretation and questioning of one's theoretical assumptions based on personal experience and insights was remarkable.

The inclusion of reflexivity and self-disclosure among sociologists, even among those who used psychoanalytic ideas in their work like Parsons (1948, 1950b, 1958, 1970), Dai (1952), and Miller and Swanson (1966), was limited. Their writings could be described as applied psychoanalysis within a structural-functionalist sociological framework. The extensive theoretical knowledge and clinical engagement as patients or analysts, so common in the 1950s and early 1960s among academics, did not alter their adherence to the positivistic rule of separation of their personal reflections from their academic writings. In the 1950s, many sociologists in departments such as Chicago, Harvard, and Columbia were being analyzed, and some, such as Smelser, Parsons, Inkeles, and Lindsey, also received psychoanalytic training. Their clinical experience was essential in using psychoanalysis in their work, yet their insights into intra-psychic and interpsychic mechanisms, the use of personal memoirs and personal insights coming from their own analysis did not get explicitly expressed in their academic writings. How can we explain such an absence?

The sociologists who underwent psychoanalysis or trained as psychoanalysts in the US were analyzed within a classical framework and exposed to orthodox Freudian formulations: ones in which the therapist is a blank screen, a neutral figure who should limit projecting their own feelings into the treatment process. Counter-transferences were to be avoided or controlled at all cost. Ironically, this concern for neutrality in the clinical setting among sociologists trained as psychoanalysts may have contributed to their concern about keeping the personal out of their sociological writings. Paranoid anxiety and paranoid thinking, together with the projection of negative affects and the marginalization of the "Other," also occurred within the psychoanalytic community. The orthodox Freudian orientation of its early practitioners was all part of the struggles for power and recognition (Zaretsky, 2004).

Despite the constant questioning, ambivalence, and reworking of his own theoretical ideas, Freud himself succumbed to paranoid fears and thinking when he resisted certain ideas and excluded dissenting voices such as Jung, Adler, and Rank among his early disciples. The disconnect of psychoanalysis from academia created knowledge gaps from fields of inquiry such as philosophy, history, sociology, religion, and art that could have supported and broadened a conception of the self within social and cultural dimensions. The psychoanalytic movement in the US sustained a drive-oriented, deterministic, and medical-based model of psychoanalysis. The fights and splits within psychoanalytic communities buttressed a view of psychoanalysis as driven by dogmatic sect-like groups. The leadership of major training institutes was put in the hands of medically trained psychoanalysts rather than more socially and culturally oriented ones. In the therapeutic community, not unlike among early sociologists, the mechanisms of exclusion and marginalization functioned as defenses against paranoid fear of loss and vulnerability. Thus, the distancing between sociology and psychoanalysis reflects a mutual sense of distrust, a misalliance. By the mid-1960s, regulatory controls and the subtle process of internalization of a positivistic unconscious made it difficult for a psychoanalytic sociology to emerge as a truly synthesized (rather than merely additive) paradigm.

Conclusion

As I complete this essay, it is hard to admit to myself that I have internalized a positivist unconscious that has limited my own involvement with alternate ways of knowing. I have come to realize that some of the issues that confronted early sociologists illustrate my own struggles and paranoid fears in attempting to link sociology and psychoanalysis. As a student of sociology at Columbia University in the mid-1960s, working under Robert K. Merton's and Paul Lazarsfeld's guidance, I had fully absorbed and internalized a positivistic methodology in studying the social from a functionalist and empirical standpoint. My training as a sociologist shaped the way I thought, taught, and did research. In the process of forging an academic career, I was aware and mindful of the institutional controls and regulations that shaped academic life. Receiving psychoanalytic training at the National Psychological Association for Psychoanalysis (NPAP) in New York and becoming an analyst was done silently, almost secretly, for fear of loss and abandonment, feelings that touched upon my own personal history.

Columbia University in the 1960s did not provide a context for collaborative work across disciplinary boundaries, as was the case at the Yale University Institute for Human Relations in the 1930s and the Institute for Social Relations at Harvard in the 1950s. The merger of sociology and psychoanalysis happened in these institutional contexts where cross-disciplinary work was expected and encouraged. It was a long time before I started questioning the assumptions underlying my sociological work, and taking into account intra-psychic conflicts and unconscious wishes as they impacted social behavior. It took my own analysis to undo the hold that positivism had on my way of thinking and feeling. By becoming the subject to my own inquiry, I could finally experience and recognize the power of the unconscious and other psychic mechanisms and confront my paranoid fears of exclusion and abandonment. But even after becoming a trained psychoanalyst, I kept my sociological and psychoanalytic writings and my professional life separate. Splitting as a defense mechanism minimized my anxiety of being rejected. The fear of professional marginalization in academia accounted for my cautiousness regarding what I would research, how I would write, and where I would publish. I was anxious about not being taken seriously and was even labeled "disloyal" by some fellow sociologists when they heard that I had trained to become an analyst.

For years, I struggled intellectually to link sociology and psychoanalysis within the framework of an empirical structural-functionalist approach based on the quantification of personality styles following Fromm's and Shapiro's traditions (Silver and Spilerman, 1990; Silver and Malone, 1993; Silver and Levey, 2006). I collected empirical data and collaborated with statisticians to analyze the impact of character structure on career choice and value orientations. The results of the research were disappointing to me, and the articles felt lifeless and voiceless. I had expected my quantitative research to be a bridge between sociology and psychoanalysis, but that did not happen. My experience as an analyst and as a therapist made me realize how distanced I was from understanding the complexities of the interaction between the psyche and the social and the role of transference and counter-transference in any interactions in and out of the clinical setting. Like many of the early sociologists, I tried to add psychoanalytic ideas to existing sociological models rather than merging the two disciplines into a new paradigm. Later in my career, I published outside of sociological journals and gradually moved toward addressing psychoanalytic questions based on clinical data and personal insights as an integral part of the research process.

After the embrace of psychoanalysis by a variety of disciplines during the 1940s and early 1950s, the 1960s saw a narrowing of interests and the isolation of sociology behind paranoid fears and paranoid thinking, making any interplay of sociological and psychoanalytic ideas and methods difficult. The lack of cross-fertilization is attributable in part to the sectarianism of the major psychoanalytic institutes at the time, which were ensconced in paranoid fears and paranoid thinking of their own, cut off from an academic culture where interdisciplinary research might have taken place. One had to wait until the feminism of the 1970s and the cultural studies of the 1980s to witness challenges to many orthodoxies about gender, sexuality, and the self—challenges in which psychoanalytic discourse played a central role. Since I started combining personal insights and clinical data into my writing and teaching,[7] I have been able to expand my theoretical reach, rethink existing sociological paradigms, and feel connected in new ways to other disciplines that use psychoanalysis. I am not dismissing the potentially creative attempts at integrating sociology and psychoanalysis within empirical models using more appropriate methodologies, but I am aware that the paranoid thinking of the 1950s and 1960s is far from over.

I end this paper on a note of openness, a paranoid laugh of sorts, by rethinking paranoid responses. I started the paper with an analysis of paranoid anxiety and paranoid thinking as responses to the fear of the loss of professional identity. I focused on the need to regulate the expression of paranoid fears and negative affects through the use of paranoid thinking. But there is also another vision of paranoia that stresses the unconscious wish to get away from such emotional and social controls. Returning to Dr. Schreber's vision, his paranoia was experienced as a revolt of the imagination (a form of madness)—a place where porous boundaries between human/(in)human/(sub)human, animate/(in)animate, man/(wo)man, wo(man)/god gave rise to less polarized conceptualizations of the self. Freud's (1911b, p. 41) analysis of mechanisms of paranoid anxiety can provide us with a vision of delusion formation "that is not the product of a pathological formation but is in reality an attempt at recovery, a process of reconstruction." From a Lacanian perspective, the pursuit of unattainable and frustrated desires is embodied in a multiplicity of broken and refracted mirrors that can potentially stimulate a creative social imagination. Bion's (1992, pp. 214–215) rethinking of Klein's paranoid-depressive position stresses the importance of such destabilizing forces/energies, which can challenge totalizing certainty through social dreaming. Klein herself saw the oscillation between schizoid and depressive positions as a way to integrate the conflictual and contradictory demands of unconscious paranoid anxiety and provide an arena for reparative work (Klein, 1937). Cultural studies, comparative literature, feminist epistemologies, and neuroscience have provided new intellectual paradigms that can incorporate a mix of psychoanalytic ideas based on a multilayered and changing view of a non-universal and non-unitary conception of the self.

The time may have come for sociologists to embrace the return of the repressed by transgressing the rules of sociological method and inventing new methodologies, or at least allowing ambivalence and social imagination to regain some ground in sociological thinking. Perhaps then there might be a chance for psychoanalytic sociology to reemerge as a discipline endowed with a multiplicity of unconscious desires.

Notes

1. The description of the coding procedures as well as a detailed history can be found in Cavalletto and Silver's article in this volume: "Opening/Closing the Sociological Mind to Psychoanalysis."
2. By splitting, I mean the ability to keep separate emotional states in ways that give the individual a sense of control over negative content. By projection, I am referring to the process by which individuals disown their negative feelings and project them onto other people (objects), usually onto people who are in marginalized or in powerless situations. By rationalization, I mean a process that minimizes or denies the existence of emotional states. By intellectualization, I mean the use of abstract ideas to avoid seeing concrete reality.
3. In the text, the use of italics are mine.
4. The new research on attachment has proven him wrong (Beebe and Lachman, 2003).
5. See, for details, Cavalletto and Silver's chapter in this volume.
6. By transference, I mean a process by which a patient will transfer onto the therapist feelings and emotions that were originally directed onto significant others. By counter-transference, I mean the process by which the therapist responds with his own emotions to the therapy interaction.
7. I should mention that later on in my career as a sociologist I was able for a number of years to teach a course on psychoanalytic sociology at the Graduate Center of the City University of New York. The course was truly cross-disciplinary and based on a variety of sociological and psychoanalytic models.

References

Adorno T. W., E. Frenkel-Brunswik, D. Levinson, and R. N. Sanford. (1950) *The Authoritarian Personality* (New York: Harper and Brothers).

Andrews, J. (2009) "Depression Today, or New Maladies of the Economy," *Social Text*, 27 (2) 99, 167–173.

Bain, R. (1936) "Sociology and Psychoanalysis," *American Sociological Review*, 1 (2) 203–216.

Becker, H. S. (1953) "Review of *Jews in Relationship to German Anti-Semitism* by of Eva Reichmann," *American Journal of Sociology*, 58 (5), 531.

Beebe, B. and Lachmann, F. (2003) "The Relational Turn in Psychoanalysis: A Dyadic Systems View from Infant Research," *Contemporary Psychoanalysis*, 39 (3), 379–409.

Bendix, R. (1952) "Compliant Behavior and Individual Personality," *American Journal of Sociology*, 58 (3), 292–303.

Bion, W. R. (1992). *Cogitations* (London: Karnac).

Bion, W. R. (1984) *Second Thoughts: Selected Papers on Psychoanalysis* (London: Karnac).

Blumer, H. (1954) "What Is Wrong with Sociological Theory?," *American Sociological Review*, 19 (1), 3–10.

Brennan, T. (2000) *Exhausting Modernity* (London: Routledge).

Burgess, E. W. (1939) "The Influence of Sigmund Freud upon Sociology in the United States," *American Journal of Sociology*, 45 (3), 356–374.

Cameron, W. B. and T. McCormick (1954) "Concepts of Security and Insecurity," *American Journal of Sociology*, 59 (6), 556–564.

Cavalletto, G. (2010) *Opening and Closing of the Sociological Mind to Psychoanalysis: The case of AJS, ASR and Parsons*. A paper presented at the Annual Social Theory Forum: Critical Social Theory: Freud & Lacan for the 21st Century, Boston, 7–8 April 2010.

Cavalletto, G. (2007) *Crossing the Psycho–Social Divide: Freud, Weber, Adorno, and Elias* (London: Ashgate).

Clough, P. T. (1992) *The End(s) of Ethnography: From Realism to Social Criticism* (New York: Peter Lang).

Clough, P. T. (2007) "Introduction," in Clough, P.T. and J. Haley (eds), *The Affective Turn: Theorizing the Social* (Durham, NC: Duke University Press), pp. 1–3.

Coser, L. A. (1950) "Review of *Essays in Sociological Theory Pure and Applied* by Talcott Parsons," *American Journal of Sociology*, 55 (5), 502–504.

Dai, B. (1952) "A Socio-Psychiatric Approach to Personality Organization," *American Sociological Review*, 17 (1), 44–49.

Devereux, G. (1939) "Maladjustment and Social Neurosis," *American Sociological Review*, 4 (6), 844–851.

Dollard, J. (1936) *Criteria for the Life History* (New Haven: Yale University Press).

Dunham, W. H. (1948) "Social Psychiatry," *American Sociological Review*, 13 (2), 183–197.

Dunham, W. H. (1954) 'Review of *Twenty years of Psychoanalysis*," *American Journal of Sociology*, 60 (1), 104.

Durkheim, E. ([1895] 1982) *The Rules of Sociological Methods*, Steven Lukes (trans.) (New York: The Free Press).

Eigen, M. (2001) *Damaged Bonds* (London: Karnac).

Eigen, M. (1999) *Toxic Nourishment* (London: Karnac).

Elliott, A. (2002) *Psychoanalytic Theory: An Introduction*. 2nd edition (Durham, N.C., Duke University Press).

Fanon, F. ([1961] 1963) *The Wretched of the Earth* (New York: Grove Press).

Faris, R. E. L. (1953) "Review of *Psychoanalysis as Science: The Hixon Lectures on the Scientific Status of Psychoanalysis*, by E. Pumpian-Mindlin," *American Sociological Review*, 18 (4), 437–439.

Freud ([1900] 1965) 'The Interpretation of Dreams' in J. Strachey (ed.) *The Standard Edition Of the Complete Psychological Works of Sigmund Freud*, Vol. 4–5 (London: Hogarth Press).

Freud, S. (1911a) "Psychoanalytic Notes upon an Autobiographical Account of a Case of Paranoia" in J. Strachey (ed.) *The Standard Edition of the Complete Psychological Works of Sigmund Freud*, Vol. 12 (London: Hogarth Press).

Freud, S. (1911b) "On the Mechanism of Paranoia" in J. Strachey (ed.) *The Standard Edition of the Complete Psychological Works of Sigmund Freud*, Vol. 12 (London: Hogarth Press).

Freud, S. (1916) "Some Character Types Met with in Psychoanalysis" in J. Strachey (ed.) *The Standard Edition of the Complete Psychological Works of Sigmund Freud*, Vol. 14 (London: Hogarth Press).

Fromm, E. (1951) *The Forgotten Language. An Introduction to the Understanding of Dreams, Fairytales and Myths* (New York: Rinehart & Co).

Fromm, E., and M. Maccoby (1970) *Social Character in a Mexican Village: A Sociopsychoanalytic Study* (Englewood Cliffs: Prentice-Hall).

Glaser, D. (1956) 'Criminality theories and behavioral images', *American Journal of Sociology*, 61 (5), 433–44.

Goffman, E. (1955) 'Review of *Children's humor: A psychological analysis*, by Martha Wolfenstein', *American Journal of Sociology*, 61 (3), 283–4.

Goffman, E. (1956) 'Embarrassment and social organization', *American Journal of Sociology*, 62 (3), 264–71.

Gold, M. (1958) "Suicide, Homicide, and the Socialization of Aggression," *American Journal of Sociology*, 63 (6), 651–661.

Goldhamer, H. (1948) "Recent Development in Personality Studies," *American Sociological Review*, 13 (5), 555–565.

Hauser, R. M. and C. Camic (2006) "Biographical Memoirs: William Hamilton Sewell," Proceedings of the American Philosophical Society, 150 (1), 201–204.

Hinkle, G. (1957) "Sociology and Psychoanalysis," in H. P. Becker et al. (eds) *Modern Sociological Theory in Continuity and Change* (New York: The Dryden Press).

Hyman, H., and P. B. Sheatsley (1954) "*The Authoritarian Personality*: A Methodological Critique," in Christie, R. and Jehoda, M. (eds) *The Authoritarian Personality: Continuities in Social Research* (Glencoe: The Free Press).

Jones, R. A. (1974) "Freud and American Sociology, 1909–1949," *Journal of the History of Behavioral Sciences*, 20 (1), 21–39.

Kaye, H. L. (1991) "A False Convergence: Freud and the Hobbesian Problem of Order," *Sociological Theory*, 9 (1), 87–105.

Kirkpatrick, C. (1939) "A Methodological Analysis of Feminisms in Relation to Marital Adjustment," *American Sociological Review*, 4 (3), 325–334.

Klein, M. ([1937] 1964) "Notes on Some Schizoid Mechanisms," in R. E. Money-Kyrle (ed.) *The Writings of Melanie Klein* (New York: Free Press).

Klein, M., and J. Riviere ([1937] 1964) *Love, Guilt, and Reparation, and Other Works, 1921–1945* (New York: W. W. Norton).

Kohn, M. L., and J. A. Clausen (1955) "Social Isolation and Schizophrenia," *American Journal of Sociology*, 20 (3), 265–273.

Lacan, J. ([1981] 1993) *Seminar of Jacques Lacan*. Book 3: *The Psychoses, 1955* (New York: Norton).

Lacan, J. (1977) "The Mirror Stage as Formative of the Function of the 'I' as Revealed in Psychoanalytic Experience" in *Écrits, a Selection* (New York: Norton).

LaPiere, R. T. (1948a) 'Review of *The psychology of ego-involvements*, by Sherif and Cantril', *American Sociological Review*, 13 (2), 231–9.

LaPiere, R. T. (1948b) "Review of Three Books on Freud," *American Sociological Review*, 13 (3), 346–348.

LaPiere, R. T. (1960) "The Freudian Ethic. An Analysis of the Subversion of the American Character," *American Sociological Review*, 25 (3), 422–423.

Laplanche, J. and J. B. Pontalis (1988) *The Language of Psychoanalysis* (London: Karnac).

Layton, L. (2006) "Attacks on Linking: The Unconscious Pull to Dissociate Individuals from Their Social Context," in L. Layton, N. Caro Hollander, and S. Gutwill (eds), *Psychoanalysis, Class and Politics: Encounter in the Clinical Setting* (New York: Routledge).

Lear, J. (1998) *Open Minded. Working out the Logic of the Soul* (Cambridge: Harvard University Press).

Levine, D. N. (1978) "Psychoanalysis and Sociology," *Ethos*, 6 (3), 175–185.

Lindersmith, A. R. and A. L. Strauss (1950) "A Critique of Culture-Personality Writings," *American Sociological Review*, 15 (5), 587–600.

Manning, P. (2005) *Freud and American Sociology* (Malden: Polity Press).

Miller, D. R. and G. E. Swanson (1966) *Inner Conflict and Defense* (New York: Schocken).

Mills, C. W. (1940) "Situated Actions and Vocabularies of Motive," *American Sociological Review*, 5 (6), 904–913.

Mowrer, E. R., and H. Mowrer (1951) "The Social Psychology of Marriage," *American Sociological Review*, 16 (1), 27–36.

Ogburn, W. F. (1925) "Bias, Psychoanalysis, and the Subjective in Relations to the Social Sciences." *ASS*, 18, 62–74.

Parsons, T. (1948) "The Position of Sociological Theory," *American Sociological Review*, 13 (2), 156–171.

Parsons, T. (1950a) 'Psychoanalysis and the social structure', *The Psychoanalytic Quarterly*, 19 (3), 371–84.

Parsons, T. (1950b) "The Prospect of Sociological Theory," *American Sociological Review*, 15 (1), 3–16.

Parsons, T. (1958) "Social Structure and the Development of Personality. Freud's Contribution to the Integration of Psychology and Sociology," *Psychiatry*, 21, 321–340.

Parsons, T. (1970) "On Building Social System Theory: A Personal History, *Daedalus*, 99 (4), 826–881.

Platt, Gerald M. (1976) "The Sociological Endeavor and Psychoanalytic Thought," *American Quarterly*, 28 (3), 343–359.

Pumpian-Mindlin, E (1952) "Review of Psychoanalysis as Science: The Hixon Lectures on the Scientific Status of Psychoanalysis", Edited by Pumpian-Mindlin (Standford: Stanford University Press).

Ricoeur, P. (1970) *Freud and Philosophy: An Essay on Interpretation* (New Haven: Yale University Press).

Roland, A. and C. Silver (2010) "Interrelating Politics and Paranoia," *The Psychoanalytic Review* (Special issue: *Politics and Paranoia: The Political Exploitation of Paranoid Anxiety*), 99 (2), 337–356.

Roustang, F. (1996) *How to Make a Paranoid Laugh*, A. C. Vila (trans.) (Philadelphia: University of Pennsylvania Press).

Rustin, M. (1991) *The good society and the inner world: Psychoanalysis, politics, and culture* (London: Verso).

Sapir, E. (1939) "The Contribution of Psychiatry to an Understanding of Behavior in Society," *American Journal of Sociology*, 62 (3), 862–870.

Sedgwick, E. K. (2003) *Touching Feeling: Affect, Pedagogy, Performativity* (Durham: Duke University Press).

Sewell, W. H. (1952) "Infant Training and the Personality of the Child", *American Journal of Sociology*, 58 (2), 150–159.

Sewell, W. H., P. H. Mussen and C. W. Harris (1955) "Relationships among Child Training Practices," *American Sociological Review*, 20 (2), 37–148.

Shapiro, D. (1965) *Neurotic Styles* (New York: Basic Books).

Smelser, N. J. (1998) *The Social Edges of Psychoanalysis* (Berkeley: University of California Press).

Silver, C. and J. Malone (Fall 1993) "A Scale of Personality Styles Based on DSM-III for Investigating Occupational Choices and Leisure Activities," *Journal of Career Assessment*, 1 (4), 427–440.

Silver, C. and T. Levey (2011) "Gender and Value Orientation – What's the difference!? The case of Japan and the United States," *Sociological Forum*, 21 (4), 659–91.

Silver, C. and S. Spilerman (1990) "Psychoanalytic perspectives on Occupational Choice and Attainment," *Research in Social Stratification and Mobility*, 9, 181–214.

Steinmetz, G. (2005) "The Genealogy of a Positivistic Haunting: Comparing Pre-War and Post-War U.S. Sociology," *Boundaries*, 2 (32), 109–135.

Steinmetz, G. (2006) "The Epistemological Unconscious of U.S. Sociology and the Transition to Post-Fordism: The Case of Historical Sociology," *Constellations*, 13 (4), 445–464.

Steinmetz, G. (2007) "American Sociology Before and After World War II: The (temporary) Settling of a Disciplinary Field" in C. Calhoun (ed.), *Socilogy in America: A History* (Chicago: University of Chicago Press), pp. 314–366.

Steward, D. and T. Hoult (1959) "A Socio-Psychological Theory of the Authoritarian Personality," *American Journal of Sociology*, 65 (3), 274–279.

Wrong, D. (1961) "The Oversocialized Conception of Man," *American Sociological Review*, 27 (2), 183–193.

Zaretsky, E. (2004) *Secrets of the Soul: A Social and Cultural History of Psychoanalysis* (New York: Alfred A. Knopf).

3
The Unconscious in Cultural Dispute: On the Ethics of Psychosocial Discovery

Thomas DeGloma

> No one knows who will live in this cage in the future, or whether at the end of this tremendous develop-ment, entirely new prophets will arise (Weber, [1905] 2003, p. 182).

In the 1970s, psychoanalysis came under attack on two fronts. On the one hand, proponents of a new biomedical model of psychiatry began pushing for a major paradigmatic shift in the 1980 revision of the Diagnostic and Statistical Manual of Mental Disorders (Cooksey and Brown, 1998; Horwitz, 2002). On the other hand, various social move-ment communities, including the North American feminist movement, the growing gay pride movement, and the anti-war Vietnam veterans' movement were advancing a "new ethos of self-discovery" involving "a politics of lifestyle" and a shared "politics of self-identity" (Giddens, 1991, pp. 209–217). These new social movements were, in various ways, deeply influenced by the psychoanalytic commitment to self-explora-tion, but they were also increasingly critical of the Freudian convention of interpreting psychological and behavioral problems as evidence of idiosyncratic personal conflicts buried in the mind of the individual sufferer. Instead, participants in these late modern political movements cooperated to interpret negative psychological experiences to be symp-toms of social problems held in common with others victimized by the same conditions. As they linked personal introspection to new ideas about critical social discovery, activists criticized psychoanalytic author-ities for ignoring, and even perpetuating, significant social problems.

In this essay, I explore the ways two new social movement commu-nities mounted a cultural challenge to psychoanalytic authority and conventional psychoanalytic conceptions of the unconscious.[1] The first case involves the evolving conflict between the gay pride movement and advocates of sexual reparative therapy over the nature of homosexuality. The second case involves the ongoing dispute between the recovered memory movement and the False Memory Syndrome Foundation over the veracity of recovered memories of child sexual abuse. I explore these *psychosocial battles* to show how late modern social movement activists promoted a new cultural *ethic of participatory democracy*—defined by the practice of collective story-sharing and the related notion of shared "consciousness-raising"—as a framework to redefine the nature of the unconscious and the roots of psychological suffering. In the process, these activists worked to undermine a more traditional *ethic of dynamic paternalism*—marked by an asymmetry of cognitive authority between analyst and client—underlying conventional psychoanalytic theories and practices. These dueling ethics provide alternative frameworks that individuals use to discover meaning in their lives as their respective proponents advance different models of the unconscious and conflicting ideas about the nature of psychological truth. Exploring these particular psychosocial battles (A) shows how claims about the unconscious and the concomitant process of psychological discovery were, and continue to be, contested, and (B) tells us something about why psychoanalysis was marginalized in the US during the late twentieth century.

From this cultural sociological perspective, the unconscious takes form as what C. Wright Mills (1940, p. 904) called a vocabulary of motive. "Rather than fixed elements 'in' an individual," Mills argued, "motives are the terms with which interpretation of conduct *by social actors* proceeds." One of Freud's most significant contributions was to introduce the personal unconscious as a vocabulary of motive. That is, Freud established the idea of a personal and even idiosyncratic unconscious (Zaretsky, 2004) as a viable explanatory mechanism—as a way for social actors to make sense out of thoughts, feelings, and actions in the world. Reacting to a particular reading of Freud, late modern activists introduced an alternate vocabulary of motive rooted in a new psychosocial notion of the unconscious. The path to psychological healing, these activists argued, involved discovering and combating previously unseen aggressive, abusive, and hostile forces underlying mainstream societal values, attitudes, actions, and relations, and part of this discovery involved unearthing the ways psychoanalysis was contributing to these harmful forces.

By considering the unconscious as a discursive endeavor (rather than treating it as an essential element of the mind), we can develop a deeper understanding of the ways individuals use claims about newly discovered psychological "truths" as they attribute meaning to their experiences, explain their actions and the actions of others, and situate their selves in relation to other individuals and communities.[2] If "psychoanalytic exploration of the unconscious involves, among other things, the *search for new narrative material*" (McAdams, 1993, p. 274), the new social movements of the late modern era launched a battle for cognitive authority (DeGloma, forthcoming) and narrative control. They fought to control the attribution of motive, intention, and agency as well as the definition of feelings and actions situated in stories about the unconscious forces shaping their lives. More, if "the ethic of our times" is "an ethic of voice" (Frank, 1995, p. xiii), these social actors set their voices within a chorus of like-minded others. As they worked in various ways to connect the personal to the political, these new psychosocial "prophets," to borrow Max Weber's famous reference to the Protestant ethic used as the epigraph of this chapter, linked the mind to community and the community to broader, if yet-to-be fully discovered, political forces in the world.

Gay pride and the psychology of sexual repair

At the May 1973 convention of the American Psychiatric Association (APA), hundreds gathered to hear panelists debate the issue of homosexuality. Irving Bieber and Charles Socarides, two prominent practitioners in the field, represented the conventional psychiatric view and defined homosexuality as a pathological condition. Both psychiatrists have published work central to the treatment of homosexuality as a mental disorder.[3] They presented theories based on psychoanalytic case studies and argued that homosexuals suffer from a psychosexual developmental disturbance caused by the impact of harmful family relationships during early childhood. On the other side, psychiatrists and activists aligned with the growing gay pride movement argued that the APA's conventional position involved a moralizing posture that had no scientific validity. They claimed that the "treatment" of homosexuals was doing more harm than good. This faction argued passionately that the APA ought to eliminate homosexuality as a diagnostic classification.[4] Robert Spitzer, then a prominent member of the association's Committee on Nomenclature and soon to lead the task force charged with drafting the DSM-III, hosted the panel. As Ronald Bayer (1981, p. 13) notes, when the APA eventually sided with the gay pride movement (at the subsequent December 15th meeting of the APA Board of Trustees), the organization,

not only placed itself in opposition to the systematic pattern of formal and informal exclusions that precluded the full integration of
homosexuals into American social life, but deprived secular society,
increasingly dependent upon "health" as a moral category, of the
ideological justification for many of its discriminatory practices.

Thus, the gay pride community effectively worked to define the modern
psychiatric practice of "curing" homosexuals to be harmful, antiscien-
tific, and morally reprehensible.

Despite the gay pride victory of the 1970s, many psychotherapists
and other counselors continue to insist that homosexuality is a treat-
able illness and the issue of sexual reparative therapy still spurs public controversy. Some practitioners of sexual reparative therapy (e.g.
Nicolosi, 1991, 1993, 2009; Byrd, 2009; Carvalho, 2009) lean more
closely to a secular, psychological view of homosexuality as illness.
The mission statement of the National Association for Research and
Therapy of Homosexuality (NARTH) describes the group as a "professional, scientific organization that offers hope to those who struggle
with unwanted homosexuality" (NARTH, 2013). Other practitioners
(e.g. Davies and Rentzel, 1993; Cohen, 2006; Chambers, 2009) and
organizations, many of which are united under the umbrella group
Exodus International, advocate or practice conversion therapy from a
more blatantly religious perspective. However, many proponents combine psychological and religious logics to deem homosexual behavior
a problem. They use psychoanalytic theory to provide an explanatory
mechanism for the rise of homosexual impulses while using a religious
framework to label homosexual acts as polluting behavior with profound moral consequences. Both paradigms are used to justify the need
to "cure" homosexuals by resolving repressed inner psychic conflicts
that proponents claim lead to problematic outward behaviors that typically exacerbate shame, pain, and suffering. The goal of analysis, then,
is to reclaim the healthy, happy, and authentic heterosexual self lying
in wait of discovery (on such a notion of heterosexual authenticity, see
especially Davies and Rentzel, 1993, pp. 93–105; Nicolosi, 2009, p. 41;
Chambers, 2009, pp. 41–65).

The complementary religious and psychoanalytic paradigms inherent
in the modern sexual reparative worldview each stem from different historical and theoretical roots. On the religious side, biblical prohibitions
against homosexuality (e.g. Leviticus 18:22; 20:13; Romans 1:27) were
later expounded and reinforced in the theological writings of Thomas
Aquinas (Summa Theologica, Question 154; see also Bayer 1981, pp. 15–18).

On the psychoanalytic side, while Freud did not believe homosexuality was a legitimate illness, was highly skeptical about the prospect or desirability of sexual conversion, and was opposed to the persecution of homosexuals (Freud, [1935] 1951, p. 787), he laid the groundwork for later efforts to define homosexuality as a psychological disorder in three important and interrelated ways. First, Freud defined homosexuality as an expression of an incomplete or perverted psychosexual development. Second, consistent with his theories of the unconscious and childhood sexuality, his explanation of homosexuality was focused on the personal psyche while essentially ignoring broader cultural and political forces. Third, Freud published case studies (most notably his "The Psychogenesis of a Case of Homosexuality in a Woman" and "Certain Neurotic Mechanisms in Jealousy, Paranoia, and Homosexuality") in which he modeled the ethic of dynamic paternalism characteristic of conventional psychoanalysis more generally, demonstrating how an authoritative analyst can interpret and define a homosexual's choice of sexual object to be, if not an "illness" *per se*, a behavioral trait stemming from abnormalities and issues of psychological concern (regardless of whether the homosexual at issue was suffering). In short, he identified unconscious and unresolved inner (personal) psychic conflicts and disturbances ("neurotic mechanisms") as the hidden motives behind his clients' sexual preferences and behaviors.

For Freud ([1920] 1963, p. 137), both hetero and homo sexualities depend "upon a restriction in the choice of object." However, "those who are restricted homosexually" (Ibid.) exhibit a "variation of the sexual function produced by certain arrest of sexual development" (Freud, [1935] 1951, p. 787). Despite Freud's sympathetic approach and compassionate manner, the notion that homosexuality stems from an arrested psychological development is loaded with the moral valuations inherent in Enlightenment notions of progress and effectively associates the homosexual adult with the psychosexual character of the child at the point of disruption. While all humans share an inherent early childhood bisexuality, in the normal and preferred course of development one comes to identify with the parent of the same sex, ultimately rejects objects of homosexual desire, and embraces heterosexual attraction. In the case of post-pubescent homosexuality, the individual is diverted "from the normal Oedipus attitude" ([1920] 1963, p. 154) and fails to sublimate the homosexual impulses that are normal in early childhood (Freud, [1922] 1963, pp. 164–165). Just as anthropologists have used historical time to split and distance their own cultural group from the otherwise contemporary culture they study (Fabian, 1983), deeming the latter to be "primitive," Freud used a normative psychoanalytic conception of progress to render homosexuality a developmental restriction. Freud details just how this proceeded for his client, a young women undergoing analysis at the behest of her parents. Explaining the psychodynamic roots of her homosexuality, Freud tells us that the young woman "was just experiencing the revival of the infantile Oedipus-complex at puberty when she suffered a great disappointment." That is, she desired a child and unconsciously "it was her father's child and his image that she desired" ([1920] 1963, p. 144). At the same time, her mother, "the unconscious hated rival," actually delivered her third child. "Furiously resentful and embittered," the young girl "turned away from her father, and from men altogether" and "foreswore her womanhood and sought another goal for her libido" (Ibid.). In other words, Freud (pp. 144–145) tells us,

> this girl had entirely repudiated her wish for a child, the love of a man, and womanhood altogether. [. . .] She changed into a man, and took her mother in place of her father as her love-object.

This move had the a further advantage, Freud writes, of allowing the young woman to defer to her mother and escape the otherwise normal contest for her father's affection ("retiring in favor of" her mother) and thus removing "something which had hitherto been partly responsible for her mother's disfavor" (p. 145). She won her mother's affection at the price of sacrificing her normal sexuality. This choice was all the easier, he explains, because "the girl had suffered from childhood from a strongly marked 'masculinity complex'," envied her brother's penis, and rebelled against the social lot of her sex (p. 156). Notably, while lesbians desire a penis in Freud's view (a notion that would be directly contested by later lesbian feminist movements), male homosexuals do too. They, however, suffer from "the inability to tolerate" ([1920] 1963, p. 168) the absence of the penis in women and a horror of women because they lack the valued male organ. Freud, however sympathetic to the homosexual's plight, provides clinical and theoretical fodder for those who would later portray homosexuality as a psychologically troubling aberration.

Further, while in Freud's care the young woman exhibited a "cool reserve" that Freud came to see as an outward display of her transference to him of "the deep antipathy to men which had dominated her ever since the disappointment she had suffered from her father" (Freud, [1920] 1963, p. 151), which ultimately rendered analysis futile. In other words, Freud interprets that the young woman unconsciously wished for revenge against her father for an equally unconscious oedipal-pubescent betrayal. With this authoritative ascription of motive, he credits his own inability to treat the subject (to convert her) as a consequence of transference stemming from the root of the sexual preference itself. Her homosexuality has been caused, we are told, by an unconscious conflict that prevents the analyst from undoing it. "So as soon as I recognized the girl's attitude to her father," Freud writes, "I broke off the treatment" (p. 151). This notion is more attractive, from the perspective of the ethic granting diagnostic and prognostic authority (and responsibility) to the analyst, than is the notion that the young woman is simply comfortable with her sexual attraction to other women (and may perhaps resent Freud, and her parents, for attempting to take it from her). The latter idea, which is implicit in the notion of gay *pride* and would take center place in later gay rights struggles to achieve social recognition and acceptance, has no place in the psychoanalytic story.

The most prominent advocates of sexual reparative therapy developed Freud's theories of psychosexual development to classify homosexuality as a mental disorder. Both Irving Bieber and Charles Socarides linked homosexuality to early childhood experiences and damaging parent–child dynamics (see Bayer, 1981, pp. 30–31). More particularly, both used Freud's (normalized) oedipal framework to argue that the disorder stems from a pathological over-identification with the parent of the opposite sex. For males, Socarides writes,

> The child persists beyond the preoedipal period in believing that the mother is all-powerful, all-controlling, and the only one to protect his interests and insure his survival [. . .] In the case of the boy, the absence of a strong father further predisposes the child to this primary identification and precludes a [normal, healthy, progressive] shift to identification with the father. The boy later [. . .] seeks partners who represent strong masculine figures and who would give him, almost by transfusion, the missing masculine attributes which diminish and deprive him, and make him feel empty, weak, and unmanly. (1978, pp. 143–144) [5]

The inability to separate from the mother, Socarides argues, leads to unhappiness as the male homosexual is locked in a tragic Sisyphus-like state, constantly seeking to absorb maleness from other men yet never feeling satisfied and never becoming truly "male." Elsewhere (1995, pp. 25-28; see also Bayer, 1991, pp. 34–35), in a psychoanalytic Social

Darwinist fashion, one formally consistent with Freud's earlier and more subtle association of heterosexuality with progress, Socarides argues that heterosexuality is the evolutionarily and anatomically favored form of sexuality and homosexuality goes against the evolutionary interests of the species.

Similarly, Irving Bieber argued that a particular triangular configuration of the family (father–mother–son) leads to homosexuality (Bieber et al., 1962, pp. 140–162). He and his colleagues presented data on over 200 patients to make the case that male "homosexual problems" commonly occurred in children raised in families with "close-binding intimate" mothers who were dominant in the family and dismissive or "minimizing toward the husband" (p. 172) along with fathers who were "detached ambivalent," hostile, or indifferent. As with later reparative theories, the homosexual in these early presentations is suffering and his/her homosexual feelings are "unwanted."[6] Homosexuality is depicted as a sad "dead-end street leading to profound despair" (Chambers, 2009, p. 10) that "no one is born with" and "no one chooses," but "people can choose to change and come out straight" (Cohen, 2006, p. xiii). By focusing on "unwanted" homosexuality, advocates of sexual repair can more easily frame their intentions as benevolent and justify treatment while interpreting difficult feelings of stigma or shame to be the burdensome consequences of unresolved psychic wounds repressed in the individual's mind. Homosexuals who suffer due to alienation or reproach from family, community, church, or state, or who express a "profound sense of emotional abandonment" (Nicolosi, 2009, p. 57), are told that the problem is internal to them. The sociopolitical dynamic is absent from the story. To embrace homosexuality, from this perspective, is to embrace illusion and to live an unexamined life.

When the gay pride movement mobilized in the 1970s against the sexual reparative worldview, they acted with an ethic of participatory democracy grounded in the culture of the New Left and its various identity based movements at the time. Public "coming out" testimonies came to be seen as integral to "breaking the silence" (Plummer, 1995) about sexual orientation and the social struggle to achieve recognition, inclusion, and equality. In other words, the act of story-*sharing*, and a simultaneous leveling of cognitive authority, was deemed crucial to the *collective discovery* of previously unacknowledged realities of social life. Notably, the very term "gay pride" links the emotional dimension of individual and community experience to the moral and political. Pride is contrasted to the "shame" and silence that activists assert is imposed on homosexuals as a direct consequence of cultural intolerance. Not only did gay pride advocates dispute the notion that homosexuality is a disorder, they identified the problem (and the cause of harm and suffering) as a social intolerance for, and hostility toward, those who lead morally legitimate homosexual lifestyles. Thus, gay pride advocates effectively undermined the reparative-oriented analyst's use of the personal unconscious as a vocabulary of motive and thereby challenged the authoritative ethic of dynamic paternalism at the core of the psychoanalytic relationship. By deeming the moral valuations at the core of the reparative therapy worldview to be unjust, gay pride activists promoted a flexible, publicly open, and democratic approach to human sexuality. Many psychoanalysts, alternatively, continued to defend the integrity of the reparative vision and charged gay rights activists with using ideology to dispute the truths of scientific study.

The gay pride community and advocates of sexual reparative therapy continue to compete for moral and cognitive authority in the public sphere. They wield contentious psychosocial frameworks with contrasting cultural (Alexander and Smith, 1993, 2003) and emotion codes (Loseke, 2009) as they seek to undermine their opponents' definition of the situation. By asserting the falseness of their opponents' claims, each side claims their own moral authority—the goodness inherent in their worldview. Today, the gay pride ethic of participatory democracy is evident in growing movements of individuals who define themselves as both homosexuals and "survivors" of sexual reparative therapy. Such an ethic is clearly expressed on the homepage of the "Beyond ExGay" community, which states, "So often healing comes through community and through sharing our stories and experiences with each other [. . .] This is your space to connect with other survivors, read survivor narratives and to share your own" (Beyond ExGay, 2013). With such a statement of purpose, this group foregrounds shared experiences and common, socially rooted sources of suffering. They individually and collectively reject the authority of the reparative therapists and embrace a more democratic form of knowledge and personal discovery that emerges from the sharing of stories and commitment to a common mission.

Memory and the trauma of child sexual abuse

In 1991, a woman writing under the pseudonym "Jane Doe" published an essay in the journal *Issues in Child Abuse Accusations* in which she reported that her daughter, who was in her early thirties at the time, had recently claimed to have recovered memories of her father (the author's husband) repeatedly molesting her during her childhood

(Doe, 1991). The accusation, the author claimed, was completely false and engineered by her daughter's psychotherapeutic encounter. Shortly after the publication of this essay, the author was revealed to be Pamela Freyd, mother of renowned University of Oregon trauma psychologist and cognitive scientist, Jennifer J. Freyd (the accuser, who was dubbed "Susan" in Pamela's account). In 1992, Pamela and Peter Freyd (the accused), working with a small number of couples facing similar accusations, founded the False Memory Syndrome Foundation (FMSF), an organization that deems recovered memories of sexual abuse to be "believed-in imaginings that are not based in historical reality" (FMSF, 2013). In 1993, Jennifer Freyd, who is well known for her work detailing the psychological mechanisms at the root of dissociative amnesia (the official psychiatric term for a prolonged "forgetting" of childhood abuse), addressed the issue at an academic conference in Ann Arbor, Michigan. Three years later, Jennifer published her now famous book, *Betrayal Trauma: The Logic of Forgetting Childhood Abuse* (Freyd, 1996), firmly establishing her position as a psychological and mnemonic authority figure of the recovered memory movement. Thus, the Freyds' intra-familial conflict played a central role in sparking the heated public "memory wars" that would unfold over the next two decades.

When Pamela and Peter Freyd founded the False Memory Syndrome Foundation, they were reacting to a relatively recent yet increasingly pervasive phenomenon. The modern notion that a victim of child sexual abuse can "forget" their abuse experiences for years and recover those memories later in adulthood originated with the convergence of feminist-led anti-rape and child protection movements in the 1970s and 80s (Davis, 2005a; Whittier, 2009). As movement activists and other self-identified survivors began telling public stories about living with the consequences of various forms of sexual assault, they were also aligning their claims with a newly formulated psychological trauma framework that linked adverse psychological symptoms to destructive worldly experiences (Alexander, 2004; DeGloma, 2011).[7] As Joseph E. Davis (2005a, p. 27) points out, "There simply were no public 'adult survivor' stories [. . .] before the 1970s." Increasingly, these stories included accounts of memory impairment and delayed discovery (recovered memory) among the consequences of sexual abuse. While some began positing new mechanisms to explain childhood dissociation and extended amnesia, these psychosocial activists also argued that sexual abuse was "a common occurrence" (Herman, 1981, pp. 7–21) yet a widely *unseen* epidemic—"the best kept secret" in the words of social worker and feminist author Florence Rush (1980). They coupled their claims about the psychological consequences of interpersonal sexual violence with a critique of entrenched patriarchal power relations and argued that the mental mechanisms of traumatic amnesia paralleled social mechanisms of denial at the level of the family and the state.[8] The link between the inner world of the individual and the dynamics of sexual politics became central to this new notion of the unconscious.

At the root of this increasingly public and vocal recovered memory movement was a feminist critique of Freud (see especially Rush, 1974, 1977, 1980; Herman, 1981, 1992; Masson, 1984). Early in his career, critics argued, Freud realized a long-forgotten and often hidden truth— that sexual assault was the prime cause of psychological suffering in women. In 1896, before the Society for Psychiatry and Neurology in Vienna, a young Sigmund Freud presented a paper titled "The Aetiology of Hysteria" in which he stated,

> I therefore put forward the thesis that at the bottom of every case of hysteria there are *one or more occurrences of premature sexual experience*, occurrences which belong to the earliest years of childhood but which can be reproduced through the work of psychoanalysis in spite of the intervening decades. I believe that this is an important finding, the discovery of a *caput Nili* in neuropathology. ([1896] 1984, pp. 263–264)

At the heart of Freud's position was the thesis that adverse psychological symptoms were caused by very real yet repressed early childhood traumas of a sexual nature. More, this was quite common in the young Freud's view (indeed, the *source* of hysteria, especially in women). The goal of psychoanalysis was to recover and reproduce the now repressed occurrences—to bring them to light so that the adult client can achieve a cathartic discovery and the previously unprocessed sexual encounter would cease to secretly motivate her affect and behavior.

However, just one year after the publication of "The Aetiology of Hysteria," Freud rejected his central thesis (which came to be known as the "seduction theory") and began to develop his more famous theory of infantile sexuality and the Oedipal complex. In other words, in a move that his later feminist critics would denounce, he traded a view that located the cause of hysteria in real occurrences of sexual abuse for one that located the cause of psychological disturbance in the repressed sexual fantasies and desires (wishes) of the suffering woman. In 1905, Freud stated that he "overestimated the frequency" of real sexual encounters and commented,

I have since learned to unravel many a phantasy of seduction and found it to be an attempt at defense against the memory of sexual activities practiced by the child himself (masturbation of children). [. . .] [Hysterical symptoms] now no longer appeared as direct derivations of repressed memories of sexual experiences in childhood; but, on the contrary, it appeared that between the symptoms and the infantile impressions were interpolated the patient's phantasies (memory-romances), created mostly during the years of adolescence and relating on one side to the infantile memories [of masturbation] on which they were founded, and on the other side to symptoms into which they were directly transformed. [. . .] the frequency of seduction in childhood was no longer assumed. ([1905] 1963, pp. 14–15)

This statement can be read alongside Freud's ([1905] 1997) analysis of Ida Bauer ("Dora"), conducted over an eleven-week period in 1900 and published in 1905. Even when Freud was still open to the possibility that his patients had real sexual experiences with adults when they were children or adolescents (as he was with Dora), he no longer viewed these events as the root matters of psychological concern. Rather, Freud attributed Dora's nervous coughing, loss of voice, and appendicitis, not to the adult Herr K.'s unwelcome sexual advances toward her in adolescence, but to Dora's own hidden (and self-denied) desire for Herr K. and her even more deeply repressed feelings for her father (which were exacerbated by her jealousy of her father's fondness for Frau K.). The idea that Herr K.'s kiss was somehow not sexually attractive to Dora was implausible in Freud's interpretation (which was now clearly shaped by his evolving ideas about the oedipal nature of child sexuality). When Dora disagrees, Freud obstinately maintains cognitive authority and interprets Dora's rejection of his account (and eventual termination of analysis) as her transference of her conflicted feelings (of both attraction and the wish for revenge) onto Freud himself.

More clearly stating that the seduction scenes reported by his patients never occurred, Freud ([1935] 1952, pp. 36–37) later reflected,

[. . .] the majority of my patients reproduced from their childhood scenes in which they were sexually seduced by some grown-up person. With female patients the part of the seducer was almost always assigned to their father [. . .] I was at last obliged to recognize that these scenes of seduction had never taken place, and that they were only phantasies which my patients had made up [. . .] I had in fact stumbled for the first time upon the *Oedipus complex* [. . .]

Thus, Freud firmly linked the phenomenon of "phantasizing" such childhood sexual encounters to normal psychosexual development, "the typical Oedipus complex in women" ([1933] 1965, p. 149; see also Herman, 1981, p. 7). As Freud moved away from his seduction theory and toward his theory of the oedipal complex, he solidified a key element of the psychoanalytic notion of the personal unconscious which shows its connection to an ethic of dynamic paternalism. That is, he no longer considered the memories of his patients to be literal reports but to have deeply personal symbolic meaning. Thus, Freud removed the testimonial authority of the analysand and secured the interpretive, cognitive, and mnemonic authority (DeGloma, forthcoming) of the analyst, establishing the latter as the legitimate voice of the new and rising science of psychiatry. The goal of psychotherapeutic intervention was no longer to discover memories of abuse but to see stories ("scenes") of abuse as encrypted revelations of the very typical yet unconscious oedipal desires of the aberrant individual.

Later, feminist activists and scholars argued that Freud denied the reality of his patient's memories of sexual abuse because of the immense controversy sparked by his initial exposure of sexual relations between upper-class Viennese men and their daughters (Herman, 1992, pp. 14–19). He betrayed his patients, they claimed, by lending scientific credence to the idea that suffering young women conjured fantasies of incestual seduction as a part of normal psychological development—that they wished to be seduced by their fathers and father proxies and failed to sublimate this wish, leading to hysterical symptoms and mounting sexually derived psychological tensions. More generally, they claimed, Freud established psychoanalysis as a patriarchal science of the mind—"a psychology of men" (Herman, 1981, p. 10) that legitimated and obscured the ongoing physical, sexual, and psychic assault on women and children. As the theories of infantile sexuality and the oedipal complex left an indelible mark on twentieth century psychoanalysis, they argued, the true causes of psychological harm were eclipsed—relegated to our collective unconscious—for decades.

By launching their criticism of psychoanalysis, feminist activists were reclaiming the basic logic behind Freud's earlier seduction theory (a logic that was now supported by the budding trauma paradigm) and reinforcing it with the ethic of participatory democracy emblematic of their era. Emerging from the "safe spaces" of semi-private consciousness-raising groups, they argued in public concert that a common type of social problem causes psychological damage to victims who share something of their suffering due to their shared experiences and common subordination.[9] Developing new theories of amnesia and recollection, these psychosocial activists reconceptualized the unconscious to fit with the practice of consciousness-raising and collective public claims-making that defined their social movement culture. Just as Vietnam veterans were typically critical of traditional notions and dynamics of therapy (Lifton, 1973, pp. 75–95; Scott, 1990), feminist consciousness-raising groups were often "conceived as antithetical to therapy" (Davis, 2005a, p. 244) and as collective, politically charged endeavors where an inward focus was always coupled with an outwardly directed pro-gram for social change. More, social change was deemed necessary for psychological health. Psychological discovery now entailed a shared enterprise of identifying previously unseen social problems; it ceased to be a truly personal phenomenon and became a moral responsibility for the betterment of an emergent and newly defined community. As they advanced their claims, these activists were also rejecting and countering the ethic of dynamic paternalism that granted interpretive power to an authoritative analyst (a dynamic that mirrored, in their view, problems central to the patriarchal family structure). Claiming the right to coop-erative self-determination and shared self-definition, they described discovering a previously hidden phenomenon of abuse simultaneously at the personal *and* political levels.

By founding the False Memory Syndrome Foundation in the early 1990s, Pamela and Peter Freyd (with others) sparked a cultural, politi-cal, and legal backlash against the recovered memory movement and thereby undermined a core mechanism behind feminist claims about the nature and frequency of child sexual abuse. While some FMSF mem-bers have been critical of Freud (because of his emphasis on repression), these activists reaffirmed the notion that claims about child sexual abuse are often more like fantasy ("false [. . .] imaginings" located in the mind) rather than reality (occurrences of the external world). These two camps wield contentious psychosocial frameworks and advance contrasting cultural codes as they seek to undermine their opponents' definition of this morally charged issue. To bolster their efforts to undermine the claims of recovered memory advocates, FMSF members actively circulate the stories of "retractors"—those who once believed they were sexu-ally abused (typically by a close family member) and now reject those once-believed memories, deeming them false and illusory (Davis, 2005b; DeGloma, 2007; Whittier, 2009, pp. 133–166). In the process, they work to transform the victim/perpetrator dynamic alleged by recovered memory activists (Davis, 2005a, p. 228). As foreshadowed by Pamela Freyd's 1991 "Jane Doe" article, FMSF activists deem feminist-inspired recovered memory therapists a new type of harmful force while considering retractors (exploited) and families (falsely accused) to be victims.

Discussion

As Freud developed the theory and practice of psychoanalysis, he provided a new vocabulary with which to understand the motives underlying our behaviors, feelings, and forms of suffering—as well as to ascribe motives and meaning to the behaviors and feelings of others. With its new emphasis on the unseen impulses of the mind, the idea of the personal unconscious provided a means of comprehending and articulating an unprecedented "separation between public and private" life and a complementary "conflict between the inner and outer worlds of human experience" (McAdams, 1993, p. 120). The inner realm, the recesses of the mind, became a frontier. However, in the second half of the twentieth century, this frontier became the focal point of both private and public psychosocial battles between camps vying for the authority to define various morally and politically salient forms of human activity, especially, though not limited to, sexual feelings and behaviors. As Joseph E. Davis (2005a, p. 237) has argued about psychotherapies more generally, psychosocial disputes—with their claims and counter-claims about the unconscious—can be seen as "a window on a culture's sources of distress."

Despite their differences, both the gay pride movement and the recovered memory movement represent a late modern cultural insurgence challenging particular psychoanalytic ideas about the unconscious. While these new social movements would not have been possible without psychoanalytic ideas, especially the notion of the unconscious as a realm of discovery, new social movement activists changed the notion of the unconscious in two fundamental ways. First, both movements worked to undermine the strictly personal inner oedipal core of the Freudian unconscious by emphasizing the link between personal well-being and widespread social forces. Thus, these activists shifted attention away from repressed personal fantasies and toward a more social and political form of unconscious aggression underlying power dynamics in the world. The gay pride movement argued that the real problem at hand was not some inner pathological disturbance in psychosexual development, but an underlying heteronormative cultural hostility and homophobia masked as moral right and scientific theory. More, failing to acknowledge the true character of the problem, they claimed, caused homosexuals to suffer and live an inauthentic life, "in the closet," or risk persecution by various authoritative forces, a persecution sanctioned by psychoanalytically aligned theories of sexual repair. Similarly, feminists and early recovered memory movement activists argued that women's suffering was not caused by unresolved oedipal drives but by oppressive power dynamics that have sheltered an unseen epidemic of abuse—an underlying cultural hostility and sexual victimization of women and children. Drawing on a new trauma paradigm, these psychosocial activists claimed that real-world conditions and experiences lead to a particular form of psychological harm. More, these traumas were often as equally unknown to the victims, due to a protective dissociative amnesia, as they were unseen by the culture at large.

Second, both the gay pride movement and the recovered memory movement rejected the asymmetry of cognitive authority inherent in the psychoanalytic ethic of dynamic paternalism. Both worked to level cognitive authority by involving multiple cooperating voices in the process of psychosocial discovery. They emphasized collective story-sharing as a means of consciousness-raising and stressed public testimony (whether "coming out" as a homosexual or as a victim) as a moral imperative (Plummer, 1995, pp. 49–61). As with the Marxian view of class consciousness, psychological discovery not only meant awakening to know one's oppressed status in the world, but also one's shared interests with a group, and the necessity of cooperative social change to achieve both personal and collective emancipation.

By exploring the cultural dynamics of the late twentieth century psychosocial battles initiated by these movements, I have outlined the contours of two alternative and widely relevant discursive frameworks with which to make sense of the human condition. (See Table 3.1)

Table 3.1   Dueling psychosocial ethics of dynamic paternalism and participatory democracy

The psychoanalytic ethic of dynamic paternalism	The new social movement ethic of participatory democracy
Focus on individual aberration—on the uniquely situated symptoms and experiences of the individual	Focus on social problems—on symptoms and experiences shared by a community
Asymmetry of cognitive authority: Analyst has interpretive authority and analysand's claims/memories have symbolic meaning	Leveling of cognitive authority: Community shares interpretive authority and voices of community members are given a testimonial character
Principal focus on the personal unconscious—the idiosyncratic inner world of the individual	Principal focus on the social unconscious—the collective discovery of previously unacknowledged realities of social life ("consciousness-raising")

Using this cultural sociological approach, I have focused on a particular dimension of the cultural impact of psychoanalysis to show (A) important reasons for its decline in popularity in the US during this era and (B) the way new social movements relied on reconceptualized psychoanalytic ideas to advance social problems claims. Thus, we need both psychoanalytic and cultural frameworks to understand these movements. The challenge for psychoanalytically inspired sociologists is to rethink the core themes of psychoanalysis (including the unconscious, repression, resistance, and transference) with respect to their social impact on our understanding of experience, identity, and memory at both the individual and collective levels of analysis. From this perspective, both psychoanalytic theories and the claims of Freud's critics are emblematic of the cultural ethics of their respective movements. With such an approach, psychoanalytic sociologists can expand a commitment to analytic (hermeneutic) interpretation while attending to the continual moral and political significance of the various ethics of personal discovery that shape our lives. As we might learn from studying the psychosocial battles between the early gay pride movement and the proponents of sexual reparative therapy, or between the recovered memory movement and the False Memory Syndrome Foundation, our inner worlds of meaning are no less relevant to the world today, yet the ways individuals understand the connection between private and public life and the ways they use claims about unconscious forces depend on the normative contours of their psychosocial worldviews. To understand how ideas about unconscious forces have changed the world, a psychoanalytic sociology needs a cultural sociology of mind.

Notes

1. There is a wealth of literature on new social movements. Foundational work includes, for example, Melucci, 1989 and Laraña, Johnston, and Gusfield, 1994.
2. c. f. Gubruim and Holstein's (2000) position on the character of the self. As opposed to taking a conventional psychoanalytic perspective, I argue that the unconscious is socially significant precisely because people believe it exists and use it to make sense of their lives and the world around them. As with speech acts more generally (Austin, 1962; Searle, [1969] 1999), when individuals do this psychosocial meaning-making work, their stories often have "some illocutionary force or performative impact" (Smith, 2005, p. 33).
3. See, for example, Bieber et al., 1962; Socarides, 1968, 1978. For an account of the APA panel, see Bayer, 1981, pp. 125–126.
4. For an illuminating and thorough account of this issue, see Bayer, 1981, pp. 101–154. In my treatment of this issue, I rely heavily on Bayer's work.

5. Bracketed comments are my own. The roots of these ideas can be seen in Freud's ([1920] 1963, pp. 167–168) discussion of the male homosexual's "fixation on the mother."

6. See particularly Hamilton and Henry (eds), 2009, *Handbook of Therapy for Unwanted Homosexual Attractions: A Guide to Treatment*. Notably, the word "unwanted" is bolded, raised, larger, and printed in a different font and color on the cover of this book. The qualifying term "unwanted" also appears in the mission statement of the National Association for Research and Therapy of Homosexuality.

7. This psychological trauma model is epitomized by the Posttraumatic Stress Disorder (PTSD) diagnosis. PTSD was first included in the Diagnostic and Statistical Manual of Mental Disorders during its 1980 revision (DSM-III) due to the work of anti-war Vietnam veterans and their allies in the psychiatric professions. See Scott, 1990; Shephard, 2001.

8. On the social logic of denial, see Zerubavel, 2006. On this point, see also Davis, 2005a.

9. From this perspective, an important reason why the "safe spaces" of the feminist movement were deemed "safe" is because they were collectively and deliberately shielded from the more entrenched cultural (including psychoanalytic) definitions of women's experiences. They were essentially spaces of cooperative meaning-making and memory work where actors constructed a new psychosocial framework with which to understand the unconscious forces shaping their lives.

References

Alexander, J. C. (2003) *The Meanings of Social Life: A Cultural Sociology* (New York: Oxford University Press).

Alexander, J. C. (2004) "Toward a Theory of Cultural Trauma" in J. C. Alexander, R. Eyerman, B. Giesen, N. J. Smelser, and P. Sztompka (eds) *Cultural Trauma and Collective Identity* (Berkeley: University of California Press).

Alexander, J. C. and P. Smith (1993) "The Discourse of American Civil Society: A New Proposal for Cultural Studies," *Theory and Society*, 22 (2), 151–207.

Alexander, J. C. (2003) "The Strong Program in Cultural Sociology: Elements of a Structural Hermeneutics" in *The Meanings of Social Life: A Cultural Sociology* (Oxford, England and New York: Oxford University Press).

Austin, J. L. (1962) *How to Do Things with Words* (Oxford: Oxford University Press).

Bayer, R. (1981) *Homosexuality and American Psychiatry: The Politics of Diagnosis* (New York: Basic Books).

Beyond ExGay (2013) Beyond ExGay, http://www.beyondexgay.com/ (Home Page), date accessed March 2013.

Bieber, I., H. J. Dain, P. R. Dince, M. G. Drellich, H. G. Grand, R. H. Gundlach, M.W. Kremer, A. H. Rifkin, C. B. Wilbur, and T. B. Bieber (1962) *Homosexuality: A Psychoanalytic Study* (New York: Basic Books).

Byrd, A. D. (2009) "The Psychological Care of Men Who Present with Unwanted Homosexual Attractions: An Interpersonal Approach," in J. H. Hamilton and P. J. Henry (eds) *Handbook of Therapy for Unwanted Homosexual Attractions: A Guide to Treatment* (United States: Xulon Press).

Carvalho, E. R. (2009) "Eye Movement Desensitization and Reprocessing (EMDR) and Unwanted Same-Sex Attractions: New Treatment Options for Change," in J. H. Hamilton and P. J. Henry (eds) *Handbook of Therapy for Unwanted Homosexual Attractions: A Guide to Treatment* (United States: Xulon Press).

Chambers, A. (2009) *Leaving Homosexuality: A Practical Guide for Men and Women Looking for a Way Out* (Eugene: Harvest House Publishers).

Cohen, R. (2006) *Coming Out Straight: Understanding and Healing Homosexuality* (Winchester: Oakhill Press).

Cooksey, E. C. and P. Brown (1998) "Spinning on its Axes: DSM and the Social Construction of Psychiatric Diagnosis," *International Journal of Health Services* 28 (3), 525–554.

Davies, B. and L. Rentzel (1993) *Coming Out of Homosexuality: New Freedom for Men and Women* (Downers Grove: InterVarsity Press).

Davis, J. E. (2005a) *Accounts of Innocence: Sexual Abuse, Trauma, and the Self* (Chicago: University of Chicago Press).

Davis, J. E. (2005b) "Victim Narratives and Victim Selves: False Memory Syndrome and the Power of Accounts," *Social Problems*, 52 (4), 529–548.

DeGloma, T. (2007) "The Social Logic of 'False Memories': Symbolic Awakenings and Symbolic Worlds in Survivor and Retractor Narratives," *Symbolic Interaction* 30 (4), 543–565.

DeGloma, T. (2011) "Defining Social Illness in a Diagnostic World: Trauma and the Cultural Logic of Posttraumatic Stress Disorder" in P. J. McGann and D. J. Hutson (eds) *Advances in Medical Sociology, Vol. 12: Sociology of Diagnosis* (Wales: Emerald Publishing Group).

DeGloma, T. (Forthcoming) *Seeing the Light: The Social Logic of Personal Discovery* (Chicago: University of Chicago Press).

Doe, J. (1991) "How Could This Happen? Coping with a False Accusation of Incest and Rape," *Issues in Child Abuse Accusations* 3, 154–165, http://www.ipt-forensics.com/journal/volume3/j3_3_3.htm, date accessed March 2012.

Donileen, R. L. (2009) "Examining emotion as discourse: Emotion codes and presidential speeches justifying war," *The Sociology Quarterly*, 50: 497–524.

Fabian, J. (1983) *Time and the Other: How Anthropology Makes Its Object* (New York: Columbia University Press).

FMSF (2013) False Memory Syndrome Foundation, http://www.fmsfonline.org (Home Page), date accessed March 2013.

Frank, A. W. (1995) *The Wounded Storyteller: Body, Illness, and Ethics* (Chicago: University of Chicago Press).

Freud, S. ([1896] 1984) "The Aetiology of Hysteria" in J. Moussaieff Masson (ed.) *The Assault on Truth: Freud's Suppression of the Seduction Theory* (New York: Farrar, Straus and Giroux).

Freud, S. ([1905] 1963) "My Views on the Part Played by Sexuality in the Aetiology of the Neuroses" in *Sexuality and the Psychology of Love* (New York: Collier Books).

Freud, S. ([1905] 1997) *Dora: An Analysis of a Case History* (New York: Touchstone).

Freud, S. ([1920] 1963) "The Psychogenesis of a Case of Homosexuality in a Woman," in *Sexuality and the Psychology of Love* (New York: Collier Books).

Freud, S. ([1922] 1963) "Certain Neurotic Mechanisms in Jealousy, Paranoia and Homosexuality," in *Sexuality and the Psychology of Love* (New York: Collier Books).

Freud, S. ([1933] 1965) *New Introductory Lectures on Psycho-Analysis* (New York and London: W. W. Norton & Company).

Freud, S. ([1935] 1951) "Letter to an American Mother," *American Journal of Psychiatry*, 107, 787.

Freud, S. ([1935] 1952) *An Autobiographical Study* (New York and London: W. W. Norton & Company).

Freyd, J. J. (1996) *Betrayal Trauma: The Logic of Forgetting Childhood Abuse* (Cambridge: Harvard University Press).

Giddens, A. (1991) *Modernity and Self-Identity: Self and Society in the Late Modern Age* (Stanford: Stanford University Press).

Gubrium, J. F. and Holstein, J. A. (2000) "The self in the world of going concerns," *Symbolic Interaction*, 23 (2): 95–115.

Hamilton, J. H. and P. J. Henry (eds) (2009) *Handbook of Therapy for Unwanted Homosexual Attractions: A Guide to Treatment* (United States: Xulon Press).

Herman, J. L. (1981) *Father–Daughter Incest* (Cambridge: Harvard University Press).

Herman, J. L. (1992) *Trauma and Recovery: The Aftermath of Violence – From Domestic Abuse to Political Terror* (New York: Basic Books).

Horwitz, A.V. (2002) *Creating Mental Illness* (Chicago: University of Chicago Press).

Laraña, E., H. Johnston, and J. R. Gusfield (eds) (1994) *New Social Movements: From Ideology to Identity* (Philadelphia: Temple University Press).

Lifton, R. J. ([1973] 2005) *Home from the War: Learning from Vietnam Veterans* (New York: Other Press).

Masson, J. M. (1984) *The Assault on Truth: Freud's Suppression of the Seduction Theory* (New York: Farrar, Straus and Giroux).

McAdams, D. P. (1993) *The Stories We Live By: Personal Myths and the Making of the Self* (New York and London: The Guilford Press).

Melucci, A. (1989) *Nomads of the Present: Social Movements and Individual Needs in Contemporary Society* (Philadelphia: Temple University Press).

Mills, C. W. (1940) "Situated Actions and Vocabularies of Motive," *American Sociological Review*, 5 (6), 904–913.

NARTH (2013) National Association for Research and Therapy of Homosexuality (Home Page) http://narth.com/, date accessed March 2013.

Nicolosi, J. (1991) *Reparative Therapy of Male Homosexuality: A New Clinical Approach* (Lanham, MD: Rowman & Littlefield).

Nicolosi, J. (1993) *Healing Homosexuality: Case Studies of Reparative Therapy* (Northvale, NJ: Jason Aronson, Inc).

Nicolosi, J. (2009) *Shame and Attachment Loss: The Practical Work of Reparative Therapy* (Downers Grove, IL: InterVarsity Press).

Plummer, K. (1995) *Telling Sexual Stories: Power, Change and Social Worlds* (London and New York: Routledge).

Rush, F. (1974) "The Sexual Abuse of Children: A Feminist Point of View," in N. Connell and C. Wilson (eds) *Rape: the First Sourcebook for Women* (New York: New American Library).

Rush, F. (1977) "The Freudian Cover-Up," *Chrysalis*, 1, 31–45.

Rush, F. (1980) *The Best Kept Secret: Sexual Abuse of Children* (New York: McGraw-Hill).

Scott, W. J. (1990) "PTSD in the DSM-III: A Case in the Politics of Diagnosis and Disease," *Social Problems*, 37 (3), 294–310.

Searle, J. R. ([1969] 1999) *Speech Acts: An Essay in the Philosophy of Language* (Cambridge: Cambridge University Press).

Shephard, B. (2001) *A War of Nerves: Soldiers and Psychiatrists in the Twentieth Century* (Cambridge: Harvard University Press).

Smith, P. (2005) *Why War? The Cultural Logic of Iraq, The Gulf War, and Suez* (Chicago and London: University of Chicago Press).

Socarides, C. W. (1968) *The Overt Homosexual* (New York: Grune and Stratton).

Socarides, C. W. (1978) *Homosexuality* (New York and London: Jason Aronson).

Socarides, C. W. (1995) *Homosexuality: A Freedom Too Far* (Phoenix, AZ: Adam Margrave Books).

Weber, M. ([1905] 2003) *The Protestant Ethic and the Spirit of Capitalism* (Mineola: Dover Publications).

Whittier, N. (2009) *The Politics of Child Sexual Abuse Emotion, Social Movements, and the State* (New York: Oxford University Press).

Zaretsky, E. (2004) *Secrets of the Soul: A Social and Cultural History of Psychoanalysis* (New York: Alfred A. Knopf).

Zaretsky, E. (2006) *The Elephant in the Room: Silence and Denial in Everyday Life* (Oxford and New York: Oxford University Press).

Part II
Are Psychosocial/Socioanalytic
Syntheses Possible?

4
Sustaining an Unlikely Marriage: Biographical, Theoretical, and Intellectual Notes

Neil J. Smelser

Readers of this volume will easily discern the difficulties of fruitful articulation between psychoanalysis and sociology on all dimensions— theoretical synthesis, collaborative research, practical applications, and no doubt friendships and visiting patterns among their respective practitioners. As a person whose primary identification has been that of a sociologist, but also as one who became a psychoanalyst and remained intellectually active in that field, I appreciate these difficulties as much as the next. Yet I have remained committed to both fields, and have made a number of efforts to use both in order to generate knowledge. In this essay, I attempt to discuss this marriage and along three dimensions:

- Biographical-personal, or how predispositions and events brought me to pursue both fields.
- Theoretical-cultural, or how the core assumptions and methods of the psychoanalytic and sociological approaches mainly discourage but leave some room for positive articulation.
- Practical-intellectual, or an account of the specifics of the avenues I actually pursued in discerning the social edges of psychoanalysis and the psychoanalytic edges of sociology.

The first is meant to illustrate the interplay between purpose and accident in life; the second to represent adversity; the third to record one scholar's attempts to overcome that adversity.

A personal account

In my pre-college years, attending Phoenix (Arizona) Union High School, I heard or learned nothing about either sociology (the high-school course in social studies was descriptive, dull and alienating) or psychology (unavailable in the curriculum), much less psychoanalysis. I entered my college years uninformed and unprejudiced about both fields.

In my freshman year at Harvard (1948–1949), I was firm in my commitment to be an academic, and that remained unchallenged. Both my parents were teachers (my father taught philosophy at the junior college level and my mother taught high-school Latin and English); all three of their sons excelled academically. My father's presence as a teacher of philosophy was pervasive; under his influence I had read some philosophy in high school and was influenced to take a history-of-philosophy course and an ethics course in college. In 1948 my older (by six years) brother Bill was preparing to go into graduate study in philosophy at Berkeley; my younger brother Philip (by three-and-one-half years) was destined to follow his father's career as a philosophy teacher in a community college in the Phoenix area.

I performed well in the philosophy courses at Harvard but did not generate much zeal about them. There were complex reasons for this, but retrospection tells me that this was part of a process of quietly distancing myself from my father. The Department of Social Relations at Harvard offered an immediate alternative attraction. The program, in its youthful enthusiastic years, combined sociology, anthropology, and social and clinical psychology. I took three courses in my freshman year: introductory psychology with Gordon Allport, who inspired me; introductory sociology with George Homans, the subject-matter of which was fascinating but Homans was not; and introductory cultural anthropology, offered by the giant Clyde Kluckhohn, who seemed bored with teaching that subject, and that dimmed my enthusiasm for anthropology.

The second and third years turned out to be decisive. I took dynamic psychology, taught by Henry Murray, who was thoroughly Freudian-Jungian in his emphases, and a course in abnormal psychology from Robert White, also heavily psychoanalytic in emphasis. Murray singled me out from the large (200 students) class, and continued to befriend me, asking me to dinner several times at his home, and recruiting me as a "guinea-pig" in a series of psychological studies at the Psychology Clinic. In the meantime, my brother Bill, still an idol in my life, had decided to go into clinical psychology, and enrolled in Berkeley's Ph.D. program. Bill and I remained in close touch during these years, and many of our discussions were about topics in depth psychology. I should also add that the entire cultural scene in Social Relations—and to some degree at Harvard in general—was much influenced by psychoanalysis in and around the 1950s. Many of the faculty—Talcott Parsons, Gardner Lindzey, and Alex Inkeles among them—were or had been in training at the Boston Psychoanalytic Institute; Murray, White, and Kluckhohn were sympathetic in different ways. Parsons in particular actively incorporated psychoanalytic theory into his own sociology. I experienced all these features of psychoanalytic culture, both as an undergraduate and later as a graduate student (1954–1958) at Harvard.

In my last two years at Harvard I took more courses in sociology. All, especially those of Parsons, were inspiring, and in those years I drifted into a full commitment to become a sociologist. "Drifted" is the right word. There was no dramatic moment. As I reconstruct it, I was genuinely enthusiastic about its subject matter, its promise, and its "fit" with my own predilections, but my drift away from clinical psychology probably reflected the presence of Bill, who occupied that seat, just as my father occupied the philosophical seat. My choice of sociology was probably both an active choice and a silent, unrecognized declaration of independence from and perhaps avoidance of direct competition with my father and brother. Despite this, my exposure to and substantive knowledge of depth psychology had been cemented in this atmosphere.

The following two years (1952–1954) were a hiatus. I had secured a Rhodes Scholarship for two years at Oxford, where there was no sociology to study. I elected to read a second B.A. in Philosophy, Politics, and Economics, still committed to an academic career and knowing that this further interdisciplinary training would serve me well. Quite by coincidence Parsons had been invited to give the Marshall lectures at Cambridge University in the spring of 1964. His chosen topic was the integration of economic and sociological theory. He was aware that I was studying economics at Oxford, and he sent me a copy of the lectures for critical comments. I was somewhat terrified by this request, but responded thoroughly and critically. Parsons was receptive, and in the course of further meetings, he encouraged me to return to Harvard for graduate studies and invited me to co-author the lectures as a book, which appeared a few years later as *Economy and Society* (Parsons and Smelser, 1956). His invitations fully cemented my commitment to sociology and assured my return to Harvard for graduate study.

It wasn't quite over, though. When I returned to Cambridge Henry Murray initiated a personal campaign for me to choose the clinical-psychology option in graduate school (and be *his* student), and he was personally wounded when I told him I wasn't inclined to change my plans. Nevertheless, during my Ph.D. years at Harvard I continued my involvement in that psychoanalytically conscious atmosphere, even taking (with some unease) a joint seminar in psychoanalytic studies with Parsons and Murray. In my first year in graduate school, I worked as a research assistant with Parsons when he was writing his most psychoanalytically oriented book (Parsons and Bales, 1955). My doctoral dissertation (published as Smelser, 1959), under Parsons' direction, was on a completely non-psychoanalytic subject—a thoroughly sociological analysis of structural changes affecting both industrial and family organization during the Industrial Revolution in Britain. At the end of my graduate studies I was recruited as an Assistant Professor of Sociology at the University of California, Berkeley (1958), launching me unequivocally on an academic career in sociology. Incidentally, one of my motives—among many—for joining the Berkeley faculty was to establish distance from Parsons, who urged me to take a similar appointment at Harvard.

In my first few years at Berkeley I threw myself avidly into teaching and research in sociology. I was completely immersed in the Sociology Department and few other parts of university life. From my Harvard years I carried with me a strong but vague feeling that I might enter psychoanalytic training (like all my role models there), but was far from acting on it. My main research in the first four years was to write a major treatise on collective behavior (Smelser, 1962). That work was explicitly sociological, and polemically cast against the social-psychological approaches to the subject matter, but in my analysis of belief systems accompanying episodes of collective behavior and social movements, I imported many psychoanalytic ingredients, especially those dealing with anxiety, aggression, and fantasy. I remained close to my brother Bill, who lived in Berkeley, practiced clinical psychology, and taught in Berkeley's Social Welfare Department. We even published a reader on psychological and sociological research and its articulations (Smelser and Smelser, 1963), not especially psychoanalytic in emphasis, but focusing more generally on personality systems and social systems.

What I did not anticipate in those early Berkeley years was a devastating personal crisis, the collapse of my first marriage in bitterness, conflict, and personal unhappiness. Matters were complicated by the fact that we had a young son and daughter. In 1963, when things were cascading toward an end, I applied for admission as a research-training candidate at the San Francisco Psychoanalytic Institute, was interviewed, was accepted, and began my personal analysis almost precisely at the time my wife and I separated. Of course my background exposure and lingering commitment to depth psychology played a role in my decision, and I chose the research- training candidacy rather than therapy alone because it was immersed in an academic program. Ninety per cent of the driving force, however, was my own despair and sense of personal failure.

At that time, recent changes in policies of the American Psychoanalytic Association permitted candidates without an M.D. to receive full training (personal analysis, an intensive seminar program, supervised analysis of others, and graduation). The only restriction was that I had to agree not to practice psychoanalysis after graduation. Even that prohibition was rescinded before I finished training in 1972, and upon my graduation most of my teachers and colleagues in the Institute encouraged me to continue in practice. In 1979 the California legislature licensed non-medical graduates of recognized psychoanalytic institutes to practice psychotherapy in that state. My training itself was an eight-year, no-turning-back commitment of an average of 12–15 hours per week, a really major investment of time and intellect. With all that, the whole journey was in the end very rewarding. I had a superb personal analyst, Stanley Goodman, and I profited greatly from the four-and-one-half years. I worked my way through the painful crisis of divorce. The analysis also enabled me to enter a second, happy, and permanent marriage in 1967, and it improved almost all my interpersonal relations with authorities, colleagues, students, and friends.

My seminars in the Institute were always with four other analysts-in-training admitted in my "class," all psychiatrists with medical training and in full-time practice. All were extremely intelligent and talented, and we formed a solidary band. We read almost all of Freud's work, as well as a great deal of contemporary psychoanalytic writing, and participated in many clinical case-study seminars. As the only non-physician in the group, I expected some marginalization. But as it worked out, my situation was quite the opposite. By virtue of my academic training and research, I was advantaged in general scientific thinking. By virtue of their medical training, my compatriots had become wedded to the complex of diagnosis and clinical treatment of a single case. In fact, the whole culture was thinking about the "clinical case" and our seminars were forever being drawn in that direction. I myself was seduced into that magic as well, much as one might be seduced into a gripping novel or drama. But I had a philosophical, theoretical, and methodological advantage.

Despite the consuming nature of my participation in the Institute, the experience had a strange marginality about it. When I entered the program I had almost no support from my colleagues in sociology, most of whom thought me some kind of fool for taking on such a major diversion from my academic career. This set up a kind of permanent double-life for me. I made many new friends and joined several social circles in the psychoanalytic world and continued a full professional and social life in the university, but with some exceptions these worlds remained separate. As I will iterate later, I made several *intellectual* efforts to build bridges between these two worlds, but there were not many social connections. A few psychoanalysts took an interest in my academic work, and I later developed some relations with a few psycho-analytically minded university colleagues and students, but mostly the two worlds were separate.

Two issues persisted after I completed my analytic training:

- Should I practice psychoanalysis? I was legally permitted and encour-aged by some psychoanalytic colleagues to do so, and some other non-medical trainees had taken that route. But by then I was an established sociologist, engaged in a great deal of research and travel, even residence abroad. I knew I could not conscientiously practice psychoanalysis without either cutting out traveling or wrecking the psychoanalyses of patients through extended absences. I came to terms with this by continuing to practice short-term psychotherapy at Cowell Hospital on the academic calendar, and, later, to supervise graduate students in the clinical psychology doctoral program at Berkeley. I thought of taking up private practice after my final retire-ment from academic life in 2001, but decided in favor of continuing scholarship full-time.
- How major and how permanent should my commitment to psycho-analytic research be? For a time I solved this problem by a policy of combined passivity and opportunism. Mainly I responded to peri-odic invitations to deliver papers at the American Psychoanalytic Association and elsewhere.

My close relationship with Erik Erikson, which began in the mid-1970s, provided another opportunity for exploring psychoanalytic processes in the context of the development in the human life-cycle (Smelser and Erikson, 1981). Then, in the 1980s my pace accelerated, for reasons that are beyond me, and I began to respond to invitations by *initiating* interdisciplinary connections (see Smelser, 1993a and Smelser, 1999) and in 1996 I decided on a major move—to make my address to the American Sociological Association on the psychoana-lytic issue of ambivalence in social life. This acceleration of inter-est prompted me to publish all my scattered essays in one volume

(Smelser, 1998b). In my post-retirement work, the psychoanalytic perspective finds ample representation (see below).

In the final section of this essay I will turn to the *substance* of these efforts I made to bridge the psychoanalytic–sociological divide, but first I will present my version of the many obstacles to building such bridges, and perhaps discern some reasons why that enterprise has not been very vibrant.

Poor prospects for marriage: Theoretical, substantive, methodological

In pondering the possibilities for productive linkages between psychoanalysis and sociology that would generate insights, problem-solving, and more comprehensive knowledge, I have developed the following thoughts on the nature of the two intellectual enterprises. Most of these thoughts concern obstacles and traps. All of the thoughts, moreover, are oversimplified because both fields have shown an internal diversification and substantive sprawl in their histories; as a result neither is any longer a coherent conceptual entity.

Basic units of analysis

For psychoanalysis, the fundamental unit of analysis is the individual personality; for sociology the reference point is sometimes the person but more often typically the social role (an interpersonal concept), institutions (systems of social roles), groups, organizations, and whole societies. Psychoanalysts have divided the person into sub-units such as unconscious-preconscious-conscious and id-ego-super-ego, and identify mainly intra-psychic forces such as impulses, their psychic representations, and defenses against them.

When sociologists regard the person it is not so much in terms of coming to terms with his or her drives as it is a matter of coping with a balance of external constraining conditions and influences on the one hand, and freedom to act (agency) in these circumstances on the other. Much of the time sociologists choose other basic units such as social problems, social and cultural structures that impinge on the individual, and sometimes on the relations of these larger structures to one another in social systems. For psychoanalysis the external world has been what individuals *make* of it in terms of denial, distortion, rationalization, avoidance—all in relation to their intrapsychic struggles; for sociologists the external world has been conceived of as an independently existing reality that impinges on people. Can investigators with such different analytic starting-points begin to talk with one another and define common intellectual problems?

Imagery of human nature

From the psychoanalytic beginnings, the "model of human nature" assumptions stressed the irrational. That is certainly the representation of the id—impulsive, insistent, uncalculating—and many adaptations to psychic conflict. The development of a psychoanalytic ego psychology muted this view, though most of the defense mechanisms still involved a rear-guard, often distorted response to anxiety and related affects. The theory of sublimation and adaptive ego-psychology at mid-century moved some steps more toward a model of positive coping. Successful psychoanalysis, moreover, was regarded as reducing enslavement to crippling conflicts, and permitting more conflict-free adaptations. Sociology has had no single, explicit model of human nature, so it is difficult either to be precise or to generalize. In general, however, one can usually discern the presence of one or more actors who strive toward purposive action in a context of constraints, sometimes debilitating. Some models, such as resource mobilization, stress the active and strategic behaviors of those in social movements, and the rational-choice approach, borrowed from economics, is explicitly and polemically rational in emphasis. In the end, it is difficult to square these contrasting ranges of first assumptions in psychoanalysis and sociology with one another.

The concept of the unconscious and its workings is a particular instance of contrasting first assumptions. It is one of the original—and enduring—features of the psychoanalytic world view, and sometimes is treated as an actual thing—"the unconscious." This notion has been the object of repeated methodological attacks from other psychologists and philosophers, but nonetheless persists. It is also difficult to square with sociological conceptions of purposive behavior, which generally afford more access to self-awareness and to consciously directed behavior. Sociologists have sometimes appropriated assumptions about the unconscious, for example in the study of racial prejudice, and have fashioned and used conceptions of false consciousnesses and the ideas of unintended effects and unanticipated consequences. However, these formulations do not coincide with the psychoanalytic notions of unconscious motivation. These differences also make fruitful synthesis difficult.

Special mind-sets

Freud's original conceptualization of psychoanalysis rested on a scientific representation of medical models of his time, and included disease and its cure as core element (Freud, [1895] 1950). Its main lines of development have rested on notions of pathology and the accompanying ideas of causation, course of development, symptoms, intervention, and cure, with the individual case as the object of attention. His early work also involved a classification of disorders. While early sociology also made use of medical analogies (for example, in Durkheim's theory of anomie, and in the "schools" of social disorganization and social pathology in the United States), the dominant approaches were different. The main thrusts of sociology were to make the field scientific, to deal with social disintegration, and to resolve social problems. With respect to social problems, the main emphasis of American sociology was reformist, focusing especially on human suffering, crime, exploitation, and inequalities. So while the medical model and the curative impulse had its representation in both fields of inquiry, it was more thoroughgoing in psychoanalysis. Furthermore in the identification of what the "diseases" or "problems" are, the two fields aimed in different directions—individual pathologies on the one side and social discrepancies on the other. The respective emphases survive to the present.

Settings shaping of the research process

The main "laboratory" for psychoanalytic inference and interpretation of its subject matter is the therapeutic setting in which the passive patient, through free-association, provides the "data" for inferences and interpretations by the therapist. Though the psychoanalytic situation is structured in many respects, it is not so from this standpoint of the production of relevant information. This circumstance, as well as the psychoanalytic view of behavior and character as products of a complex pattern of forces—impulses, affects, defenses, and adaptations—is what gives the clinical, or configurational, or "case" method its magic. Both the production of information and the substantive view of causation in the field dictate that method of inference and drawing conclusions. The clinical method has continuities with anthropological preoccupations with "culture," which is also represented as a complex patterning of determinants. The method is also appreciated in "qualitative sociology," which often relies on case studies of individuals (biographies), communities, or events. But that method is a minor, ofen devalued one in sociology. More typically, sociologists, along with other social scientists, employ a method of *aggregating* data on many people (for example, religious preferences, years of education, or rates of unemployment) and using these independent variables to explain some outcome (such as the occurrence of protest, election results, spending behavior). A few sociologists accomplish this aggregation in laboratory settings. The explanatory variables and their outcomes are linked by using some intervening psychological assumption (for example, relative deprivation). Using aggregates, statistical analyses can be employed, and different variables can be "controlled" and explanations made more "scientific." When they can, social scientists also employ formal mathematical models (stochastic, network, for example) that are not found in the psychoanalytic repertoire of explanations. Such methodological differences also generate criticisms that the psychoanalytic (and other clinical) methods are scientifically "soft" and that aggregative explanations sacrifice the idiosyncratic, contextualized, and meaning-based characteristics of behavior. This abiding tension also makes for not only differences in methodological approach, but also differences in claims to scientific status.

Causal models

This style of thinking spills over into contrasts in causal thinking in the two enterprises. The manifestation in psychoanalysis is primarily that of clinical prediction, or the positing of probable lines of individual behavior on the basis of the confluence of a pattern of interrelated forces. The "experienced" or "skilled" analyst is the prototype. Though this method has been subjected to harsh criticisms by more "scientific" psychologists as inferior to statistical inference (for example, Meehl, 1955), it has remained the mainstay of psychoanalytic reasoning. More varied models of thinking appear in the psychoanalytic study of literature, social organization, psychobiography, and psychohistory, but the case method is the typical one. Sociological researchers more often opt for research methods and modes of explanation based on larger numbers and using quasi-laboratory methods of controlling for variation, even in the comparative analysis of societies. Such differences in arriving at judgments of reliability and validity of truth claims do not facilitate comfortable collaboration.

Separate institutionalization

Through a series of historical and political processes, academic psychology, psychiatry, and psychoanalysis ended up in different organizational and institutional places. Psychology developed in academic departments of colleges and universities, and followed a predominant experimentalist-scientific model, and while it also came to include personality, developmental, social, and clinical variants, these proved to be disadvantaged because they were regarded as "softer" scientifically than experimental psychology. Psychiatry, including some psychoanalytic emphases, developed mainly in departments of medical schools. Psychoanalysis proper, however, while yoked to medical practice (lay analysis is relatively recent in this country), became installed in psychoanalytic institutes, separated from universities and medical schools as professional training grounds. Historically this meant, through spatial and institutional separation, less opportunity for conversations and cooperation among psychoanalysts and *all* other behavioral and social scientists. These circumstances also help explain the distance of psychoanalysis and sociology from one another.

Reviewing this array of substantive, methodological, and institutional obstacles, one arrives at a pessimistic conclusion with respect to the prospect of *general* intellectual syntheses between the psychoanalytic and sociological perspectives. Respectively, they approach human behavior from perspectives that defy merging into a coherent and inclusive scheme. This conclusion is, in my estimation, unfortunate but inevitable. I conclude further that fruitful integrative efforts must be more pointed, that is more oriented to specific scientific and intellectual *problems*. Furthermore, as I review my own attempts to bridge the fields, I have followed this strategy without articulating it. I turn now to these efforts.

Trying to nurture a marriage

I list these intellectual efforts as analytic topics but present them mainly in chronological order. Representing them thus may convey an impression of intentionality of purpose on my part. That would be misleading. I mainly responded *ad hoc* to invitations, and my topics were formulated and my analyses executed for those occasions.

Two early theoretical-methodological explorations

I wrote little—only three essays—during my research-training candidacy. Two of these were mainly theoretical-methodological in character—in retrospect rather general, throat-clearing and programmatic in nature. The first essay was a collaboration with Robert Wallerstein, a training analyst in the Institute and already a respected psychoanalytic scholar, at his invitation in 1967. He had been requested to write a theoretical piece for the fiftieth anniversary publication of *The International Journal of Psycho-Analysis* (Smelser and Wallerstein, 1969). We worked well together, and produced an article that stressed the nature of disciplined inquiry in both fields, and developed the idea of "complementary articulation" (my terminology) between the two fields in relation to specific topics, for example, the study of suicide. We also raised some familiar philosophical topics, especially the limitations on deriving value-preferences on the basis of scientific findings and knowledge. A recent re-reading of this essay (forty-five years later) led me to the conclusion that we presented arguments that remain sound, but that the essay was more optimistic and programmatic than demonstrative of results, and that we were both preoccupied with presenting a respectful attitude to both fields and observing a scientific and methodological correctness in our explorations.

Also during my candidacy, I wrote a general essay on psychological and social dimensions of collective behavior for a research group at the Psychoanalytic Institute (later published in Smelser, 1968). It was a direct dialogue with my prior theoretical work on collective behavior. In retrospect I also regard this as a polite and correct essay, giving a respectful, balanced place to both perspectives but also articulating the limitations of each approach (I used Freud's group psychology as the psychological emphasis). This essay also was heavy in self-conscious theoretical and methodological commentary. I mention two more specific themes in this essay:

- I developed one critical point that was to hound me for decades. I pointed out that the analysis of an episode of collective behavior or a social movement typically involve an account of prior, determining conditions (for example, collective threat, or mass unemployment), and the analysis of some kind of outcome (correspondingly, a panic or reform movement). The link between conditions and outcome was that the former excited a common *psychological* reaction or mechanisms that connected conditions and outcome and "made sense" of that connection. My critical point was that an error is typically involved: determining conditions have a uniform or identical psychological impact on the individuals who ultimately mobilize, whereas in reality we know that the greatest diversity of psychological effects are generated by, for example, unemployment. This dilemma was to recur frequently, for example in subsequent work on cultural trauma (Smelser, 2004a).
- Toward the end of the essay, I developed a straightforward Oedipal interpretation of many elements of student protests, including the variables of hostility (toward academic administrators) and seduction

(of hoped-for faculty supporters). My eye was on the Free Speech Movement that had recently engulfed the Berkeley campus. My analysis was, I thought, presented as objective, and did not contain the vitriol of other psychoanalytically inspired attacks on the student movement (Feuer, 1969; Bettelheim, 1970), which is probably the reason why my account excited little attention. Nevertheless, it represented my first *substantive* effort to apply psychoanalytic principles to explaining a social phenomenon. On other occasions I have been critical of what I regard as excessive psychologism in the explanation of terrorist phenomena, invoking general determinants such as "narcissistic rage," "terrorism-prone individual," and "terrorist personality" (Smelser, 2007).

A theoretical reformulation and extension of psychoanalysis

Toward the end of my psychoanalytic training I was required by the Institute to write a "thesis" as the final requirement for graduating. The requirement wasn't much of a thesis, having been watered down over the years because of difficulties that candidates had had in completing it (much like the language requirements for the Ph.D.). In all events, I didn't know what to write, and stewed for a long season over the matter. In the end I decided to do something on the idea of defense mechanisms, which I had found from the beginning to be one of the most engaging ingredients of the psychoanalytic worldview. As it turned out, it was a both a theoretical codification and substantive extension. I reviewed the entire, sprawling list of what were called defense mechanisms in the psychoanalytic literature, omitted some that I thought were fanciful or repetitive, and codified the remaining list systematically according to where they could be located in the impulse→psychic representation→behavioral response sequence. I also classified the defenses into directional tendencies, or vectors: blocking, reversal, shift in reference, and insulation. Perhaps more important, I extended the classification to include *external* as well as internal-impulse threats, thus incorporating "reality" into the picture and building a set of orientations and reactions to the social world. I believed it to be an extension of the "adaptive" approach in psychoanalysis.

As I recall, when I presented this to my Institute seminar, it fell, like one of Hume's philosophical treatises, "still-born." I received polite compliments from my peers that it was very "scholarly," but almost no further substantive reactions. I recall that the faculty director of the seminar was hostile to its message, reminding me sternly that defense-mechanism theory dealt with internal-instinctual conflicts, not external reality. Neither did I seem to be very excited by the paper at the time, taking it home and stashing it in a file. I reactivated it only fifteen years later, when I was organizing in and participating in a German-American conference on the macro-micro link in the social sciences. I updated and reworked it as my contribution (Smelser, 1987) to the volume that emerged. In that same volume Richard Munch and I laid out a critical catalogue of scholars' efforts in the history of the social sciences to make transitions between the micro (psychological) and macro (social) levels of analysis (Munch and Smelser, 1987).

Psychoanalytic analyses of cultural and social phenomena: The power of ambivalence

In 1980 the American Psychoanalytic Association was holding its meetings in San Francisco. Jerome Oremland, my teacher and colleague at the Institute, invited me to give a plenary address of my choice. The invitation came as a surprise, and I had no topic at hand. As it happened, I was at that time participating in a longer-term discussion group at Berkeley's Institute of Governmental Studies on the topic of California's economy, society, and culture. I had come across a number of "California novels" and cultural commentaries, so I decided to explore something in that context. As an approach my effort resembled psychoanalytic studies of culture and efforts in the "culture-and-personality" approach in anthropology. As I continued my explorations, I was forcefully struck by both positive and negative themes in California symbolism: on the one hand the themes of plenty, ease, effortless get-rich-quick possibilities, and the good life, and on the other the themes of corruption, craziness, and social anomie. The main insight I pursued was to link these opposites to one another, and I used the conceptual avenue of ambivalence to do so. I interpreted the self-indulgence theme as a negative mirror of the Protestant work ethic as an American cultural value, and the darker side as a guilt-ridden renunciation of the greed, plenty, and passivity. That framework proved very powerful. Years later when I was on a major lecture tour of eight universities around the country, I used that talk on "the myth of the good life in California" as my centerpiece. Audiences loved it because they regarded it as California-bashing by a Californian—missing the point but enjoying the message. Yet I let that analysis lie around as well, publishing it only several years later (Smelser, 1983), when requested for a contribution by the editor of the *Humboldt Journal of Sociology*.

I had always regarded the notion of ambivalence as one of the most powerful and least discredited aspects of classical psychoanalysis, and its "payoff" in the California study strengthened that conviction. On three separate occasions during the next decade, I made it the center of a publication, each prepared in response to an invitation.

The first of these was a request to prepare an essay for a conference on contemporary problems in the American research university. The requested topic was diversity and multiculturalism, but I was given complete freedom to develop my own line of thinking. My starting-point for this was also a perception of an ambivalence evident in the political positions of many academics. Up to that time they had been friendly to the ideals of both egalitarianism and equality of opportunity (based on merit), but the movements for affirmative action and diversification based on social categories constituted a threat to the merit criteria, and left many ambivalent about those projects. I took up this theme of ambivalence and carried it further, interpreting the collegiate and university experiences of administrators, faculty, and students alike. The interpretation was mainly about the characteristics of political struggles when contestants hold ambivalent attitudes toward the issues at hand— thus the actual title, "The Politics of Ambivalence" (Smelser, 1993a).

On the basis of the arguments of that essay, I believe, I was invited in 1996 to give a presentation of my choice on the contentious issue of affirmative action at the celebration of the 250th anniversary of Princeton University's founding. Once again the starting-point of my analysis was a perplexity: why has not affirmative action, like so many reforms, become routinely institutionalized, and, in the same spirit, why has it been such a running conflict? Again I chose the theme of ambivalence to organize a long and complicated essay around the sources of cultural, political, social-structural, and social-psychological conflicts. The argument was complex but held together under the umbrella of that concept. Since the nation was in the middle of the 1990s backlash against affirmative action in many states—which I also analyzed—the essay was a timely one.

I now rediscover, in reflecting, that in all three of these intellectual adventures—the California myth, the diversity paper, and the affirmative action paper—I began with an anomaly or paradox that neither common sense nor conventional social-science notions of culture and conflict could readily handle. In all three I found great power in the idea of ambivalence. At the same time, each essay was fully interdisciplinary in that psychoanalytic ideas were combined with historical, cultural, social, and political perspectives.

When elected as President of the American Sociological Association in 1996, I had to begin thinking immediately the topic of my Presidential Address, to be delivered one year hence. I wrote down six general topics, all standard sociological ones except for the sixth, "ambivalence." I was genuinely uncertain which to pursue, so I showed the list to Christine Williams, a former student at Berkeley and now faculty member at the University of Texas, Austin. She looked at the list for five seconds, and said, with conviction, "it has to be ambivalence." She convinced me, but that topic frightened me most, not least because of my awareness of widespread indifference and some hostility to psychoanalysis in my own field of sociology.

The starting-point for this address (Smelser, 1998a) was a series of critical reflections on various assumptions of rationality that dominate the field of economics but are found in the other social sciences and in other areas such as law, management, and organizational analysis. I listed a range of limitations of rational postulates and models, but focused mainly on the assumptions of the full availability of information to the actor, the downplaying of affect as a determinant of behavior, and, above all, on the assumption of *univalence*, that is, that an actor, that is, a level of either positive (utility) or negative (disutility) orientation but *not* simultaneously *both* toward the same object at the same time, that is, ambivalence. The remainder of the essay involved a theoretical explication of ambivalence and its application to a wide range of phenomena that appear to demand an assumption of ambivalence as part of their understanding. Some of these topics were more or less self-evident: death of and separation of loved ones, attitudes toward authority, in-group and out-group orientations. But I expanded those illustrations into less obvious ones, including the play of public opinion, the obligations of citizenship, and the institutionalization of sacred values. It is impossible (especially for an author) to assess the interest and impact of this intellectual effort, but at least a few commentators have cited it as among the most influential of my later writings.

Exporting and applying psychoanalysis: Problematics

Twice in the 1990s Wallerstein and I offered a course on social applications of psychoanalysis to advanced psychiatry students at the University of California, San Francisco. He initiated the collaboration, but I took some leadership in shaping the substance of the course. We made no plans to publish any results emanating from the course. However, in 1990, Jeffrey Prager, a former Berkeley Ph.D. student of mine who had taken a teaching position at UCLA and entered psychoanalytic training, asked me to contribute to a book on psycho-analytic sociology he was co-editing for publication in Great Britain. With the memory of that course still in mind, I decided to undertake a systematization of some of its themes in the proposed essay. Unlike previous and subsequent efforts, however, I decided to take an explicitly theoretical and methodological direction. I asked, initially, what kind of enterprise is psychoanalysis from several standpoints: its theoretical structure, its empirical situation (the treatment setting), and the kinds of data (clinical) from which its inferences and explanations were made? To extend this analysis, I raised a further question: what kinds of results can be expected and what kinds of problems are generated when psychoanalytic interpretations are empirical-historical situations that *differ* from the clinical situation and yield different kinds of non-clinical data?

With this question in mind I dissected several studies that employed the tools of psychoanalysis but in non-psychoanalytic situations. These were:

- A study of a community disaster resulting from a flood in Buffalo Creek, West Virginia, conducted by Erik Erikson's son, Kai, a sociologist (Erikson, 1976).
- A study of authority and interpersonal dynamics in a mental hospital (Hodgson et al., 1965) foreshadowing the growth of another area of scholarly interest—emotions in organizations.
- Several studies of the psychoanalytic investigation of cultural products such as novels and dramas (for example, Jones, 1954).
- Several studies in psychohistory, a briefly flourishing intellectual movement stimulated in large part by the work of Erikson (for example, 1958).

In all these cases I analyzed as best I could the kinds of empirical information these kinds of inquiry yielded, and attempted to specify *both* the power that psychoanalytic interpretations could bring to these settings *and* the limitations that those settings entailed with respect to generating reliable and valid psychoanalytic interpretations. (Smelser, 1993b).

Psychologizing at the cultural level: The idea of cultural trauma

In late 1990s, when I was directing the Center for Advanced Study in the Behavioral Sciences at Stanford, Jeffrey Alexander (a former student) and a number of European scholars applied to come to the Center with a special intellectual project: the study of cultural values and collective memory. I was personally interested in the topic, and secured Hewlett Foundation funds to sponsor it. I also decided, with Alexander's permission, to join the project myself, as if I were one of the visiting Fellows. During the fellowship year itself (1998–1999) we converged on the special topic of cultural trauma, which had in the previous couple of decades become a focus of interest in psychology, anthropology, and history.

Participants in the special project agreed that we should put together a volume on cultural trauma, each contributing a chapter. Most of the chapters were case studies (for example, American slavery, the holocaust, and post-Communist traumas in Eastern Europe). I decided to write a theoretical essay, exploring and comparing the idea of trauma as a psychoanalytic concept (remembering its central place in Freud's early writings) and the adaptation of that idea at the social and cultural levels (Smelser, 2004a). Using Freud's characterization as a starting point, I found the idea of individual trauma to be an extremely powerful analogy in suggesting and elucidating the characteristics of cultural traumas—their embeddedness in larger systems; their indelibility; the compulsive interplay of affect and defense; and their claim on psychic energy. In these regards, genuine parallels could be observed. However, at the same time I argued against pressing the analogy too far. In particular, I emphasized that collective coping with cultural traumas was an analytically different process than individual coping that demanded analysis at the social level. In particular, I argued that collective coping involved distinctly different mechanisms—the play of public opinion, group contestation and conflict, and claims of "ownership" of the trauma—that were distinctively at the social-cultural level, and did not have direct counterparts in individual adaptations to traumas, or even in "mass" adaptations, which refers to like responses of large numbers of individuals.

We submitted the manuscript emanating from the special project to the University of California Press. They found it worthy, but the sponsoring editor, writing to us in the spring of 2002, more or less demanded that we include a chapter on the recent 9/11 attacks as a cultural trauma. Since, by chance, I was working on several committees on terrorism in the National Research Council at the time, it fell to me to prepare that chapter. It was a tough chapter to write, because in spring of 2002 we were still in the hot phases of that trauma. Nevertheless, I developed an interpretation of many of the early reactions as those of cultural trauma, assessed them in light of distinctive features of American culture, and generated a number of predictions about the ways the events would become embedded in collective memory and shape future political decisions (Smelser, 2004b). My analysis was interdisciplinary, but it did involve a distinctively psychoanalytic interpretation of socio-cultural phenomena.

Psychoanalysis as an instance of a generic social-psychological process

During my career I experienced some of my own education and some sabbatical leaves abroad. In addition I was director of an education-abroad program for students of the University of California, UK-Ireland (1977–1979), and director of the Stanford Center (1994–2001), where scholars gathered for a year of free research away from their own academic institutions. Over the decades I became fascinated with the psychological and social dynamics of these "years away" from status, structure, and routine. I came to call them "Odyssey experiences." After my retirement in 2001 I decided to undertake a major analysis of these "destructured moratoria," and wrote a monograph that included analyses of religious pilgrimages, tourism and travel, religious conversion, academic leaves, many rites of passage, the honeymoon, and coercive experiences such as military training and even brain-washing (Smelser, 2009). I also incorporated "psychoanalysis-as-journey" into this generic analysis, and made an effort to demonstrate its continuity as a period finite of withdrawal-destructuring-regenerating. This was a different kind of "articulation" of the psychological and social worlds, namely treating psychoanalysis as a generic social process.

Coda

No coherent summary of this essay is needed, or is indeed possible. I have presented a biographical history and an intellectual history as they unfolded in quite unsystematic ways. To attempt a rational recapitulation of these histories would be an error, because they were not in intention, plan, or sequence. To generalize this observation, I regard attempts at forging articulations between the sociological and the psychoanalytic enterprises to be necessarily piecemeal, given the massive difficulties of general syntheses. Such piecemeal attempts appear to be analogous to attacking a granite rock with one's bare hands. One never achieves a conquest in that enterprise, but from time to time one may gain a definite grasp and achieve a palpable increment of progress.

References

Bettelheim, B. (1970) *Obsolete Youth: Towards a Psychography of Adolescent Rebellion* (San Francisco: San Francisco Press).

Erikson, E. H. (1958) *Young Man Luther: A Study in Psychoanalysis and History* (New York: Norton).

Erikson, K. (1976) *Everything in its Path: Destruction in the Buffalo Creek Flood* (New York: Simon and Schuster).

Feuer, L. S. (1969) *The Conflict of Generations: The Character and Significance of Student Movements* (New York: Basic Books).

Freud, S. ([1895] 1950) "Project for a Scientific Psychology" in J. Strachey (ed.) The Standard Edition of the *Complete Psychological Works of Sigmund Freud*, Vol. 1 (London: The Hogarth Press).

Hodgson, R., D. J. Levinson, and A. Zeleznik (1965) *The Executive role Constellation: An Analysis of Personality and Role Relations in Management* (Boston: Harvard Graduate School of Business Administration).

Jones, E. (1954) *Hamlet and Oedipus* (Garden City: Doubleday).

Meehl, P. E. (1954) *Clinical vs Statistical Predictions: A Theoretical Analysis and a Review of the Evidence* (Minneapolis: University of Minnesota Press).

Munch, R. and N. J. Smelser (1987) "Relating the Micro and Macro," in J. C. Alexander, B. Giesen, R. Munch, and N. J. Smelser (eds) *The Micro-Macro Link* (Berkeley: University of California Press).

Parsons, T. and R. F. Bales, in collaboration with J. Olds, M. Zelditch, Jr., and P. E. Slater (1955) *Family, Socialization, and Interaction Process* (Glencoe: The Free Press).

Parsons, T. and N. J. Smelser (1956) *Economy and Society: A Study in the Integration of Economic and Sociological Theory* (London: Routledge and Kegan Paul and Glencoe: The Free Press).

Smelser, N. J. (1959) *Social Change in the Industrial Revolution: An Application of Theory to the British Cotton Industry* (Chicago: The University of Chicago Press and London: Routledge and Kegan Paul).

Smelser, N. J. (1962) *Theory of Collective Behavior* (New York: The Free Press and London: Collier-Macmillan).

Smelser, N. J. (1968) "Social and Psychological Dimensions of Collective Behavior," in *Essays in Sociological Explanation* (Englewood Cliffs: Prentice-Hall).

Smelser, N. J. (1983) "Collective Myths and Fantasies: The Myth of the Good Life in California," *Humboldt Journal of Social Relations*, 2 (1), 1–35.

Smelser, N. J. (1987) "Depth Psychology and the Social Order," in J. C. Alexander, B. Giesen, R. Munch, and N. J. Smelser (eds), *The Micro-Macro Link* (Berkeley: The University of California Press).

Smelser, N. J. (1993a) "The Politics of Ambivalence: Diversity in the Research Universities," *Daedalus*, 122 (4), 37–53.

Smelser, N. J. (1993b) "The Psychoanalytic Mode of Inquiry in the Context of the Behavioral and Social Sciences," in J. Prager and M. Rustin (eds) *Psychoanalytic Sociology*, Vol. 1 (Aldershot: Edward Elgar Publishing).

Smelser, N. J. (1998a) "1997 Presidential Address: The Rational and the Ambivalent in the Social Sciences," American Sociological Review, 63 (1), 1–15.

Smelser, N. J. (1998b) *The Social Edges of Psychoanalysis* (Berkeley: University of California Press).

Smelser, N. J. (1999) "Problematics of Affirmative Action: A View from California," in E. Y. Lowe, Jr. (ed.) *Promise and Dilemma: Perspectives on Racial Diversity and Higher Education* (Princeton: Princeton University Press).

Smelser, N. J. (2004a) "Psychological Trauma and Cultural Trauma," in J. C. Alexander, R. Eyerman, B. Giesen, N. J. Smelser, and P. Sztompka (eds) *Collective Trauma and Collective Identity* (Berkeley: University of California Press).

Smelser, N. J. (2004b) "Epilogue: September 11, 2001, as Cultural Trauma," in J. C. Alexander, R. Eyerman, B. Giesen, N. J. Smelser, and P. Sztompka (eds) *Collective Trauma and Collective Identity* (Berkeley: University of California Press).

Smelser, N. J. (2007) *The Faces of Terrorism: Social and Psychological Dimensions* (Princeton: Princeton University Press).

Smelser, N. J. (2009) *The Odyssey Experience: Physical, Social, Psychological, and Spiritual Journeys* (Berkeley: University of California Press).

Smelser, N. J. and E. H. Erikson (eds) (1981) *Themes of Love and Work in Adulthood* (Cambridge: Harvard University Press).

Smelser, N. J. and T. W. Smelser (eds) (1963) *Personality and Social Systems* (New York: John Wiley & Sons).

Smelser, N. J. and R. S. Wallerstein (1969) "Psychoanalysis and Sociology: Articulations and Applications," The International Journal of Psychoanalysis. 50, 693–710.

5
Why Is It Easy to Be a Psychoanalyst and a Feminist, But not a Psychoanalyst and a Social Scientist? Reflections of a Psychoanalytic Hybrid

Nancy J. Chodorow

I was asked to make these reflections on my dual identity and location as academic and psychoanalyst personal and informal, and so they are. I see them, in some ways, as both a continuation of and a contrast to our last meeting: my thinking was sparked by Paul Schwaber's presentation, "The Pleasures of Mind," in which Schwaber, a psychoanalyst and humanities professor, described the happy combination he has been able to make of psychoanalysis and literature. Here, I describe what I have found to be, from both sides, a not-so-happy combination.

I write as sociologist, feminist, and psychoanalyst, and in this context, it is important to warn readers that, as with all expressions and behaviors, my way of seeing—calling myself a hybrid and describing how difficult it is to have a dual psychoanalytic and social scientific identity—is overdetermined and early-determined. Several recent writings have "hybrid," "margin," or "cusp" in their titles. The introductory chapter of my recent *Individualizing Gender and Sexuality: Theory and Practice* (Chodorow, 2012) is called "Psychoanalysis and women from margin to center" (2004b). I have written about "relational individualism" (1986), I have created the name "intersubjective ego psychology," not two-person relational, not one-person classical, to define my own psychoanalytic location (2004a), and I have located myself as a feminist psychoanalyst on the "modern–postmodern and classical–relational divide" (2005). *The Power of Feelings* (Chodorow, 1999a) advocates "both-and" rather than "either-or," when it comes to competing psychoanalytic theories, past and present determinism, meaning as cultural and personal, life as psychically and socially created, and academia and psychoanalysis.

In "Born into a World at War," an essay about being a member of the World War II birth cohort (the paper itself an Eriksonian hybrid psyche-culture-society paper), I note that I always feel like an outsider. I was the only Jewish girl in my class and describe myself as "a Jewish New Yorker who grew up in California and who as a preschooler wanted to be a cowgirl (or cowboy)" (Chodorow, 2002, p. 304). I was Jewish not Gentile, yet, as I remarked in the autobiographical component of my application to the San Francisco Psychoanalytic Institute, an Eastern European rather than a German Jew.

Virginia Goldner, a leading relational psychoanalyst, couples therapist, and gender theorist, was in my "consciousness-raising" group, a group that formed in 1969 as part of the women's movement. Recently, she has observed that I am driven to locate myself on the margin, that I am a person who walks a perfect tightrope of conflicting identities and ambivalence without ever losing her balance. She is right: I see myself in an in-between way and had almost entitled my presentation "From Margin to Margin and Back Again." My chapter, then, has both psychodynamic and substantive origins.

My sense of marginality, or insider-outsiderness, can be empirically supported. I turn from the self-understanding of a psychoanalyst to the observations of a sociologist. It was 1992 or 1993, at the first or second yearly meeting of the University of California Interdisciplinary Psychoanalytic Consortium, as of this writing (2014) a now 20-plus yearly meeting, organized originally by UCLA historian and psychoanalyst Peter Loewenberg, UCSD psychiatrist-psychoanalyst Robert Nemiroff, and myself. The goal of the UCIPC is to bring together psychoanalytically interested faculty and graduate students from throughout the University of California system. It attracts people from well over fifteen academic disciplines, many of whom have trained as CORST analysts and all of whom find a welcome retreat where everyone takes psychoanalysis seriously. Karin Martin, then a student of mine, was among the attendees. Karin has herself worked on the psychoanalysis–sociology boundary. Now Professor of Sociology at the University of Michigan, she wrote a dissertation entitled "Puberty, Sexuality, and the Self" (Martin, 1996) and gave a job talk, miraculously welcomed in a very traditional sociology department, entitled "My Hair is My Accomplishment." Since then, she has done research on, among other topics, gender and body image in preschoolers, feeling rules for women giving birth, and birth stories told to children by lesbian and straight parents. At the meeting, Karin said, "Nancy, have you noticed? All of the feminists here are in the humanities, except you, and all the social scientists except you are men."

For a second example, skip to May, 2004, one month before this presentation. The psychoanalyst-sociologist hyphen had snapped, and in 2005, after thirty years of teaching, I was planning to leave academia and to focus on clinical work, analytic teaching, and writing. As a favor and an honor, Peter Evans, my department chair, suggested that I teach, for my final semester, a graduate seminar on my own work. I called it "Chodorow on Chodorow: Theorizing and Theory." For many years, I had taught slightly insurgent graduate courses: among classical and contemporary theory electives, "Freud and Beyond" and "Feminist Theory," and among methodology courses our graduate interviewing methods course under the title, "Clinical Interviewing for Social Scientists," as well as feminist methodology. My undergraduate courses included "Feminism and Psychoanalysis," "Individuality and Society," and "Psyche, Culture, and Society." At a department reception, I ran into the staff assistant to the graduate program, who, knowing of my upcoming retirement, said, "I hear you're going to teach next fall. I *hope* you're doing *something* that the students *want*, and not just *Freud!*" I told her about "Chodorow on Chodorow," in which we would be talking about feminist theory, sexuality, gender, theory construction, and the history of theory, along with substantive issues I had written about—terrorism and masculinity, mothering, homophobia, and so forth. Her response: "Yes, but I hope it will be broad and interesting to our students, and not just about Freud and analysis."

A final vignette about why it is not easy to be a psychoanalyst and a social scientist takes us back to the beginning of my career. Consider a symposium on *The Reproduction of Mothering* which took place at the American Sociological Association Meetings in 1979. At those meetings, the book also shared the first Jessie Bernard Award for its contribution to understanding women and society. The symposium was published in its entirety in *Signs*, the premier women's studies journal of the time. Sociologist Judith Lorber writes, "When I read *The Reproduction of Mothering*, I found to my disappointment that it is primarily an exegesis of psychoanalytic theory and therefore, in my eyes, a lesser contribution to the sociology of gender than Nancy Chodorow's earlier, short pieces" (Lorber et al., 1981, p. 482). In like vein, Alice Rossi notes, "I was not prepared for so extended an exegesis of psychoanalytic theory, past and present, or for the nearly total embeddedness of her theory in psychodynamic terms. . . . what constitutes 'evidence' in Chodorow's book. . . . does her central insight require the burden of so much psychoanalytic theory and so harsh a rejection of theories in biology and developmental psychology?"

(6: 493).[1] By contrast, the third discussant, Rose Coser, was a great supporter of the book and of me, did not take issue with its psychoanalytic underpinnings, and in fact, found it easy to read the book as a treatise on modern family structure. For several years thereafter, until I stopped going to sociology meetings in the late 1980s, I found myself wandering into one session after another on topics that interested me—mothering, gender roles, feminist theory, socialization—and someone would be declaiming, "we can take seriously five different understandings of women's mothering, but Chodorow's individualistic psychology is not one of them."

Meanwhile, even as my sociological colleagues were excoriating my "individualistic psychology," colleagues in the humanities—in literature, philosophy and political theory—were writing books and dissertations based on my work ("all of the feminists here are in the humanities, except you"). My focus on the internal mother–daughter world and the mother in the male psyche opened new vistas for understanding women authors, characters, and patterns of interaction depicted in women's novels, imagery, metaphor, and other characteristics of women's writing, and fear of women and the feminine in writings by men. My characterization of the female psyche as based in relation and connection, preceding Gilligan and self-in-relation theory, and my theorizing the defensive denial of connection and dependency in men, served as a basis for thinking in moral philosophy and epistemology and for critiques of normal science and classical political theory. In anthropology, an ideographic discipline that studies people as well as structures and organizations, the work served as underpinning of several ethnographic investigations.

Thus, my work, even where it was criticized, was taken very seriously throughout the academy, and I did become "famous."[2] I note, though I won't address further, another contribution to the comparative ease of being a psychoanalytic feminist in contrast to a psychoanalytic sociologist. In those pre-postmodern, pre-poststructuralist times in which I first wrote, all feminists had to acknowledge that Freud, along with Levi-Strauss, was one of only two classical grand theorists to take gender seriously. Several early first-wave feminist books excoriated Freud, but at least until the poststructural turn, within the academic humanities and in feminist anthropology my work was almost idealized (except when it was being criticized for its purported psychoanalytically inspired "difference feminism" and "universalizing and essentializing"). In short, it was universally considered a founding and foundational feminist theory.

I turn now from it is easy to be a psychoanalyst and a feminist to "all the social scientists except you are men." My early academic training, and my first intellectual home, was in psychological anthropology. This discipline had been at the forefront of American anthropology in the 1930s through the 1950s, influencing and influenced by our native-grown Sullivanian and Eriksonian psychoanalysis. Not negligibly, it had, like psychoanalysis, many leading women practitioners. In the 1940s and 1950s, there was also a vision, found throughout the social sciences, and given institutional expression by Parsons, Kluckhohn, Murray, and Allport in the Harvard Department of Social Relations, of an integrated social science that incorporated the macro-societal questions and methodology of sociology, the on-the-ground ethnography of cultures, the study of psychological anthropology and personality and culture, and clinical and personality psychology. You find the legacy of such integrative thinking—a familiarity with Freud along with Weber, Durkheim, George Herbert Mead, Malinowski, and Boas—in anthropologists and sociologists Clifford Geertz, Neil Smelser, Robert Bellah, and Victor Turner, in political scientists like Gabriel Almond, and in other leading thinkers of a certain American social science generation. You find it in those of us who studied as undergraduates and graduate students in the Social Relations Department.

By my time, however, psychological anthropology was on the margins of anthropology, where it has remained. Much of the discipline has redefined its location to be within the postmodern or critical postcolonial humanities; it is extremely anti-psychological, and it thinks of cultures as texts. The leading feminist anthropologists are not psychoanalytic. At the same time, I want to acknowledge that within anthropology, psychoanalytic anthropology has been an extremely strong margin. When I conclude these reflections by turning to the perspective from psychoanalysis concerning why it is hard to be a social scientist and a psychoanalyst, that is also part of my story: these disciplines—psychological and psychoanalytic anthropology, and ethnography more generally, that are as close epistemologically, theoretically, methodologically and substantively as any discipline to psychoanalysis, and that include several CORST analysts—are mainly not noticed by psychoanalysts.

The reader can see from what I have written so far that my "field" has always been, basically, psychoanalysis, or psychoanalysis-hyphened. I have always been interested in the complexities of individuality and by extension in intersubjective epistemologies and methodologies—ethnography, the qualitative sociologies, the analytic encounter. I am a sociologist who has never studied groups, organizations, stratification, collective behavior, institutions beyond the family, or any other typical sociological topic, and I am a theorist, interested in the complexities of theory and in writing about others' theories and creating my own.

I think of psychoanalysis as the human science of individuality or subjectivity. It is the only field that studies and theorizes about how we constitute ourselves as whole beings, through our innate constitutional givens, our relationships, our material and social reality, and our history of psychic reactions, defenses, and compromise formations. Its methodology is intersubjective. At my retirement ceremony in 2005, I remarked that if I had another thirty years in the university, I would advocate for a missing discipline, probably in the social sciences, called individuology.

Given my passions and subsequent history, I have sometimes wondered why I didn't follow some of my closest undergraduate friends straight into clinical psychology. Like most of our choices, mine was probably over-determined. I had grown up in an academic world, was a very good student, loved anthropology and then social and psychoanalytic theory, and have always been, for personal psychodynamic reasons, quite autonomous when it comes to my thinking. Though I found it of course challenging, I simply assumed, over those early years, that I could incorporate psychoanalytic theory, ethnography, Marxism, the study of gender, and so forth. I used to tell my graduate students that they should not bother to become an academic unless they were absolutely passionate about it and could not imagine doing anything else (and I would say the same thing to anyone who wants to become a psychoanalyst). I was completely fortunate in getting away with this, being in one of the few leading sociology departments in the country to take theory seriously, and in a department where there was one professor senior to me, Neil Smelser, who had himself trained as an analyst and who encouraged me in my interests and pursuits well before I had met him.

Moving from the personal and autobiographical, my contribution to a *festschrift* for Neil Smelser (Chodorow, 2004c) expresses at some length my substantive observations and reflections about the incompatibilities between sociology and psychoanalysis and therefore my own tensions living within these two fields (I make similar observations in *The Power of Feelings*):

To look specifically at sociology: sociologists usually interest themselves in structures, practices, processes, and social relations that characterize groups, organizations, and other supra-individual entities.

They tend to think that individual experience is created, shaped, or structured through these social dynamics and structures and to see sociological actors in terms of a single dimension of action, for example, rational choice, impression management, measured and scaled attitudes, political or economic actor. When sociology theorizes individuals, it is in terms of social categories, according to their race, class, gender, ethnicity, and so forth. Sociology envisions both individual and collective agency through the lens of these social categories and socially oriented action, so that both individual and collective behavior are portrayed in terms of their relations to institutions and social processes rather than in terms of individually idiosyncratic goals or beliefs. Similarly, agency and resistance are evaluated not in terms of personal goals or interpretations, but in relation to structures of inequality or domination, and intersectionality theory leads us to conceive not of unique individuals who internally experience and help to shape their lives but of individuals only as joint products of race, gender, and class forces. Practice theory describes culturally and situationally embedded, goal-oriented enactment.

Sociologists are trapped by a legacy that separated individual experience, subjectivity, and action from structures and institutions and that construed the former as determined by the latter. This legacy began with structural-functionalism but continued with most Marxisms. Postmodernism-poststructuralism argues against cultural holism and for the complexity, contingency, and historicity of cultures, as well as for the multiple contradictions, rather than functional interrelations, among cultural elements. But at the same time, these theories agree with traditional structuralism about the autonomy of the cultural. Poststructuralism may have made central to its critique of structuralism the absence of a subject, but it argues that subjectivity is constructed discursively and politically from without. The "structure-agency" problem is itself an artifact of this construction of theoretical reality: if traditions like symbolic interactionism or pragmatism had been more hegemonic, if Mead, Cooley, Simmel, and Freud had been as canonical as Marx, Weber, and Durkheim, social scientists would not need to look for a connection between structure and individual or collective action.[3]

Like sociology, although with more apparent tension, anthropology has also minimized individual selfhood. This tension develops because, while the ethnographic encounter makes the individuality of informants palpable, such that from its earliest moments anthropology has described individuals, the goal of most ethnography has been to make generalized claims about particular cultures, even if these claims are based on information observed and gathered in particularized interactional moments. Like most accounts in qualitative sociology, contemporary anthropological accounts that portray a person in relation to culture may or may not have a complex view of culture, but they often have an unelaborated concept of the person— of an internally differentiated self, an inner world, and complex unconscious mental processes. By looking only at elements of meaning that are culturally shared and not those that are individually particular, anthropologists and qualitative sociologists abstract out of how meaning is personally experienced, skimming off one part of experience, so that experience becomes less rich than it actually is. They lose understanding of how individual psychologies enact or express cultural forms and give these forms emotional force, depth, and complexity.

I believe that the core of individuality is in the realm of personal meaning. As with social determinism, thinkers from a variety of fields have tended to assume that cultural meanings have determinative priority in shaping experience and the self. Even those who think in a more constructionist vein claim that actors create meaning by drawing upon available tangles or webs of cultural meaning. Meanings still come entirely from a cultural corpus or stock. I suggest that people create and experience social processes and cultural meanings psychodynamically—in unconscious, affect-laden, non-linguistic, immediately felt images and fantasies that everyone creates from birth, about self, self and other, body, and the world—as well as linguistically, discursively, or in terms of a cultural lexicon. Social processes are given, and they may lead to some patterns of experiencing in common, but this experiencing will be as much affective and non-linguistic as cognitive. All social and cultural experiences are filtered, shaped, and transformed through a transferential lens. In order fully to understand human social life, we need to theorize and investigate personal meaning.

I am suggesting, then, that people are historically and biographically changing individuals who create psychodynamically their own multi-layered sense of meaning and self, that consciousness determines life just as much as life determines consciousness. Individuals are interesting and complex in themselves and worthy of study for this reason alone. All the people we study have inner lives and selves that affect and shape how they act and feel. They may not always be aware of this inner life, which is experienced unconsciously as well as consciously, but you cannot understand or interpret what they are telling you if you think that they always say what they mean—as I tell my students, whom I try to help to see themselves not as tape-recorders of interviews but as listeners and interpreters of meanings communicated through affect and transference as much as through language (of course, it is also difficult to get clinical student super-visees not to rely on tape-recorded sessions or note taking in the hour). Also, we as researchers have complex inner lives. As one of my students in a course on feminist methodology put it, reflecting upon a field experience in which she had tried to study shop floor labor process according to the precepts of Marxist ethnography, "the difficulty was that I had beliefs and a personality."

In addition to its being interesting in its own right, studying indi-vidual subjectivities gives us an enriched and fuller understanding of society and culture. All social scientists whose theories and findings make assumptions about human nature and human motivation need to address individual experience and agency, and one major compo-nent of that experience and agency is psychodynamic. Approaches to agency and practice that assume only conscious, rational, strategic goals, and maneuvers do not comprehend the action they purport to explain. Personal meaning is a central organizing experience for each individual, and society or culture does not precede or determine these lives. Rather, there are complex relations between personal meaning and cultural meaning and between individual lives and society. In any individual life, many different social and cultural elements interact. Also, each person herself or himself puts together these elements and elements of self and identity in idiosyncratic, conflictual, contradictory, changing, personalized ways. It is a rev-elation to sociology students to try to account for a single life in all its social, historical, and familial context and personal uniqueness. Individuality is important in any social science context that involves interaction with others or observation of them.

Even those few social scientists who do study the emotions, con-ceptions of self, and unconscious life seem suspicious of and do not tend to pay attention theoretically and ethnographically to psycho-logical individuality. These scholars tend to turn emotions and self into something else. Anthropologists of self and feeling claim that emotions are pragmatic, linguistic and discursive, employed for cul-tural communication and practice. Their investigations ask how the web of cultural emotion- and-self meanings interrelates with, gives further meaning to, and gains meaning from, other cultural webs of meaning or meaning-imbued practices, but not with other webs of personal meaning. Sociologists of emotion focus on the feelings rules that are imposed by the culture and that people react to. But if you read the sociologists of emotion and the anthropologists of self and feeling, the striking palpable anxiety, pain, and confusion of people engaged in cultural emotions and feelings is not theorized—the "I" of the experiencer, if you will, rather than the "me" whose emotional life is being shaped and reshaped according to cultural patterns.

Finally, being a psychoanalyst as well as a sociologist, I would suggest that the psyche itself plays a part here. In many cases thinking in terms of individual action and fantasy is, simply, terrifying. If we keep things impersonal, call something "racism," or "nationalism," or "misogyny," or "homophobia," we do not need to keep in the front of our minds that individuals, with conscious and unconscious intentions, with, indeed, conscious reasons and rationalizations that make such behaviors all right, engage, in specific instances, in lynching, mass murder or genocide, rape (or, in the case of the intersection of "nationalism" and "misogyny," mass rape of women and girls), or the murder of homosexuals.[4]

Moreover, I speculate that people attracted to the social sciences have a pretheoretical, emotional predilection to feel and believe that things come *from society* or *from culture*. This unquestioned belief is reinforced through studying the social sciences, but the social sciences resonate in turn with an already present inner sense of truth. For people who naturally look at the world like this, it is very difficult and anxiety-provoking fully to consider that we also create our psychological life and consciousness, rather than this life and consciousness being determined by external conditions, or to consider that our consciousness, psyches, and modes of being, and social and cultural conditions, may be mutually shaping. As I put it in *The Power of Feelings*, "By character, perhaps, those who become social scientists tend intuitively to be paranoid externalizers who projectively see troubles and opportunities as coming from without; those who become analysts tend intuitively to be omnipotent (or depressive) narcissists who see the world as created from within" (1999a, p. 221).

My contribution here compares the difficulty of being a psychoanalyst and a sociologist, as elaborated in the preceding long extract, with the comparative ease of being a psychoanalyst and a feminist. I have suggested that psychoanalysis was not for the most part welcomed by sociological feminists, and I now turn to the psychoanalytic reaction to psychoanalytic feminism. I describe this reaction briefly and conclude by returning to my first dyad, in order to explore the reciprocated ignoring of and blindness toward the social sciences on the part of psychoanalysis. From both sides, why is it easier to be a psychoanalyst and a feminist than a psychoanalyst and a social scientist?

When I published my first articles and book, I of course wanted to get the same rewards and recognition from psychoanalysis as from the academy. I wanted, contradictorily, instant acclaim for a work that in fact posed a fundamental challenge to many elements in psychoanalysis (most writers are closet or not-so-closet narcissists). With hindsight, knowing now with what (glacial) speed new ideas, especially those from outsiders but even those from within, receive acceptance in psychoanalysis, I would say that psychoanalysts took up my work and drew upon it with extreme seriousness. It was not, after all, simply that I was an outsider, and an outsider with quite absolutist second-wave feminist notions about the non-existence of the psychic body and sexuality. I also located myself psychoanalytically as a British object-relations theorist during the mid-1970s to mid-1980s, when American psychoanalysis was still steeped in classical ego psychology and not open to neo-Kleinian thinking. Yet, as a feminist and thinker about gender and sexuality, I became, along with several other people, central in the psychoanalytic revaluation of the theory of femininity. On my side, from the moment I finished *The Reproduction of Mothering*, I knew that if I wanted to go any more deeply into the understanding of psychic life and psychoanalysis, I needed clinical training (I had *some* respect for the empirical bases of theory!).

By the mid-1970s, and largely, I believe, in response to second wave feminism, psychoanalysis began slowly to reappraise the theory of femininity (I discuss this more fully in Chodorow, 2004b). We can recall a bit of history here. After the active debates about female sexuality and femininity in the 1920s and 1930s, there followed what Fliegel (1986) noticed as a repression of memory of the debate—a "quiescent interval" of lack of investigation of or interest in femininity. Between the 1940s and the 1970s, a very few psychoanalysts—Chasseguet-Smirgel, Kestenberg, and Stoller—explored femininity, and in the 1950s, Benedek and Bibring wrote about pregnancy and childbirth, which, ironically, had never been central to psychoanalytic thinking (see Balsam, 2012).

For the sociologist of knowledge, it is not surprising that the reemergence of psychoanalytic interest in the psychology of women did not arise simply from within psychoanalysis through "normal science." Rather, theorizing and critique mainly from without came slowly to generate rethinking from within, spurring major breakthroughs in understandings of gender and sexuality, generating changes in psychoanalytic attitudes towards mothers, increasing attention to, revaluation, and depathologization of "preoedipal" levels of functioning, and probably leading to greater American acceptance of relational theories— both the native-grown Sullivanian and Horneyan schools and British object-relations thinking.

I am looking back here on the mid-1970s to mid-1980s, when the feminist critique moved into the center of psychoanalysis, and of course I cannot even begin to name the large number of important contributors who made gender and a critique of classical psychoanalysis central in their work. They included classically trained American analysts like Carol Nadelson, Malkah Notman, Ethel Person, Rosemary Balsam, and many others, all of whom did extensive writing and thinking about women. Unlike the classical analysts of a previous generation, these analysts, without giving up their commitments to the intrapsychic world and the centrality of the psychic sexual body, thought that culture played a part in the psychology of gender and in psychoanalytic understandings of gender and sexuality (I have called them "cultural school ego psychologists," Chodorow, 2004a). Similarly, all the contributors to a 1976 special issue of the *Journal of the American Psychoanalytic Association* were aware, explicitly or implicitly, of the feminist ferment going on around them. Soon, feminism as a social and political force propelled greater numbers of women into the professions, and psychoanalytic institutes began accepting more women candidates. Eventually, the field itself refeminized (in the 1920s and 1930s, a large proportion of psychoanalysts were women). As a psychoanalyst and a feminist, then, I have always found myself at the heart of things, sometimes in disagreement with my colleagues but always in overlapping dialogue, central rather than peripheral, feeling that there is much to learn from each and every one of them and feeling, in turn, appreciated by them.

This welcoming of me and of other psychoanalytic feminists by feminist psychoanalysts stands in sharp contrast to what I have observed to be the impact upon psychoanalysis of, and interest of psychoanalysts in, the social sciences. I conclude with some observations and speculation about this divide, about psychoanalysts' reciprocal suspicion of and simple disinterest in social science. In my extended quotation from "The sociological eye and the psychoanalytic ear," I make some suggestions about why social scientists are so critical of psychoanalysis: *the basic premise of psychoanalysis is antagonistic to the social sciences*. To recapitulate, among social scientists, there is, quite simply, professional suspicion, ambivalence, and even antipathy toward personal individuality, to the idea that the individual is not a tabula rasa affected by social and cultural forces. Economics is the only social science that even thinks in terms of individual motivation, but it deals with individuals, not individuality. Social scientists fear that a consideration of psychological factors in experience and behavior psychologizes away the institutional and sociohistorical forces of globalization, sexism, homophobia, and racism and blames the victim. I am not as clear about the reverse.

In lieu of conclusions, I draw in what follows on my qualitative social science background, and some speculative license about motivation, to make some initiating ethnographic observations. Psychoanalysts, as I observe them, have had and continue to have a love affair with, or a crush on, almost every even vaguely connected academic discipline in the sciences and the humanities—on the scientific side, psychiatry, medicine, and neuroscience, on the side of the humanities, philosophy, literature and literary criticism, opera, music, painting, and sculpture. We find several ongoing discussion groups at the meetings of the American Psychoanalytic Association on creativity, novels and novelists, art, and music. Analysts admire poets and publish articles about the poetic elements in the analytic experience, and there is a poetry column in the newsletter of the American Psychoanalytic Association. Many analysts spend years studying the philosophy of mind, and some brave souls steep themselves in Derrida, Lyotard, Heidegger, or Stanley Cavell.

By contrast, analysts do not notice that the clinical consulting room is always partly a psychodynamically inflected instantiation of society, culture, and politics, as is the transference-countertransference field.[5] They do not read the psychoanalytic anthropology literature—Kracke, LeVine, Spiro, Hollan, Johnson, and Paul all fully trained psychoanalysts, or Briggs, Obeyesekere, Crapanzano, Herdt, Ewing, and Levy, all steeped in psychoanalytic thinking and modes of observation, Levy a psychiatrist as well as anthropologist (in contrast to psychoanalyst-anthropologists and the long history of psychoanalytic anthropology, we notice that there are only three CORST sociologists,[6] a few political scientists, and one CORST economist, though there are a fair number of CORST historians—a field that is, depending on the particular university, classed either as a humanity or as a social science).

All of these ethnographers theorize and observe the psychological and cultural lives of individuals, dreams, transference and countertransference in the intersubjective encounter of anthropologist and informant, minute mother–child interactions, permissible and non-permissible emotions and the anxieties and defenses that are engaged to enforce these, and concepts of person, self, and feeling. They try to elicit and assess unconscious fantasies and individual patterns of projection and introjection, and they explore how cultural groups collectively enforce feeling rules and engage in projective othering and dehumanizing. They describe cases—cases of the individuals whom they study and cultures or families as cases.

You cannot, then, find a field as epistemologically, methodologically, and substantively near to psychoanalysis as ethnography. Indeed, all of the reflexive social sciences are close methodologically and epistemologically to psychoanalysis (compare Loewald, 1970), yet it is only within anthropology that we see not only reflexive methods but also interest in psychoanalysis.[7] A quote from the anthropologist Obeyesekere could, with a few word changes, have been written about psychoanalysis by an analyst. Obeyesekere says, "Ethnography highlights, more than any other human science, the intersubjective relationship between the scholar and the subject of his study, by focusing on a single individual, or a couple at most, hopelessly trying to make do in an alienating field situation" (1990, p. 225).

For thirty years, there was a two-day psychoanalysis and anthropology workshop at the time of the New York Meetings of the American Psychoanalytic Association, but, as I discovered the first time I attended, this workshop competed with the meetings themselves: you could not attend both psychoanalytic and psychoanalytic anthropology meetings. In January 2004, at the meetings of the American Psychoanalytic Association, I chaired a panel on the legacy of Bloomsbury, but as far as I know, no one has thought to have a panel on the legacy of 1930s psychological anthropology, on the 1920s anthropological debates about sexuality and the Oedipus complex, or even about the role of anthropology in 1940s American psychoanalytic politics, in which splits so often developed over the role of culture in psychic life. In psychoanalysis, further, we have a substantial research tradition in process and outcome, infant observation, and mother–infant interaction, but it is my impression that our roots and connections do not reach far into academic psychology–to cognitive and developmental psychology, social psychology, and so forth.

There are, of course, a few exceptions, and I am sure that I am guilty (both in 2004 and 2014) of sins of omission and distortion. History, like ethnography and some qualitative interviewing, often draws on a case methodology and creates a narrative rather looking for general theories, and historical biography has been influenced by psychoanalysis, just as many psychoanalysts have tried their hand at psychobiography. A few psychoanalysts are social activists and occasionally write books about their work, on analysts in the "inner city" (Altman, 2004), the "trenches" (Sklarew et al., 2004), or in international mediation and ethnic violence (Volkan, 1997), and these colleagues draw upon studies of race and poverty, political science, small group theory, and international relations.[8]

The final question that I bring to these reflections then, is, what are the dynamics, prejudices, or scotomas from the side of psychoanalysis that distance it from those fields that seem to have so much in common with it, methodologically, epistemologically, and substantively and that, in their topics of inquiry, bear on our psychoanalytic work? Is there a reciprocal suspicion, ambivalence, or antipathy among psychoanalysts to the social, political, historical, and cultural, one that mirrors the attitudes of traditional social scientists toward personal individuality and personally created meaning from within? Is there a narcissism of minor differences, or a diffidence, because psychoanalysts cannot study other cultures or historical periods on the ground, because it is too time-consuming to do a qualitative interview study with multiple interviews, or because psychoanalysts are not trained to do sociological or political science research and could not do so without an institutional base? By contrast, we can all read a novel, watch a movie, or go to an opera, and think about our experience in psychoanalytic terms. Is it a matter of snob appeal? Are psychoanalysts more interested in being cultured cosmopolitans who know high culture? Have psychoanalysts, traditionally the handmaidens of psychiatry, a low prestige fields within medicine, noticed that with the exception of economics, the social sciences have lower academic and social prestige than the sciences or the humanities?

These concluding observations take me back to my initial question: why is it easy to be a psychoanalyst and a feminist but not a psychoanalyst and a social scientist? For me, discovering social science, originally anthropology, was a great relief. I found a home. Now, I know I have a good ear and a lot of knowledge about music and opera, and, unlike in my youth, I have confidence in my literary and artistic taste. I recognize that I am a good theorist—a psychoanalytic, a social, and a feminist theorist. When I do not understand something I am reading, as is inevitable, and often the case with postmodernism, philosophy, or Lacan, I assume either that if I wanted to train myself to understand, I could, or that there is something wrong with the writing itself. And as is obvious, I am ambivalent about the social sciences. Yet, I still notice that psychoanalysts seem to operate as if the social sciences did not exist and did not have a contribution to make either to psychoanalysis itself or to our lives as intellectuals and citizens. And I still notice that sociology seems to reciprocate in kind, to operate as if psychoanalysis either does not exist or is a suspect theory and practice, a theory and practice to be, except in volumes such as this one, dismissed, disparaged, and ignored.

Notes

This chapter is drawn, with minor editing, from a presentation that I made at the Meetings of the American Psychoanalytic Association in June, 2004 to the discussion group, "Psychoanalysis and the Humanities and Social Sciences: The CORST Contribution." In conjunction with recognition as the 2004 CORST honoree, I was asked to give a personal and autobiographical account about combining a professorial with an analytic career. I have edited for clarity and have added a few 2014 notes and some updated references and reflections. The chapter goes between bibliographic citations and lists of authors, when their names are mainly for illustrative purposes. I am grateful to the editors of this volume for allowing me to contribute these informal reflections.

CORST, the Committee on Research and Special Training, oversees administratively the psychoanalytic clinical training of academics and occasionally other non-clinicians, organizes lectures, prizes, and discussion groups that bring together letters and sciences and psychoanalysis, and provides one identity and home for academic analysts. In an earlier era, when you needed to be a physician to become a psychoanalyst in the United States, CORST was the rubric under which (a relatively few) clinical psychologists, as well as academics with analytic interests analytic interests, could become analysts.....the rubric under which (a relatively few) clinical psychologists, as well as academics with analytic interests, could become analysts.

1. As I myself acknowledge in the forward to the book's second edition (Chodorow, 1999b), I am in agreement with Rossi on this last point. In the 1970s, it was imperative for feminists (and social scientists!) to distance ourselves from any hint of biological determinism. A book that argues, however persuasively, that there is no biological contribution to maternal feelings has itself a psychopolitical agenda.
2. 2014 postscript: It is also the case that younger sociologists—often students at U.C. Berkeley where a strong feminist professoriate included sociologist of emotions Arlie Hochschild and everyday life ethnographer of childhood Barrie Thorne, as well as myself and several other feminists—drew extensively upon the work (though other UCB feminist students claimed that I was blind to class and cultural difference).
3. 2014 addendum: My "Brandeis" sociological training, where my theory teachers were German-Jewish refugees whose idea of sociology foundationally included Mannheim and Simmel, and where my dissertation director, Egon Bittner, was an ethnomethodologist with roots in the phenomenology of Husserl, has been fundamental to all of my writing as a psychoanalyst. In addition to writing on gender and sexuality, itself investigating the taken-for-granted (women mother; heterosexuality is unstudied and unnoticed), I have

written extensively about and been influenced in my clinical practice by the psychoanalyst Hans Loewald, whose initial intellectual formation was generationally and geographically similar to my professors (Chodorow, 2003b, 2007, 2009; Loewald, 1980).

My plenary address to the American Psychoanalytic Association, "Beyond the dyad: Individual psychology, social world" (Chodorow, 2010) argues, partly in relation to my roots in sociology, that psychoanalysts need to keep our focus on the individual, that when everything is "two-person" or "relational," we fall into an ultimately social-interpersonal determinism of everything in the clinical relationship. There, I also notice that analysts do not understand, and in fact have no theoretical way to understand, the nature of those very dyads that compose the analytic relationship and analytic training. I claim that knowledge of Simmel's and Slater's writings on dyads would greatly improve the profession and its practice.

4. 2014 addendum: I describe this in "Hate, humiliation and masculinity" (2003a).
5. I address this scotoma and, drawing upon ethnomethodology, look at the taken-for-granted infrastructure of the consulting room, the sociology of the dyad, and the structure and organization of psychoanalytic training and practice in "Beyond the dyad."
6. 2014 note: all contributors to this volume.
7. 2014: As I notice in "Beyond the dyad," however, a disproportionate number of foundational ethnomethodology, symbolic interactionism, and sociological ethnography studies overlap with psychoanalysis–studying mental hospitals, psychiatric clinic records and decision-making, definitions of mental illness, and medical and psychiatric training.
8. 2014: My citations and references here are not updated. As I write, the upcoming meetings of the International Psychoanalytic Association, thanks to Chair Sverre Varvin, a psychoanalyst who has worked with torture victims and has done mediation work in Gaza and elsewhere, is entitled "Facing the pain." The meetings will focus on political trauma and violence as well as on the personal.

References

Altman, N. (2004) *The Analyst in the Inner City: Race, Class and Culture through a Psychoanalytic Lens* (New York and London: Routledge).

Balsam, R. M. (2012) *Women's Bodies in Psychoanalysis* (New York and London: Routledge).

Chodorow, N. J. (1986) 'Toward a Relational Individualism: The Mediation of Self through Psychoanalysis' in T. C. Heller, M. Sosna and D. E. Wellbery (eds) *Reconstructing Individualism* (Stanford: Stanford University Press).

Chodorow, N. J. (1999a) *The Power of Feelings: Personal Meaning in Psychoanalysis, Gender, and Culture* (New Haven: Yale University Press).

Chodorow, N. J. (1999b) 'Preface to the 2nd Edition of *The Reproduction of Mothering*' in N. J. Chodorow (ed.) *Individualizing Gender and Sexuality: Theory and Practice* (New York and London: Routledge).

Chodorow, N. J. (2002) 'Born into a World at War: Listening for Affect and Personal Meaning', *American Imago*, 59 (3), 297–315.

Chodorow, N. J. (2003a) 'Hate, Humiliation and Masculinity' in N. J. Chodorow (ed.) *Individualizing Gender and Sexuality: Theory and Practice* (New York and London: Routledge).

Chodorow, N. J. (2003b) 'The Psychoanalytic Vision of Hans Loewald', *International Journal of Psychoanalysis*, 84, 897–913.

Chodorow, N. J. (2004a) 'The American Independent Tradition: Loewald, Erikson, and the (Possible) Rise of Intersubjective Ego Psychology', *Psychoanalytic Dialogues*, 14, 207–232.

Chodorow, N. J. (2004b) 'Psychoanalysis and Women from Margin to Center' in N. J. Chodorow (ed.) *Individualizing Gender and Sexuality: Theory and Practice* (New York and London: Routledge).

Chodorow, N. J. (2004c) 'The Sociological Eye and the Psychoanalytic Ear' in J. C. Alexander, G. Marx, and C. L. Williams (eds) *Self, Social Structure and Beliefs: Explorations in Sociology* (Berkeley: University of California Press).

Chodorow, N. J. (2005) 'Gender on the Modern-Postmodern and Classical-Relational Divide: Untangling History and Epistemology' in N. J. Chodorow (ed.) *Individualizing Gender and Sexuality: Theory and Practice* (New York and London: Routledge).

Chodorow, N. J. (2007) 'Reflections on Loewald's "Internalization, Separation, Mourning, and the Superego', *Psychoanalytic Quarterly*, 76, 1135–1151.

Chodorow, N. J. (2009) 'A Different Universe: Reading Loewald through "On the therapeutic action of psychoanalysis"', *Psychoanalytic Quarterly*, 78, 983–1011.

Chodorow, N. J. (2010) 'Beyond the Dyad: Individual Psychology, Social World', *Journal of the American Psychoanalytic Association*, 58, 207–230.

Chodorow, N. J. (2012) *Individualizing Gender and Sexuality: Theory and Practice* (New York and London: Routledge).

Fliegel, Z. O. (1986) 'Women's Development in Analytic Theory' in J. L. Alpert (ed.) *Psychoanalysis and Women: Contemporary Reappraisals* (Hillsdale: The Analytic Press).

Loewald, H. W. (1980) 'Psychoanalytic Theory and Psychoanalytic Process', in *Papers on Psychoanalysis* (New Haven: Yale University Press).

Lorber, J., R. L. Coser, A. S. Rossi, and N. J. Chodorow (1981) 'On *The Reproduction of Mothering*: A Methodological Debate', *Signs*, 6, 482–514.

Martin, K. A. (1996) *Puberty, Sexuality and the Self: Boys and Girls at Adolescence* (New York: Routledge).

Obeyesekere, G. (1990) *The Work of Culture* (Chicago: University of Chicago Press).

Sklarew, B., S. W. Twemlow, and S. M. Wilkinson (2004) *Analysts in the Trenches: Streets, Schools, War Zones* (New York and London: Routledge).

Volkan, V. D. (1997) *Bloodlines: From Ethnic Pride to Ethnic Terrorism* (New York: Farrar, Strauss, & Giroux).

6
The Narcissism of Minor Differences: The Status Anxiety and Disciplinary Intolerance between Sociology and Psychoanalysis

Siamak Movahedi

In this essay, I show how arbitrary the disciplinary boundary is between psychoanalysis and sociology, how psychoanalysis can complement sociology, how structural analysis in one discipline needs the other to explain its causal efficacy, how symbolic interaction relates to psychoanalysis, and how many psychoanalytic concepts—including the analytic situation—can be expressed in sociological language. My analysis is a form of deconstruction of *social fact* versus *the social subject*: searching for the "psyche" in the discourse of "social" is the idea of deconstruction. Deconstruction exposes the conceptual tension between the arbitrary categories of individual versus society, personal troubles and public issues, or psychoanalytic versions of the individual mind and the individual life.

Here, though, I am more interested in using the concept of deconstruction as a conceptual tool in the sociology of knowledge to argue that much of the sociological animosity toward psychoanalysis stems from what Freud called "the narcissism of minor differences," and Donald Campbell (1969) referred to as "disciplinary ethnocentrisms," a symptom of tribalism or cross-disciplinary partisanship. For it seems that the more similar two disciplines are, the greater the likelihood that there will be conflict and tribalism. Fear of the loss of self and identity motivates the ethnocentric's and xenophobe's fear of strangers. Similarly, the threat of losing distinct disciplinary boundaries is proportional to the proximity of the areas of inquiry that different disciplines seek to colonize. For example, while human sciences avoid systematic intercourse with their neighboring fields, they all seem to engage in amorous courtship with biology, genetics, and neuroscience. The need for difference seems to rest on the threat of identity.[1]

Freud used the concept of the "narcissism of minor differences" in three different places in his work, in the contexts of both individual and group psychology. The phrase first appeared in *The Taboo of Virginity* (1917), based on his interpretation of the writings of the British anthropologist Ernest Crawley. Much of Freud's preoccupation with the narcissism of minor differences had to do with his attempt to explain the battle of the sexes, while more recently we might use the term to explain the battle between in-groups and out-groups. In group psychology, the concept speaks to group members' need to see their group as radically different from other groups. Freud considered our needs for maintaining identity to be behind many exaggerated perceptions of differences among groups (Freud, 1930, p. 104). And fear of the influence of the imaginary other was taken to be behind the need for the maintenance of identity.[2]

It is precisely the minor differences in people who are otherwise alike that form the basis of feelings of strangeness and hostility between them. It would be tempting to pursue this idea and to derive from this 'narcissism of minor differences' the hostility which in every human relation we see fighting successfully against feelings of fellowship and overpowering the commandment that all men should love one another. Psychoanalysis believes that it has discovered a large part of what underlies the narcissistic rejection of women by men, which is so mixed up with despising them, in drawing attention to the castration complex and its influence on the opinion in which women are held. (p. 199)

Applying the concept of the narcissism of minor differences to the context of intergroup conflicts, he wrote in 1930:

It is always possible to bind together a considerable number of people in love, so long as there are other people left over to receive the manifestation of their aggressiveness. . . . It is precisely communities with adjoining territories and related to each other in other ways as well, who are engaged in constant feuds and in ridiculing each other—like the Spaniards and the Portuguese, for instance, the North Germans and South Germans, the English and Scotch, and so on. I gave this phenomenon the name of 'the narcissism of minor differences,' a name which does not do much to explain. (p. 114)

The ritual of boundary maintenance in sociology, which is couched in terms of the binary opposition (and, as such, a pseudo distinction) between individual behavior and social phenomenon, may be viewed as a mechanism of territorial battle against possible influence by neighboring disciplines such as psychoanalysis, psychology, and even cultural studies. This academic tribalism is, to Scheff (2011, 2013), responsible for much of the backward status of the human sciences. He sides with Wilson (1998) when he argues that "biology would have remained stuck in its 1850 position if it had stayed at the level of the whole organism, refusing to include cells and molecules. Perhaps in the beginning, pure sociology was a virtue, but treating it as the only way has become a vice" (Scheff, 2013, p. 2).

The relationship between sociology and psychoanalysis—or its unhappy divorce—is itself a sociological question worthy of critical analysis in the sociology of knowledge. The critical social theory of the Frankfurt School embraced Freud, while contemporary American sociology has chosen to ignore psychoanalysis. This raises questions about the nature of and changes in the unchallenged preconceptions that underlie our claims about knowledge and practices. Knowledge as process and product is part of cultural worldviews and practices. Freud comes to the US, for instance, and becomes the ego-psychologist, the psychologist of the autonomous individual, the agent of capitalism, and the purveyor of individualistic ideology; he goes to France to become part of the structuralist intellectual capital of Foucault, Lévi-Strauss, and Althusser and a friend of Marx and leftwing revolutionary students.

Bourdieu (Steinmetz, 2006) maintains that sociology and psychoanalysis are concerned with similar givens, but they construct them differently. However, I do not see the alienation of psychoanalysis from sociology as a simple matter of different constructions of similar disciplinary interests; psychoanalysis does not seem to be the only hated object of intellectual inquiry. Sociologists are reported to exhibit a similar dismissive attitude toward cultural studies and history. Lee (1999) attributes the hostile reception of cultural studies to factors that are endogenous to American sociology. More than forty years ago, Wax (1969), addressing the same problem in the disciplinary relationship between anthropology and sociology, encouraged us to critically examine the myths that, as social scientists, we all promulgate about our discipline and be cognizant of the personal and ideological dimensions of our research. He rightly argued that "pure theoretical" analysis of the interdisciplinary boundaries between various fields of social sciences results in a dull discussion, "since so often they represent either the ideology of the discipline or the ambitions of a scholar who wishes to impose upon his [or her] colleagues his [or her] program of investigation" (p. 77). He also advocated adoption of the perspective of the sociology of knowledge or the anthropology of knowledge when analyzing interdisciplinary relations in academe.

Sociologists are keen to remind us that all knowledge is socially constructed—which, of course, includes what counts as sociology and the relationship between *that* sociology and other discourses of knowledge. "The heart of capitalism and materialism alike," writes Mukerji (1983), "lies in the shape of objects—in pens, books, chairs, and tables, cities and fields, warships and satellites—the theories and dreams we have embedded in matter perhaps less for the glory of God and tomorrow's profits than for the advancement of states and today's pleasures" (p. 261). This includes the shape of our theories and the objects of our disciplinary endeavors that, in mainstream American sociology, have become the study of "things" rather than the human *subject*, and the study of "rates" rather than the study of human experience.

The dominant research practice of mainstream sociology today revolves around analyses of prefabricated data sets, rates, and percentages rather than time-consuming, intensive case studies or theoretical explanation of what is reported as "social facts." The goal is to explain variance rather than human action. The domain of sociological research is justified by appeal to Durkheim's (1951) classic study of suicide. The preoccupation with technique and overestimation of the value of empty statistical data mining—often packaged as applied sociology—has worked at the expense of the capacity for theoretical thought.

I once had a colleague who was interested in studying sexual offenders; most of her papers and presentations at least touched on the topic. I asked if she would be interested in talking with or interviewing inmates who had been committed by the courts for sexual offenses. At the time I was working at a mental health facility that housed a number of such offenders, and I could easily arrange for my colleague to meet with them. She was not interested in my offer, replying "I study data sets." Aside from some friend or relative who had perhaps awakened her interest in the topic, she had not spoken with a single sexual offender. She was studying "rates," but I am sure she would have been eager to express her "professional views" on the air if some radio or television reporter had called on her for an interview about, for instance, an ongoing investigation of a sexual assault.[3]

The social psychological context in which Freud created psychoanalysis—the study of the bourgeois character, as portrayed by Marcuse (1955)—was certainly not the same as our present social context, characterized now by attention deficit disorder and a fast-food mentality.

The Frankfurt School tradition, which is amiable to psychoanalysis, does not resonate with the intellectual ambiance of much of the academic sociology today. There is no time or reward for traditional scholarship in a discipline that is preoccupied with training technical specialists in criminal justice, terrorism, substance abuse, alcoholism, family violence, and program evaluation. Mainstream American sociology is now much closer to American psychiatry than to French structuralism, the intellectual culture of the fathers of sociology. Typical sociologists' acquaintance with Freud and psychoanalysis rarely goes beyond the caricature of id, ego, and superego—hardly enough to foster connections between the two fields of scholarship. They have fallen for the popular culture's misrepresentation of psychoanalytic theory as psychiatry or psychology, an error that was perpetrated by the Americanization of psychoanalysis into a culture of disease, diagnosis, and medicine in line with the ideological tenet of individualism.[4]

We should add here that psychoanalysis today is not a monolithic viewpoint. Some schools, for instance, see the subject—the self—as embedded in and constituted by relationships, and some see our unconscious phantasies and desires to form relationships and mediate our experience of the external (Frosh, 1989). Other psychoanalytic schools, such as American ego psychology—with its emphasis on an autonomous ego—are significantly more alien to a sociological perspective than that of the French psychoanalyst Lacan, whose theories may in fact be seen as sociological: for Lacanians, the *subject* and the unconscious are discursive and transindividual, as opposed to the *ego* in ego-psychology, which—echoing familiar political parlance—can pull itself up by its bootstraps.

Durkheim's (1951) work in *Suicide* was an exercise in thinking about the social nature of human life rather than the presentation of a sociological method; his aim was to call attention to the manifestation of a phenomenon that may appear to be principally psychological. As Thompson (1982) points out, Durkheim was more interested in theorizing about the nature of human beings as presented in suicide along the dimensions of "integration" and "regulation" than in defining sociology as a study of the statistical idea of rates. Douglas (1967) has even argued that Durkheim's typology of suicide was not based on the analysis of his data: he had an explanation for the "facts" of suicide before he had begun to look at the numbers. In this regard, Durkheim's (1951, p. 213) conception of human beings is a double-homo duplex (Hynes, 1975) comprised of a biological base with insatiable desires and a social base keeping drives in check and is not much different from Freud's. In fact,

Lacan's interpretation of Freud's (1920) theory of *beyond the pleasure principle* as jouissance—the pursuit of one's desire despite prohibitions of the symbolic order—is an extension of Durkheim's notion of anomie.

Much of the blame for the stifling in-group/out-group mentality can be laid at the door of the academy rather than a particular discipline, for example, sociology. Robert Dentler (2000), in reminiscing about his early encounter with psychoanalysis in graduate school, places disciplinary tribalism and ethnocentrism at the core of academe's intellectual culture. He used to think, he writes, that liberal studies entailed reading widely in different fields and making frequent cognitive transfers from one intellectual domain to another. As a graduate student in English, for instance, he had begun to read Freud, Jung, Adler, Horney, and Sullivan, and had noticed the extent to which many German and French scholars of literature drew on psychoanalytic ideas in their literary criticism. His fascination with Marx and Freud's work in the spirit of critical theory had even inspired him to research the functions of obscenity and pornography in Elizabethan satire. It was then, however, that the chairman of the English Department at Northwestern called him into his office to praise him for his scholarship and urge him to continue his doctoral studies—but also to warn him that if he wanted to continue at Northwestern, he would have "to learn to avoid psychoanalytic and socialistic ideas and to concentrate exclusively on the texts. We do not attend to other disciplines and ideologies, you see. What do you say?"

Later, when he had decided to do his doctoral work at Harvard and wrote Gordon Allport to express interest in the Department of Social Relations, he faced a similar reaction:

Allport invited me to visit him. He was very cordial and had a marked up version of my little textbook on his desk. He complimented me on the contents, adding his disappointment that I had relied heavily at some points on psychoanalytic sources. This might change, he suggested, in the course of my doctoral studies at Harvard. 'You will be concentrating on social psychology under me, of course,' he said. I replied that I had not made up my mind about a concentration and would plan to do so in the course of the first year of required courses that covered most of the social sciences. He became insistent about my commitment to his specialty and I became politely insistent in return. Allport then stood up, walked to his window, and turned his back on me. 'You will have to compete with all of the other applicants and we'll see how you do on the Graduate Record Examination,' he said. Failing to recognize that he had really already rejected me, I rose to his challenge and spent four months cramming intensively in preparation for the exam. . . . And, of course, as Gordon Allport locked the door, I joined the thousands of those whose resumes report that they have been rejected by Harvard. Again, I found myself reading in psychoanalysis, this time reaching Wilhelm Reich, discovering that Talcott Parsons had been psychoanalyzed and had drawn on his experience in developing his theory of socialization, and finding the work of Alfred Adler. (p. n/a)[5]

Ironically, ethnocentrism and partisanship have plagued psychoanalysis itself from its inception. Intellectual intolerance, ideological paranoia, demands for theoretical loyalty, in-group fighting, and institute splitting have been rampant in psychoanalysis, beginning with Freud himself. Fromm, Sachs and others have written about Freud's intolerance for those members of the International Association who were not completely loyal to the party line; Jones (1957) wrote about Freud's blessing of a purge of the London Society's Jungian members, and Sachs reported on the secret, ring-wearing committee of seven who were to guard the movement from internal dissidents.

Ideological schisms and splintered institutes have followed psychoanalysis almost everywhere in the world—Austria, Germany, England, France, Spain, Sweden, Norway, Brazil, Mexico, Argentina, Venezuela, and the US (Eckhardt, 1978; Eisold, 1994, 1998). In the US, schism and splitting—or, as Henry Murray of the Boston Psychoanalytic Society, has described it, "humorless hostility, cultism, rigidity in thought, and ruthless rivalry for power have been the characteristic ambiance of many psychoanalytic institutes [throughout the country]." Although other things have changed, this feature of the discipline appears to have remained the same. Kirsner (2000) believes that the seed of this intellectual intolerance can be traced to the cultural-organizational level of the analytic societies and institutes. He feels that the conflicts are not merely matters of theoretical opinion; the bitterness that accompanies these events has to do with the political nature of theoretical dissension.

Here, in the context of the ongoing battles over the proper boundaries between and within different disciplines, we can more fully appreciate Freud's notion of the narcissism of minor differences, which was written more than a hundred years ago. Defensive action against a fear of influence may explain lack of tolerance not only for others but also for their ideas. Such a fear, ironically, is rampant in the academy and may be responsible for much of the in-group fighting, intellectual intolerance, ideological paranoia, and demand for theoretical or disciplinary loyalty.

In searching for synthesis and attempting to bring sociology and psychoanalysis back together—the theme of this volume—one should consider how much of the discord or méconnaissance between sociology and psychoanalysis may be over different ways of seeing the same (discursively constructed) thing. Are "words" the things we fight over, or is there some "real" difference somewhere that structure and molds our "words" and "theories?"

On a surface level, there are many commonalties between psychoanalysis and sociology in terms of theoretical interests, status anxiety, and methodological consciousness—and more of an affinity, in my opinion, between psychoanalysis and sociology than between psychoanalysis and psychology.[6] In psychoanalysis, for instance, social constructionism is now a popular conceptual model. Much of what goes on between the analyst and the analysand, including both actors' dreams, reveries, and fantasies, are said to be co-constructed. The past is a reconstruction, the memory is a perception, and the perception is a fantasy. The person's conviction of the validity of recall is much more important than its factual authenticity; the patient's beliefs or fantasies about the experience of a sexual seduction, for instance, have greater impact than the seduction itself. If one defines a seduction fantasy as real, it will become real in its consequences. Similar to W.I. Thomas and other symbolic interactionists, Freud was concerned not with the situation but with the individual's interpretations of it (Movahedi, 2007). Deconstructing such interpretations is the goal of psychoanalysis.

The therapeutic situation today is considered to be a social situation—a particular frame within which the analyst and the analysand interact. It is in reference to this analytic frame that many analysts rely on the works of sociologists Alfred Schütz (1945) and Erving Goffman (1974) as models for the contextual understanding of the experience of the analytic dyad (Bass, 2007; Bauknight and Appelbaum, 1997; McLaughlin, 1983; Spruiell, 1983).

Although psychoanalysis has undergone profound changes since Freud, it continues to present an elegant mode of listening to a patient or reading a text. Contrary to other psychotherapeutic techniques, the analyst does not ask the patient to change, to give up his symptoms, to be "normal," or to adapt or behave in a particular way. The analyst is not to have any desire or plan for the patient but to help him discover his own desires rather than being enslaved by others' demands. In one sense, the goal of analysis is to help the analysand discover the extent to which he is trapped in social and cultural structures. Psychoanalysis is concerned primarily with the patient's mind—that is, the subject's intersubjective experience within the interactive matrix of the analytic situation. Inferences about the patient's experience are to be made through the social interaction within the session, including narrative activities in the here and now of the psychoanalytic frame. The analyst focuses attention not so much on the content of life narratives as on their communicative functions and on what is omitted, disowned, avoided, or unattended.

Although "mind" is not clearly defined in operational terms, it is assumed to reflect the joint analytic activities in the session. The patient comes to analysis with a conscious expectation that the analyst will help her search for the sources of her trouble, which are presumed to be unconscious. Thus a sharp distinction is made between the manifest (explicit) and the latent (implicit) meanings of the individual's communications. There is a great deal of overlap between sociological and psychoanalytic theories of the self in which the self is considered as a fantasy emanating from the mirror reflection in the face of the (m)other. Sullivan's, Winnicott's, and Lacan's notions of the self come very close to those of Mead, Cooley, and Goffman. Sullivan's (1953), Winnicott's (1956) and Lacan's (1977) notions of the self come very close to those of Mead (1934), Cooley (1902), and Goffman (1959).

Methodological debates in psychoanalysis are also similar to those in sociology. For instance, a lively debate is in progress in psychoanalysis between those who call themselves "scientists" and those who maintain that psychoanalysis is inherently interpretive and hermeneutic. Those adopting the natural science position are hopeful that, by reducing meaning to some form of brain functioning, they can become biologists of the mind rather than analysts of the soul. In turn, members of the hermeneutic circle reduce psychoanalysis to textual analysis, subject only to the requirement of internal coherence. There are also those who agree with the interpretive tradition but maintain that psychoanalysis goes beyond the hermeneutic method, in that interpretation of the text in psychoanalysis changes the text itself. Since psychoanalytic data consist of emotional exchanges in the analytic situation, the primary method of investigation in psychoanalysis remains participant observation and case study. The analytic setting is considered to be both a laboratory and an operating room for scientific and clinical work. The emotional climate of the analytic context is of critical importance in interpreting any exchange during the analytic hour (Movahedi, 2012).

What, then, would explain the alienation of sociology from psychoanalysis—fields that take great interest in their disciplinary domains and have inherited, from their German and French ancestors, so much shared intellectual capital? Can this primarily be attributed to sociologists' struggle, as suggested by Huber (1995), to prove their relevance in academia during the recent fiscal crises by a blind pursuit of positivistic methods that could render respectability to pedestrian research endeavors?

The discursive deadlock between the two disciplines seems to center on the question of *the subject* versus *the social*. This is a discursive deadlock, in that we are speaking not about theoretically or empirically embedded concepts that sharply define distinct fields, but rather about how we use the terms "the subject" and "the social." For instance, the subject that to Foucault (1970) is supposed to be "dead," decentered, or dissolved by the structuralist's analysis—rather than being a meaningful theoretical concept—is simply an empty place in the discourse adopted by a locutor (Benveniste, 1968; Funt, 1973; Parker, 1994). The problem of building a bridge between psychoanalysis and sociology and the reason why most attempts to achieve any meaningful dialectical synthesis of individual and society have failed is related, according to Carveth (1982), to a false dichotomy that that has been introduced between the self and society and the private and public. To treat the social as a reified "thing" that is independent of its members—or as a set of individuals who are the subject of psychoanalytic understanding—or to view the social as an enormous individual with its own unconscious, core conflicts, and defenses will not get us out of a discourse in which the individual is defined in opposition to the social: as two independent, self-contained entities interacting antagonistically, each subject to its own laws (Parker, 2003). To place the individual in an antagonistic position vis-à-vis the social points to a conflict internal to the subject and the social rather than to one between the two (Žižek, 2000). Such contentious academic exercises, in Castoriadis's words (1989), are nothing more than pseudo-theoretical covers for an evasion of thinking. Even on a semiotic level, the distinction between the personal or private and its public or social meanings of cultural objects is problematic and tends to break down. In fact, the distinction between public and private semiotics should be made only for analytic purposes (Movahedi and Homayounour, 2012, 2013).[7]

Although psychoanalysis has traditionally concentrated on the individual person, a number of contemporary analytic schools, particularly the Lacanians, take theoretical positions that are essentially sociological. They have not relinquished interrogating the subject; however, the subject is no longer equated with the individual or ego but rather a sociocultural position that structures the person's desires and relationships to self and the other. In that sense, the subject is enslaved by history, language, and culture. Freud was highly cognizant of the subject's cultural and historical context, as quotes like the following one indicate:

Without the assumption of a collective mind, which makes it possible to neglect the interruptions of mental acts caused by the extinction of the individual, social psychology in general cannot exist. Unless psychical processes were continued from one generation to another, if each generation were obliged to acquire its attitude to life anew, there would be no progress in this field and next to no development. This gives rise to two further questions: how much can we attribute to psychical continuity in the sequence of generations? And what are the ways and means employed by one generation in order to hand on its mental states to the next one? (Freud, 1913, p. 157).

To Freud (1921), the chief subject of psychoanalytic practice and research was necessarily social:

The contrast between individual psychology and social or group psychology, which at first glance may seem to be full of significance, loses a great deal of its sharpness when it is examined more closely. It is true that individual psychology is concerned with the individual man and explores the paths by which he seeks to find satisfaction for his instinctual impulses; but only rarely and under certain exceptional circumstances is individual psychology in a position to disregard the relations of this individual to others. In the individual's mental life someone else is invariably involved, as a model, as an object, as a helper, as an opponent; and so from the very first individual psychology, in this extended but entirely justifiable sense of the words, is at the same time social psychology as well. The relations of an individual to his parents and to his brothers and sisters, to the object of his love, and to the physician, in fact all the relations which have hitherto been the chief subject of psychoanalytic research may claim to be considered as social phenomena. (pp. 69–70)

The aim of both sociology and psychoanalysis is to look beyond the manifest representations of things to discover—or construct—the rich layers of social or psychic reality that underlie the illusory appearances. A sociological encounter requires one to look some distance beyond the commonly accepted explanation of the goals of human actions (Berger, 1963). A psychoanalytic engagement requires one to get to the reality behind appearances. For both disciplines, one either pursues the truth behind appearances or pursues the truth inherent in appearances

(Levenson, 1985). Sociology thus shares with psychoanalysis the objective of understanding the surface structure of events in terms of deep structure. Both sociology and psychoanalysis aim at deciphering the codes of the dead that have structured our present by trapping us in a past. Marx, Freud, and Durkheim all challenged the wisdom of the past as packaged in the sacred beliefs and rituals surrounding God and religion as illusion—nothing but the "opiate of the people." Who could give a better description of a dynamic that defines the core concern of psychoanalysis than the father of sociology himself, Emile Durkheim (1977)? He wrote:

> In each of us, in varying proportions, there is part of yesterday's man: it is yesterday's man who inevitably predominates in us, since the present amounts to little compared with the long past in the course of which we were formed and from which we result. Yet we do not sense this man of the past, because he is inveterate in us: he makes up the unconscious part of ourselves. Consequently we are led to take no account of him, any more than we take account of his legitimate demands. Conversely, we are very much aware of the most recent attainments of civilization, because, being recent, they have not yet had time to settle in our unconscious. (p. 11)

To Foucault (1970), a theory of discursive practice—rather than the theory of "the knowing subject"—should inform our historical analysis of social life. The notion of "the knowing subject" (the subject of human sciences) is considered illusive, as "self-consciousness." We can now replace the "knowing subject" with the "speaking subject" whose discourse we may take as the focus of our analysis. We may thus listen to the discourse, taking the subject and the subject's mind and consciousness as strictly discursive. The subject the analyst listens to is the subject of the Freudian unconscious—which, according to Lacan, is the discourse of the Other and is structured like language. This reinterpretation of Freud's concept of the unconscious connects psychoanalysis with structuralism, Marxism, and sociology. The unconscious thus becomes a sort of a structuring code that provides syntax for the organization of one's ideas, wishes, feelings, and memories (Lévi-Strauss, 1949). In other words, the unconscious provides syntax for a "discourse" for which the "vocabulary" comes from the subject's biography.

Almost every introductory sociology text begins with C. Wright Mills's famous (1961) distinction between personal troubles and public issues, and gives examples of how individuals blame themselves or others for much of their problems of living—divorce, unemployment, poverty, mental illness, and so on—while remaining unaware that their fates are structurally determined. In Lacan's and Lévi-Strauss's views, the deep structure seems to provide an infrastructure for the formation of the individual's personal myth, that is, his or her biography. Furthermore, the individual's biography provides deep structures with contents. The task of psychoanalysis is to decipher the code of the deep structure by listening to the individual's personal narratives.

For Lacan, who was influenced by Marx, Hegel, Saussure, and Lévi-Strauss, the unconscious is "the aggregate of structural laws by which individual experiences are transformed into living myth." What this means is that we construct the personal myths of our biography in terms of the transindividual's structural syntax of the symbolic order, within which we are born. The individual's biography as content is unfolded within the deep structure as form. That is, the unconscious is transindividual and culturally shared by individuals, whereas the preconscious is individual and contains the person's history (Skelton, 1993). Here the distinction between the transindividual unconscious structure and the preconscious personal history comes close to Mills's distinction between history and biography or structural issues versus personal troubles.

Lévi-Strauss, Lacan, and even Carl Jung borrowed their notions of deep structure from Marcel Mauss (Mauss and Hubert, 1902–1903), Durkheim's nephew and collaborator. Mauss's thesis of symbolic codes as the structuring link between the personal and the public spheres of mental and social activities has always been a bridge joining psychoanalysis, anthropology, sociology, and politics that must be crossed intellectually. Some have used the term "cultural unconscious"; Fredric Jameson (1981) uses the term "political unconscious" to refer to what the social unconscious *does* rather than *means*. Texts and artistic expressions may represent symbolic solutions to real but unconsciously felt social and cultural problems. Reconstructing the problematic condition for which the text as symbolic act was a solution is the task of a social or cultural critic.

In related vein, Cornelius Castoriadis (2010), the French-Greek psychoanalyst, philosopher, and social theorist, argues that the truth of the social and psychic life should be sought in imaginary significations. For him, the human psyche has never been separate from society: there is no personal way of thinking. There has never been a state of nature à la Hobbes or, à la Rousseau, a "coming together to form a contract." Castoridas says that what causes societies to "hang together" is the nature of imaginary significations—social meanings—that cannot be reduced to something real or to some rational, functional dimension. What holds everything together and seems to give a semblance of order, even in the chaos of war, is the outcome of the internal cohesion of interwoven significations or meanings that pervade life in society. Social significations are not constructed in terms of logic or rationality; social systems—and even bureaucratic organizations, in which collective activities are run by an impersonal, hierarchically organized apparatus—are haunted by inherent irrationality and contradictions. To Castoriadis, any distinction between the subject and the social makes no sense. To him, the man, the woman, and the child, when taken not as biological categories, are all social institutions, each of which is almost the society as a whole. In their concrete content, they reflect the entire fabric of imaginary significations. This idea is basically a reformulation of Durkheim's conception of the symbolic nature of psychic reality as presented in *The Elementary Forms of the Religious Life* (1912) in that society is symbolically expressed in the individual in the form of religious beliefs and practices.

Frosh (1987), similar to Castoriadis, sees the unconscious as the bridge between psychoanalysis and sociology. Most of our social institutions and their ideologies, according to him, are structured by a social unconscious.

The problem is then how to translate or connect the realm of the psyche/individual to the realm of the social or structural. Similar to Lacan's argument for the impossibility of a translation of sexual difference into a set of symbolic oppositions (Žižek, 2000), any attempt to force the individual and society into a set of symbolic oppositions is equally impossible. If the individual is defined in opposition to the social, the accentuation of the difference between the two is simply tautological and, as such, uninformative. Regarding the relation between the individual and the social, even the claim that one is constitutive of the other seems problematic, because it postulates two different entities that influence one another in some causal, temporal, and linear dialectical process. To that extent, both sociology and psychoanalysis—particularly the Durkheimian notion of "social facts" and the American ego-psychology notion of ego's "conflict-free" zone of practice—are involved in some hegemonic struggle to justify their illusionary binary oppositions of individual and society, intrapsychic and interpsychic, or intrapsychic and interpersonal. In fact, Durkheim's structural and Hartmann's (1939) "individualistic" frameworks simply represent the ideological components of the two intellectual climates. As we can see in contemporary intellectual debates across the continent, the American Freud is a right-wing ego-psychologist and the French Freud—as read by Lacan—is a left-wing sociologist.

More than a half-century ago, Max Born (1953) observed that in physics, the attributes of physical things are properties of processes, events, or relationships. He argued that although the theory of relativity never abandoned attempts to assign properties to matter, "often a measurable quantity is not a property of a thing, but a property of its relation to other things" (p. 143). This observation can clearly be applied to the question of interdisciplinary discourses of identity and difference, where identity and difference reflect ways of doing rather than being—that is, ways of relating to the world rather than actual similarities or differences among entities. The shift from one pole of this binary opposition to the other may represent nothing but an illusory shift in the discursive mode of encounter with the object world.

Notes

1. Contrary to Samuel Huntington's (1996) so-called theory of the "clash of civilizations," the New Conservatives and the Christian right are the close soul mates of "terrorists" and Islamic fundamentalists. They look very much like Eric Hoffer's (1951) "true believer" and religious fanatic, Adorno's (1950) fascist or authoritarian personality, and Eysenks's (1975) tough-minded character, and they should all score high on psychoticism and Machiavellianism. Their battle has partly grown from the narcissism of minor differences rather than out of concern for human dignity or liberty.
2. In the context of the ongoing violent crusade against evil by equally fanatic and reactionary worriers dressed up differently in the right-wing fundamentalist uniforms of the three major religions of the world, we can more fully appreciate Freud's ideas: You are either with us or against us; you are either with us or with the terrorists. The paradox here is that the other can't be with us, since it is the container of our disavowed, disowned, and unacceptable part of the self—yet it is with us because it has to be too similar to us to function as the container of our projected fantasies.
3. The trained incapacity to go beyond descriptive statistical analyses is not a new phenomenon in sociology. Wakefield (Mills, 2000) writes about C. Wright Mills's typical encounters with graduate students at departmental events:

    "I simply sat in a chair in a corner," he said, "and one by one these guys would come up to me, sort of like approaching the pariah—curiosity stuff. They were guys working on their Ph.D.'s, you see, and after they'd introduced themselves I'd ask, 'What are you working on?' It would always be something like 'The Impact of Work-Play Relationships among Lower Income Families on the South Side of the Block on 112th Street between Amsterdam and Broadway.' And then I would ask—Mills paused, leaned forward, and his voice boomed, 'Why?'"

    At least in Mills's time, some sociologists or graduate students made an effort to meet and talk to some lower-income families on the south side of the block on 112th Street between Amsterdam and Broadway. Today, thanks

to voluminous data sets on the Internet, "scientific" sociological thinking and research have been reduced to computerized data mining.
4. Freud feared the medicalization of psychoanalysis in America. He was worried that psychoanalysis would be "swallowed up by medicine." He dreaded that psychoanalysis would find its "last resting place in a textbook of psychiatry under the heading 'Methods of Treatment', alongside of procedures such as hypnotic suggestion, autosuggestion, and persuasion" (Freud, 1926, p 248).
5. The Harvard Department of Social Relations was not only allergic to psychoanalysis; when it came to culture, the intellectual ambiance of the department was permeated by ethnocentrism. Writing about his experience at Harvard, Sherif (1969) refers to the preoccupation of Allport's crowd with experimental social psychology at the expense of any appreciation for cultural values, social institutions, or ideologies.
6. Freud himself felt that "Individual Psychology [had] very little to do with psychoanalysis but, as a result of certain historical circumstances, [led] a kind of parasitic existence at its expense" (1933, p. 140). Lacan was much more dismissive of individual psychology. He contended that "To enclose the Freudian interrogation within the field of psychology is to lead it to what I call a psychogenetic delirium" (1994, p. 412).
7. Fredric Jameson (1986) has controversially argued for the inclusion of Marx along with Freud in the analysis of third-world texts. To him, the third world narratives, "even those which are seemingly private and invested with a properly libidinal dynamic—necessarily project a political dimension in the form of national allegory: the story of the private individual destiny is always an allegory of the embattled situation of the public third-world culture and society" (pp. 69–70).

References

Adorno, J., E. Frenkel-Brunswik, D. Levinson, and R. N. Sanford (1950) *The Authoritarian Personality* (New York: Harper).
Bass, A. (2007) "When the Frame Doesn't Fit the Picture," *Psychoanalytic Dialogues*, 17, 1–27.
Bauknight, R. and Appelbaum, R. (1997) "AIDS, Death, and the Analytic Frame," *Free Associations*, 7, 81–100.
Benveniste, E. (1969) *Problèmes de Linguistique Générale* (Paris: Gallimard).
Berger, P. (1963) *Invitation to Sociology* (New York: Doubleday).
Born, M. (1953) "Physical Reality," *Philosophical Quarterly*, 3, 141–149.
Campbell, D. (1969) "Ethnocentrism of Disciplines and the Fish-Scale Model of Omniscience" in M. Sherif and C. W. Sherif (eds) *Interdisciplinary Relationships in the Social Sciences* (Chicago: Aldine).
Carveth, D. L. (1982) "Sociology and Psychoanalysis: The Hobbesian Problem Revisited," *Canadian Journal of Sociology*, 7 (2), 201–229.
Carveth, D. L. (1984) 'Psychoanalysis and Social Theory', *Psychoanalysis & Contemporary Thought*, 7 (1), 43–98.
Castoriadis, C. (1989) "The State of the Subject Today," American *Imago*, 46 (4), 371–412.

Castoriadis, C. (2010) *Society Adrift: Interviews and Debates, 1974–1997* (New York: Fordham University Press).
Cooley, C. H. ([1902] 1964) *Human Nature and the Social Order* (New York: Schocken).
Cooley, C. H. ([1909] 1962) *Social Organization* (New York: Schocken).
Danziger, K. (1997) *Naming the Mind* (Thousand Oaks: Sage publications).
Dentler, R. A. (2000) "Fifty Years of Brief Encounters with Psychoanalysis: A Sociologist's Memoir," A paper presented at the Year 2000 Annual Meeting of the Eastern Sociological Society in Baltimore, Maryland.
Douglas, D. (1967) *The Social Meanings of Suicide* (Princeton: Princeton University Press).
Durkheim, E. ([1912] 1995) *The Elementary Forms of Religious Life*, in K. E. Fields (trans.) (New York and London: The Free Press).
Durkheim E. (1951) *Suicide: A Study in Sociology*, J. A. Spaulding and G. Simson (trans.) (New York: Free Press).
Eckhardt, M. H. (1978) "Organizational Schisms in American Psychoanalysis: Origins and Development" in J. M. Quen and E. J. Carlson (eds) *American Psychoanalysis: Origins and Development* (New York: Brunner/Mazel).
Eisold, K. (1994) "The Intolerance of Diversity in Psychoanalytic Institutes," *International Journal of Psychoanalysis*, 75, 785–800.
Eisold, K. (1998) "The Splitting of the New York Psychoanalytic and the Construction of Psychoanalytic Authority," *International Journal of Psychoanalysis*, 79, 871–885.
Eysenck, H. J. (1975) "The Structure of Social Attitudes," *British Journal of Social and Clinical Psychology*, 14 (4), 323–331.
Foucault, M. (1970) *The Order of Things: An Archaeology of the Human Sciences*, A. M. Sheridan (trans.) (London: Tavistock).
Freud, S. (1913) "Totem and Taboo" in J. Strachey (ed.) *The Standard Edition Of the Complete Psychological Works of Sigmund Freud*, Vol 13 (London: Hogarth Press).
Freud, S. (1920) "Beyond the Pleasure Principle" in J. Strachey (ed.) *The Standard Edition Of the Complete Psychological Works of Sigmund Freud*, Vol. 18. (London: Hogarth Press).
Freud, S. ([1921] 1955) "Group Psychology and the Analysis of the Ego" in J. Strachey (ed.) *The Standard Edition of the Complete Psychological Works of Sigmund Freud*, Vol. 18 (London: Hogarth Press).
Freud, S. (1926) "The Question of Lay Analysis" in J. Strachey (ed.) *The Standard Edition of the Complete Psychological Works of Sigmund Freud*, Vol. 20 (London: Hogarth Press).
Freud, S. ([1930] 1961) *Civilization and Its Discontents, Standard Edition*, Vol. 21. (London: Hogarth Press).
Freud, S. (1933) "New Introductory Lectures on Psychoanalysis" in J. Strachey (ed.) *The Standard Edition of the Complete Psychological Works of Sigmund Freud*, Vol. 22 (GW 15) (London: Hogarth Press).
Frosh, S. (1989) "Melting into Air: Psychoanalysis and Social Experience," *Free Associations*, 1 (16), 7–30.
Funt, D. P. (1973) "The Question of the Subject: Lacan and Psychoanalysis", *Psychoanal. Rev.*, 60, 393–405.
Goffman, E. (1959) *The Presentation of Self in Everyday Life* (Garden City: Doubleday).

Goffman, E. (1974) *Frame Analysis: An Essay on the Organization of Experience* (New York: Harper and Row).

Grosskurth, P. (1991) *The Secret Ring: Freud's Inner Circle and the Politics of Psychoanalysis* (Reading: Addison Wesley).

Hartmann, H. ([1939] 1958) *Ego Psychology and the Problem of Adaptation* (New York: International Universities Press).

Huber, J. (1995) "Institutional Perspectives on Sociology," *American Journal of Sociology*, 101 (1), 194–216.

Hoffer, E. (1951) *The True Believer: Thoughts on the Nature of Mass Movements* (New York: Harper Collins).

Huntington, S. (1966) *The Clash of Civilizations and the Remaking of World Order* (New York: Simon & Schuster).

Hynes, E (1975) "Suicide and Homo Duplex an Interpretation of Durkheim's Typology of Suicide', *The Sociological Quarterly*, 16 (1), 87–104.

Jameson, F. (1981) *The Political Unconscious: Narrative as a Socially Symbolic Act* (Ithaca: Cornell University Press).

Jameson, F. (1986) "Third World Literature in the Era of Multinational Capitalism," *Social Text*, 15, 65–88.

Jones, E. (1957) *The Life and Work of Sigmund Freud*, Vols. 1–3 (New Brunswick/ London: Transaction Publishers).

Kirsner, D. (2000) *Unfree Associations: Inside Psychoanalytic Institutes* (London: Process Press).

Lacan, J. (1968) *The Language of the Self: The Function of Language in Psychoanalysis* (Baltimore and London: Johns Hopkins University Press).

Lacan, J. (1977) "The Mirror Stage as Formative of the Function of the I as Revealed in Psychoanalytic Experience" in A. Sheridan (trans.) *Écrits: A Selection* (New York: Norton).

Lacan, J. (1994) *La relation d'objet* (séminaire, IV, 1956–1957) (Paris: Seuil).

Lee, O. (1999) "Social Theory across Disciplinary Boundaries: Cultural Studies and Sociology," *Sociological Forum*, 14 (4), 547–581.

Levenson, E. (1985) "The Interpersonal (Sullivanian) Model" in A. Rothstein (ed.) *Models of the Mind: Their Relationships to Clinical Work* (Workshop Series of the American Psychoanalytic Association).

Lévi-Strauss, C. ([1951] 1963) *Structural Anthropology*, C. Jacobson and B. Schoepf (trans.) (New York: Basic Books).

Lévi-Strauss, C. ([1949] 1963) "The Effectiveness of Symbols," in C. Jacobson and B. Schoepf (trans.) *Structural Anthropology* (New York: Basic Books).

Long, S. (2013) *Socioanalytic Method: Discovering the Hidden in Organizations and Social Systems* (London: Karnac).

Marcuse, H. (1955) *Eros and Civilization* (New York: Random House).

Mauss, M. and H. Hubert (1902–1903). *Esquisse d'une Théorie Générate de la Magique Année Sociologique*. Série 2.

McLaughlin, J. T. (1983) "Some Observations on the Application of Frame Theory to the Psychoanalytic Situation and Process," *Psychoanalytic Quarterly*, 52 (2), 167–179.

Mead, G. H. (1934) *Mind, Self and Society* (Chicago: University of Chicago Press).

Mills, C. R. (1961) *The Sociological Imagination* (New York: Grove Press).

Mills, C. R. (2000) "C. Wright Mills: Letters and Autobiographical Writings," in K. Mills (ed.) with Pamela Mills (Berkeley: University of California Press).

Movahedi, S. (2007) "Psychoanalysis," in G. Ritzer (ed.) *The Blackwell Encyclopedia of Sociology* (Oxford: Blackwell Publishing).

Movahedi, S. (2012) "Quantitative and Qualitative Analysis of Reported Dreams and the Problem of Double Hermeneutics in Clinical Research," *Journal of Research Practice*, 8 (2), http://jrp.icaap.org/index.php/jrp/article/view/303/274, date accessed 22 September 2013.

Movahedi, S. and Homayounpour, G. (2012) "The Couch and the Chador," *International Journal of Psychoanalysis*, 93, 1357–1375.

Movahedi, S. and Homayounpour, G. (2013) "Fort!/Da! through the Chador: The Paradox of Women's Visibility and Invisibility," in W. Muller-Funk, I. Scholz Strasser, and H. Westrink (eds) *Psychoanalysis, Monotheism and Morality: The Sigmund Freud Museum Symposia 2009–2011* (Belgium: Leuven University Press).

Mukerji, C. (1983) *From Graven Images: Patterns of Modern Materialism* (New York: Columbia University Press).

Parker, I. (1994) "Reflexive Social Psychology," *Free Associations*, 4D, 527–548.

Parker, I. (2003) "Lacanian Social Theory and Clinical Practice," *Psychoanalysis and Contemporary Thought*, 26, 195–221.

Sachs, H. (1945) *Freud: Master and Friend* (Cambridge: Harvard University Press).

Saussure, F. de ([1916] 1966) *Course in General Linguistics*, C. Bally and A. Schehaye (eds), W. Bakin (trans) (New York: McGraw-Hill).

Scheff, T. (2011) "Parts and Wholes: Goffman and Cooley," *Sociological Forum*, 26 (3), 694–754.

Scheff, T. (2013) "Getting Unstuck: Interdisciplinary As a New Discipline," *Sociological Forum*, 28 (1), 179–185.

Schutz, A. ([1945] 1973) "On multiple Realities," in R. Zaner and H. T. Engelhardt, Jr. (trans.) *Collected Papers* (Evanston: Northwestern University Press).

Sherif, M. (1969) "If The Social Scientist Is to Be More Than a Mere Technician," *Journal of Social Issues*, 24, 41–61.

Sherif, M. and Sherif, C. W. (eds) (1969) *Interdisciplinary Relationships in the Social Sciences* (Chicago: Aldine).

Skelton, R. (1993) "Lacan for the Faint Hearted," *British Journal of Psychotherapy*, 10 (2), 419–429.

Spruiell, V. (1983) "The Rules and Frames of the Psychoanalytic Situation," *Psychoanalysis Quarterly*, 52 (1), 1–33.

Steinmetz, G. (2006) "Bourdieu's Disavowal of Lacan: Psychoanalytic Theory and the Concepts of 'Habitus' and 'Symbolic Capital'," *Constellations*, 13 (4), 445–464.

Sullivan, H. S. (1953) *The Interpersonal Theory of Psychiatry* (New York: Norton).

Thompson, K. (1982) *Emile Durkheim* (New York: Routledge).

Wax, M. L. (1968) "Myth and Interrelationship in Social Science: Illustrated through Anthropology and Sociology," in M. Sherif and C. W. Sherif (eds) (1968) *Problems of Interdisciplinary Relations in the Social Sciences* (Chicago: Aldine).

Wilson, E. O. (1998) *Consilience* (New York: Knopf).

Winnicott, D. W. (1956) "The Mirror Role of Mother and Family in Child Development," in *Playing and Reality* (New York: Basic Books), 1971, pp. 111–118.

Žižek, S. (2000) "Holding the Place," in J. Butler, E. Laclau, and S. Žižek (eds) *Contingency, Hegemony, Universality: Contemporary Dialogues on the Left* (London: Verso).

Part III
The Unfulfilled Promise of Psychoanalysis and Sociological Theory

7
Escapes from Freedom: Political Extremism, Conspiracy Theories, and the Sociology of Emotions

Neil McLaughlin

Although sociology and psychoanalysis have a troubled history and relationship, Erich Fromm's theory of social character is a good entry point for reconciling and reviving dialogue between the two traditions. Ironically Fromm—who can be characterized as a "forgotten intellectual"—had a conflicted relationship with empirical sociology, the Freudian tradition and the Frankfurt School within which his theory of character was forged (McLaughlin, 1998). To many sociologists, he was perceived as a second-rate thinker within two discredited traditions, Marxism and psychoanalysis. And Fromm was also discredited among some psychoanalytic theorists, particularly those holding to mid-twentieth century "drive" orthodoxies as well as language-oriented Lacanians who thought his work undermined core Freudian insights into the unconscious and human emotions.

Yet, against this conventional wisdom, I argue for renewed sociological engagement with Fromm's psychoanalytic and social insights. For Fromm was once a significant figure in the sociological canon, and mid-twentieth century sociologists like Robert Merton, C. Wright Mills, and Talcott Parson drew appreciatively from his ideas (Burston, 1991; Friedman, 2013; McLaughlin, 1998). Moreover, even though his theories fell between the disciplinary cracks of sociology and social psychology, Fromm's work remains paradoxically relevant, and promises a way forward for contemporary sociologists interested both in emotions and in psychoanalytic insights. It provides a more direct path connecting psychoanalysis and contemporary empirical sociology than available in the critical theory of Adorno, Marcuse, or Lacanian-influenced theories used in the humanities or social sciences (Steinmetz, 2006).

More specifically, drawing on Neil Smelser's American Sociological Association Presidential address on the "rational and irrational,"

I contend that, more than other Frankfurt School ideas, Fromm's concept of social character is most compatible with empirical sociology (Smelser, 1998a). By attempting to merge psychoanalytic insights with social issues, Fromm's work is distinguishable from that of "critical theorists" like Adorno, Marcuse, and Lacan who used psychoanalytic ideas in highly speculative ways irreconcilable with empirical sociology (Jay, 1973; Steinmetz, 2006). To show how his social psychological theory usefully connects the sociological tradition and contemporary theory, I suggest three "macro" research topics that would gain from Fromm's version of sociological psychoanalysis: authoritarianism in contemporary extremist movements (the American Tea Party and new versions of European fascism); destructiveness among genocidal leaders and "loose" terrorists in the West (i.e. the Boston Marathon bombers and Canadian based terrorist plots); and automation conformity of the sort manifested through conspiracy theories in North America.

Research on contemporary societies needs to compellingly analyze widespread mass movements' promotion of irrational hatreds and emotions—whether in the form of anti-Muslim hysteria around the "Ground Zero" mosque, broader Tea Party extremism, the re-emergence of neo-fascist movements in Western and Central Europe, or Islamic extremism. We are living in a moment when social psychological analyses of emotions are in order, and when social and political turmoil has given rise to rapid spread of bizarre conspiracy theories blaming Muslims, Jews, or either George Bush or George Soros for all the world's problems. The freedoms created by modernity, the rights revolutions, and democracy in the early years of the twenty first century have paradoxically led to increased anxieties and the potential for, and actuality of, violence.

Of course, Fromm's social psychology cannot replace empirical sociological analyses of these complex phenomena. However, in the spirit of Smelser's argument for delimited applications, I assert that Fromm's work suggests mechanisms better capable of explaining these topics than the more conventional tools of social scientific analysis. After arguing for modest sociological application of Fromm's psychoanalytic ideas to these examples, this essay ends with cautionary thoughts about how contemporary sociology—generally speaking—can draw on psychoanalytic ideas. To preserve the distinction between professional academic sociology and Fromm's version of critical "public sociology," I contrast Fromm's ideas with Bourdieu's reflexive sociology, arguing that psychoanalytic and sociological levels of analysis must remain in a creative and ultimately unresolved tension. Let us begin, then, with some intellectual history about when sociology and psychoanalysis first parted company in the golden years of both, that is, mid-twentieth century America.

The forgotten psychoanalytic sociologist

Born in 1900, Erich Fromm became a major public intellectual, known throughout the world during the 1940s, 1950s, and 1960s. Fromm's classic *Escapes from Freedom* (1941), a powerful and influential analysis of Nazism's rise in the 1930s provided a social psychological basis for thinking about the complexities of freedom and laid a foundation for later writings on varied topics like *The Sane Society* (1955), *The Anatomy of Human Destructiveness* (1970), and *Social Character in a Mexican Village* (1973). Despite assertions otherwise (Coser, 1984; Friedman, 2013), *Escape from Freedom* (1941) was not Fromm's most academically well-developed piece of scholarship. Yet it contains the core of his major theoretical contribution to any contemporary dialogue between sociology and psychoanalysis.

Despite millions of books sold and widespread fame, Fromm was a "forgotten intellectual" by the late 1960s (McLaughlin, 1998); by then, he had gone from a famed intellectual to a neglected figure read by few serious intellectuals in the US or Canada (Burston, 1991; McLaughlin, 1998). But, despite "origin myths" that obscured his role in pioneering empirical psychoanalytic sociology, Fromm was a central player in the emergence of the Frankfurt School in Germany and New York in the 1930s (Burston, 1991; Friedman, 2013; McLaughlin, 1999; McLaughlin, 2008; Wheatland, 2009). These myths also erased Fromm from histories of the school now known to sociologists largely by the names of Horkheimer, Marcuse, Adorno, and Lowenthal (for example, Jay, 1973, but see Bronner, 1994; Burston, 1991; Wheatland, 2004a; Wheatland, 2004b; Wheatland, 2009; Wiggershaus, 1994).

Yet, we know from recent archive-based research that when Frankfurt School scholars left Nazi-ruled Germany to come to the US, they were invited to the Columbia University Department of Sociology largely because of Fromm's empirical research program (Friedman, 2013; Wheatland, 2009). Not only did Fromm direct the Institute's campaign for affiliation with Columbia (Wheatland, 2004b), but his empirical research agenda was the main reason sociologist Robert Lynd intervened with the Columbia administration to gain the scholars affiliation with the university and housing on Morningside Heights. As Wheatland summarizes Fromm's reputation in the 1930s, "in the eyes of Columbia's faculty, he was the central figure guiding the Horkheimer circle's most significant work" (Wheatland, 2004a). Fromm was also pivotal in research for the "authoritarian personality" study published in 1950, the most important contribution the critical theorists made to contemporary empirical social science.

Moreover, Fromm was deeply sociological. Trained at Heidelberg as a sociologist by Alfred Weber (Max Weber's less famous, but still accomplished, younger brother), Fromm's sociological pedigree and relevance was widely acknowledged in mid-century American social science. For instance, Robert Merton taught Fromm's *Escape from Freedom*; C. Wright Mills saw his ideas about social psychology partly shaped by Fromm, this most sociological of the "neo-Freudians." Later, famous sociologist Paul Lazarsfeld worked as a statistical consultant for Fromm as he completed a study on the "working class in Weimar Germany," while David Riesman's influential 1950s analysis of conformity of the "lonely crowd" was forged through dialogue with Fromm, his intellectual mentor and life-long friend (Burston, 1991; Friedman, 2013; McLaughlin, 1998). Although Fromm moved to a career as a psychoanalyst, interdisciplinary scholar and social critic, his appeal to these sociologists was hardly accidental. At the height of the dialogue that took place between sociology and psychoanalysis in the 1945–1968 period, it was Fromm's work which was found the most sociological because empirically useful—much more so, by contrast, than the work of other psychoanalytically oriented theorists like Wilhelm Reich, Erik Erikson, or Lacan. Thus, Fromm is an indispensable figure for restarting a conversation between two complementary traditions.

How to think about psychoanalysis in sociology?

While certainly a theoretical school in crisis, the death of psychoanalysis has been exaggerated (Hale, 1995; Stepansky, 2009). Yet, despite the sway of Freudian-influenced scholars from Talcott Parsons through Dennis Wrong and Nancy Chodorow (Chodorow, 1999), psychoanalysis remains relatively marginal in sociology. As Neil Smelser stated in his 1997 Presidential address to the American Sociological Society, "many elements of Freud's psychoanalytic theories have been discredited: eros and thanatos, universal dream language, the psychosexual stages of development, the primal horde" (Smelser, 1998a, p. 5). Still, the Freudian tradition provides a useful conceptual tool kit from the notion of ambivalence stressed by Smelser through others equally important like repression, transference, resistance, and the dynamic concept of character, concepts sociologists can use to develop a more sophisticated model of human action than possible with either a neo-classical economic model or a sociological structuralism.

Of course, Freudians are not alone in analyzing emotions and irrationality: academic psychologists, evolutionary theorists, and neuroscientists have much to add as well (Katz, 2001; Turner, 2000). But if a self-contained "psychoanalytic sociology" is outdated and unviable, quality sociological analysis is possible which would draw selectively on the Freudian tradition's insights into relationships between psyche and society. Indeed, the great strength of Smelser's argument is in shifting attention beyond counterproductive paradigm wars (Smelser, 1998b). Trying to disprove either currently influential rational-choice theory, or the relatively unfashionable psychoanalytic accounts of the human actor, makes little sense. More sensible, by comparison, is to view both rational calculation *and* emotional ambivalence as important aspects of human motivation (Smelser, 1998a). Doing so allows for focusing on how sociological context and emotional dynamics relate in ways that point beyond either/or thinking; in other words, it is possible to preserve psychoanalytic insights while avoiding Freudian dogmatism.

Thus it seems wrong, for example, to psychoanalyze the participants of far-right-wing movements in Hungary without first analyzing the history of fascist movements in the region with attention to the structural character of global and domestic as well as economic and political forces at play. But ignoring psychoanalytic insights in such a situation would also be limited and one-dimensional, leaving important social psychological dynamics unexplored. Similarly, while rational choice theories work reasonably well for explaining market choices, they are wholly inadequate for analyzing the emotional dynamics of dependence which create ambivalence within longstanding intimate relationships as well as within closed networks and organizations with high exit costs (Smelser, 1998a).

Still another case in point: Randall Collins rightly critiques attempts to explain the recruitment and motivation of suicide bombing on the basis of psychological dynamics when conscious political motivations and objectives, and organized interaction ritual chains creating violent political action against civilians, offers a better explanation (Collins, 2008). And surely revenge and strategic rationales are central to organized cycles of terrorist and counter-terrorist violence (Brym and Araj, 2006) Yet what of the "loose individuals" (Nisbet, 1989) who are Western born or recent immigrants, and who are drawn through complex personal motives and hatred spread by the Internet yet operate relatively free-lance? Is this not the kind of terrorism where psychoanalytic perspectives are useful in ways not fully covered by traditional political sociology? Collins' interaction ritual chains theories would again be useful here, too, but falls short of comprehending the process before it picks up emotional energy because Collins lacks a psychological micro-foundation. While a useful and growing literature exists on violence and terrorism, not so a sociologically informed theory of emotions that can help to ground this research. Smelser has provided a sociological manifesto for the sensible and eclectic use of Freudian theories and, indeed, this general sensibility has surfaced within varied sociological subfields. For example, social movement scholars are recently interested in integrating psychoanalytic ideas (Goodwin, 1997; Goodwin, Jasper and Polletta, 2000) since emotional appeals, deep hatreds, and passionate commitments are central to political action. But where does Fromm, and the ideas developed in *Escape from Freedom*, play a role in developing broader theoretical frameworks useful for contemporary research?

Escapes from freedoms: Theoretical framework

In Fromm's view the modern world brought both new freedoms and increased anxieties. In Germany, defeat in war and economic depression destroyed the legitimacy of democratic institutions and set the stage for Nazism in the 1930s; at a horrible human cost, Hitler's "evangelism of self-annihilation" showed millions of Germans a way out of cultural and economic collapse (Fromm, [1941] 1969, p. 259). Thereby, to Fromm, the Nazi Party's racism, nationalism, militarism, and "spirit of blind obedience to a leader" represented an "escape from freedom" (Fromm, [1941] 1969, p. 235).

Historical analogies with the 1930s and the present merit serious reflection. The 1991 fall of Communism in the former Soviet Union was a victory for modern freedoms, but emerging markets, openness, and elections soon thereafter created countervailing trends toward authoritarian rule, political dogmatism, and cultural chaos. Elements of an "escape from freedom" mark the contemporary resurgence of Islamism, as the fall of autocrats and the spread of freedoms opened political space for new forms of Fromm's "evangelism of annihilation." Within North America and Europe, new cultural liberties, the breakdown of traditional family forms, and ethical and religious diversity have also generated feelings of crisis and confusion especially post 9/11.

Fromm's *Escape from Freedom* is useful in highlighting ever-present searches for meaning alongside economic and political forces. This is so

past and present, from Fromm's powerful depictions of social psychological quests for certainty in Weimar Germany through more recent
social dynamics set in motion, for example, through the Internet. Social
media facilitates an unprecedented global spread of conspiracy theories and radicalization, something far slower to spread, and nationally
bound, at the time of German, Japanese, and Italian fascisms.

Fromm criticized Marxist theories of fascism that reduced Nazism
to the "expansionist tendencies of German imperialism." While he
understood the role of German militarism, Junkers, and opportunist
right-wing industrialists in the rise of Hitler, he thought Nazism did not
simply result from a "minority's trickery and coercion of the majority
of the population," from the victory of madman Hitler or from a capitalist plot. Instead, Fromm insisted that analyses of Nazism's mass base
needed to avoid both "over-socialized" explanations and psychological
reductionisms (including instinctually based explanations of, say, violence) (Wrong, 1961).

Escape from Freedom traces Nazism's origins to economic changes
transforming medieval Europe over centuries into a modern market
society. Hardly an orthodox Marxist, Fromm held that the nineteenth
century Enlightenment tradition influencing Marx could not explain
horrifying incarnations of violence, power, and yearnings for submis-
siveness as surfaced with Hitler: in other words, Nazism was inexplica-
ble in purely rationalistic terms. But Freud's theory of the unconscious
helped to fill gaps in Marxist theory about the mass irrationality of
World War I as well as Hitler's rise. Fromm asserted that, while Freud
and most of his disciples "had only a very naive notion of what goes
on in society, and most of his applications of psychology to social
problems were misleading constructions" (Fromm, [1941] 1969, p. 23),
psychoanalytic ideas were nonetheless essential for theory to come to
grips with the destructiveness of a movement like Nazism.

An existentialist revision of psychoanalysis

To adapt psychoanalytic insights for sociology, Fromm favored revising
psychoanalysis to reject ahistorical, and biologically oriented aspects
of Freud's theory. According to Jay Greenberg and Stephen Mitchell
(1983), Freud's formulations reflect the "influence of now outmoded
neurological conceptions" as well as "hydraulic metaphors." In fact,
the mainstream of psychoanalytic thought was shifting from the original Freudian model of humans as "drive-regulating animals" to object
relations perspectives viewing people as "meaning generating animals"

(Mitchell, 1993, p. 23). It is this focus on emotions and meaning which recommends psychoanalytic perspectives to contemporary sociologists, especially those interested in understanding the power of irrationality within recent extremist movements.

Tapping Kierkegaard, Nietzsche, and Dostoevski, Fromm opined that the very conditions of human existence bring about "the need to be related to the world outside oneself, the need to avoid aloneness" ([1941] 1969, p. 34). Kierkegaard, Fromm continued, "describes the helpless individual torn and tormented by doubts, overwhelmed by the feeling of aloneness and insignificance" (p. 154). Nietzsche foresaw the "approaching nihilism which was to become manifest in Nazism," and his "superman," Fromm thought, was meant to negate the insignificance of the individual in the modern world (p. 154). In Dostoevski's *The Brothers Karamazov*, people are described as having no more pressing need than "the one to find someone to whom he can surrender, as quickly as possible, that gift of freedom which, he, the unfortunate creature was born with" (p. 173). For Dostoevski, too, eliminating the self also eliminates the burden of freedom—precisely the thesis of *Escape from Freedom* ("Moral aloneness" and "lack of relatedness to values, symbols, patterns" is as "intolerable as psychical aloneness") (p. 33). Even more than instincts, the need to relate to the world is a powerful driving force, and people will turn to religion or nationalism for refuge from "what man most dreads: isolation" (p. 34). And self-consciousness—awareness of oneself as distinct from nature and also from others—is what makes the fear of isolation so strong.

Against critics who saw his Marxism marred by idealism, Fromm understood the need to ground social analysis in concrete sociology and history. As Fromm later said, unlike Kierkegaard and many others in the existentialist tradition, Marx saw "man in his full concreteness as a member of a given society and of a given class, aided in his development by society, and at the time its captive" (1961, p. vi). Whereas existentialists wrote abstractly about the human condition, dread, and death, then, Fromm used existentialist insights and a Marxist philosophical anthropology to psychologically ground a historically informed and empirical social science. And, unlike most existentialist philosophers, Fromm envisioned modernity with historical specificity rather than as a simply abstract human condition. In addition, for Fromm, the history of the human species is a progressive move away from instinct-determined behavior (Cortina and Maccoby, 1996, and Cortina, 1996). As he put it, "Man" is "the most helpless of all animals at birth. His adaption to nature is based essentially on the process of learning, not on instinctual determination" (Fromm [1941] 1969, p. 41) and "human existence and freedom are from the beginning inseparable."

Thus in Fromm's theorization, by bequeathing "an unbearable feeling of isolation and powerlessness," separation and individuation could lead to defensive psychic mechanisms (p. 47). Indeed such mechanisms, as they emerged in modernity, cannot be understood in purely structural terms. Fromm was explicitly critical of Durkheim for trying to "eliminate psychological problems from sociology" and neglecting the "role of the human factor as one of the dynamic elements in the social process" (p. 29). While much of *Escape from Freedom* is a polemic against Freudian instinct, Fromm also derided sociological thinking "tinged with Behaviorism"—that is, what we now call rational choice theory. While his Marxism led him to highlight the role of economic relations in shaping human behavior, Fromm also insisted utilitarian models were insufficient for understanding the complex sources of human action.

Clinical evidence on masochistic and sadomasochistic behavior raises serious questions about contemporary social and political theory (Chancer, 1992). "From Hobbes to Hitler," said Fromm, "the lust for power has been explained as a part of human nature which does not warrant any explanation beyond the obvious" blurring, for Fromm, an understanding of the "personality structure which is the human basis of fascism" ([1941] 1969, pp. 169, 186). In the late 1920s and early 1930s, with the Institute for Social Research, Fromm had conducted an empirical study on the social character of the German working class.[1] The study concluded that the most important aspect of an individual with an authoritarian character was his or her attitude toward power: this person tends to have contempt for the weak and powerless while also submitting to those more powerful.

After laying this theoretical foundation, Fromm returned to a discussion of the political and psychological basis of Nazism. Following the humiliation of the Versailles Treaty post-World War I, unemployment and inflation accelerated the loss of legitimacy caused by the collapse of the monarchy. The older generation was bewildered by such rapid cultural changes, while young people rebelled against the authority of their discredited elders. In this context Hitler's hatred, which might otherwise have been relatively harmless, found a mass base as he rallied people as the ideological representative of a humiliated but now resurgent Germany. Following Reich, then, Fromm became primarily interested not in individual pathology but the "mass psychology of fascism." But whereas Reich stressed the passing on of authoritarian values through sexual repression in the German family, Fromm insisted that a full explanation of Nazism had to account both for psychological dynamics and larger social and political realities such as the indignation people experienced—and Hitler channeled—at the felt injustice of the Versailles Treaty.

In other words, the authoritarian character Fromm claimed was dominant among Protestants and the lower middle class came to comprise a potential mass base exploitable by the "radical opportunism" of the Nazi Party (Fromm, [1941] 1969, p. 245). Again, inflation played both an economic and psychological role in the rise of fascism: it was, as Fromm points out, "a deadly blow against the principle of thrift as well as against the authority of the state" (p. 239). Consequently just as Luther expressed the social and psychological insecurities of his supporters during the Reformation, Hitler was a representative of the threatened and marginalized lower middle class as well as of a humiliated nation.

Escapes reformulated: Psychoanalysis and empirical sociology

Arguably at the core of Fromm's existentialist-psychoanalytic theory is the insight that emotional dynamics affect the search for meaning in the modern world. In the concrete social context of German fascism, Fromm assertion that its base of mass support lay primarily with the urban lower middle class of shopkeepers, artisans, and white-collar workers is almost certainly wrong. However, with the benefit of decades of modern research, historian Richard Hamilton has persuasively shown that scant empirical evidence exists to document a lower middle-class affinity for Nazism, particularly in urban areas (Hamilton, 1996).[2] He describes a linear positive relationship between social class and the Nazi vote in major German cities, contending that the upper middle class, not the lower middle class, was more likely to vote for the Nazi Party relative to their numbers in Germany at the time. While the evidence is not as clear when one considers party membership instead of voting (Kater, 1983), Hamilton nevertheless cast doubt on the presumption that both the Nazi vote and party cadre were disproportionally drawn from the lower middle class (Hamilton, 1982, 1996). To wit: Fromm and the 1950s' and 1960s' conventional wisdom about the mass base of Nazism were probably wrong, and most certainly simplistic.

But Fromm was right that Protestantism is the single best predictor of Nazism, a point blurred by a Marxist-influenced orthodoxy that likewise accepted that the lower middle class was the mass base of fascism. And while Fromm stressed that uprooting community produced Nazism, Hamilton's data showed that rural, not urban, Protestants were the single most important stratum voting for the Nazis. As Barrington Moore stressed in *The Social Origins of Dictatorship and Democracy* (1968), fascism likely emerged more from the militaristic values of rural Germany than desires to escape from freedoms created by the conditions of urban mass society.

The current period is also one wherein desires to escape from freedom abound, but the tools Fromm developed in the context of Nazi Germany require updating and refinement. To reformulate Fromm's ideas, it would be crucial to use Randall Collins' work—stressing the organizational structure of respective churches as key to their political stances—in a more disciplined manner. Doing so would offer a more compelling thesis than Fromm's Weber-influenced explanation of Nazism largely in terms of ideas. Just as Fromm's emphasis on the lower-middle-class origins of Nazism may have been ideologically more than empirically based, *Escape from Freedom*'s identification of Nazism's early roots with the Reformation overlooks the extent to which other religious contexts also gave rise to fascistic movements. Focused on the authoritarian aspects of Lutheran and Calvinist doctrines in Germany as it was, Fromm's account was empirically one-sided in overlooking the emergence of fascism in Italy, Spain, and Japan, as well as its widespread support in Catholic Bavaria and Austria. In contemporary context, too, authoritarianism needs to be understood in a wider frame as we confront Islamist movements and the deadly dialectic between extremist ideologues and Western economic power and neo-colonial violence. A focus on authoritarianism embedded in the ideas of certain religious traditions can easily slip into simplistic associations between Islam and violence, as if religious traditions can be understood without serious attention to historical context, geo-politics, and institutional dynamics.

With this caveat, Fromm's existentialist-influenced sociology of emotions provides a useful foundation which, combined with organizational models, can provide an intellectually powerful way to understand the rise of Nazism. Hamilton is again helpful here, explaining Nazism via an organizational model that treats Hitler's movement as a right-wing ex-military cadre which gained access to potential followers in places with the least organizational resistance (Hamilton, 1996). Along with Randall Collins, Hamilton argues the central difference between the Catholic and Protestant churches was organizational, not doctrinal as Fromm posited. The relative individualism of Protestant communities left people less tied to church culture and institutions, and provided an opening for mobilization from the far right (1996).[3] These dynamics, not the economic and social squeeze of the lower middle class between workers and industrialists, explain the social base of the Nazi movement. The upper middle class supported the Nazi party partly to protect their privilege from the left, a political force Hitler promised to destroy.

Despite these empirical strengths, Hamilton's account of the motivations of the Nazi cadre is inadequate. Certainly demobilized officers and soldiers were socialized into a militaristic culture, angry at their defeat in war, and in need of jobs. But what explains the level of anger, hatred, and far-right commitment and sacrifice these cadres exhibited over the many years it took for the Nazi Party to gain power? What explains the level of irrationality and fanaticism exhibited by Hitler and the Nazis once they controlled the state, and the emotional hatred that made the Holocaust possible? For further explanation, Randall Collins's analysis of interaction ritual chains that sustain and focus the emotions of warriors, soldiers, and extremist activists is useful and necessary at an analytic level between macro-politics and individual social psychology.

In other words, the psychoanalytic level of emotions requires disciplined scholarly attention. For contemporary historical accounts of the Nazi Party and other extremist movements' rise seem to rest on under-theorized analyses of these movements' emotional appeals—a pitfall Thomas Scheff's *Bloody Revenge: Emotions, Nationalism and War* (1994) effectively acknowledges in making a case for collective shame and humiliated fury as central to the Nazis' rise. But such theoretical claims, too, require evidence and to be tested; likewise, contemporary theories about class, religious, status, "power-knowledge," gender, sexuality, and/or racial mechanisms offer propositions testable by gathering context-specific data (Alford 1998). Simultaneously, a major aim of research on violence and irrationality should be to posit general theories (albeit modestly) rather than simply counting, testing, and criticizing theories as Hamilton tends to do.

Then too, to draw usefully on Fromm's existential psychoanalysis, it is worth synthesizing historical-comparative sociology, organizational analysis, interaction ritual chain theory, and psychoanalytic insights. Randall Collins has convincingly demonstrated analytic pay-offs from examining the roots of violence between macro-historical structures and the micro dynamics of individual psychology (Collins, 2008). Sociological theory can add to our understanding of far-right extremism, militant ultra-nationalism, non-state actor violence, and the social psychology of conspiracies both through careful attention to macro, organizational, and situational contexts, and by highlighting the micro-level roots of social action in an existentialist-psychoanalytic theoretical foundation.

A modest depth psychology: Three mechanisms of escape

At the center of Fromm's theoretical framework is an extended discussion of "mechanisms of escape": authoritarianism, destructiveness, and automation conformity (Fromm, 1941). Fromm's analysis of varied mechanisms by which people deal with existential anxiety arising in sociological and historical contexts can be more easily integrated into current sociological theories than other versions of psychoanalytic theory (for a discussion of mechanisms, see Gross, 2009). While other approaches are more influential—for example, the orthodox Freudian focus on instincts or Lacanian tradition's almost exclusive emphasis on language—Fromm's is arguably the most sociological.

Fromm's existential psychoanalysis is also more compelling. The human condition is anxiety producing at its core, and authoritarianism is but one mechanism by which people escape existential uncertainty. Thus Fromm's analysis of Nazism exemplifies social processes and sets of mechanisms to explore the social psychological bases of Stalinism (both Soviet and Chinese versions) (Fromm, 1961), colonial and neo-colonial rule, and non-democratic development models in the global South (Fromm and Maccoby, 1970). Destructiveness takes authoritarianism to another level—*Escape* was written, after all, before the Holocaust and post-war revelations about Stalin—as humans destroy what they cannot control, and hatreds and passions drive social actors to kill, main, and commit genocide. And finally, in a book written partly to encourage the US to enter World War II to defeat Hitler, Fromm refused to promote Western propaganda, arguing that escapes from freedom also operate in democratic societies. Excessive consumerism, the tyranny of the majority, and the decline of rationality and reason provide escapes from anxieties created by the need for independent judgment and democratic participation among people who are formally free. Fromm's larger agenda in social theory can be read as a filling out of each of these three mechanisms of escape as they apply to Western democracies, totalitarian regimes, and the Global South.

The mechanism of authoritarianism

The contemporary relevance of authoritarianism as a mechanism of escape hardly needs spelling out. Reason is on the defensive in the West with right-wing anti-immigrant racist movements on the rise throughout

Europe, and the Tea Party wing of the Republican Party creating a political climate of fear and hysteria in the US. Certainly, the rise of radical Islam also offers an often violent and reactionary challenge to modern freedoms. This historical moment is not dissimilar to the cultural climate of the doomed Weimar Republic of the 1930s discussed in *Escape from Freedom* (1941) though there are important differences. In the US, Canada, and throughout the European Union, Parliamentary and Presidential systems of elections, independent courts, and free presses exist formally; these remain strong despite the rise of far right movements attacking the legitimacy of democratic states and the liberal status quo. Thus, democracy is at once under threat and more deeply rooted now than in the 1930s. Moreover, major differences separate the Tea Party in the US, the British National Party, and the English Defence League in the UK, and Jobbik in Hungary. Simultaneously, these diverse movements share an authoritarianism that arguably offers varied escapes from the uncertainty and widespread social changes under foot in these respective national contexts.

In the 1930s, Fromm did a respectable job building on relevant literature about the rise of Nazism. Contemporary scholars interested in exploring psychoanalytic insights, though, have a more difficult task in mastering existing literature on the historical, political, and sociological topics at hand. Any attempt to insert psychoanalytic insights into the debate must be modest and carefully crafted: the dangers of repeating some of Fromm's earlier errors are real. Take, for example, Lauren Langman's otherwise useful account of the US Tea Party: Langman creatively uses Fromm's insights but also repeats the "lower-middle class" analysis, something almost certainly wrong in the Nazi case but which should be treated only as a hypothesis when thinking about the US Tea Party (Langman, 2010). Langman suggests social psychological mechanisms at play, with some people reacting to confusion and crisis amidst US economic declines and massive post-1960s cultural changes with calls to restore a mythical America that never existed (Langman, 2010). An empirical literature on these issues has emerged and no social psychology of the Tea Party ought to quickly jump, as Fromm did over 70 years ago, to assuming the lower middle class to be the base of this movement.

Of course Fromm's social psychological insights are helpful here but only if left biases are reflected upon critically rather than taken for granted. Instead, careful empirical analysis of the Tea Party's base is needed; as already shown, this was a serious omission in Fromm's *Escape from Freedom*'s account of Nazism that Langman tends to repeat.

Langman is right to stress that the election of an African-American President in the US may have stirred social anxieties: however, this kind of Frommian analysis may understate the centrality of sexual politics to right-wing reactions, a seeming salient point given Tea Party obsessions with gay marriage, feminism, and modern sexual freedoms (Langman, 2010). An important lesson from Fromm through the present, then, is that psychoanalytic sociology must engage with and not ignore empirical sociological research and debates (see Fetner and King, 2014, and Williamson, Skocpol, and Coggin, 2011).

The Tea Party is not fascism but some European examples, such as the rise of a neo-fascist movement in Hungary alongside a far-right-wing government now in power, offer concerning cases in point. In the Hungarian instance, the crisis of democracy should be carefully analyzed with regard to local economic, political, and historical dynamics as well as further destruction of democratic traditions during the post-World War II Communist occupation. At a minimum dreary economic trends and lack of opportunities for young people, as well as analysis of specific right-wing parties and their platforms, are needed to seriously analyze threats to democracy in this important Central European nation (Cohen, 2011). While simplistic psychohistory should be rejected, probing how social psychological mechanisms contributed to a rise of a new authoritarianism in Europe and North American is a useful scholarly project. Does the powerful pull of a mythical Hungarian past, and scapegoating of Jews, Roma, and foreigners in a country emerging from Communist tyranny, attest at least in part to national desires for escaping from freedom?

The eclectic sociological theorizations running through Fromm's work also help to think about other recent right-wing movements in psychoanalytic terms. Although Marxist thinking about class and far-right movements can be simplistic—sometimes telling us as much about the researcher as the research subject—investigation is nonetheless needed into classes and class dynamics, movements of economic capital, and booms and busts of economic insecurity. In addition, empirical attention needs be paid historical differences in far right and extremist movements in places as diverse as (say) Holland, France, or Russia; as empirical cases demand, it is important to look for religious, status, class, economic gender and sexuality, or historical-cultural variables to predict participation in extremist movements.

Beyond empirical patterns, social psychological mechanisms merit investigation. The social psychological dynamics of rationalization and projection set in motion as Germans sought to comprehend their 1930s national decline could apply again as economic insecurities, rapid changes in cultural norms, and new religious and ethnic diversity shake contemporary world views and the meaning systems of millions. Of course, political dynamics behind the scapegoating of Jews and Roma in post-Communist Hungary or Russia, or the situations of Muslims and married gays in France and Britain, are all different: yet the psychological dynamics of diverse escapes from freedom can be similar enough to offer benefits from their being theorized together.

Then too, ever the Weberian, Fromm also had an historical psychoanalytic and sociological side useful for analyzing destructive individuals like Hitler and Stalin without descending into simplistic rhetoric about evil (Wolfe, 2012). A one-dimensional focus on individual leaders does not substitute for political analysis but, surely, the emotional power and psychological motivations of charismatic but hateful leaders like Geert Wilders in Holland and Csandad Szegedi in Hungary belong within sociological accounts. Analysis of both leaders, and how they connect with mass publics drawn to ideologies favoring destruction and killing, may point to deeply emotional desires to escape social change and uncertainty through imagined returns to simpler days.

The mechanism of destructiveness

When leaders move beyond authoritarianism to hate-filled violence, analyzing the mechanism of destructiveness is necessary. This mechanism emerges at a national level when authoritarian political parties or movements gain control of states and pursue aggressive wars and/or engage in genocide. The Nazis are the paradigmatic example in *Escape from Freedom*, but Fromm also developed a larger research agenda in his classic *The Anatomy of Human Destructiveness* (1973). Here, he argued that the debacle of twentieth century Communism and the horrors of Nazism could not be understood without analyzing the pathologies of Stalin and Hitler even though these political tragedies were irreducible to a matter of personalities. Fromm produced detailed case studies on the social psychology both of Stalin and major Nazi leaders. Regardless of one's assessment of the specifics of his analyses (Fromm, 1973), Fromm makes a compelling case that character matters in the political and social sphere, and that one can study and debate these issues without descending into overly easy psychohistories.

Surely a social psychology of destructiveness pertains when exploring high-profile events like the public suicide of the 78-year-old, far-right-wing French historian Dominique Venner, who shot himself in Notre Dame Cathedral in May 2013 to protest the pending legalization of gay marriage (Chrisafis, 2013). One would need to understand recent French politics, and Venner's long history of far-right extremism, even before attempting to explicate this highly dramatic, deeply emotional and symbolic event. While a political act in the context of French far-right politics, class could not simply explain Venner's protest against gay marriage's legalization, nor can culture analysis, network theory, or organizational dynamics alone provide adequate illumination. For Venner saw in gay rights not further freedoms arriving in France, but chaos and disorder. In response, he chose an ultimate escape through a violent symbolic act which would have been hard to comprehend through a rational choice theorist's stress on self-interest: on the contrary, Venner's motivations point much more strongly to powerful emotions and a search for meaning. Recall, from *Escape from Freedom*, that the rise of Nazism in the 1930s was also a deeply emotional response to a loss of meaning and order in a world turned upside down; Venner's statement gives us a parallel glimpse of the mechanism of destructiveness in a culturally conservative Catholic, rural, and nationalistic France disappearing before the powerful forces of modernity.

However, Fromm's existential-psychoanalysis is even more salient for analyzing destructive individuals less linked than Venner with political movements. Just as Smelser drew on ambivalence to examine emotional dynamics in intimate relationships, Fromm's psychoanalytic mechanism of destructive escape applies to "loose individuals" driven to killing for emotional reasons more than actors well integrated within violent political movements, gangs, or armies. Take a case such as the deadly Boston Marathon bombing, possibly lending itself to social psychological analysis: perhaps Islamic radicalism becomes appealing in situations where immigrants, freed from closely integrated communities in their violent homelands, are relatively disconnected to roots in their new homes and face barriers to mainstream success (McVeigh, 2013). In no way does this suggest the Boston killers are simply crazy, or insane; no analysis of this event can fail to examine the mobilizing tactics and ideological belief systems of radical Islam, nor the coinciding persistence of Chechen culture and wars (Reitman 2013). Yet, as in many cases of young Canadians recruited to terrorism in recent years, political consciousness is relatively low and organizational commitments and ties to radical organizations relatively weak (Austen and Johnston, 2006; Doucet, 2013; Collins, 2004, 2008). This leaves important work to be done by examining interaction ritual chains that bind young men to destructive ideologies, leading them to kill or plan to kill for no rational defensive reason (as in the case of the recent brutal

London stabbing of a British soldier in the streets) (Travis 2013). Thus, again, a purely structural interactional account can miss the power of emotions which leads people to annihilate others and ultimately themselves even when living in the relative freedom of liberal democracies.

The mechanism of automation conformity

The third mechanism of escape involves individuals giving up commitments to reason and rationality in a frenzy of automation conformity, and following the crowd within the contemporary consumerist and entertainment-driven culture of liberal democracies. Fromm developed this analysis in *The Sane Society* (1955). Little explicit mention of conspiracy theories appears in either *Escape from Freedom* or *The Sane Society* (1955). Rather, Fromm's work in the 1930s and 1940s shared the broader Frankfurt School inattention to theorizing anti-Semitism (even though Adorno and Fromm addressed the omission once the urgent reality of the Holocaust became clear). But Fromm's theory of automation conformity offers a social psychological foundation for reflecting on how irrationality can take over reason in modern societies where people, free to think for themselves, are often drawn to irrational claims promoted by radio, TV and now, especially, on the Internet (the latter rife for updating this third Frommian mechanism).

In the US, the paranoid style of American politics has long been noted (Hofstander, 2012); recently "Birther," 9-11 Truther, and Glenn Beck's Soros and Piven and Cloward conspiracy theories, among others, exemplify the pattern (Kay, 2011; Beck, 2010). Although applicable to some cases more than others, the intensification of paranoid fantasies and conspiracy theories in early twentieth century America is precisely the kind of social phenomena that psychoanalytic sociology can help to illuminate. For what can one say in rationalistic terms about racist fantasies which insist Barak Obama to be a Kenyan-born Muslim radical, or about the theory (tinged with anti-Semitism) that the Hungarian born multi-billionaire George Soros is funding a radical world government take-over of the US (Horowitz, 2006; Bacon, 2007)? Or about the even more bizarre claim that well-known social work professors—the late Columbia University Professor Richard Cloward and City University of New York Professor Frances Fox Piven—were attempting to bring down the US economic and political system (the Piven-Cloward strategy, as Glenn Beck has ranted) (McLaughlin and Trilupaityle, 2013)? These are psychological fantasies partly explicable as psychological escapes from freedom and reason.

These political fantasies operate on the margins of mainstream politics but they are not irrelevant; their resonance surfaces in the context of emboldened right-wing politics in the US, including economic power manifested in mass media outlets like the Fox network. Relatedly, the right-wing appeal of a media pundit like Glenn Beck seems incomprehensible short of a social psychological analysis of fear and confusion felt by millions of Americans living in relative freedom but struggling to come to terms with massive cultural and political changes in the decades since the 1960s. While the 60s brought new freedoms to African-Americans, women, gays and various religious and racial minorities, the current era is one of longstanding economic decline where the cultural rules have been turned upside down. It is easier to blame a black intellectually oriented President, an eccentric Jewish billionaire, and two radical professors for problems in the US than look structurally and historically at the challenges the nation faces amidst economic decline, military overextension, and massive cultural changes.

Most political movements and electoral campaigns are explicable by standard sociological models based on opportunity structures, resource mobilization, political analysis, and historical knowledge of past elections. But the simplicity of conspiracy theories appeals to social psychological needs to avoid thinking for oneself in societies formally free but not operating in fully rational and democratic ways. Thus, Fromm's insights about the decline of critical thinking in modern democratic societies—prefigured in *Escape from Freedom* (1941) but developed in *The Sane Society* (1955), *May Man Prevail (1961)*, *The Revolution of Hope* (1968), and *To Have or To Be* (1976)—aids in developing a theoretical framework to understand irrational conspiracy theories.

A distinction can be made between right-wing individuals who can be understood as political actors with identifiable goals—attempting to win elections (like Reagan or Thatcher), or sell books (like Ann Coulter), or promote a social movement campaign against Muslims' political influence (like Pam Gelner) —and those whose emotions dominate their political strategy. Former Fox TV commentator and now radio celebrity Glenn Beck exemplifies the latter category, not the former, because of the manic nature that is a large part of his far-right Republican agenda. Thus, for example, Beck had "tree of revolution" segments on his now cancelled Fox TV shows where he targeted radicals from Karl Marx, Che Guevara, Bill Ayers, George Soros, and Frances Fox Piven, among others, as having allegedly infiltrated US society and shaped the Obama administration's allegedly socialist revolutionary agenda (Beck, 2009, 2010).

Of course, it can be dangerous to pathologize political opponents with psychological categories—as Fromm himself was sometimes guilty of doing (Pietikainan, 2004). (Indeed, in public, Fromm polemically attacked the psychology of both Herman Kahn, an American nuclear war strategist, and his former Frankfurt School colleague Herbert Marcuse.) It is not possible or desirable to produce a scientific account of someone's psychology from their lectures, writings, and public statements as if psychoanalysis was a "science." Yet Glenn Beck is virtually a textbook case of someone whose appeal demands explanation not only in terms of his personality and the emotional manipulation apparent in his media strategy, but in terms of the mechanisms of escape widespread in modern free societies. Even more central, though, is that Beck's bizarre conspiracy theories attract mass audiences in a society facing confusion, anxiety, and crisis. Just as German society in the 1930s went through a cultural breakdown as it attempted to restore a mythical Thousand Year Reich, Glenn Beck is the great ideologist of a break with reality in early twenty first century America. The differences between Beck and 1930s fascists are largely structural and historical: while Beck has millions of followers, basic democratic structures are in place in the US even if eroded by the Patriot Act, the NSA, and a general climate of authoritarianism. In the end, Beck's conspiracy theories have been consigned to the margins of political discourse after even the Fox network decided he went too far and cancelled his show. Still, these margins are wide enough that millions listened long to Beck ranting about billionaire philanthropist George Soros as the puppet master and funder of a vast left-liberal conspiracy (McLaughlin and Trilupaityte, 2013).

Finally, Fromm's version of the authoritarian personality tradition is more useful than the history of social psychology version institutionalized by the Frankfurt School precisely because it leaves more room for analyzing left-wing as well as right-wing irrationality. Fromm's original study of working-class support for Nazism led him to theorize authoritarianism on the left, something other critical theorists rejected. But automation conformity is certainly found on the left, one example being the contemporary "9-11 Truther" movement; this movement suggests that the planes which flew into the Twin Towers on September 11, 2001, were part of a false flag operation by the US government (Kay, 2011). Of course, this conspiracy theory is not taken seriously by mainstream left movements and intellectuals in the West; in addition, politically conservative 9-11 Truthers also appear on the far-right. However, the majority of the social movement which holds that a missile, not a plane, hit the Pentagon on 9/11 and that the Twin Towers were brought down by planted explosives, fall on the left liberal side of the political spectrum (2011).

For example, in Canada, most prominent "Truthers" are left-liberal Canadian professors who have become "public intellectuals" spreading bizarre conspiracy theories. Here, again, automation conformity can be illustrated by looking at their writings and speeches about 9/11; these suggest psychological dynamics at work behind this mechanism as individuals in a free society believe uncritically what they hear rather than thinking for themselves. Paranoid thinking pushes for-merly rational left-wing 9-11 Truthers to think what is theoretically possible is probable (Fromm, 1961; Kay, 2011). Take, for example, one Canadian academic who appeared on national television to argue that the US government faked cell phone calls to family members made by passengers on the doomed flights; another spent his retirement speak-ing and writing to convince people the Twin Towers were brought down by explosives placed inside the buildings (see, again, Kay, 2011). Rationalizations assist these professors to avoid obvious evidence against their theories (Fromm, 1941; Fromm, 1961).

One could not illustrate emotional projection more clearly: the obvi-ous hatred of the US exhibited by Muslim extremists is attributed to George W. Bush or other American officials who allegedly engineered the attack. Jonathan Kay's excellent account of the world of 9/11 and other conspiracy theorists provides rich, thick description of people giving up rational thought in a modern society to follow a cult-like movement partly created by the dynamics of new media (Kay, 2011). Fromm's theo-ries identify such social psychological mechanisms of escape operative in democratic societies, and place them in broader sociological context (Fromm, 1941; Fromm, 1961).

Conclusion: A structural and relational sociology of emotions

Fromm's mechanisms of escape provide a valuable entry point for integrating psychoanalytic ideas into sociology, but the obstacles to a sociology of emotions giving adequate weight to depth psychology are considerable. Sociology's identity as an academic discipline was formed largely in opposition to economics and psychology, two highly scien-tistic forms of academic discourse; as such, it may not be open to inte-grating the insights of an increasingly marginal and even discredited theory like psychoanalysis.

To move forward, psychoanalytically oriented scholars must do three major things: look closely for psychoanalytic ideas within sociology that have been smuggled in; engage, not simply criticize, sociological orthodoxy; and, last, move beyond pathologizing tendencies of the organized psychoanalytic traditions. With these broad principles in mind, Fromm's ideas offer potential for sociological application in new and useful ways, including both scholarship in critical theory and psychoanalytic history as well as openings for a critical public sociology. Let me address each point in turn.

Psychoanalytic insights are real and powerful: as a result, sociologists have tended to import them in repackaged and domesticated forms. An obvious example of a sociologist who was hostile to the psychoanalytic tradition on the surface but shaped by its insights is Pierre Bourdieu (Cheliotos, 2011a; Steinmetz, 2006). Bourdieu argued for a sociological science in opposition to more speculative theories like psychoanalysis but, as George Steinmetz has argued, habitus and other concepts related to bringing the social into the psyche and body can broadly be understood as psychoanalytic. Steinmetz relies on Lacan to make this case, thereby overlooking possible affinities with Fromm's notion of social character which was arguably similar to the idea of habitus (Steinmetz, 2006). Moreover the way Fromm developed his own ideas through an extensive multi-method study of a Mexican village could be read, in Bourdieu's terms, as studying how the habitus of a colonized, underdeveloped nation with a coopted revolutionary tradition contributed to the reproduction of poverty, alcoholism, and fatalism (Fromm and Macoby, 1970). Thus, a key task for psychoanalytically oriented sociologists is to find places in the sociological field which are open to these ideas, and where opportunities exist to build on them in sociologically rigorous ways.

Important, too, is avoiding repetition of older explanations as to why sociology has not engaged the psychoanalytic tradition. Like Chodorow's work, some of sociology's great thinkers created the sociological perspective in *opposition* to psychological or psychoanalytic analysis: for example, Durkheim's social account of suicide or Merton's later concept of *sociological* not psychoanalytic ambivalence. But sociology has evolved enormously since its origins, and now is a good time for psychoanalytically oriented sociologists to fill in gaps and blinders that the orthodox sociological lens bequeathed. While Dennis Wrong's *ASR* essay "The Oversocialized Conception of Man" work did not take up gendered object relations like Chodorow's (Chodorow, 1999), it was a major manifesto, warning against over-using sociological perspectives in ways that blind us to Freudian concerns about the psyche, biology, emotions, and the unconscious (Wrong, 1961). But Wrong himself may have been overly influenced by orthodox Freudian emphases on instincts and the fashionable new leftism of Herbert Marcuse. Instead this essay argues, building on Wrong's important analysis, Fromm offers even greater potential for sociological engagement with the psychoanalytic tradition. But, while a psychoanalytic perspective should be inserted into the sociological perspective, it should be done so using concrete examples rather than general—even ideological—arguments for so doing.

But how then, given the history of divisions between sociology and psychoanalysis, should we approach the Freudian tradition? Over half a century ago, Lewis Coser held that positivism, Marxism, and psychoanalysis—three great intellectual traditions of Western modernity—emerged from intellectual sects, and were thereafter shaped by their own origins in ways that bequeathed both insights and tendencies toward dogmatism and sectarianism (Coser, 1965). Can anyone look at debates in psychoanalysis between orthodox Freudians, Jungians, neo-Freudians, Lacanians, object relations theorists, and ego psychologists and deny this? Though this essay contends Fromm's psychoanalytic perspective is the best place to begin a dialogue between psychoanalysis and sociology in the mainstream of our discipline, I hope to evade rather than reproduce stale sectarian divisions that have made mainstream sociologists wish to avoid the discussion altogether. And, while I am not convinced that Lacan or Marcuse offer theoretical insights useful to sociology, this should be resolved not through polemics but concrete studies and examples. New work needs to be done, not old intellectual battles repeated. In a contemporary world permeated with irrationality and strong emotions, few intellectual tasks are more pressing.

We do not need a psychoanalytic sociology but a sociological imagination which draws selectively and carefully on the Freudian intellectual tradition. Nor do we need 'critical theory' that institutionalizes its own political biases into the very categories it creates. This was certainly what occurred within the Frankfurt School 'authoritarian personality' tradition, one that recognized right wing extremism but was largely blind to authoritarianism on the left (Shils, 1954). But we do need sociological theory that, rather than disavowing or under-theorizing psychoanalytic concepts (as did Bourdieu), taps them selectively and carefully (Steinmetz, 2006).

In Fromm's case, new openings exist for re-incorporating his ideas. Fromm because a forgotten intellectual precisely because, within elite intellectual and academic networks, reputational entrepreneurs did not exist with incentives to promote his ideas (Fine, 2001). As a result, "Frommian" followers have been marginal and even sect-like, his theories thereafter remaining far from the cultural capital and intellectual energy that maintains and recreates ideas and influential schools of thoughts (Collins, 2008). Over the last twenty years, though, serious scholarly studies have emerged that have started to create space again for his socio-logical version of psychoanalytic ideas (Chancer, 1992; Cheliotos, 2011a; Cheliotos, 2011b; Cortina, 1996; Wilde, 2004). Moreover, the conven-tional wisdom within psychoanalysis has fundamentally changed with revisionist theories challenging previously dominant schools of ortho-dox Freudian theory (Greenberg and Mitchell, 1983; Mitchell, 1983).

Lawrence Friedman's recent biography of Fromm, *The Lives of Erich Fromm: Love's Prophet* (2013), considers his place within a larger canvas of twentieth century intellectual and political history. Friedman adds to our knowledge by detailing Fromm's influence on President John Kennedy regarding nuclear disarmament, and Fromm's role in funding Amnesty International in its formative years. Previously I have advocated for Fromm's version of critical theory in contrast with competing versions offered by Adorno, Marcuse, and Horkheimer (McLaughlin, 1999); more recently, to allow for middle ground, I have taken a sociological approach to the debates themselves (McLaughlin, 2008) that complicates the story of Fromm and the Frankfurt School. While Fromm's psychoanalytic sociology is the most empirically oriented, enough time has elapsed that any version of critical theory can and should be used selectively to better interrelate sociology and psychoanalysis.

Last, the sociological terrain itself has changed dramatically in the years since Fromm's psychoanalysis disappeared from the sociological canon. For example, in 2004, former ASA President Michael Burawoy called for valuing critical and public sociology within the discipline, thereby offering new opportunities for scholars to take sophisticated sociological ideas public. This is precisely what Fromm did with his many best-selling classics—from *Escape from Freedom* (1941) and *The Sane Society* (1955) through *To Have or To Be* (1976)—at a time when this public sociological orientation was more common. Indeed Fromm men-tored David Riesman, one of the great public sociologists as Burawoy and others have recognized (Burawoy, 2004). Simultaneously, Fromm's willingness to make his ideas public generated scholarly limitations as well, suggesting the need to evaluate his work with these tradeoffs in mind.

Fromm's critique of excessive rationalism in mainstream social science and of excessive reliance on "scientific" psychology and economics paradigms provides a model of "critical" social science. Critical sociology of this kind may fit best on what I have called the "optimal margins" of academic discourse, and Fromm's insights could not have been formed closer to the core of the then-professionalizing sociology of the 1940s, 1950s, and 1960s (McLaughlin, 2001). But with professional sociology relatively well established, at least in the US, the role of a "critical sociology" informed by psychoanalysis is now more vital than ever as the limitations of social science become clearer to all concerned about responding effectively to outbursts and movements of irrationality all around us.

Notes

1. Fromm published a summary of this research in German as part of Horkheimer's edited collection *Studien über Autorität und Familie* (1936). By the late 1930s, however, Fromm had broken with the other members of the Frankfurt School, for intellectual, personal, political, and financial reasons (Friedman, 2013). The full text of the original authoritarian character study was not published until after Fromm's death, when German sociologist Wolfgang Bonss pulled the uncompleted manuscript together as *The Working Class in Weimar Germany: A Psychological and Sociological Study* (1984). Adorno developed Fromm's ideas with much better empirical methods (helped by a group of social psychologists at Berkeley) in *The Authoritarian Personality* (1950). Adorno and Horkheimer both underplayed Fromm's contribution to this research tradition, although the history of Fromm's involvement was quite widely known in the 1940s and 1950s.
2. For a somewhat different view see Kuechler (1992). Thomas Childers also modified the conventional wisdom, arguing "the nucleus of the NSDAP's following was formed by the small farmers, shopkeepers, and independent artisans of the old middle class" (1983, p. 264).
3. Unions and left parties in the cities and the Catholic Church in the countryside complicated the Nazi mobilization, while rural Protestants and the anti-socialist and anti-communist upper middle class were the obvious source of potential recruits.

References

Adorno, T. W., E. Frenkel-Brunswik, D. J. Levinson, and R. N. Sanford (1950) *The Authoritarian Personality (Studies in Prejudice)* (New York: Harper & Row).

Alford, R. (1998) *The Craft of Inquiry: Theories, Methods, Evidence* (New York: Oxford University Press).

Austen, I. and D. Johnston (2006) "17 Held in Plot to Bomb Sites in Ontario," *The New York Times.* June 4, 2006.

Bacon Jr., P. (2007) "Foes Use Obama's Muslim Ties to Fuel Rumors About Him,"*The Washington Post*, November 29, 2007.

Beck, G. (2009) *Remember to Look at the Big Picture by Glenn Beck*, Fox News, September 18, 2009.

Beck, G. (2010) *Soros Poised Profit?* Fox News, June 22, 2010.

Bourdieu, P. (1988) *Homo Academicus* (Stanford: Stanford University Press).

Bourdieu, P. (1989) 'Social Space and Symbolic Power," *Sociological Theory*, 7 (1), 18–26.

Bronner, S. E. (1994) *Of Critical Theory and Its Theorists* (London: Blackwell).

Brym, R. and B. Araj (2006) "Suicide Bombing as Strategy and Interaction: The Case of the Second Intifada," *Social Forces*, 84 (4), 1969–1986.

Brunner, J. (1994) "Looking into the Hearts of the Workers, or: How Erich Fromm Transformed Critical Theory into Empirical Research," *Political Psychology*, 15 (4), 631–650.

Burston, D. (1991) *The Legacy of Erich Fromm* (Cambridge: Harvard University Press).

Chancer, L. (1992) *Sadomasochism in Everyday Life: The Dynamics of Power and Powerlessness* (Rutgers: Rutgers University Press).

Cheliotos, L. K. (2011a) "For a Freudo-Marxist Critique of Social Domination: Rediscovering Erich Fromm through the Mirror of Pierre Bourdieu," *Journal of Classical Sociology*, 11 (4), 438–461.

Cheliotos, L. K. (2011b) "Violence and Narcissism: A Frommian Perspective on Destructiveness under Authoritarianism," *Canadian Journal of Sociology*, 36 (4), 337–360.

Childers, T. (1983) *The Nazi Voter: The Social Foundations of Fascism in Germany, 1919–1933* (Chapel Hill: The University of North Carolina Press).

Chodorow, N. (1999) *The Power of Feelings: Personal Meaning in Psychoanalysis, Gender, and Culture* (New Haven: Yale University Press).

Chrisafis, A. (2013) "French Historian Kills Himself at Notre Dame Caherdral after Gay Marriage Rant," *The Guardian*, May 21, 2013.

Cohen, N. (2011) "Who will Confront the Hatred in Hungary? The European Union Seems Happy to Ignore the Repression That Is Happening under Viktor Orbán," *The Observer*, January 2, 2011.

Collins, R. (2004) *Interaction Ritual Chains* (Princeton: Princeton University Press).

Collins, R. (2008) *Violence* (Cambridge: Harvard University Press).

Cortina, M. (1996) "Beyond Freud's Instinctivism and Fromm's Existential Humanism" in M. Cortina and M. Maccoby (eds) *A Prophetic Analyst: Erich Fromm's Contributions to Psychoanalysis* (Northvale: Aronson).

Cortina, M. and M. Maccoby (1996) *A Prophetic Analyst: Erich Fromm's Contribution to Psychoanalysis* (Northvale: Jason Aronson Inc).

Coser, L. (1984) *Refugee Scholars in America: Their Impact and Their Experiences* (New Haven: Yale University Press).

Coser, L. (1965*) Men of Ideas* (New York: The Free Press).

Doucet, I. (2013) 'Two Arrested in Canada over Alleged Passenger Train Terrorist Plot," *The Guardian*, April 23, 2013.

Fetner T. and B. King (2014) "Three-Layer Movements, Resources, and the Tea Party." in Nella Van Dyke and David S. Meyer, (eds). *Understanding the Tea Party*. (Farnham, UK: Ashgate).

Friedman, L. (2013) *The Lives of Erich Fromm: Love's Prophet* (New York: Columbia University Press).

Fromm, E. (1973) *The Anatomy of Human Destructiveness* (New York: Holt, Rinehart, and Winston).

Fromm, E. ([1941] 1969) *Escape from Freedom* (New York: Holt, Rinehart, and Winston).

Fromm, E. (1955) *The Sane Society* (New York: Holt, Rinehart, and Winston).

Fromm, E. (1976) *To Have or To Be?* (London: Abacus).

Fromm, E. (1961) *May Man Prevail?* (New York: Anchor Books).

Fromm, E. and M. Maccoby [1970] (1996) *Social Character in a Mexican Village* (Edison, NJ: Transaction).

Fine, G. A. (2001) *Difficult reputations: Collective memories of the evil, inept, and controversial* (Chicago: University of Chicago Press).

Goodwin, J. (1997) "The Libidinal Constitution of High-Risk Social Movement: Affectual Ties and Solidarity in the Huk Rebellion," *American Sociological Review*, 62 (1), 53–69.

Goodwin, J., J. M. Jasper, and F. Polletta (2000) "The Return of the Repressed: The Fall and Rise of Emotions in Social Movement Theory," *Mobilization: An International Journal*, 5 (1), 65–83.

Greenberg, S. and S. Mitchell (1983) *Object Relations in Psychoanalytic Theory* (Cambridge: Cambridge University Press).

Gross, N. (2009) "A Pragmatist Theory of Social Mechanisms," *American Sociological Review*, 74 (3), 358–379.

Hale, N. G. Jr. (1995) *Volume II: The Rise and Crisis of Psychoanalysis in the United States: Freud and the Americans, 1917–1985* (New York: Oxford University Press).

Hamilton, R. F. (1982) *Who voted for Hitler?* (Princeton, NJ: Princeton University Press).

Hamilton, R. F. (1986) "Review of Erich Fromm *The Working Class in Weimar Germany'*, *Society*, March/April, 82–83.

Hamilton, R. F. (1996) *The Social Misconstruction of Reality: Validity and Verification in the Scholarly Community* (New Haven: Yale University Press).

Hofstadter, R. (2012) *The Paranoid Style in American Politics* (New York: Random House).

Horowitz, D. (2006) *The Shadow Party: How George Soros, Hillary Clinton, and Sixties Radicals Seized Control of the Democratic Party* (New York: Thomas Nelson Inc.).

Jay, M. (1973) *The Dialectical Imagination: A History of the Frankfurt School and the Institute of Social Research, 1923–1950* (Berkeley: University of California Press).

Kater, M. H. (1983) *The Nazi Party: A Social Profile of Members and Leaders, 1919–1945* (Cambridge: Harvard University Press).

Katz, J. (2001) *How Emotions Work* (Chicago: University of Chicago Press).

Kay, J. (2011) *Among the Truthers* (Toronto: Harper Collins).

Küchler, M. (1992) "The NSDAP Vote in the Weimar Republic: An Assessment of the State-of-the-Art in View of Modern Electoral Research," *Historical Social Research/Historische Sozialforschung*, 61 (17), 22–52.

Langan, L. (2010) "Cycles of Contention: The Rise and Fall of the Tea Party," *Critical Sociology*, 38, 469–494.

McLaughlin, N. (1996) "Nazism, Nationalism and the Sociology of Emotions: Escape from Freedom Revisited," *Sociological Theory*, 14 (3), 241–261.

McLaughlin, N. (1998) "How to Become a Forgotten Intellectual: Intellectual Movements and the Rise and Fall of Erich Fromm," *Sociological Forum*, 13 (2), 215–246.

McLaughlin, N. (1999) "Origin Myths in the Social Sciences: Fromm, the Frankfurt School and the Emergence of Critical Theory', *Canadian Journal of Sociology*, 14 (1), 109–113.

McLaughlin, N. (2001) "Optimal Marginality: Innovation and Orthodoxy in Fromm's Revision of Psychoanalysis," *Sociological Quarterly*, 42 (2), 271–288.

McLaughlin, N. (2008) "Collaborative Circles and Their Discontents: Revisiting Conflict and Creativity in Frankfurt School Critical Theory," *Sociologica*, 2 (2), http://www.sociologica.mulino.it/doi/10.2383/27714

McLaughlin and S. Trilupaityte (2013) "The International Circulation of Attacks and the Reputational Consequences of Local Context: Soros's Difficult Reputation in Russia, Post-Soviet Lithuania, and the United States, *Cultural Sociology*, 7 (4), 431–446.

McVeigh, K. (2013) "Tamerlan Tsarnaev and Radical Islam: Friends and Neighbours Seek Answers," *The Guardian*, April 27, 2013.

Mitchell, S. A. (1983) *Object Relations in Psychoanalytic Theory* (Cambridge: Harvard University Press).

Moore, B. (2003) *Social Origins of Dictatorship and Democracy: Lord and Peasant in the Making of the Modern World* (Boston: Beacon Press).

Nisbet, R. (1989) *The Present Age* (New York: Harper & Row).

Pietikainen, P. (2004) "'The Sage Knows You Better Than You Know Yourself': Psychological Utopianism in Erich Fromm's Work," *History of Political Thought*, 35 (1), 86–115.

Reitman, J. (2013) "Jahar's World," *Rolling Stone*, July17, 2013.

Scheff, T. J. (1994) *Bloody Revenge: Emotions, Nationalism, and War* (Boulder: Westview).

Shils, E. (1954) "Authoritarianism: 'Right' and 'left'," in R. Christie and M. Jahoda (eds) *Studies in the Scope and Method of the Authoritarian Personality* (New York: Free Press).

Smelser, N. (1998a) "The Rational and the Ambivalent in the Social Sciences: 1997 Presidential," *American Sociological Review*, 63 (1), 1–16.

Smelser, N. (1998b) *The Social Edges of Psychoanalysis* (Berkeley: University of California Press).

Steinmetz, G. (2006) "Bourdieu's Disavowal of Lacan: Psychoanalytic Theory and the Concepts of 'Habitus' and 'Symbolic Capital'," *Constellations*, 13 (4), 445–464.

Stepansky, P. E. (2009) *Psychoanalysis at the Margins* (New York: Other Press).

Travis, A. (2013) "Woolwich Killing: The 'Rules of the Game' Still Changing," *The Guardian*, May 26, 2013.

Turner, J. H. (2000) *On the Origins of Human Emotions: A Sociological Inquiry into the Evolution of Human Affect* (Stanford: Stanford University Press).

Wheatland, T. (2009) *The Frankfurt School in Exile* (Minneapolis: University of Minnesota Press).

Wheatland, T. (2004a) "Critical Theory on Morningside Heights," *German Politics & Society*, 22 (4), 57–87.

Wheatland, T. (2004b) "The Frankfurt Schools Invitation from Columbia University," *German Politics & Society*, 22 (3), 1–32.

Wiggershaus, R. (1994) *The Frankfurt School: Its History, Theories and Political Significance*, M. Robertson (trans.) (Cambridge: Harvard University Press).

Wilde, L. (2004) *Erich Fromm and the Quest for Solidarity* (Basingstoke: Palgrave Macmillan).

Williamson, V., Skocpol, T., and J. Coggin (2011) *The Tea Party and the Remaking of Republican Conservatism* (New York: Oxford University Press).

Wolfe, A. (2012) *Political Evil: What It Is and How to Combat It* (New York: Random House).

Wrong, D. H. (1961) "The Over-Socialized Conception of Man in Contemporary Sociology," *American Sociological Review*, 26, 183–193.

Wrong, D. H. (1994) *The Problem of Order: What Unites and Divides Society.* (Cambridge: Harvard University Press).

8
C. Wright Mills, Freud, and the Psychosocial Imagination

Lynn Chancer

The sociological as personal: An introduction

The name "C. Wright Mills" may be best known to twentieth century students through the book *The Sociological Imagination* (1958) and through Mills' commonly quoted statement that sociology can be defined by how "personal troubles" and "public issues" interrelate. However despite two new works by Stanley Aronowitz and Jock Young about the ongoing relevance of Mills' ideas (Aronowitz, 2012; Young, 2011) to sociology and criminology, Mills seems less influential in contemporary US sociology than, by contrast, the relatively more fashionable (at present) French theorists Pierre Bourdieu and Michel Foucault.

Yet *The Sociological Imagination* inspired the ideas and vision of thousands of scholars, in and beyond the US, from the time of Mills' untimely death in 1962 at age 45 through the present. In thinking of Mills myself, I oscillate between the sociological and the personal, wishing I had met, studied, and been able to talk with him especially given his social psychological inclinations. In my projective imagination, at least, we would have shared common interests. Mills was a leftist and passionately anti-Stalinist, a progressive tradition within which I place my own political and intellectual background. I also relate to Mills' background teaching sociology at Columbia University. But most germane to this essay is that my first book *Sadomasochism in Everyday Life* was fueled, in retrospect, by a "Millsian" preoccupation with linking personal biography and public issues. It began with two intimate relationships significant to me in my 20s, and moved from psychological introspection to socio-analyses of the sadomasochistic texture of both capitalist and patriarchal dynamics on individual as well as group levels.

Was the strategy I followed in *Sadomasochism in Everyday Life* argu-ably "Millsian" insofar as moving from the personal to the sociologi-cal and back again? (Chancer 1992) In this dual sense, yes; in another way, hardly would Mills have opened with so revealing a personal example, a direction my own work took after exposure to social and feminist theories, and to psychoanalysis. *Sadomasochism in Everyday Life* was indebted to Marx, Hegel, and Simone de Beauvoir as well as to Erich Fromm and Sigmund Freud; Freud, though, was not one of Mills' overtly acknowledged heroes. But what did motivate Mills' distinctive "social psychology," then, and how does it continue to inform our per-sonal and sociological imaginations?

Mills, Freud, and social psychology: Ambivalence and the sociology of sociology

Only at intellectual risk can Mills' "social psychology" be isolated from the rest of his work all told. Take the well-known *Sociological Imagination* which begins from within, with individuals: "The facts of contemporary history are also facts about the success and failure of individual men and women . . . Neither the life of an individual nor the history of a society can be understood without understanding both" (Mills, 1958, p. 1). Throughout his opus of writings, Mills was interested in exam-ining "personal troubles" as well as "public issues"; he contended, in effect, that the "personal was sociological." And explicitly in 1953, with Hans Gerth, Mills co-authored *Character and Social Structure: The Psychology of Social Institutions* (1953), arguably his most detailed state-ment of how "social" and "psyche" interconnect.

The volume is significant for what it reveals as well as omits. In *Character and Social Structure*, Gerth and Mills theorized four dimen-sions needed to understand the "human individual." These were, first, the level of the human "organism" or "man as a biological entity"; second, "psychic structures" involving feelings, sensations, and impulses "anchored in the organism"; third, the "person" who is a player of "roles" influenced by societal objectives and values at the same time his or her psychic structure is also incorporated in its operations (pp. 21–22). Last, Gerth and Mills defined "character structure" as a combination of psychic structure and social roles. In their words, "On the one hand, a character structure is anchored in the organism and its specialized organs through the psychic structure: on the other hand, it is formed by the particular combination of social roles which the person has incorporated from out of the total roles available to him in his society. . . . The uniqueness of a certain individual, or a type of individual, can only be grasped by proper attention to the organization of these component elements of the character structure" (p. 22).

Although thus presenting a four-part structure (organism, psychic structure, person, and character structure), Gerth and Mills' framework is reminiscent of George Herbert Mead's tri-partite understanding of "mind, self and society." Certainly, and as Gerth and Mills state in the book's introduction, Mead influenced their ideas as did a burgeoning symbolic interactionist emphasis on 'roles' as set forth by Herbert Blumer in the 1940s and 1950s. Clearly, Gerth and Mills sought to account for individual psychic and biologically based uniqueness while giving theoretical pride of place to social institutions and history in shaping "interactions." Just as evidently, they did not want to reduce individuals' organic and psychic structures to the social. The vision they proffered was therefore intended to be multi-dimensional–a goal, to some extent, they achieved.

Yet it is also intriguing that Gerth and Mills entitled their magnum opus "character structure," a term associated with the Frankfurt School's concerns with Nazism in general but also with the work of Wilhelm Reich in particular. Reich remains a "forgotten intellectual," as Canadian sociologist Neil McLaughlin coined the phrase in reference to Erich Fromm. In 1933, though, Wilhelm Reich was a recognizable name after writing *Character Analysis* (1958); it was a work translated from German to English in the 1940s, and with which Gerth and Mills could have become familiar while working on their own social psychological study. Like Mills, Wilhelm Reich's use of "character" aimed at connecting the social/historical and the psychological; he, too, considered himself a Marxist. Unlike Mills, though, Reich was not a sociologist but a Freudian-trained analyst. He sought to integrate Marxist with Freudian ideas that he believed had radical and liberatory potential–even though Reich broke from Freud with his intensifying insistence on linking cultural and political freedoms with bio-sexual orgasmic happiness. Yet the objectives of "early" Reich were kindred to those of Frankfurt School theorists insofar as combining social analysis with Freudian drive-based insights. Indeed, it is precisely the kind of Freudian-based concepts picked up and reworked by Reich in his discussion of "character"— that is, repressed drives and sexuality, defense mechanisms, emotions involving anxiety and guilt and, most central, the unconscious and its manifestations at both individual and social levels—that are almost entirely absent from Gerth and Mills' rendering of "character structure."

By no means are references to Freud entirely missing from Gerth and Mills' treatment of social psychology. Rather, in the Gerth and Millsian version of *Character and Social Structure*, guarded references are made to Freud—at once respectful and seeking to differentiate from Freudian and post-Freudian developments. On the respectful side, and as though would-be (albeit pragmatic, Americanized) Frankfurt School types, Gerth and Mills assert that one cannot write a social psychology unless citing Freud on "psychic" structure and Marx on "social" structure. And they compliment Freud, declaring that "It was Freud's contribution to raise the question of the nature of human nature in its larger framework" (Gerth and Mills, 1953, p. xiv).

Soon afterward being acknowledged, though, one senses Freud subsumed under the aegis of the authors' preferred theoretical framework: symbolic interactionism. Gerth and Mills note that Freud's super ego is analytically similar to George Herbert Mead's idea of the "generalized other," allowing us to understand "the social anchorage of conscience" in the family even as Freud does this "from a logical and unhistorical point of view" (p. xvi). Barely mentioned, though, are Freud's insights into the unconscious, repression, sexuality, and defense mechanisms. The word "unconscious" does not even appear in the index to the Gerth and Mills version of *Character and Social Structure*, though it does appear in a chapter on "motivations" where they rather hazily theorize that people sometimes do not understand their own thoughts and feelings even as these can be revealed and made "conscious" in social situations and conversations. Again, these passages bring Mead to mind while suggesting an only simple-to-simplistic understanding of Freud's notions of drives, repression, defenses, and the unconscious. Thus, the ontological status of the unconscious is left relatively undefined and the possibility of a "social" or collective unconscious only superficially explored in *Character and Social Structure*.

Why this under-theorizing of the unconscious and its intercourse with the social? And why the only half-hearted and unenthusiastic nod to Freud both in Gerth and Mills' work on social psychology narrowly conceived and later in Mills' writings overall? Suggested here are a set of reasons why Mills, despite his political radicalism, was not particularly ahead of his time in recognizing both the conservative aspects of Freud's ideas and their potentially more radical and liberatory dimensions. Despite Mills' tendency toward nuanced and radical intellectual analyses elsewhere, he sounds rather conventional when it comes to Freud. In this regard, Mills may have subscribed and even contributed to a dominant and ongoing tendency in American sociology toward marginalizing psychoanalysis as contrary to the discipline's central social concerns.

Before suggesting four reasons for Mills' relative disinterest in Freud, let me make another prefatory observation: Mills, like other American sociologists of his time and later, *could* have gone in a different direction vis-a-vis Freud. From an historical perspective, Mills knew the work of Horkheimer, Adorno, and Fromm, among other Frankfurt School theorists. He *could* have shared their orientation toward deeply integrating Marxist and Freudian ideas to unlock the problems of creeping authoritarianism and mass cultural apathy that Mills—in sync with Frankfurt School thinkers—agreed were worrisome in the extreme. Moreover I can imagine theoretical reasons within American sociology, not only historical and political reasons beyond it, why Mills *might have* accorded Freudian ideas—especially the idea of the unconscious—closer attention than he did.

As I have argued elsewhere (Chancer, 2013), something like a collective "unconscious" has long been present in the classical tradition of American sociological theory. It strikes me that without the presumption of something like a social or sociological unconscious, major arguments made by Durkheim, Marx, and Weber—obviously thinkers fundamental to the dominant or 'hegemonic' sociological canon—would lack power and theoretical coherence. This is not to say, of course, that Marx, Weber and Durkheim used the unconscious in exactly the same manner as did Freud—or even that they themselves were aware of their reliance on an invisible sociological unconscious for their arguments' persuasiveness. Nonetheless, each classical "founder" of sociology in his own distinctive way presumed motivational forces operating en masse behind-the-backs—or let us say without the conscious awareness—of social actors. Thereafter, couldn't Durkheim's, Marx's, and Weber's treatment of sociodynamics have been construed by later sociologists not as alien to but kindred with—as though second or third cousins several intellectual generations and European borders removed—from the expressly psychodynamic concerns of the later Austrian-born Freud? Then, too, Mills' own work—take, for instance, *White Collar* (1951) and *The Power Elite* (1956) —contains analyses of in effect unconscious attitudes held by a newly professionalized middle-class strata and by political, military, and financial elites quite collectively unaware (as Mills himself noted) of their interconnected motivations and practices.

Given the implicit reliance on notions of sociological unconsciousness both in the classical tradition and his own writings, then, what explains the ambivalence and relative superficiality of Mills' attitudes toward Freud? Moreover, by investigating this question, can we uncover why Freudian ideas remain at the edges of, rather than central to, American sociology decades after Mills' sadly premature death? Despite important exceptions in the figures of contemporary sociologists like Neil Smelser, Nancy Chodorow, and Thomas Scheff (none of whom can be linked together as though a "school," though, comparable with, say, symbolic interactionism), overall, it is ambivalence at best and marginalization at worst that best describes the ongoing reception of psychoanalytic ideas in US sociology.

Take the decades of the anti-war and anti-institutional protests of the 60s and 70s that Mills himself never lived to see. During those tumultuous years, a leading figure in American sociology was Erving Goffman who, following Blumer, publicized his antipathy toward Freudian ideas as he penned the important interactionist texts *Stigma* (1963), *Asylums* (1961), and *The Presentation of Self in Everyday Life* (1959). In the 80s and 90s, Foucault and Bourdieu became towering post-Millsian theorists influencing both European and American sociology. Like Goffman, Foucault was famous for objecting to Freudian ideas (though Foucault's attitudes were complex and not simply/simplistically hostile). Bourdieu's attitudes can also be characterized not so much as hostile but a virtual case study in ambivalence toward Freud and the psychoanalytic tradition. Even though Bourdieu's work might have benefited from drawing on Lacanian psychoanalytic ideas (Steinmetz, 2006), Bourdieu generally distanced himself from Freud and most brands of post-Freudianism until the last years of his life when, as in *Pascalian Meditations* (2000), one has the impression his thought may have headed in directions more indebted to and recognizing of Freud.

For argument's sake, though, let us treat Mills as a figure whose very ambivalence toward Freudian ideas may have had historical repercussions. Given his radicalism and ongoing influence, had Mills explicitly used Freud's work—treating Freudian ideas as important elements of a multi-faceted exploration of questions like why socialism didn't take hold in the US, and why Americans were becoming politically ever more quiescent—U.S. sociology might have itself developed differently. On the other hand, if we view Mills from within his own place and time, this account would itself be insufficiently nuances without exploring how Freudian psychoanalysis must have looked to him in the distinctively American academic milieu he inhabited from the late 1940s and 1950s. With this, I turn to four possible reasons behind Mills' ambivalence toward Freud which link Mills own "personal biography" and public issues. Indeed why would not the biographically "personal" also be historical and sociological for Mills himself?

First, Mills in his time would have deemed many of Freud's ideas as sociologically conservative. As he complained in *Character and Social Structure*, Freud tended to universalize drives as though biological and pre-given "essences" of human personality. By contrast, from Mills' perspective, both constructionism and symbolic interactionism were relatively new and seemed comparatively liberating. Relative to Freud, constructionism and interactionism defied oppressive notions of "biology as destiny" and seemed comparatively more open to possibilities of individual and social change. Mills' view of Freudian ideas as conservative was likely also influenced by the particular version of Freudianism to which he would have been exposed as a Columbia sociology professor in the 1940s and 50s. He could not have read object relations treatments of Freud later written by, for example, Jessica Benjamin or Nancy Chodorow, nor did he live long enough to know of Lacanian interpretations of Freud. Rather, within US sociology, the closest interpreter of Freud who would have been familiar to Mills was Talcott Parsons. And, while a trained psychoanalyst in "private," in the "public" realm of academic sociology, Parsons tended to subordinate Freud not so much (like Gerth and Mills) to symbolic interactionism but to Durkheimian structural functionalism. Mills thus might well have agreed with Dennis Wrong's well-known critique of Parson's treatment of Freud (1961). As Wrong argued, in Parson's hands, Freud became not a dynamic theorist of subjective and social change but a theorist who fit into the static and arguably tautological model presented in *The Social System* (1961).

Secondly, Mills was likely to have deemed Freud's views politically conservative in effect if not intention. Not only in *Character and Social Structure* but in other writings, Mills referred to Freud's biological essentialism on the subject of gender. Here, one imagines that had Mills in fact lived through the 70s and 80s, he would have been extraordinarily influenced by and sympathetic to unfolding feminist movements and theories. More than likely, he would have agreed with the majority of "second wave" feminist criticisms of Freud as patriarchal and essentializing in attitudes toward women's roles and their supposedly innate "masochism." Mills might or might not have noticed an exception to widespread feminist criticisms of Freud in Juliet Mitchell's early work on *Psychoanalysis and Feminism* (2000), wherein Mitchell took the brave position that feminists had thrown out the "baby with the bathwater" by depicting Freud as merely reactionary. Mitchell advocated a more nuanced understanding of Freud that included the potential of Freudian analysis to free women from sexual repression and unconsciously reproduced forms of subordination.

Similarly, had he lived, Mills would also have appreciated Goffman's anti-Freudian critiques of prisons, mental hospitals, and other total institutions. Likely, he would have resonated with critiques of the use of Freudian-influenced psychiatry and psychotherapies as techniques of social and political control. Such critiques foreshadowed—and for Mills might have given further credence to—understanding the role of discourses in cementing social controls that Foucault eventually described in now-classic texts including *Discipline and Punish* to *The History of Sexuality.*

The first and second factors identified attribute of Mills' ambivalence to the skepticism of a radical 1940s sociologist toward an apparently conservative theory. By comparison, the next two reasons are more introspectively and biographically oriented. Third, then, Mills' marginalization of Freudian ideas may have been influenced—even if at a paradoxically unwitting, even unconscious level—by hopes of status recognition. For why wouldn't Mills himself have been shaped by the cultural milieu, including the academic environment, of which he was part? US sociology in the 40s and 50s remains marked by an empiricist proclivity, even an empiricist bias, and certainly at the most elite and prestigious top rungs of the academic hierarchy where Mills found himself as a Wisconsin graduate student at Wisconsin and then a Columbia Department of Sociology professor. Among what might be ironically deemed an interlocking "academic power elite" in American sociology of the 1940s and 1950s, including the renowned and powerful Robert Merton, empirical research of the kind Paul Lazarsfeld oversaw at the Bureau of Applied Social Research was a sine qua non for sociologists to be recognized, and approved, as such.

Of course Mills, too, prioritized empirical evidence. Like other sociologists he held, and for some good reasons, that studies like *White Collar* (1951) should be based on and backed up by systematically collected social science data. Still Mills could also be said to have been first-and-foremost a theorist with the scope, vision, and inclination toward large ideas. Hardly was Mills a positivist or conventional sociologist: by both Russell Jacoby and later Michael Burawoy's definitions, he was a "public intellectual," a "public sociologist" impatient with the failure of other academic colleagues to engage with pressing political issues of the time. It is this theoretically "big" side of Mills which makes it possible to imagine that—under other biographical circumstances and in a more open academic climate—Mills *might* have found Freudian ideas about unconsciousness, defense mechanisms, and drives worthy of further exploration, whether or not falsifiable by social scientific methods of his day.

With this, a different facet of Mills' ambivalence toward Freudian ideas appears: he may have been conflicted as a result of his own personal/biographic place in the US academy; iconoclastic in one respect, he may have been seduced by status in another. If so, then responding to the more radical theoretical and methodological ideas of Freud (had his theoretical side led him in this direction) might have placed Mills at odds with the *sociological* "power elite" on whom he had relied for advancement, and with whom he had agreement on other social/sociological questions. This "sociological power elite" would have needed to have been theoretically and methodologically open minded for Freudian concepts to be deemed legitimate alongside the survey methods and "middle range" theories predominant at the time. This is so especially since Freudian concepts like the unconscious, libido, repression, and defense mechanisms do not lend themselves, then or now, to an empirical test: for a "social fact" to exist, it must be visible, measurable, and quantifiable. To take on empiricist biases or close-minded methods would thus have been difficult indeed for a young sociologist, likely to earn him (or her) more enemies than friends, and hardly apt to pave a smooth path toward tenure, promotions, and professional stability, bringing to a final factor conceivably germane for investigating Mills' attitudes toward Freud.

Fourth, and last, Mills may have inclined away from Freud's ideas because psychoanalytic approaches direct one's attentions inward rather than outward. Taking Freud seriously might have pushed psychic and emotional introspection into deeper territory than Mills, in his time, was comfortable or willing to venture. This could have led to noticing conflicted feelings toward status, as just speculated, or toward probing a broad range of psychosocial effects wreaked by one's own gender, race, and class background. By extension, perhaps this unwillingness to look inward—to question the "personal biographical" as well as historical and social effects of his own "political" background—partly explains Mills largely omitting gender and racial analyses from his primarily institutionally oriented writings.

For as noted by Eli Zaretsky in *Secrets of the Soul* (2005), Freudian ideas and methods are profoundly connected with introspection. As Zaretsky describes, Freud drew on his own recollected dreams as "data" for *The Interpretation of Dreams* (1932), wherein he theorized night-time meanderings as windows into unconscious wishes and fears. Just as for a Buddhist, Eastern philosophy is inadequately comprehended unless one meditates oneself so, perhaps analogously, Freudian and post-Freudian ideas are hard to grasp unless explored and found persuasive from within. Why, though, might Mills have been reluctant to turn inward for a psychosocial theory-and-method aimed at linking personal troubles and public issues?

One response draws on insights from feminist theories from the 60s onward about which Mills could not possibly have known. But, published in the US in 1951, Mills *could* have read Simone de Beauvoir's *The Second Sex* (DeBeauvoir 1952); already, this would have identified systematic effects of gender which skew the range of characteristics human beings are permitted to explore and express and discourage men from expressing and exploring their feelings. Here, then, a fascinating conjuncture arises between feminist theory and psychoanalytical theory insofar as *both* were likely to have been poorly received among sociological theorists of Mills' time, and to have encountered marginalization due to their common tendency to point analytic attentions inward-and-outward, toward simultaneously subjective-and-objective levels of awareness. For example, the controversial but influential feminist phrase "the personal is political" alludes to power dynamics pervading bedrooms as well as boardrooms, homes as well as workplaces. Applied to sociology, we might conclude it should be routine—not unusual—to marry socio- and psycho-analyses so as to reflect on our own internal and external connections with what we study. But the (unconscious?) effects of socialized masculinity might have made personal/biographical explorations which became intellectually well-founded for feminists—for example, how I opened my own *Sadomasochism in Everyday* Life—relatively alien for a figure like Mills, however, boldly radical in other respects.

Another reason Mills was unlikely to start introspectively with himself, as did Freud, entails US sociology and its own more extroverted than introverted orientation. (It should be noted, though, that this also applies to the work of Bourdieu in France: Bourdieu who in theory wished to interconnect the subjective and the objective, analogously to Mills seeking to interweave an emphases on personal troubles and public issues, was also loathe to begin a book with himself.) Hardly would Mills have been alone in responding ambivalently to Freudianism because of the latter's associations with introspection. Rather one might say that sociologists as a group, then as now, have been socialized to study subcultures, nations, races, ethnicities, genders, but not—occupationally or personally speaking—ourselves. A tendency to look outward than inward has been the "norm," not the exception, through much of the history of American sociology which has only recently begun to integrate people of varied genders and races at its heights. Thus, perhaps it should not be surprising that Mills was ambivalent toward Freud but that he mentioned Freud as much as he did.

By now, this essay has explored myriad reasons for Mills' symbolic interactionist rather than Freudian orientation: to wit, the sociological and political conservatism he believed to inhere in many of Freud's ideas; Mills' own socialization within sociology to value visible empirical evidence and away from more internally oriented (or autho-ethnographic) approaches; and the unanalyzed effects of Mills' own gendered predispositions and attitudes. But why does this matter when Mills obviously bequeathed sociology powerful and insightful works from *White Collar* and *The Power Elite* through *The Sociological Imagination*?

Why Mills' ambivalence toward Freud matters

In concluding, I offer three reasons why Mills' attitude affected diverse forms of social psychological analyses—including but not limited to psychoanalysis—failing to take hold, and to become broadly legitimized, within US sociology. For one Mills' disinterest (at best) or rejection (at worst) of Freudian perspectives affected how, in turn, Frankfurt School perspectives integrating Marx and Freud were received (or not) in US sociology. Again, Mills' *Character Structure* was quite consistent with symbolic interactionist perspectives which did attain sociological recognition. But had Mills called for further Frankfurt School-style studies—marrying his sympathy for Marxist theory with arguably kindred Freudian emphases on contradictions and returns-of-the-repressed—sociologists later influenced by Mills might have continued in that direction. This might have mitigated against the kind of "overlooking" that Neil McLaughlin (1998) claims characterizes relatively forgotten Frankfurt School intellectuals from Fromm to Marcuse, both obviously influenced by Freud.

Secondly, why *this* matters—this relative forgetting of Frankfurt School theorists—is that sociologists' ability to illuminate major social issues may have been concomitantly compromised. For instance, Mills' *White Collar* posited a robotic-like consumerism pervasive across 1950s middle-class America but how was this consumerist mentality able to take hold, and did Mills' work provide any hope that change and protest could replace such one-dimensionality (as Marcuse called it)? One could reference capitalism's systemic by way of assisting Mills, but this is a potentially functionalistic reply that misses precisely the interconnected relationship of "public issues" and "personal troubles" that he—at least in theory—aimed to theorize within his presciently "structure and agency" social psychology. Had Mills been willing to tap Freudian ideas, though, he might have seen how repressed angers and anxieties exist—and are likely to persist, and return—even at seemingly quiescent moments in social history. Indeed Freudian ideas may be even more useful now than in the 50s when diverse protests (or lack thereof) raise questions about psychosocial conditions of social movement emergence in some places and times rather than others.

Last, and perhaps most crucially, Mills' overlooking of Freud may have had the ongoing effect of over-simplifying the actual multi-dimensionality of human experiences and motivations. Unconscious dynamics and feelings rooted in childhood are often seen as the province of psychologists, not sociologists, leaving theoretical lacunae perhaps avoidable if the field routinely drew on combined "psychosocial" ideas. For example, consider Bourdieu's central notion of habitus as transposable dispositions: how could this *not* be substantially influenced by the "psychic" character of childhoods that reach into adulthood, thereafter (unconsciously) coloring not only bodily but emotional and mental patterns reinforced over long years in a given home or family? Yet, despite Bourdieu's brilliance, he rather curiously avoided exploring childhood's powerful contribution to the development of habitus(es). Perhaps Bourdieu, like Mills, did not wish to be negatively associated with the "conservative" Freudian tradition were he to incorporate, too much, the ethnographic contribution of childhood(s) to habitus(es). By 2014, though, such oversimplification in otherwise sophisticated social theory should itself be rendered outdated. For those who follow Bourdieu and Mills, it is no longer necessary to throw the Freudian baby out with the bathwater. Instead let it be a tribute to C. Wright Mills to no longer divorce sociology and psychoanalysis, and that we can finally incorporate Freudian-inspired ideas and methods into our own sociological imaginations.

References

Aronowitz, S. (2012) *Taking it Big: C. Wright Mills and the Making of Political Intellectuals* (New York: Columbia University Press).
De Beauvoir, S. (1952) *The Second Sex* (New York: Knopf).
Bourdieu, P. (2000) *Pascalian Meditations* (Stanford: Stanford University Press).
Chancer, L. (1992) *Sadomasochism in Everyday Life: The Dynamics of Power and Powerlessness* (New Brunswick: Rutgers University Press).
Chancer, L. S. (2013) "Sociology, Psychoanalysis, and Marginalization: Unconscious Defenses and Disciplinary Interests," *Sociological Forum*, 28 (3), 452–468.

Freud, S. (1932) *The Interpretation of Dreams* (London and New York: Allen and Unwin).

Gerth, H.H. and C. W. Mills (1953) *Character and Social Structure: The Psychology of Social Institutions* (New York: Harcourt, Brace and Company).

Goffman, E. (1961) *Asylums; Essays on the Social Situation of Mental Patients and Other Inmates* (Garden City: Anchor Books).

Goffman, E. (1963) *Stigma: Notes on the Management of Spoiled Identity* (London: Penguin).

Goffman, E. (1990) *The Presentation of Self in Everyday Life* (New York: Doubleday).

McLaughlin, N. (1998) "How to Become a Forgotten Intellectual: Intellectual Movements and the Rise and Fall of Erich Fromm," *Sociological Forum*, 13 (2), 215–246.

Mills, C. W. (1951) *White Collar: The American Middle Classes* (New York: Oxford University Press).

Mills, C. W. (1956) *The Power Elite* (New York: Oxford University Press).

Mills, C. W. (2000) *The Sociological Imagination* (Oxford and New York: Oxford University Press).

Mitchell, J. (2000) *Psychoanalysis and Feminism: A Radical Reassessment of Freudian Psychoanalysis* (New York: Basic Books).

Reich, W. (1958) *Character Analysis* (London: Vision).

Steinmetz, G. (2006) "Bourdieu's Disavowal of Lacan: Psychoanalytic Theory and the Concepts of 'Habitus' and 'Symbolic Capital'," *Constellations*, 13 (4), 445–464.

Wrong, D. H. (1961) "The Oversocialized Conception of Man in Modern Sociology," *American Sociological Review*, 26 (2), 183–193.

Young, J. (2011) *The Criminological Imagination* (Cambridge and Malden: Polity).

Zaretsky, E. (2005) *Secrets of the Soul: A Social and Cultural History of Psychoanalysis* (New York: Vintage).

9
From Sociology to Socioanalysis: Rethinking Bourdieu's Concepts of Habitus, Symbolic Capital, and Field along Psychoanalytic Lines

George Steinmetz

According to Vincent de Gaulejac, a French sociologist and clinician, "Far from being hostile to psychoanalysis [Bourdieu] reckoned that there was no fundamental difference between his conception of the unconscious and Freud's." (de Gaulejac, 2004, p. 83). Indeed, prior to Bourdieu, European sociology engaged intensively with psychoanalysis for almost a century, starting with Kolnai's *Psychoanalyse und Soziologie* (1921), through to the mid-century writings of Fromm (1989), Bastide (1950), Ginsburg (1947), Elias,[1] and Adorno, and continuing to the present (Maître, 1994, 2000; de Gauljac, 1987, 1996; Elliott, 2004). French academic and intellectual culture has been especially open to psychoanalysis in the postwar period, due in no small part to the efforts of Jacques Lacan and the Lacanian school (Roudinesco, 1990). A Middletown-style study of a small city in the Paris suburbs sponsored by UNESCO in 1949 included a number of psychoanalytic hypotheses and methods and was designed and carried out by a group of sociologists and psychoanalysts (Dampierre, 1956). French academic bookstores specializing in "les sciences humaines" usually carry a large section on contemporary psychoanalytic theory and it is often located right next to sociology. De Gauljac speaks of an entire group of "socioanalysts" like himself who see "the social and the psychic" as "two scenes, both autonomous and interdependent" and who are interested in "understanding the interaction of social, familial and unconscious determinants" (1999, pp. 9–10, 16, see also Lapassade 1975).

How does Pierre Bourdieu fit into this landscape? In the English-speaking world Bourdieu is sometimes described as "a theorist who will have no truck with Freudian psychoanalytic theory" (Witz, 2004, p. 217). But Bourdieu seemed to recognize, especially during the last decade of his life (1930–2002), that psychoanalysis was both similar and intrinsic to his own project. In a dialogue with the psychoanalytically oriented sociologist Jacques Maître, Bourdieu embraced "a kind of social psychoanalysis" (Bourdieu, 1994, pp. v–xxii). Bourdieu gestured repeatedly toward such a merger through his reliance on psychoanalytic terminology, ideas, and arguments, through his embrace of the idea of socioanalysis (*la socioanalyse*).

One barrier to completing the move from sociology to socioanalysis and a merging of disciplines, however, is rooted in Bourdieu's highly allergic response to any serious engagement with Jacques Lacan, whose ideas can contribute to a rethinking of the core Bourdieuian concepts. Bourdieu's gradual rapprochement with Freud and certain ego-analytic traditions contrasts sharply with his studious avoidance of any open engagement with the distinctively French school of psychoanalysis.

Many of Bourdieu's formulations during the 1980s and 1990s could be drawn directly from Freud or Lacan, although when they are hedged about with a *cordon sanitaire* of Bourdieu's own coinages. In *The Rules of Art*, Bourdieu asks "What indeed is this discourse which speaks of the social or psychological world *as if it did not speak of it*; which *cannot speak* of this world except on condition that it only speak of this world as if it did not speak of it, that is, in a *form* which performs, for the author and the reader, a *denegation* (in the Freudian sense of *Verneinung*) of what it expresses?" (1996a, p. 3). Bourdieu introduces at this same moment the idea of the "social *libido* which varies with the social universes where it is engendered and which it sustains (*libido dominandi* in the field of power, *libido sciendi* in the scientific field, etc.)" (p. 172).

This opening to psychoanalysis becomes even more explicit in *The Weight of the World*, which declares sociology and psychoanalysis to be identical enterprises: "This is not the place to question the relation between the mode of exploring subjectivity proposed here and that practiced by psychoanalysis. But, at the very least, it is necessary to guard against thinking of these relationships as alternatives to each other. *Sociology does not claim to substitute its mode of explanation for that of psychoanalysis*; it is concerned only to construct differently certain givens that psychoanalysis also takes as its object" (Bourdieu et al., 1999, p. 512, emphasis added). This book also contains extensive analyses of the problem of *disjunctures* between an individual's inherited social position and her subjectivity. Bourdieu writes of the "limitation of aspirations" which "shows up in cases where the father has been very successful" but which "assumes all its force when the father occupies a dominated position . . . and is therefore inclined to be ambivalent about his son's success as well as about himself. . . . At one and the same time he says: be like me, act like me, but be different, go away. . . . He cannot want his son to identify with his own position and its dispositions, and yet all his behavior works continuously to produce that identification" (p. 510). In psychoanalysis, the young boy's first symbolic identification is with the imago of the father, but the Oedipal structure makes this identification fundamentally impossible, or at least contradictory: "There issues forth an impossible double command: to be like the father, but not to be like the father with respect to his sexual power" (Bryson, 1994, p. 233). According to Freud, the relationship of superego to ego is not exhausted by the precept, "You *ought to be* like this (like your father)," but also comprises the prohibition: "You *may not be* like this (like your father)" (Freud, 1962, p. 34). Freud's analysis does in fact suggest the centrality of social class in generating psychic variations, for example, in his discussion of the "family romance" (Freud, 1953, pp. ix, 238–239). But Freud was less explicit than Bourdieu about the different conditions in which parents either occupy "a dominated position" or are "very successful," and this is one of the reasons sociology needs to be integrated into psychoanalysis and vice versa. De Gaulejac, drawing on Bourdieu, recognizes this and focuses specifically on the ways in which children's class position determines their interest in "correcting reality" through family romances and in which class position in general shapes "the transmission of family history" (1999, p. 15).

At first glance, the influence of psychoanalytic theory in Bourdieu's thought might seem overstated. His work can be mined for any number of theoretical influences. For instance, the key influences on the way Bourdieu poses the phenomenological problem at the core of his work—the relationship between the subject and the social/material environment—come from Cassirer, Merleau Ponty, and Canguilhem, not from Freud. Bourdieu also relies heavily on the language of Marxism, although here again his work is marked by deep ambiguity as to whether he is embracing a Marxist definition of terms like *capital* (Calhoun, 1993; Steinmetz, 2009; Desan, 2013). Cultural capital is not extracted via an exploitative process, however, and cultural domination in Bourdieu is governed by the monopolization of cultural capital rather than the accumulation and expansion of cultural capital. Bourdieu's core theoretical projects of analyzing the irreducible interdependence of subject and *Umwelt* and the logics of semiautonomous fields of practice can stand alone without these Marxian concepts.

Yet, Bourdieu's theory cannot do without psychoanalysis, whose concepts go to the very heart of the sociologist's main concerns. Of course

Bourdieu does emancipate sociology from over-sociologized models of the self such as Althusser's interpellation theory. Against overly rationalist models he insists that practice is often guided "unconsciously." Bourdieu also rejects accounts focused on objective lived environments as conditioning or socializing subjects uni-directionally, without attending to "the different manners in which the world is constructed by social agents" (Mead, 2013, p. 221). Against overly sociological models Bourdieu argues that habitus is not a mechanistic structure leading simply to repetitive behavior, since that would not allow subjects to adapt to changing conditions and would therefore lead to constant "mismatches" between action and context, as the world changed. Nor is social action mechanically reactive, as in behavioralist accounts. Equally problematic is the voluntaristic belief that "one's construction of the world has no antecedents" or that "social conditions always remain subject to agents' willingness to acquiesce to them" (Mead, 2013, pp. 60, 197). The constructive capacities of habitus offer a way out of these metaphysical dead-ends.

Nonetheless, something is still missing in this theory of subjectivity that is not provided by the phenomenological literature. This becomes glaringly evident in the fact that Bourdieu does not really have a theory of the unconscious. Indeed his habitus concept seems to be located in the nebulous no-man's land popularly referred to as "the subconscious." Bourdieu cannot explain subjectivity and its combined dependence on and autonomy from the social environment without a more complete and adequate theory of the psychic. Psychoanalytic theory is not so much an unrecognized influence on Bourdieu's thought as an essential component for a reconstructed version of his theory.

Bourdieu frames his theory of subject formation in terms of the internalization, incorporation, and embodiment of societal conditions and the reconstitution of those external conditions through the regulated improvisations of individual and collective practice.[2] In its broad sweep, this model tracks the psychoanalytic narrative of the individual's interiorization of social history (Freud) and incorporation into the symbolic order (Lacan). Indeed, one of Bourdieu's more remarkable openings to the *logic* of psychoanalysis occurs in the section of *Pascalian Meditations* (2000) in which he addresses the genesis of subjects who are suited to operate competitively in social fields. In a passage that tracks the shift in an individual's transition from self-love toward a "quite other object of investment" that "inculcate[s] the durable disposition to invest in the social game," Bourdieu works through a development described by

Freud as the Oedipal story and by Lacan as the entry into the Symbolic order:

Sociology and psychology [*sic*] should combine their efforts (but this would require them to overcome their mutual suspicion) to analyse the genesis of investment in a field of social relations, thus constituted as an object of investment and preoccupation, in which the child is increasingly implicated and which constitutes the paradigm and also the principle of investment in the social game. How does the transition, described by Freud, occur, leading from a narcissistic organization of the libido, in which the child takes himself (or his own body) as an object of desire, to another state in which he orients himself towards another person, thus entering the world of 'object relations', in the forms of the original social microcosm and protagonists of the drama that is played out there? (Bourdieu, 2000, p. 166)

As we will see below, Bourdieu locates the motor of this shift in the 'search for recognition,' a phrase that brings his interpretation even closer to the Lacanian (and Žižekian) reading of Freud through G. W. F. Hegel's *Phenomenology*. It follows that another key Bourdieusian concept, *field*, also makes sense only when it is reconstructed with psychoanalytic underpinnings. For fields cannot be understood solely as agonistic *Kampfplätze* but are always also arenas of mutual identification, libidinal investment, recognition, and even love (Steinmetz, 2008).

The pressure of the Freudian tradition was first revealed in Bourdieu's writing by the recurrence of the words "unconscious"—used both as adjective and as noun—and "misrecognition" (*méconaissance*), a concept that received its most powerful formulation in the writing of Lacan. Over time, Bourdieu's oeuvre accumulated a growing psychoanalytic vocabulary. His writing includes the following terms: unconscious, misrecognition, projection, reality principle, libido and libidinal investment, ego-splitting, negation (*dénégation*), repression (*refoulement*), return of the repressed, compromise formation, anamnesis, phallonarcissism, and collective phantasy. In his *Self Analysis* (published first in German in 2002 and in French in 2004), he uses the phrases "disavowal, in the Freudian sense" and "community of the unconscious" (2004, p. 19).[3]

Nonetheless, Bourdieu's relationship to this tradition was not untroubled. Indeed, the conditions in which Freudian concepts appear in Bourdieu's work can be partly understood as forms of denegation in which the ideational aspect of a repressed idea is reintroduced to consciousness, accepted intellectually, and named, while the condemning affective judgment toward the idea is retained (Freud, [1923] 1961).

In some writings, especially the earlier ones, Bourdieu rejects psychoanalysis outright. In *Outline of a Theory of Practice* (1977, pp. 92–93) psychoanalysis is portrayed as a form of biological reductionism. More often Bourdieu's treatment takes the form of admitting Freudian psychoanalytic terminology and arguments while surrounding these passages with rhetorical devices that seem to condemn psychoanalysis.[4] In *Masculine Domination*, Bourdieu reveals his debt to Freud immediately when he mentions that he is focusing on the same Mediterranean cultural matrix emphasized by psychoanalysis. Where Freud drew on ancient Greek myth, Bourdieu deploys Kabyle society as a "paradigmatic realization" of the tradition he calls "phallocentric." Striking an explicitly psychoanalytic tone, Bourdieu interprets masculine domination as being rooted in unconscious structures that are centered on "phallonarcissism." Bourdieu asserts that the "the link (asserted by psychoanalysis) between phallus and *logos*" is "*established*" here (2001, p. 17, my emphasis). In his discussion of the "somatization of the social relations of domination" in the process of creating sexed bodies, the difference to psychoanalysis vanishes altogether:

> The work of symbolic construction is far more than a strictly *performative* operation of naming . . . it is brought about and culminates in a profound and durable transformation of bodies (and minds), that is to say, in and through a process of practical construction imposing a differentiated definition of the legitimate uses of the body, in particular sexual ones, which tends to exclude from the universe of the feasible and thinkable everything that marks membership of the other gender—and in particular all the potentialities biologically implied in the 'polymorphous perversity,' as Freud puts it, of every infant. (2001, p. 23)

Bourdieu argues that male domination, rather than class domination, "constitutes the paradigm (and often the model and stake) of all domination" (1990a, pp. 30–31). Bourdieu takes as a given Freud's analysis of infantile sexuality and ego-analytic arguments about the denial of "the female part of the male" and "severing attachments to the mother" (p. 26). Whereas Bourdieu had reframed sociology as *socio-analysis* in some of his earlier works, here the hyphen is dropped altogether in favor of *socioanalysis*, a coinage that points even more insistently to a psychoanalytic template (2001, p. 3). At the same time, however, Bourdieu begins this text with one of his characteristic defensive moves, categorizing psychoanalysis *tout court* as "essentialist" and "dehistoricized" (2001, p. viii).

Psychoanalytic theory has long been concerned with the problem that Bourdieu sets out to explain here, namely, the ways in which masculine domination is *historically* reproduced as a *dehistoricized* form. The meaning of the psychoanalytic expression "the unconscious does not have a history" underscores the ways in which the past is constantly being "actualized" within the unconscious through the "return of the repressed" and other mechanisms. It expressly does *not* mean that the unconscious takes the same form everywhere or that it is eternal because of some biological foundation. Likewise, for Bourdieu, the (masculine) habitus is historical—a "product of all biographical experience"—while presenting itself in an *eternalized* form (2001, p. viii.).

In general then, Bourdieu's strategy allows him at least to discuss Freud's ideas openly and to give them names, even if he sometimes takes back with one hand what he has given with the other. His treatment of Lacan is a different matter entirely. Bourdieu's avoidance of Lacan is problematic because so many of Bourdieu's ideas require integration with psychoanalysis—especially the Lacanian version. Lacan provides the key to understanding the psychic foundations of the key mechanisms theorized by Bourdieu: *symbolic capital, habitus,* and *field.*

Symbolic capital, social fields, and the Lacanian symbolic

Psychoanalysis is well suited for analyzing the transformation of originally *symbiotic* subjects into agents equipped with the desire to compete in social "fields"—agents who can sublimate, in Freud's phrase, or submit to the demands of the big Other in the field of the Symbolic, in Lacan's terminology. Lacanian theory allows us to reground Bourdieu's concept of *symbolic capital* in Lacan's notion of the *symbolic order* and in the related dynamics of *recognition* and *misrecognition* that are so central to symbolic identification. The symbolic in Lacan is the realm of language, difference, metonymy, and the Law, an arena of socially sanctioned, official *ego ideals.* The relationship of the subject to the symbolic is thus a relation of "dependence on the Other, locus of signifiers" (Julien, 1994, p. 167). Symbolic identification is linked to an ego-ideal (*Ichideal*), which "constitutes a model to which the subject attempts to conform" (Laplanche and Pontalis, p. 144). In Lacan's later writings, symbolic identification is understood more specifically as identification with *the place from which we are observed,* the location from which we "look at ourselves so that we appear to ourselves likeable, worthy of love" (Žižek, 1989, p. 105). The "demand of the *Ichideal*," according to Lacan, thus "takes up its place within the totality of the demands of the law" (Lacan, 1988, p. 134). The ego-ideal for Lacan is the "position of the subject within the symbolic, the norm that installs the subject within language." (Butler, 1997).

According to Lacan subjects seek to *recognize* the normative injunctions of the symbolic order, and they seek *to be recognized* by those who issue these injunctions. There is a dialectic of *recognition* between the Subject or Law of the Father and the subject who is inducted into the Symbolic Order, recalling the master–slave dialectic in Hegel's *Phenomenology of Spirit*. In his *Jena Realphilosophie* Hegel observes that "in recognition, the self ceases to be this individual," and he adds that "Man is necessarily recognized and necessarily gives recognized. . . . he *is* recognition" (Hegel, 1983, p. 123). In Kojève's summary of Hegel's *Phenomenology*, "all human, anthropogenetic Desire—the Desire that generates Self-Consciousness, the human reality—is, finally, a function of the desire for 'recognition'" (Kojève, 1969, p. 7).

Although *Pascalian Meditations* begins to pose as a problem the individual's reorientation from narcissism to an orientation toward recognition from others, and to see this transition as a precondition for the operation of the competitive "field," Bourdieu never acknowledged the relevance of the Lacanian Symbolic for his analysis of "symbolic domination." But why did Bourdieu feel the need to complement his category of "cultural" capital with "symbolic" capital? None of his other categories take this doubled form. Of course, other influences are named: Bourdieu refers to Durkheim as a sociologist of symbolic forms and attributes to Cassirer the idea that "symbolic form" is the equivalent of forms of classification (1991, p. 164). Bourdieu first defined *symbolic capital* as capital "'insofar as it is represented, i.e., apprehended symbolically, in a relationship of knowledge' (1986a, p. 255, note 3). This suggests that "symbolic" is just another word for the semiotic. Several years later, however, Bourdieu noted that symbolic capital is "cultural capital which is acknowledged and *recognized*. . . . in accordance with the categories of perception that it imposes"; it "is the power granted to those who have obtained sufficient recognition to be in a position to *impose recognition*" (Bourdieu, 1990b, pp. 135, 138). By the time he published *Pascalian Meditations* in 1997, Bourdieu had connected the topic of symbolic capital directly to the "search for recognition," and he seemed to make the crucial (Hegelian) corrective observation that it is not only the dominated but also the dominant who depend on the "esteem, recognition, belief, credit, confidence of others." Symbolic capital, he argued here, can be perpetuated only so long as it succeeds in generating a system of mutual interdependence in which all the actors in the field depend on recognition from all of the others and grant all of the others recognition—even if this is recognition of an inferior status.

Or at least, that is what Bourdieu *almost* said. The passage quoted above locates the motive behind the emergence of social subjects and symbolic violence in what Bourdieu calls the *"search for recognition"*:

> Absorbed in the love of others, the child can only discover others as such on condition that he discovers himself as a 'subject' for whom there are 'objects' whose particularity is that they can take him as their 'object.' In fact, he is continuously led to take the point of view of others on himself, to adopt their point of view so as to discover and evaluate in advance how he will be seen and defined by them. His being is being-perceived, condemned to be defined as it 'really' is by the perceptions of others. . . . Symbolic capital enables forms of domination which imply dependence on those who can be dominated by it, since it only exists through the esteem, recognition, belief, credit, confidence of others. (2000, p. 166)

But while Hegel posits a reciprocity or universality in the search for recognition, in Bourdieu the hunger for recognition is located mainly on the side of the dominated. This is undercut somewhat in *Masculine Domination*, where we are told that manliness "is an eminently relational notion, constructed in front of and for other men" in a kind of *field* of men (p. 53). For the most part, however, Bourdieu instinctively falls back on a populist political vision that prevents him from noticing that his own concept of symbolic capital requires a universalization of the desire for recognition to all players in a given social field. The dominated may develop a "taste for necessity," preferring their own (dominated) tastes to those of the elite. But they recognize the dominant as holding more valuable cultural capital. Dominated and dominant recognize the same principle of domination. The dominant are granted recognition not just by their elite peers but also by the dominated participants in the field. In Hegel's words, lord and bondsman "recognize themselves as mutually recognizing one another" (Hegel, 1967, p. 235). Where this is not the case—where the dominated and dominant fail to mutually recognize shared definitions of distinction—there is an ongoing struggle over the "dominant principle of domination" (Bourdieu, 1996b, p. 265). Fields can become unsettled; practices may fail to cohere in fieldlike ways.[5]

Lacan allows us to reformulate this problem. Lacan borrows the notion of "desire" (*Begierde*) from Hegel, "who argued that desire was the 'desire for another desire'" (Hegel, 1967, p. 235). Bourdieu's notion of symbolic capital is based on the premise of reciprocal demands for recognition by all actors in a field—recognition of the variable cultural positions, habituses and tastes, and recognition of their hierarchy. But why should the dominant partner in a hierarchical relation seek recognition from the dominated other? The answer is that both dominant and dominated are subjects of an encompassing system that is itself structured around a hierarchical system of recognition: the Symbolic order. Individuals are inducted into the Symbolic in a posture of subordination to the principle that Lacan calls the big Other—that is, "the anonymous symbolic structure" of Law and language (Žižek, 1997, p. 8). Within this law "is established and presented all human order, i.e. every human role" (Althusser, 1971, p. 209). Every future member of the "ruling class" enters this system of symbolic recognition in a subordinate status, just like every member of the dominated class. As Judith Butler observes, every individual is presumed guilty before the rule of the Law/the Symbolic order, and needs to "acquit" himself, declare his innocence, and be "tried and declared innocent" (Butler, 1997, p. 118). The subjectivity of even the future bourgeois is structured by desire for the Law's recognition. The Law is coterminous with the Symbolic and the social; the dominated members of a social field are just as integral to this system of expectations and offers and denials of recognition as are the dominant.

What we have then are two axes of recognition and misrecognition. On the one hand there is the axis along which the Law confronts the "infinity of individuals." Among the "infinity of individuals," however, are diverse social classes and groups, each of which can "contemplate its own image" in the social mirror of the other classes and groups. The Symbolic order demands recognition *from* the subject and grants him a sliver of recognition. The dominant and the dominated both demand recognition of their respective tastes and practices. These tastes and practices differ from and reciprocally implicate one another. Recognition is also doubled by *misrecognition*, both with respect to the subject's overarching relationship to the Symbolic Order and with respect to its relationship to other classes and groups in the social fields. This is a relation of misrecognition insofar as the image offered up for the purposes of ego-formation and identification is always generated elsewhere, outside the subject, and it is always an inverted, reversed, or otherwise distorted representation of the real. It is a relation of misrecognition insofar as the dominated tend to embrace their own condition of domination, and insofar as the dominant believe that their tastes and practices are genuinely superior in an absolute sense.

There is a paradox in the desire among dominated groups for the approval of, or recognition by, those who dominate them, and neither Bourdieu nor Hegel makes sense of this paradox. Bourdieu called attention repeatedly to crucial contribution to social reproduction of the "taste for necessity" or *amor fati*. By failing to account for this taste, however, Bourdieu ran the risk of functionalism. By contrast, psychoanalytic theory offers an account of the way in which the desire for submission emerges from the very genesis of the subject. It emphasizes the contradictory demand to be both *like* and *unlike* the Father. Psychoanalysis offers a definition of the masochist as one who "locates enjoyment in the very agency of the Law which prohibits the access to enjoyment," suggesting another account of this desire for recognition— one that is always controversial because it is so damaging to a different sort of *amour propre* (Žižek, 1997, p. 35).

Lacan's theory of the Symbolic Order thus sketches out some of the "microfoundations" or better, the "psychofoundations" which permit the operation of the Bourdieuian fields and govern the production of subjects suited for working in those fields. The subject's ineluctable entry into the Symbolic explains the *desire* to have one's cultural capital recognized as well as the recognition by others of that capital (either as exalted or as paltry). The "social libido" that Bourdieu invokes without ever defining (thereby leaving it open for recuperation by biological reductionism) needs to be thematized within this wider theoretical framework.

Habitus and the imaginary

A second key concept in the Bourdieuian theoretical universe is *habitus*. This concept has been praised for overcoming the mind–body and objectivity vs. subjectivity distinctions that have been so deeply engrained in Western philosophy. The habitus is also attractive as a concept because of its putative *integrative* power: Given the vast array of fields and realms of practice in which humans participate and the historical layering of experiences and moments of socialization, corporeal and psychic integration must be seen as an achievement rather than taken for granted. Bourdieu initially mobilized the idea of habitus to make sense of this seemingly magical integration of the disparate experiences that make up a biography (Bourdieu, 1986b). In *The Weight of the World* he turned to the question of the habitus that is internally contradictory and fragmented. In his "Autoanalysis" he summarized his own experience as giving rise to a split or *cloven habitus* (*l'habitus clivé*), "'inhabited by tensions and contradictions' (2004, p. 127). But while "postmodern" theory does not do justice to the fact that many people suffer from an atomized sense of identity rather than reveling in it, Bourdieu's theory tends to make the opposite error, underestimating the travails of integration. Most importantly, no matter how often Bourdieu restated his definition of habitus he never seemed to come any closer to explaining how and why this integration occurs, or why it sometimes fails.

Here again, Lacan provides a crucial missing link, a picture of a mechanism that can help to elaborate the concept of habitus. Just as the Lacanian concept of the Symbolic Order makes sense of the subjective dynamics underpinning Bourdieuian symbolic capital, so the Lacanian concept of the Imaginary illuminates the subject's ability to integrate disparate experiences and identifications such that identity and practice are not always disjointed. A cluster of linked Lacanian concepts—the *mirror stage*, the *bodily ego* and *ideal ego*, and *imaginary identification*—suggest a possible solution to this problem.

The starting point for human individuals is not a Hobbesian condition of competitive individuality but a state of symbiotic helplessness with no clear boundary between inside and outside, self and other. According to Lacan, this primordial experience is connected to a fragmented body image, which reappears in adult fantasies of the "body in pieces" along the lines of the "return of the repressed." Lacan discusses the production of a "succession of phantasies that extends from a fragmented body image to a form of its totality that I call orthopaedic." Similarly, Freud had written that "the ego is first and foremost a bodily ego; it is not merely a surface entity, but is in itself a projection of a surface" (Freud, 1962, p. 26). Habitus in Bourdieu thus appears as a sociological reworking of the psychoanalytic concept of a roughcast "bodily ego." Lacan writes:

> Whatever in man is loosened up, fragmented, anarchic, establishes its relation to his perceptions on a plane with a completely original tension. The image of the body is the principle of every unity he perceives in objects. . . . Because of this. . . . all the objects of his world are always structured around the wandering shadow of his own ego. They will all have a fundamentally anthropomorphic character. . . . Man's ideal unity, which is never attained as such and escapes him at every moment, is evoked at every moment in this perception. . . . The

very image of man brings in here a mediation which is always *imaginary*, always problematic, and which is therefore never completely fulfilled.

The key word here is *imaginary*. For Lacan, the initial identifications that constitute the subject begin with the mirror phase, when the watery subject—the *hommelette* or man-omelette—identifies with the totalizing and alienating external image of itself. This need not be a literal reflection in a mirror but can also be the image or even the voice of another human, perhaps a mother or caretaker (Silverman, 1988). The core structure of *specular* identity in the realm of the *imaginary* is this sense of plenitude and wholeness. Imaginary identification is identification with an image that Lacan (following Freud) calls the ideal-ego (*Idealich*), that is, an image representing 'what we would like to be'" (Žižek, 1989, p. 105). The earliest imaginary identifications in the mirror phase provide a template for later ones that are similarly characterized by a striving for wholeness.[6] The notion of imaginary identification can be connected to the overarching psychoanalytic concept of *phantasy/fantasy*. Fantasy scenarios express a conscious or unconscious wish. Imaginary identification is one site for such wishful scenarios.

Lacan illustrated some of these ideas with the experiment of the phantom flower bouquet and the concave mirror. The flowers in the vase are a real image, but also an illusion, like a rainbow; for Lacan this suggests misrecognition of the real. Moreover, the phantom bouquet can only be perceived from a specific position or 'subject position'. The Subject is precipitated by this setup. Similarly, the 'human subject only sees his form materialized, whole, the mirage of himself, outside of himself' (Lacan, *The Seminar, Book 1*, pp. 139–140).

Although Lacan initially located imaginary identifications in the mirror phase, he soon realized that the imaginary was not a separate stage or realm but rather a dimension of subject-formation that is dominated by the symbolic. In Althusser's words (1971, p. 214), the 'imaginary …. is stamped by the seal of Human Order, of the Symbolic.' The imaginary is a realm of signifiers like the symbolic. The Symbolic Order channels subjects toward specific images for imaginary identifications, and the subject continually slips from symbolic identifications back into imaginary ones. Although neither realm is more 'estranged' than the other, the imaginary offers forms of identification that deny difference, estrangement, and the loss of symbiotic plenitude; they disavow their debt to the Other. The imaginary is thus a sort of estrangement from the 'inevitable estrangement' of the Symbolic (Weber, 1991, p. 106). There is a perpetual 'oscillation of the subject' between ideal egos and ego ideals (Lagache, 1961, p. 41).

My suggestion is that the sense of embodied "ideal unity" that is expressed in bodily "habitus" is generated in the realm of the Imaginary and imaginary identifications. Bourdieu alludes to this when he writes that "habitus of necessity operates as a *defence mechanism* against necessity" (2000, pp. 232–233). This comes very close to the psychoanalytic ideas of fantasy and the ideal-ego. But this also explains why a "cleft" habitus is just as likely as a unified one. Habitus is an ideological effect that is threatened by the Real and the Symbolic. The Imaginary is forever overcoded by the Symbolic, which pushes against integration and toward fragmentation and difference. All of this is haunted by the repressed memory of the "body in pieces."

'Why, in short, such *resistance* to analysis?' (Bourdieu, 1996a, p. xvii)

I have been more interested in sketching a possible reconstruction of Bourdieu than in analyzing the reasons for his defensive relationship to Lacan, an avoidance that I have argued was somewhat damaging to his theory. Lacan's combination of "nobility," his externality to the academic field, and his disregard for rational scientific discourse were obviously distasteful to Bourdieu. A deeper reason, however, can be found in Bourdieu's statement that "*Sociology does not claim to substitute its mode of explanation for that of psychoanalysis*; it is concerned only to construct differently certain givens that psychoanalysis also takes as its object" (1999, p. 512, my emphasis). If Bourdieu had explored this relationship in more depth he might have seen that they were not alternatives, but that psychoanalysis filled some of the lacunae in his own theoretical approach. His sociology did not so much construct the same object in a different manner as to construct it inadequately. Bourdieu's signal contributions, including the concepts of habitus, symbolic capital, and field, can profit from further interaction with psychoanalytic theories of the imaginary integration of bodily imagery and symbolic recognition and misrecognition.

Notes

1. Elias, whose *Civilizing Process* is a sociological version of *Civilization and its Discontents* and is perhaps "the most Freudian of sociologists" (Lahire, 2013).

Elias was one of the co-founders of the Group-Analytic Society in London, together with S. J. Fuchs (later Foulkes) of the Frankfurt Psychoanalytic Institute, and Freud was one of the first persons to whom Elias sent a copy of *Über den Prozeß der Zivilisation* in 1938 (Waldhoof, 2007, p. 329). Many versions of an essay on Freud that Elias reworked countless times can be consulted in the German Literature Archive in Marbach.
2. It is important to recognize in this context that Bourdieu is far from the ahistorical "reproduction theorist" he is sometimes made out to be. Both social reproduction *and* social change, constraint *and* freedom, are at the core of Bourdieu's project. See Steinmetz (2011). The same is true of Freud, for whom two individuals confronted by the same Oedipal drama may make very different sense of it, even if the Oedipal constellation is universal.
3. The phrase "community of the unconscious" is my translation of "une communauté des inconscients" (2004c, p. 19) and "*eine Gemeinschaft von Unbewußten*" in the German version, *Ein soziologischer Selbstversuch* (2002).
4. Fourny and Emery (2000) also notes the uneasy status of psychoanalysis in Bourdieu's work but suggests that a more systematic reception of Lacan would threaten Bourdieu's approach, while I argue the opposite.
5. I have developed the idea of unsettled and settled fields in various places, starting with Steinmetz (2002).
6. Freud (1955) already recognized that identifications need not involve explicitly erotic cathexes.

References

Althusser, L. (1971) *Lenin and Philosophy* (New York: Monthly Review Press).
Bastide, R. (1950) *Sociologie et Psychanalyse* (Paris: PUF).
Bourdieu, P. (1999 [1977]) *Outline of a Theory of Practice* (Cambridge: Cambridge University Press).
Bourdieu, P. (1986a) "L'illusion Biographique," *Actes de la Recherche en Sciences Sociales*, 62/63, 69–72.
Bourdieu, P. (1986) "The Forms of Capital" in J. C. Richardson (ed.) *Handbook of Theory and Research for the Sociology of Education* (Westport: Greenwood Press).
Bourdieu, P. (1990a) "La Domination Masculine," *Actes de la Recherche en Sciences Sociales*, 84 (September), 2–31.
Bourdieu, P. (1990b) "Social Space and Symbolic Power," *In Other Words* (Stanford: Stanford University Press).
Bourdieu, P. (1991) *Language and Symbolic Power* (Cambridge: Harvard University Press).
Bourdieu, P. (1994) "Avant-Propos Dialogué" in J. Maître, L'Autobiographie d'un Paranonoïaque: L'abbé Berry (1878–1947) *et le Roman de Billy Introïbo* (Paris: Anthropos).
Bourdieu, P. (1996a [1992]) *The Rules of Art: Genesis and Structure of the Literary Field* (Stanford: Stanford University Press).
Bourdieu, P. (1996b [1989]) *The State Nobility: Elite Schools in the Field of Power* (Stanford: Stanford University Press).
Bourdieu, P., Accardo, A., Balazas, G., Beaud S., Bonvin, F., Bourdieu, E., Bourgois, P., Broccolichi, S., Champagne, P., Christin, R., Faguer, J.-P., Garcia, S., Lenoir, R.,

Œuvrard, F., Pialoux, M., Pinto, L., Podalydés, D., Sayad, A., Soulié, C. and Wacquant Loïc J. D. (1999 [1977]) Outline of a Theory of Practice. (Cambridge: Cambridge University Press).
Bourdieu, P. (2000 [1997]) *Pascalian Meditations* (Stanford: Stanford University Press).
Bourdieu, P. (2001 [1998]) *Masculine Domination* (Paris: Seuil).
Bourdieu, P. (2001) *Masculine Domination.* Translated by Richard Nice (Stanford: Stanford University Press).
Bourdieu, P. (2004) *Esquisse pour une Auto-Analyse* (Paris: Raisons d'Agir).
Bourdieu, P. et al. (1999 [1993]) *The Weight of the World: Social Suffering in Contemporary Society* (Stanford: Stanford University Press).
Bryson, N. (1994) "Géricault and 'Masculinity'," in N. Bryson, M. A. Holly, and K. Moxey (eds) *Visual Culture: Images and Interpretation* (Hanover: University Press of New England), pp. 228–258.
Butler, J. (1997) *The Psychic Life of Power* (Stanford: Stanford University Press).
Calhoun, C. (1993). "Social Theory as Habitus." In C. Calhoun, E. Li Puma, M. Postone (eds.) Bourdieu: Critical Perspectives (Chicago: University of Chicago Press).
Calhoun, C. J. (1993) "Habitus, Field, and Capital: The Question of Historical Specificity," in C. Calhoun, E. LiPuma, and M. Postone (eds) *Bourdieu: Critical Perspectives* (Chicago: University of Chicago Press) pp. 61–88.
Dampierre, E. de (1956) "Malvire-sur-Desle. Une commune aux franges de la region parisienne." *L'information geographique,* 20: 68–73.
Desan, M. H. (2013) "Bourdieu, Marx, and Capital: A Critique of the Extension Model." *Sociological Theory,* 31: 318–342.
Elliott, A. (2004) *Social Theory since Freud: Traversing Social Imaginaries* (London: Routledge).
Fourny, J. and M. Emery (2000) "Bourdieu's Uneasy Psychoanalysis," *Substance,* 29, 103–112.
Freud, S. (1953) "Family Romances," in J. Strachey (ed.) *The Standard Edition of the Complete Psychological Works of Sigmund Freud.* Vol. 9 (London: Hogarth).
Freud, S. (1955) "Group Psychology and the Analysis of the Ego" in J. Strachey (ed.) *The Standard Edition Of the Complete Psychological Works of Sigmund Freud,* Vol. 18 (London: Hogarth).
Freud, S. ([1923] 1961) "Negation," in J. Strachey (ed.) *The Standard Edition Of the Complete Psychological Works of Sigmund Freud,* Vol. 19 (London: Hogarth Press).
Freud, S. (1962) *The Ego and the Id* (London: Hogarth Press and the Institute of Psycho-Analysis).
Fromm, E. (1989) "Psychoanalysis and Sociology," in S. E. Bronner and D. M. Kellner (eds.) *Critical Theory and Society. A Reader* (New York and London: Routledge).
de Gaulejac, V. (1987) *La Névrose de Classe* (Paris: Hommes et groups).
de Gaulejac, V. (1996) *Les Sources de la Honte* (Paris: Desclée de Brouwer).
de Gaulejac, V. (1999) *L'Histoire en Heritage. Roman Familial et Trajectoire Sociale* (Paris: Desclée de Brouvier).
de Gaulejac, V. (2004) "De l'inconscient chez Freud à l'inconscient selon Bourdieu: Entre Psychanalyse et Socio-analyse," in P. Corcuff (ed.) *Pierre Bourdieu: les Champs de la Critique* (Paris: Bibliothèque Centre Pompidou).
Ginsberg, M. (1947) "Psychoanalysis and Sociology," *Politics and Letters,* 2–3, 74–83.

Hegel, G. W. H. (1967) *Phenomenology of Mind*, J. B. Baille (trans.) (New York: Harper).

Hegel, G. W. H. (1983) "Jena Lectures on the Philosophy of the Spirit," in Leo Rauch (ed.) *Hegel and the Human Spirit: A Translation of the Jena Lectures on the Philosophy of Spirit (1805–1806) with commentary* (Detroit: Wayne State University Press).

Julien, P. (1994) *Jacques Lacan's Return to Freud. The Real, the Symbolic, and the Imaginary* (New York: NYU Press).

Kojève, A. (1969) *Introduction to the Reading of Hegel* (New York: Cornell University Press).

Kolnai, A. (1921) *Psychoanalyse und Soziologie. Zur Psychologie von Masse und Gesellschaft* (Leipzig: Internationaler Psychoanalytischer Verlag).

Lacan, J. (1988) *The Seminar of Jacques Lacan Book I. Freud's Papers on Technique 1953–1954* (New York: Norton).

Lagache, D. (1961) "La Psychanalyse et la Structure de la Personnalité," *La Psychanalyse*, 6, 5–58.

Lapassade, G. (1975) *Socianalyse et potentiel humain* (Paris: Gauthiers-Villars).

Lahire, B. (2013) "Norbert Elias and Social Theory," in F. Dépelteau and T. S. Landini (eds), *Norbert Elias and Social Theory* (Houndmills, Basingstoke: Palgrave).

Maître, J. (2000) *Anorexies Religieuses, Anorexie Mentale: Essai de Psychanalyse Sociohistorique : De Marie de l'Incarnation à Simone Weil* (Paris: Cerf).

Maître, J. (1994) *L'Autobiographie d'un Paranoïaque: L'Abbé Berry (1878–1947) et le Roman de Billy Introïbo* (Paris: Anthropos).

Mead, G. (2013) "Sense of Structure and Structure of Sense: Pierre Bourdieu's Habitus As a Generative Principle," PhD thesis, School of Social and Political Sciences, The University of Melbourne.

Roudinesco, E. (1990) *Lacan & Co.: A History of Psychoanalysis in France, 1925–1985* (Chicago: University of Chicago Press).

Silverman, K. (1988) *The Acoustic Mirror: The Female Voice in Psychoanalysis and Cinema* (Bloomington: Indiana University Press).

Steinmetz, G. (2002) "Precoloniality and Colonial Subjectivity: Ethnographic Discourse and Native Policy in German Overseas Imperialism, 1780s-1914," *Political Power and Social Theory*, 15, 135–228.

Steinmetz, G. (2008) "The Colonial State as a Social Field." *American Sociological Review* 73, pp. 589–612.

Steinmetz, G. (2009) "How Bourdieu's theory of symbolic capital might be more fruitfully utilized to study global inequality." Conference on "The Cultural Wealth of Nations," at the University of Michigan, March 27–28.

Steinmetz, G. (2011) "Bourdieu, Historicity, and Historical Sociology," *Cultural Sociology*, 11 (1), 45–66.

Waldhof, H. P. (2007) "Unthinking the Closed Personality: Norbert Elias, Group Analysis and Unconscious Processes in a Research Group: Part I," *Group Analysis*, 40, 323–343.

Weber, S. (1991) *Return to Freud. Jacques Lacan's Dislocation of Psychoanalysis* (Cambridge: Cambridge University Press).

Witz, A. (2004) "Anamnesis and Amnesis in Bourdieu's Work: The Case for a Feminist Anamnesis," *Sociological Review*, 52, 211–223.

Žižek, S. (1989) *The Sublime Object of Ideology* (London: Verso).

Žižek, S. (1997) *The Plague of Fantasies* (London: Verso).

10
The Ethnographic Spiral: Reflections on the Intersection of Life History and Ideal-Typical Analysis

Philip Manning

Introduction

Following Gananath Obeyesekere, himself following Max Weber, this essay argues that ethnographers do not really study social worlds or even social groups. Instead, they move back and forth between abstract models and life histories: according to Obeyesekere, ". . . my thoughts are conditioned by the data that I deal with, as the data themselves are conditioned by my abstractions." (Obeyesekere, 1990, p. 3) Sometimes, ethnographers present abstract information. But at other times, when gathering life histories of their informants, ethnographers are immersed in the empirical details of "who," "what," "why", and "when." In this life historical phase, the ethnographer studies what can be, in a sense, photographed; ethnography, then, has a narrative as events are structured through time. Also, when gathering life histories, ethnographers are very aware of motivational issues: why did someone choose this course of action, not another? Life historical research is then, by its character, akin to psychoanalytic investigation.

By definition and contrast, ethnographers also develop abstract models, typologies, classifications, and ideal types as they resolve the messiness of their actual research sites and describe structural rather than actual situations observed. Then, too, they describe types of people rather than actual informants. At this analytic rather than experiential moment, the world they describe cannot be photographed; there is no image to be captured. Instead, they identify general features of a situation or they characterize a type of person in that situation. The ethnographer thinks this abstract information pertains to the elements of group life or to the social world of the group. But, at this point, ethnographers are actually a long way from a narrative, motive-oriented, and arguably psychoanalytic view of the world. It is a stage when ideal types, composite models, can be used at a later date to make sense of specific events. The ethnographer's ideal types are therefore measuring rods of sorts through which they see the world.

I call this back-and-forth process between the psychoanalytically kindred level of the "life world" and the making of sociological generalizations an "ethnographic spiral." It is a spiral through which ethnographers initially organize their many inchoate observations of informants into ordered categories before returning, later, to the field to see whether new or existing life histories confirm, or contradict, these categories. The interweaving of the ethnographer's categories with his or her life-historical investigations is the art of the ethnographic enterprise.

Motives and utilities

Any social scientific project that does not contain narrative and motive will appear "flat" and out of time. Insofar as ethnographers need models as measuring rods, an ethnographic moment when the messiness of fieldwork is cleaned up and made manageable through classifications is bound to happen. Thus, as this essay later discusses, Elijah Anderson initially presented two models of "decent" and "street" families in confronting the messiness of family organization in poor Philadelphia neighborhoods. Simultaneously, he understood that neither ideal type actually described any particular family. Nonetheless, ideal types are useful conceptual tools for thinking about the particular families Anderson introduces in the course of his *Code of the Street* research (1999).

Once we switch back from model to life history, though, ethnographers need to consider motivation. Giddens (1984) has developed an interesting way to think about this by characterizing most of our experiences as "routinized and predictable." As he suggests, we live our day-to-day lives walking down well-trodden tracks; events unfold more or less as we expect. This process happens, for example, when someone returns from a trip to the shopping mall and reports "nothing happened": much happened, of course, in many ways and with varying consequences, but the person is correct in the sense of the trip having been like many others (so that nothing newsworthy stands out).

What produces routinization and predictability, though? By definition, the former requires regular repetition such that actions can be carried out on something like autopilot. We brush our teeth, drive to work, exchange pleasantries with little thought, as long as the day is itself just another day. Predictability is related to routinization but involves an additional step. We find our world predictable precisely because things happen as they did yesterday, and the day before that, but also in part because the motivations of people around us can be identified and understood.

Rival social sciences explore these motivations through their own distinctive vocabularies. Thus, for economists, motivations are utilities expected to be maximized although the risk averse might "satisfice." Knowing what someone wants becomes a way of making that person's behavior, again, understandable and predictable. This might entail something more complicated than the preference ordering of a payoff matrix (as in the prisoners' dilemma, an ultimatum game or many other ingenious if artificial economic thought experiments). Instead, some economists suggest the utility that is either maximized or satisficed might be identity itself (Akerloff and Kranton, 2010). Some economists have also wondered about a person's conscious recognition of these identity utilities, and of other utilities as well. Here, they have had to confront psychoanalytic concerns: for example, the economist George Ainslie attempted to present Freud's structural model so as to be compatible with mainstream economic theory.

Sociologists have their own theories of motivation. Those influenced by Weber (2002), Parsons (1951, 1964, 1975), and Blumer (1969, 1975) tend to assume that motivations are derived from norms. Following Elster (1989), norms are understood as "concrete guides to action" that specify what people should do in given circumstances. Elster believes the formula "in these circumstances do X" is a good test for a norm's presence: a norm is present only if the person can give a content to the "X." Thus, some sociologists believe people are motivated to follow norms either because they know what is expected of them or because they internalized and hence identify with the norms themselves (in Freud's term, they have introjected them). For instance, tipping in restaurants (even ones to which we will never return) is a routinized and predictable normative behavior both because we know it is expected of us and because we want to be the kinds of people who leave tips in restaurants.

Similar across economists and sociologists is that both use external indicators (utilities or norms, respectively) to understand motivations that make the world routine and predictable. Here, an example emerges from Weber's *The Protestant Ethic and the Spirit of Capitalism* (2002): Weber claimed sixteenth and seventeenth century Calvinists were motivated to work hard at their callings to assuage fears about salvation; in turn, this understanding of motivation predicted Calvinists' general behavior.

In Weber's example, motivations began as the possessions of individuals only to be averaged out among like-minded group members. Is this an example of the ecological fallacy? This is when a claim about an individual is based on what we know about a group. We can contrast statisticians who have no knowledge of the individuals in their sample but know something in general about a group, with ethnographers who have no knowledge of the group but know something (possibly a great deal) about their individual informants. Ethnographers strive to understand what motivates informants in the hope that these motivations are shared by others. Is it enough for them then to report simply this? Or do they need to make additional extrapolations of the kind Weber undertook?

Reading ethnographies

> The anthropologist never has a chance of sampling a range of native opinions, though ethnographies are peppered with pronouncements indicating that this is indeed the case [. . .]. In reality the anthropologist works with select or key informants who for the most part make themselves available to the investigator. An 'emic' perspective in this situation? The classic monographs that claim to present the natives' point of view in fact have constructed ideal types of X or Y culture, based on a point of view, taken implicitly or explicitly, by the ethnographer. (Obeyesekere, 1990, p. 220)

Ethnographies teach us about cultures and/or groups but, to do so, they report on the actions and motivations of individuals. Of course, we cannot see cultures and groups, only individuals. Many ethnographies begin by describing a key informant, a gatekeeper, who guided his or her ethnographer through the intricacies of group life. This gatekeeper is part teacher, part representative specimen even though, in practice, s/he may turn to be less a teacher than propaganda expert with an agenda to pursue. The gatekeeper may also turn out to represent no one other than himself, or herself. Duneier's view of this issue is noteworthy. When commenting on his own fine ethnography *Sidewalk* (1999), he acknowledged that individuals figure in his ethnography as representatives of certain positions or attitudes. Duneier emphasized that the people he described had more complicated views and motivations, though, than he credited them with publicly; yet some degree of simplification was necessary to evoke the cultural context overall. This is exemplified in Duneier's NSF documentary when he mentions how Andrew Manshel—a lawyer representing the interests of local business owners, and portrayed in *Sidewalk* as antagonistic to the homeless street vendors on whom his ethnography focuses—was actually a very sensitive man, and one of the few people who took time to get to know the vendors themselves.

As stated at the outset, I propose ethnographers should make use of an "ethnographic spiral": again, this can be defined as ethnographers confronting the messiness of their social worlds by imposing an order on their data, an imposed order which has both the practical advantage of clarity and the limitation of over-simplification, as Max Weber knew and depicted well in his (1913) discussion of the ideal-type. Ethnographers are well served to challenge their own ideal-typical formulations by "spiraling back" to their field of inquiry to measure ideal-typical formulations against the observable behaviors and motivations of key informants, as in this essay's later analysis of Elijah Anderson's *Code of the Street* (1999).

After introducing key informants, ethnographies gradually often erase them. This involves refocusing from individuals to social practices, recurrent behaviors, trajectories, and so on, which in turn involves removing narrative (though, sometimes, the illusion of narrative remains). Erving Goffman's *Asylums* (1961) exemplifies this point: in one sense, Goffman clearly separates his ethnography from the individuals he observed at St. Elizabeth's Hospital in Washington D.C. in the 1950s. No key informants are introduced or even mentioned, and there is not a whiff of a gatekeeper influencing or aiding his famous analysis of total institutional life. However, it is also the case that in *Asylums*, Goffman presented an overall career model for patients at St. Elizabeth's as well as at total institutions generally. He identified a trajectory for new inmates, and outlined three stages of total institutional life. Each of these stages showed inmates responding rationally to institutional pressures and, insofar as this was the case, inmates maximized their utilities under normative constraints. *Asylums* therefore presents an ideal-typical narrative. Indeed, it is ideal-typical in exactly the way Weber anticipated: not a description of anyone or anything in particular but a composite of similar cases. Goffman's ethnography therefore exists in the ideal-typical nowhere world: it is not a description of St. Elizabeth's or of any other specific total institution, nor does it account for why particular inmates acted in certain ways.

Goffman, like other ethnographers, gathered detailed observations over an extended period of time to produce generalized descriptions. The widely perceived "flatness" of *Asylums* is arguably a consequence of his decision to provide only generalized descriptions. His ethnography contains almost no descriptions of actually occurring events or of patients, staff, or physicians Goffman actually met. The odd exceptions are nearly all vignettes from his field notes that make their way into *Asylums* as footnotes. In brief, then, Goffman's own ideal-typical formulations are protected from the messiness of day-to-day life at St. Elizabeth's. As a result, sociologists often read *Asylums* not as an ethnography of a hospital but as a contribution to social theory. Elsewhere I have suggested that, in *Asylums*, Goffman combined an ethnographic study of St. Elizabeth's with an ethnography of the concept of the total institution (Manning, 1992, 2005). Perhaps it is worth adding that both Goffman and his readers have tended to emphasize the latter project at the expense of the former.

Elijah Anderson's *Code of the Street* (1999) provides an excellent test case of what I call the ethnographic spiral. The ethnography extends his earlier study *Streetwise* (1990), and explores conceptions of decency as well as threats of violence in Philadelphia neighborhoods. After describing the urban layout of Philadelphia, Anderson drew a contrast between "decent" and "street" families and introduces the reader to the city's street life. His introduction to the project is a concrete, realistic description of the physical and social organization of Philadelphia through a journey down Germantown Avenue where the reader encounters both gentrified and drug-ridden neighborhoods. Given his intentions, and that others have taken this step, it is surprising that Anderson did not include photographs in this chapter: two examples are, again, Duneier who recently made extensive use of professionally taken photographs to add clarity and confirmation to his ethnography of New York's homeless, and Loic Wacquant, whose writing about the role of boxing clubs in poor neighborhoods in Chicago used photographic evidence for an analogous purpose (Wacquant, 2004). Indeed, Wacquant made full use of dismal images of urban decay to bring alive the plight of people in his study.

For my purposes here, though, the issue is not whether photographs add significantly to ethnographic validity but the path Anderson wove between concrete observation and the conceptual categories of "street" and "decent" families (1999, p. 35). This key component of Anderson's argument does not rest on specific observations of this street family and this decent family. Rather Anderson developed a Weberian composite, an ideal-typical construction of the constitutive features of these two family types—and, as such, Anderson's argument is "utopian" in the etymological sense of "existing nowhere." He is not describing actual families and so could not, for example, photograph them. The family structures he describes are models or tendencies.

According to Anderson (1999, pp. 35–65), a decent family is a composite of the following three constitutive features: they are future-oriented and optimistic; accept mainstream and religious values; and accord importance to hard work and sacrifice, especially for their children. By contrast, a street family has the following two broad elements: family members are inconsiderate to strangers and there is a weak sense of family and community; and family members are committed to the code of the street that endorses normative uses of violence, or at least the threat of violence.

Since these ideal types are not descriptions of actual families, later case studies may reveal that in practice families may incorporate elements from both, either permanently or intermittently. Particular families may also "code-switch" in that they recognize that on certain occasions they should embody the role of either a decent or street family. Anderson emphasized that just about all inner city residents recognize that the threat of violence is used as a means to enhance self-image and that an unwillingness to at least threaten violence in settings widely perceived to be appropriate will be understood as displays of weakness.

Anderson was able to construct these ideal types of family organization because he had observed many actual family members' lives in inner city "Philly" neighborhoods. But, ironically, the sociological product from these observations is no longer an observation itself. Certainly it is not comparable to a photograph of a social world nor is it straightforwardly descriptive, as was the opening to *Code of the Street*. Instead, to present a clear account of the underlying structure of family organization Anderson, as Weber recognized a hundred years ago, had to "peel away" the empirical content of the case studies from which his ideal types had been developed.

Without the conceptual clarity afforded by Anderson's ideal-typical formulation, *Code of the Street* would read as simply the stories of the trials, tribulations, and sometimes successes of the many people he encountered in the course of his research. It would be reminiscent of the task facing the reader of Thomas and Znaniecki's *The Polish Peasant* ([1917] 1958), in which we are confronted with hundreds of verbatim letters between young Polish men living in Chicago and their families back home. Each letter offers its own fascination, but the sensation of reading them together is akin to drowning.

The challenge for Anderson is that ideal-typical clarification is not in and of itself ethnography. As Weber understood, it is a tool for analysis rather than analysis itself. The next step is to explore ethnographically, through detailed observations and interviews, the extent to which particular people living their lives adhere to or deviate from the constitutive features of the sociologist's ideal types. This is the ethnographic spiral displayed so well in *Code of the Street* as Anderson integrates case studies and ideal-typical formulations. While this strategy is built into every chapter as we encounter "decent daddies" and inner city grandmothers, it comes into sharpest relief in the lengthy, revealing case study of "John Turner."

Empirical fog: The case study of John Turner

I use Anderson's case study of John Turner (1999, pp. 237–289) to highlight the complexity of empirical examples. It would be simplistic and misleading to say that the John Turner case contradicts or disproves Anderson's earlier analysis, even though Turner does not readily fit into any of the ideal types or typologies the ethnography develops earlier. Rather, let us say that Anderson should be judged by the extent his ideal types illuminate the discrepancies between life histories and his theoretical model.

John Turner was an important informant for Anderson but not one he sought out. On the contrary, Turner approached Anderson at a local restaurant where Anderson was a regular customer and Turner had a job. Turner wanted Anderson's help to resolve a recent run-in with the police. How he knew that Anderson might be able to help him, or even what he knew about Anderson, was never clarified. I doubt John Turner knew that Anderson was a sociologist studying urban neighborhoods ethnographically, but he did realize Anderson was highly respected and well connected. Turner wanted practical, not clinical, help and Anderson for him was a get-out-of-jail free card.

Anderson described Turner as a 21-year-old high school graduate, a former athlete with a muscular physique: 5'9', 165 pounds. He wore fashionable designer clothes. When they first met, he was the father to four children by three different women. He later fathered two more children by a fourth woman. He lived at home with his mother, his 16-year-old epileptic brother and 17-year-old sister (1999, p. 238).

Initially, Turner wanted Anderson to help him get out of trouble with the police, who had arrested him for carrying a gun with no permit. Turner told Anderson a complicated story that involved his concerns to protect then-girlfriend Audrey from neighborhood harassment. His self-presentation was a man guilty of naivety and an impetuous predisposition to help others in need. He was, he admitted, guilty as charged, but he had acted with the best of intentions.

Anderson decided to help Turner. In part, he did so because he saw it as the right thing to do and, in part, because Turner was a case study and life history. Over an unclear period of time, Anderson acted on Turner's behalf, finding him a lawyer willing to work pro bono, work, and lending him money. He pleaded his case in front of a judge and a probation officer. Anderson appears to have understood Turner as a young man struggling to make good on his life and his commitments, and someone who could be naïve, thin-skinned and a victim of racial discrimination. Anderson also understood that Turner could be impulsive and unwilling to think through the consequences of his decisions.

After losing contact for about a year, Anderson discovered another side to Turner. Viewed in this new light, Turner was a prominent drug dealer, a skilled liar, and clever manipulator. Anderson reports being shocked by this news, even though he knew it was plausible (1999, p. 264). Following this revelation, the tone of the discussion changed and Turner appears less manipulative and more forthcoming. He described the pharmacological draw of crack cocaine as well as its economic benefits, sometimes upwards of $1500 a night. The description of these grand paydays was a prelude to a request: Turner wanted Anderson to lend him $5. How the mighty had fallen.

At this point, Anderson was still trying to restore Turner to the world of the decent family by finding him a regular job. Soon, however, Anderson realized it was useless. After Turner quit his latest job, he asked Anderson for $150. This was, in reality, a severance payment and both men seemed to understand it would never be repaid nor would they ever meet again. This proved true though Anderson was told Turner had been shot, perhaps in a drug-related incident in Baltimore.

Anderson claimed he had a "rather complete picture" of Turner, and that there was little more to learn. Understandably, he was also "uneasy" about the risks involved in his relationship with a once prominent drug dealer (1999, p. 285). In his concluding comments on this case study, Anderson transformed John Turner back into an ideal type of the alienated male, drawn to the hip allure of the street and unable to benefit from meaningful employment and the wise counsel of an "old head" (1999, pp. 285–289).

But this essay's point here is that perhaps Anderson missed an opportunity. By the time he had severed contact with Turner, a threshold had been reached; Turner no longer had much to gain from Anderson and had little reason to lie or rationalize. Whatever hope Anderson once had of saving a misunderstood youth was long gone. There was no longer a Good Samaritan role for Anderson to play since he knew Turner was not going to be saved by him or anyone else. However, could not an ethnographer in such a case also seek to explore key informants' complex "psychosocial" motivations? As Prager (1998) has demonstrated, sociologists can investigate the world with a degree of psychoanalytic sophistication but this has to include readiness to confront counter-transferential tensions that regularly follow. As just mentioned, Anderson already felt uneasy around John Turner and prolonged exposure, coupled with inevitably unpleasant discoveries likely to follow, posed an additional burden (see also Chodorow, 1999; Manning, 2005, 2009).

Conclusions

Whenever sociologists and ethnographers write about specific people encountered in their research, they are drawn into debates about life histories and motivation. They also present ideal types linked to normative and social structural aspects of their analyses which, as with Goffman's research on *Asylums*, can render their ethnographies oddly flat, even shallow and simplistic. In frustration, sociologists and ethnographers might be tempted to abandon their ideal-typical formulations all together. However, this would be a mistake as they remain valuable tools even if they are in and of themselves inadequate.

With this, let us segue back to Freud whose later structural model portrays a person's ego battling to reconcile the competing demands from the id for instant gratification with the super-ego's conscience and desire to adapt to external demands. For sociologists, this is not too far from Mead's (social) behaviorism (1962), as Mead himself realized. Mead portrays the self as the site of an internal conversation between the "Me" who is very aware of the "attitude of the generalized other" (that is, roughly, community standards) and the "I" who resists and reflects upon these external demands. Mead was aware that the group and its members were usually not as tight as had often been assumed, meaning that internalization was not a straightforward process. As he reasoned, people belong to multiple groups simultaneously and therefore possessed one "I" but more than one "Me" (Mead, 1962, pp. 142–143). Indirectly, Mead's "multiple selves thesis" suggests it may be difficult to use a group member as a guide to the group because he or she is likely to have competing commitments to other groups.

Mead's speculation about its being common for each of us to possess more than one "Me" suggests our intuitions about how ethnography works is right some of the time but also often misses the mark: indeed, few of us are tightly connected to only one group. Instead we choose and are able to "float" between them. Since competing meanings and norms are common, both Mead's and Freud's versions of inner conversations are weakened. And, as a result, ethnographers who gather life histories may better record weaker ties between the group and group member, but at the expense of generalizations. The clinical roots of psychoanalysis mean that its primary unit of analysis is the case study and so this "revelation" is consistent with its established practice. For symbolic interactionists and most qualitative sociologists, though, the "revelation" that each group member may have a personal, complicated web of internalizations drawn from different and sometimes competing group memberships, seems to undermine their research endeavor entirely.

Here, it is worth revisiting the life history of John Turner in light of both Freud and Mead. Using Mead's vocabulary, we can speculate that Turner was torn between competing "Me" identities and competing sets of internalized norms. From a psychoanalytic perspective, John Turner's life experiences had brewed up a powerful concoction of competing energies, fears, transferences, and norms. The result was the convoluted narrative that Anderson guided us through. This potent brew was also, tragically, the cause of Turner's undoing.

Many sociologists will be tempted to "explain" Turner's behavior dramaturgically rather than psychoanalytically. Understood as an example of dramaturgy, Turner is an actor who is cynically trying to manipulate everyone around him. He is an "operator" who will con anyone and connive his way out of many disasters, all of his own making. The dramaturgical task for the ethnographer is to see through Turner's presentations of self to another man behind the mask who is a mid-level drug dealer. Viewed this way, it looks like Turner got one over on Anderson. Dramaturgically, then, the person is a set of public performances and a hidden manipulator.

On the other hand, this view of the self is rationalistic and calculating: it lacks psychoanalytic nuance. I doubt Turner was simply lying to Anderson as did, for example, Agnes in Garfinkel's (1967) famous life history (of sorts). Rather, and more in line with a Freudian interpretation, it may not be surprising that Turner was capable of interpreting events—and himself—in radically different ways, at different times, with different audiences, and when facing very different kinds of pressures. Perhaps the psychoanalytic term "splitting" is a useful and complementary way of capturing Turner's life history so as to balance the dramaturgical focus on hidden manipulations.

In the second of his five lectures on psychoanalysis (1909), Freud suggested that splitting involves the dynamic conflict of opposing forces that are "actively struggling" against each other (SE Vol. XI, p. 26). The concept of splitting is part of Freud's earlier "topographic" thinking, and was present in his writings (in collaboration with Joseph Breuer) on hysteria. At this point, Freud accorded a greater role to hard-to-access unconscious memories than in his later structural writings. Of course Turner was aware that his different performances were inconsistent: thus, it cannot be said he was consciously acting in one way at one time and unconsciously acting differently at another. But perhaps Turner was able to believe some or all of a story as he was telling it, even if he also knew there was more than one story to tell.

If we only judge Anderson by his ideal-typical framework, we will likely be disappointed in Turner's story. But the strength of Anderson's analysis is that it facilitates a more nuanced reading of Turner's life history since the task of composing this life history can be separated from—even though it is also related to—ideal-typical forms of analyses. At the level of life histories, though, both Mead and Freud in different but complementary ways show us how ethnographers can achieve more complex readings.

This essay depicts how ethnographers move back and forth between their ideal types and their informants, between the abstract and un-photographable and the concrete image. Anderson addresses this interplay in his well-known response to Wacquant's critique of *Code of the Street*. Anderson claimed that Wacquant had a "theoretical" axe to grind that led him to misread his ethnography (2002, p. 1533). According to Anderson, Wacquant was predisposed to certain ideas because of his pre-commitment to the ideas of his mentor, Pierre Bourdieu. Instead, Anderson saw his own work as "more inductive" (2002, p. 1536) and concluded his rebuttal with the following summation: "I try to write about the ghetto poor in a way that is *faithful to their understanding of themselves*. I know full well that this is impossible to achieve completely, but it is a worthy goal toward which to strive" (2002, p. 1549, emphasis in original).

Perhaps everything this paper is trying to clarify is connected to the understanding of Anderson's attempt to rebut Wacquant. In this passage Anderson uses qualifiers to emphasize that the attempt cannot fully succeed: he is at pains to say he "tried" to write, that it is a worthy goal, but that it is not possible to remain faithful to the understanding the ghetto poor have of themselves. I want to stress that Anderson's reference to the "ghetto poor" is itself an ideal type, illustrating the inescapability of conflict between sociological concepts and the lived experiences of men and women to whom the concepts applied. This leaves the following question, at once sociological and psychologically attuned: can ethnographers tell the story of either a group or ideal type (the ghetto poor) or even of an informant (like John Turner) without recourse to their own sociological understandings of the world as well as their own psychic feelings and dispositions? If not, what does it mean to claim faithfulness to the understanding the ghetto poor have of themselves?

The John Turner case study demonstrates that the "ghetto poor" is an ideal type, comparable to the street or decent family, which remains a valuable analytical construct. However, a fog confusing to even as talented an ethnographer as Anderson still surrounds John Turner's actions and motivations. To unravel this complexity necessitates a combination of insights from Weberian-inspired sociology, social behaviorism a la Mead and Goffman, and a psychoanalytically attuned awareness of internal tensions, defenses, energies, denials, and transferences which often surface both in an informant and in the sociological and ethnographic enterprise overall.

References

Akerlof, G. and Kranton, R. (2010) *Identity Economics: How Our Identities Shape Our Work, Wages, and Well-Being* (Princeton: Princeton University Press).

Anderson, E. (1990) *Streetwise: Race, Class and Change in an Urban Community* (Chicago: University of Chicago Press).

Anderson, E. (1999) *The Code of the Street: Decency, Violence and the Moral Life of the Inner City* (New York: W.W. Norton & Company).

Anderson, E. (2002) "The Ideologically Driven Critique," *American Journal of Sociology*, 107 (6), 1533–1550.

Blumer, H. (1969) *Symbolic Interactionism* (California: University of California Press).

Blumer, H. (1975) "Exchange on Turner, 'Parsons as a Symbolic Interactionist,'" *Sociological Inquiry*, 45 (1), 59–68.

Chodorow, N. (1999) *The Power of Feelings* (New Haven: Yale University Press).

Duneier, M. (1992) *Sidewalk* (New York: Farrar, Straus and Giroux).

Elster, J. (1989) *Nuts and Bolts* (Cambridge: Cambridge University Press).

Freud, S. (1966) *The Standard Edition of the Complete Psychological Works of Sigmund Freud*, J. Strachey et al. (eds), 24 Volumes (London: Hogarth Press).

Giddens , A. (1984) *The Constitution of Society* (Cambridge: Polity).

Goffman, E. (1961) *Asylums* (Harmondsworth: Penguin).

Manning P. (1992) *Erving Goffman and Modern Sociology* (Stanford: Stanford University Press).

Manning, P. (2005) *Freud and American Sociology* (Cambridge: Polity Press).

Manning, P. (2009) "Three Models of Ethnography," *Theory and Psychology*, 19 (6), 1–22.

Obeyesekere, G. (1990) *The Work of Culture* (Chicago: University of Chicago Press).

Parsons, T. (1951) *The Social System* (New York: The Free Press).

Parsons, T. (1964) *Social Structure and Personality* (New York: The Free Press).

Parsons, T. (1975) "Exchange on Turner, 'Parsons as a Symbolic Interactionist,'" *Sociological Inquiry*, 45 (1), 59–68.

Prager J. (1998) *Presenting the Past: Psychoanalysis and the Sociology of Remembering* (Boston: Harvard University Press).

Thomas, W. and F. Znaniecki ([1917] 1958) *The Polish Peasant in Europe and America* (New York: Dover Publications).

Wacquant, L. (2002) 'Scrutinizing the Street: Poverty, Morality and the Pitfalls of Urban Ethnography', *American Journal of Sociology*, 107 (6), 1468–1532.

Wacquant, L. (2004) *Body & Soul: Notebooks of an Apprentice Boxer* (Oxford: Oxford University Press).

Weber, M. (2002) *The Protestant Ethic and the Sprit of Capitalism*, Stephen Kalberg (trans.) (Los Angeles: Roxbury Publishing Company).

Willis, P. (1977) *Learning to Labor* (New York: Columbia University Press).

Part IV
The Psychosocial (Analytic)
In Research and Practice

A. The Psychoanalytic Underpinnings of Subject (Object) Selection

11
Persona: Psychodynamic and Sociological Dimensions of a Project on US Activism and Political Violence

Gilda Zwerman

In 1985, I began a series of interviews with Judy Clark, a 1960s radical serving a 75-year to life prison sentence. Over three decades, the project evolved into a four-nation, longitudinal study of clandestine organizations, political violence, and New Left protest. This self-reflexive narrative essay revisits the study's psychodynamic origins, and illustrates how fantasy was a motivational force in selecting the research subject. It uses the psychoanalytic concept of "splitting" to explain how Clark and the cohort of women engaged in insurgency politics tried to balance the irreconcilable demands of their obligations as a revolutionary and their personal lives as wives, daughters, and mothers. It describes how processes of transference and counter-transference operated in building a transformative relationship between Clark and myself through which Clark began to address this "split" and nurture parts of a "new" self. Finally, the essay reveals how disciplinary pressures and incentives within academic sociology and, more specifically, in the field of social movement research, suppressed—but could not erase—the psychodynamic dimensions of the study.

Acting out

On October 20, 1981, a small racially mixed group of radicals led by the Black Liberation Army attempted to rob 1.6 million dollars at gun-point from a Brinks truck in Nyack, New York. When the action went awry, one Brinks guard and two police officers were killed. Two men and two women were apprehended while fleeing the scene. Several others escaped.

Of the four initial suspects, three—Kathy Boudin, David Gilbert, and Judy Clark—had been high-profile dissidents in the radical student and anti-Vietnam War movements of the 1960s. In 1969, they joined a small splinter group called the "Weathermen." While the mass movement receded, this faction redoubled their commitment to insurgency politics and turned to violence. The Weathermen's place in infamy was secured in 1970 when an attempt at bomb manufacturing went awry, killing three members and blowing to bits the New York City townhouse where they had been hiding. When the Weathermen disbanded in 1977, Judy Clark persisted. With others, she founded the May 19th Communist Organization, a group of white revolutionaries even smaller in size than the Weathermen and composed mainly of women who supported Third World guerrilla movements and US-based Black and Puerto Rican nationalist movements. Boudin and Gilbert remained underground, and maintained associations with this group.

For myself, as for some of my contemporaries living in New York—all veterans of the 60s turned professionals in the 80s—the Brinks defendants' crimes evoked intense responses. We were astonished to learn that members of the Weathermen and Black Liberation Army—an urban guerrilla group formed in 1971 after the Black Panther Party dissolved—had survived an entire decade. We were repulsed by the violence. We were outraged by their claims to have "expropriated" the Brinks money for the purpose of creating a "Republic of New Afrika" and to have killed two police officers and a guard in "self-defense."

Did the radicals actually believe that a separate nation, comprised of five former slave states in the South, was the solution to racism in America? In 1981? Or were their claims to building a black nation merely a cover-up for genuinely criminal motives? Even more intriguing were the motivations of the women participating in the action. The alliance between the black men—a cabal of radicals, Muslims, and ex-convicts—and the white women was fraught with confusing innuendo. Was ideological conviction the only connection between them? Had feminist criticisms of male-dominated, violent models of revolution completely missed these women?

"Brinks" remained in the headlines for months. During that time, my friends and I established a ritual. We met in a Greenwich Village cafe after work, sipped cappuccinos, read the dailies out loud, and tried to predict tomorrow's headline about which character in the Weather Underground or the BLA would be arrested next and which act of criminal incompetence would lead the FBI to their doorstep. It was difficult for those of us who had "known" the radicals to contain our sarcasm and disparaging comments. But beneath the outrage, Brinks had tapped into a well of anxiety not only about those who were "still at it," but about ourselves who weren't.

In ten short years—1971 to 1981—my peers' fevered commitment to radical social change had been replaced with not-so-passionate commitments to careers, kids, co-op purchases, therapy, and jogging. While many of us continued to participate in more moderate "new" social movements of the 1970s, activism was relegated to an increasingly peripheral zone in our lives. Certainly, no one believed that the re-emergence of Judy Clark and Kathy Boudin from the underground shouting "Free the Land!" offered a solution to the political dilemmas of the 1980s. But our response to the 80s—burying ourselves in work, domesticity, and work-outs at the gym—was not a solution either. Whereas the Brinks defendants had acted out their fantasy of revolution, we had succumbed to the risks and frustrations of radical protest. We had allowed our fantasies to be destroyed.

Along with my peers, I initially did not think too seriously about the relationship between them and us. Personally, I felt entitled to keep my distance. At the height of the 60s, I was a cautious player; I did not believe the revolution was around the corner, nor was I comfortable imposing my radical views on others. Under no circumstances could I have participated in the sessions of groupthink and the type of political frenzy requisite for committing a violent action, not in the 60s and certainly not in the 80s. Even wearing a political button or chanting at a demonstration made me feel tribal and simple-minded.

Moreover, I had compelling life obligations. In 1981, I had a dissertation to finish; the tenure clock for my teaching position was ticking; I was seeing a psychoanalyst three times a week; and, of course, there was a co-op to buy and miles to jog. I became the first to drop out of the ritual at the cafe. I left the day the headline read, "Brinks Hold-Up Opens Study of Terror Group Network." "That's just wonderful," I thought, "a new domestic security investigation led by the kingpins of political repression, Edwin Meese and Ronald Reagan." Now, I imagined, every progressive social movement in this country will be investigated for a possible link to terrorism: this was the Weathermen and company's final contribution to radical politics. At that moment, I really didn't give a damn what happened to them; I stopped paying attention to the case.

But in 1983, when Judge David Ritter pronounced his sentence on Judy Clark, something snapped. Media coverage was extensive, and reporters reviewed her path over the previous two years. Clark had participated in armed robbery and three men were dead. During legal proceedings, she showed no signs of remorse. She refused to stand when the Judge entered; she feigned sleep when the prosecutor spoke; she referred to the marshals assigned to accompany her from the jail to the courthouse as "fascist pigs"; and she ignored any reference to her as "defendant," insisting instead on "freedom-fighter." Two weeks before the trial opened, Clark and three others filed a pro se petition to act as their own counsel but did nothing to prepare a defense. During the voir dire, Clark used this privilege to question members of the jury pool, drawn from the small rural town of Goshen in upstate New York, about their opinions on John Brown and the armed slave rebellions of the nineteenth century. When the Judge cut her off, she demanded to leave. "I am an anti-imperialist freedom-fighter. The court representing the United States government has no right to try me." Clark continued this self-imposed absence through most of the trial, doing crossword puzzles and sit-ups on the floor of her cell in the basement of the court-house. Without defendants or defense attorneys, the trial proceeded swiftly. Judy Clark and two others were found guilty of all three counts of felony murder and six counts of armed robbery.

On the day of sentencing, October 6, 1983, Clark reappeared. One reporter described her as being "in a jovial mood." "(She) laughed and chatted casually with her co-defendants. (She) exchanged clenched fist salutes and calls of 'Free the Land' with friends in the courtroom" (Hanley, 1983). Before the sentence was pronounced, Clark was permitted to read a highly inflammatory statement bearing a close resemblance to Fidel Castro's "History shall absolve me" speech. When she was finished, the irate Judge expressed regret that the death penalty could not be imposed. Each defendant received three 25-year-to-life sentences to be served consecutively with no possibility of parole. In a final show of defiance, Clark waived her right to an appeal and vowed to continue the armed struggle behind bars.

A recounting of this scene was enough to hold anyone's attention. However buried beneath the description of Clark's theatrics was a detail about her life that was mentioned only in passing. Just eleven months before the Brinks robbery, Judy had given birth to a baby girl. Her daughter was now almost three years old. The image of this little girl going into a maximum security prison to visit her mother, a jovial anti-imperialist freedom-fighter, wrapped itself around some very painful experiences in my own past. While I couldn't imagine myself in Judy's place, I had no trouble identifying with that little girl.

Into the fantasy

When I was fourteen, my own mother was incarcerated, not in a state prison, but in a state mental hospital. Like Judy, she had an unusually strong identification with black people and their struggle for equality. Through the 1950s and early 1960s, she was an ardent integrationist. As the black movement turned militant, she tagged along. For a white woman supporting the emergent Black Power movement, risks were high. And, like Judy, she took more risks than necessary. Her behavior became increasingly bizarre. The proposals she suggested were outlandish. During meetings, the black militants found themselves having to calm **her** down. Finally she broke: just like in the movies, four men in white coats forced her into a strait jacket, shoved a hypodermic needle in her arm, and carted her away to the Psychiatric Ward at Kings County Hospital.

As a child, I had often felt embarrassed by my mother's behavior and frightened by the extremity of her political views. When she was incarcerated, the message communicated to me by doctors and social workers, and more kinesthetically by the steel bars on her room, was that EVERYTHING my mother had done, thought and believed was a symptom of her craziness. In many ways, this view was comforting. It was a relief to know that something was wrong with her, not me. But even at the age of fourteen, this psychiatric view of her politics seemed simplistic. As I looked around at poverty and racism with my own eyes, I could not quite dismiss her political commitments as entirely pathological. I also suspected that her sensitivity to social injustice and her frustration with the inadequate response of most others had a role in causing her to go crazy. But this awareness on my part did not diminish the pain of separation, the injustice of being robbed of my adolescence, or the trauma of having to go into that institution, week after week, month after month, year after year, and pretend, for her sake, that this woman was still being my mother.

Judy Clark's story is not my mother's story but, from the child's eye-view, it was close enough. Both women had catapulted into an outland where radical politics collides with inner emotional turmoil. In a manic psychotic state, my mother believed she was going to be given the Nobel Peace Prize—by Lady Bird Johnson, no less—for eliminating racism in all of New York City. Within the hermetically sealed environment of a clandestine organization, Judy Clark believed herself a loyal lieutenant in a black army, building a land base where African-Americans could live in sovereignty and socialism. Leaving their daughters at home, both women set out to turn their visions into reality.

Eventually, I went out of my way to talk with people who knew Judy. I became more systematic in my efforts to collect details about the case and Judy's trial—or lack of one. I began to imagine visits between Judy and her daughter inside prison. I imagined the time when her daughter would demand an explanation of why she had been abandoned for the sake of the Black Liberation Army and for a revolution that did not exist. I imagined she would ask Judy questions about why three men were killed, one of whom was black, all of whom were fathers—and why, if she hadn't killed anyone and had only been driving a getaway car, she had received a triple life sentence. I also imagined that for someone with Judy's background—white, middle-class, Jewish—it would be easier to face bullets than to face the compelling inquiries of her child. Although I certainly did not admit this to anyone at the time, beyond these ruminations lay the wildest imagining of all: if I could get to Judy, pose these questions and provide a context for her to hear what I anticipated would be the absurdity of her answers, before she imposed them on her daughter, I could possibly change the child's story. In the process perhaps I could understand my own story a little better, and have an interesting story to tell others. I decided to write "something" about Judy Clark.

Finding Judy's compatriots was not difficult. We were not entirely strangers. In 1974, I had locked horns with a group of the Weather Underground's aboveground supporters at an alternative "Women's School" in Brooklyn. Fresh out of college, working at a menial job and uncertain what to do with the rest of my life, I was approached by the School's steering committee—a collective of women who defined themselves as "socialist-feminists"—and invited to teach a course on "Marx, Freud and Feminism." Allies of the Weather Underground were instrumental in establishing the School but their goals were hardly academic. Rather, their intention was to recruit women who enrolled in courses to support the insurgency politics of the Weather Underground. When the FBI learned of this connection, the School was placed under surveillance and the militants organized a campaign to "resist" the FBI investigation. I refused to get involved. That year was my last in the movement. In 1975, I began graduate school and pursued my interest in Freud, Marx, and feminism within the confines of academic sociology.

So while not someone they liked, I was someone they "knew." I gave them a copy of my CV and asked if they would communicate my interest in writing "something" about Judy to Judy based on personal interviews. A week later, Judy signed on: she had reserved the right to review what I wrote before it was published and the right to challenge quotes attributed directly to her. With a mixture of apprehension and relief, I abandoned the proverbial pre-tenure plan to turn what now seemed a bearably boring dissertation into a book, and prepared to enter Judy's world: a world of guns, getaway cars and safe houses; of robberies and bombings; of collective identities and collective fantasies; and of jail cells and lockdowns. Into this world I would bring a tape recorder and notebooks, the theoretical tools of a critical sociologist, a set of psycho-analytically oriented interview techniques, my own experiences as an activist, and an intense identification with the little girl whose radical mother had come unraveled.

Into the prison

On August 1, 1985, I was "cleared" for my first visit to the Bedford Hills Correctional Facility. While anticipating bureaucratic red tape to obtain official authorization to conduct interviews with an individual prisoner, the actual process seemed unending. I quickly learned that Judy was classified as a "special" inmate, and as an exceptionally high security risk. Prison officials at Bedford Hills and at the New York State Department of Corrections (DOCS) expressed concerns about permitting her to participate in a process not subject to their direct supervision. They did not want anyone—inside or outside the prison—to get "too close." Delusional as it seemed to me, Judy's self-proclaimed identity as an anti-imperialist freedom fighter was apparently taken quite seriously by the authorities. My negotiations with the Director of Program Planning, Research and Evaluation, and the Director of Public Relations at DOCS continued for over fifteen months. It is probably the case that nothing less than an intense and emotionally based motivation, bordering on obsession, could have generated the tenacity it required to get through the gatehouse of the prison for an authorized visit with Judy Clark. Finally, I was assigned the status of a "special" visitor, a classification that stood ambiguously between "journalist" and "researcher."

Having arrived, it was now necessary to shift to a lower gear. I had no intention of unpacking my own history or emotional baggage at Judy's feet or of crashing into her defenses. But neither was I going to feign interest in the formation of a separate black nation. Now it was up to Judy to inject herself in the process—or not.

During our first two-hour visit, we traversed the realms of the formal and the unspoken, reviewing the obstacles I had encountered in arranging the visit, discussing possibilities for this "something" I planned to write, modifying our suspicions of each other, and otherwise overcompensating for the contrivance of this encounter. Ultimately Judy seemed intrigued, although by no means fully comfortable, with the prospect of being studied.

In fact, a precedent existed for this type of interview. In the late 1970s Jeanne Knutson, a clinical psychologist at the University of Texas, obtained permission from the Federal Bureau of Prisons to study US prisoners convicted of committing crimes for political purposes. The first article she wrote was based on in-depth interviews with a young Croatian nationalist incarcerated in the US on charges of air piracy (hijacking) resulting in the death of an officer (Knutson, 1981). Rooted in the theories of Erik Erickson, Knutson explored with her respondent both the subjective motivations and the external pressures pushing him toward violence. Her work was thoughtful, sensitive, and inspiring.

As we parted, agreeing to schedule the next interview in a month, Judy asked if I had read Kim Chernin's new book *In My Mother's House* (Chernin, 1983). I had not but, needless to say, the mere title sent me straight from the prison to the library. I pulled it from the shelf, sat down in the narrow aisle between the stacks, cracked it open, and read from cover to cover. To my astonishment, the book Judy had recommended was about the reconciliation between a daughter, Kim, and mother, Rose, whose relationship had been estranged due to the mother's life-long commitment to left-wing politics. To my further amazement, the reconciliation takes place through a series of visits in which the daughter interviews her mother and uses the pretext of writing "something" to confront difficult issues of their past and, most explicitly, Rose's prioritizing politics over parenting. When I closed the book, I felt Judy and I were in sync, our fantasies compatible, the timing right, and that "something" already was happening.

However, when arriving at the prison gatehouse for the second interview, the guard told me there was a "problem": my clearance was being "reviewed." The Public Relations Director was called to the gate and said Judy's status was "changing," that security had been "tightened" and she now required an "escort," and that all this could take "quite a while—hours maybe." But her tone was dissuasive rather than prohibitive, and I persisted. My tape recorder was disassembled and searched, my pencils and pens confiscated (due to sharp edges), and I was kept waiting at each checkpoint. But I got inside.

When Judy arrived, she was in cuffs and flanked by two officers. She seemed genuinely surprised to see me. The cuffs were removed. One guard left and the other remained, saying she had been assigned to supervise the interview. After some negotiation, she agreed to supervise while seated outside—instead of inside—the small cubicle. I had assumed once the door was closed, an outpouring of information, if not emotion, would come from Judy. Instead, her face was blank. She pinned the microphone to her shirt and indicated she was ready to proceed.

I was stunned. Judy was reacting to the ordeal as a minor inconvenience. "What's going on?" I asked.

"Nothing," she replied, still looking blank.

I had planned to use this interview to begin taking Judy's life history; I intended to focus on her parents' background, her childhood and adolescence, and her entry into the movement. But I had read enough psychoanalytic theory and taken enough courses on method to know I had to find some way of addressing the "disconnect," that is, Judy's dismissal of this foreboding situation as "nothing." A distracting discussion would enable the disconnection to remain intact. This was no time to be talking about her childhood.

I verbalized the difference in our perceptions and pressed for an explanation.

Judy responded by telling me a story. It was about her arrival at Bedford Hills prison on the day she was sentenced. The entire prison had been turned upside down. Special task forces were brought from Albany to test the electricity on all the wired fences. Guards were placed in bulletproof vests. And helicopters hovered overhead as the van transporting her from the reception area to the "State Shop" where all incoming inmates are issued clothing.

"The area, usually one of the most chaotic spaces in the prison, was totally silent. All the other inmates were cleared out and the four guards assigned to process me were literally shaking. Then they handed me a uniform. I unfolded it and held it against my body. It was a size 18." Judy is a size 6. "One of the guards started to laugh and that broke the silence. She said that given what they had heard about me and all the security measures that were in place, they were expecting to see a 9 foot tall fire-breathing amazon come stalking through the door. So they had pulled down the largest uniform they could find."[1]

But what was I supposed to conclude from this story? That today's security extravaganza was just more of the same? That out of nowhere prison officials had concocted a fantasy about the urban guerrilla in their midst? Significantly, Judy's story had omitted any reference to the inflammatory statements she made at her sentencing earlier that day including the threat to continue the armed struggle from behind bars.

I quickly shifted focus. "Let's go back to October 20, 1981," I suggested. "Tell me about your treatment in the hands of the state authorities from the time of your arrest to the present."

The interactions Judy described held to a consistent narrative line. For four years—in detention, in court, and in prison—Judy seized every opportunity to demonstrate her identity as an anti-imperialist freedom fighter although she had not "done" anything violent. In fact she basically had not "done" anything. She huffed and she puffed and threatened to blow the house down. Yet the state reacted as if she had actually done everything she had threatened to do. Any competent civil law attorney could have contested the restrictions the state imposed on Judy as a result of her speeches and empty threats. But Judy was invested in the punishment. In the absence of a revolutionary movement, the government's draconian response was a crucial source of affirmation for her identity as a revolutionary. Without it, she was just a criminal—an incompetent getaway driver in a botched bank robbery. So Judy provoked and then she endured by sleeping, daydreaming, engaging in distractions, and going blank. Still, just as in the story about her arrival at Bedford where she omitted reference to her own provocations during court sentencing, Judy declined to mention any provocation leading to the upped security.

After three hours, someone knocked at the door. "Time's up." The guard poked her head into the cubicle, and instructed Judy to remain seated. The elephant remained seated in the room as well.

"So I'll see you next week." My tone was tentative.
"Not much chance of that," Judy was shaking her head. "If you want to see me, you'll have to fight."

I started packing my gear and, when I reached to unhook the microphone from Judy's shirt, our eyes met. Judy was well aware that throughout the interview, I had been attuned to the silence—to the omission of reference to provocations on her part. She knew I knew "nothing" was not exactly nothing. But from the stories she shared about her experiences in detention and court, as well as my own experience that day, I now knew that the state's response to "not exactly nothing" was likely something harsh and excessive. By structuring the interview around the present situation, our respective emotional states were now far more in sync than three hours prior: we were both worried about "nothing."

"Will you fight?" Judy asked. It was not exactly an emotional plea, but it was not a blank space either.

I had no idea how to respond since I had no idea what the "nothing" was. I shrugged. "Take care of yourself" were the only words I could muster.

The next morning the header on *The New York Times'* front page "Metro" section read: "Escape Plot Laid to Brink's Convict." I would later learn what, in this instance, "not exactly nothing" had meant (UPI, 1985).

Three months prior, the FBI's Joint Terrorist Task Force had raided a safe house in Baltimore and found a stack of notes wherein a plan to escape from the Bedford Hills prison was outlined. Handwriting samples implicated Judy in the plan. Her would-be liberators were arrested on charges unrelated to the escape. While the plan never materialized (and a careful read of evidence showed it had had no chance of materializing), Judy was charged with "co-conspiring to escape." By the time I had arrived at the prison the previous day, she had already been removed from general population and was in a cell awaiting a hearing on the charges. Since she had not yet been convicted, though, I was permitted to proceed with the interview. When I left she was taken directly from interview cubicle to a "disciplinary hearing," found guilty and sentenced to two years in solitary confinement—the longest sentence ever given to a female inmate in New York State—even longer than the sentences given those who HAD escaped.

So as I was reading the paper, Judy was waking up in a stripped-down isolation cell herein referred to as "the box" with one day down and 729 days to go. The Deputy Superintendent informed me my "special" visits were being terminated due to rules limiting access to inmates in solitary confinement. I would fight.

Onto the couch and out of the canon

The circumstances surrounding initial interviews with Judy led to an expansion of the research. For the prison officials' efforts to deter my contact with *her* had served only to heighten my interest in *them*: I became curious about the correctional system, its decisions concerning security, and what influenced officials' assessments of the "risks" posed by a "political" prisoner. They seemed to equate Judy's advocacy of political violence and verbal defiance with a proclivity for physical confrontation. Moreover, Judy's identity as a woman seemed to accentuate rather than diminish their fears. They did not seem to "get" that simply ignoring Judy's bluster would be the most effective punishment of all. I became committed to understanding the bases of their policies, continuing my research, and challenging their decision to terminate my access to Judy. However, the primary reason for expanding the project was the availability of more "data."

Before the break in my interviews, Judy referred to a growing number of radicals like herself arrested for actions—bombings, bank robberies, prisons escape—involving violence. Some were related to the Weathermen and the Black Liberation Army, but others made the turn to violence with lesser-known protest groups. Among them were the Puerto Rican Independentistas as well as a small self-styled group of Vietnam veterans, and their wives and children, radicalized by their experiences in the military and later in prison. As a result of new domestic counterterrorism measures and increased funding for national security during the Reagan years these fugitives, some of whom managed to survive underground for years, were all in lock-up at the Metropolitan Correctional Center (a federal detention facility in Lower Manhattan). I composed a letter and short proposal requesting participation of eighteen of the women associated with the groups in a series of interviews. The documents were delivered via their attorneys and, by April 1986, fourteen of the women had responded affirmatively.

Although I had only conducted two interviews with Judy, from a psychoanalytic perspective, I had been involved with her at the level of fantasy for several years. But as the relationship transitioned from fantasy to reality, I gained greater clarity about the "something" I wanted to study. From the first interview, it was clear Judy possessed an uncanny ability to separate the political dimension of her identity from personal interactions. The disparity between the two was often glaring. In the political realm, Judy's views were extreme: she saw herself as a leader, her actions willful, her commitments unwavering. When she shifted to the personal, the fanatic vanished: in its place was a real person who was warm, funny, articulate, aware of current events, cultural fads, the latest books and films, worried about gaining weight and consumed with concerns about her daughter. The ease with which Judy shifted, even in the course of a single conversation, suggested she was well practiced in juggling the demands of two irreconcilable identities, one based in "personal" attachments and the other cemented to a long-standing commitment to revolution. Given the violent direction Judy's revolution had taken, it would appear that the revolutionary had triumphed and that she was willing to sacrifice all. But a close look at her role in the robbery, especially in the context of the material she provided in the interview about her interactions with the state, begged for a more complicated interpretation.

Judy did not participate directly in the violence: she was not at the scene of the hold-up nor did she shoot or try to shoot anyone. Her role was secondary, as a driver of a getaway car assigned to follow as "another car, just in case." Yet, her defiant behavior in court and the sentence she received as a result belied this subordinate role. What was she trying to hide? Cowardice? Inability to master the skills of an urban guerilla? Moral ambivalence? The intense pull of personal attachments and responsibilities? All of the above?

Freud's short essay "Splitting of the Ego in the Process of Defense" provides the thin horizon of an explanation. Freud noted that when confronted with two irreconcilable realities, the psychotic will simply deny one of the realities exists; alternatively, the "splitter" experiences tension (discomfort and anxiety). However instead of seeking a resolution to an untenable situation, s/he will effect a cleavage. "On the one hand, with the help of certain mechanisms, he rejects reality and refuses to accept any prohibition; on the other hand, in the same breath, he recognizes the danger of reality, takes over the fear of that danger as a symptom, and tries subsequently to divest himself of the fear" (1938, p. 373). Later examinations of "splitting" (see work by Melanie Klein and Otto Kernberg) specify how the process is expressed: by inventing half-measures; investing in convoluted rationales; or detaching from emotion. In the end, both realities are compromised (1938).

While Freud and Freudians view splitting in adults as a pathology derived from an individual's incapacity for synthesis, my training in critical theory allows me to view this dilemma dynamically, that is, as a symptom of conflict between two opposing forces that can be "social" in nature, in this case personal attachments at one end and a revolutionary identity requiring participation in violence on the other. I suspected that in the absence of a real insurgency movement wherein an extensive support system exists, splitting one's personal life from the requisites of a revolutionary identity becomes an occupational hazard. I also suspected that among the women, especially the mothers, a further splitting—of the revolutionary identity into "primary" and "secondary" roles—was essential for sustaining their participation in the armed struggle over time. Draconian responses from the state and projecting a one-dimensional, "terrorist" identity onto the women camouflaged the split. Given the opportunity to interview more women, it was this three-way splitting process I wanted to understand.

Despite meeting in a high-security detention center, I approached these women neither as criminals nor terrorists but as social movement actors. We discussed their family background and how they became politically conscious; recruitment into the protest arena; factors that led to going underground; daily routines underground as wives, mothers, lovers, and neighbors; and their role participating in high-risk, violent actions. I searched for signs of conflict and ambivalence beneath the choices they made, what it meant for them to be revolutionary and their roles vis-à-vis the violence. I listened to their responses with the proverbial "third ear," paying close attention to inconsistencies between expressed emotional states and perceived obligations in relation to their political roles and identity (Harding, 2006). Ultimately I explored how they "commuted" between these dimensions of the life-sphere and the role of state responses in "facilitating" the process.

At the time, I recognized that sociologists unfamiliar with psycho-analytic theory might construe my focus on emotion and splitting as "reductionist." But the vulnerabilities the women revealed and doubts they expressed provided a window into the "black box" of political con-sciousness among an entire cohort of high-risk, high-intensity political militants whose commitments and actions seemed unintelligible other-wise. Moreover, in the process of detailing the women's split between emotion and action, larger questions concerning the state's response to political violence in this era came to the fore. These included the uses of the "terrorist" label and an array of excessive measures deployed in arresting, detaining, prosecuting, and incarcerating these women. As a result, a secondary focus of the work was established: to document the policies and practices that determined treatment of these women in the criminal justice system, and to ascertain the degree to which extreme measures applied to the women in captivity were a function of fantasies and fallacies held by their captors (Zwerman, 1988, 1989).

In sum, analyzing this material was informed by a combination of theoretical frames including critical sociology, feminist theory, psy-choanalysis, and radical criminology. I contrasted the publicly projected self-perceptions the women had as defiant revolutionaries with the personal/emotional dimension of their lives as wives, lovers, mothers, and daughters. Speaking personally, they expressed reticence to partici-pate directly in the violence. This split was "managed" through a series of half-measures involving the mundane, emotionally fraught, and in many cases subservient roles they played in the underground regarding the violence. I then juxtaposed this disparity with the images of the "female terrorist" held by state officials, thereby discovering an interest-ing paradox: while the two sides were locked in an intensely adversarial relationship, both the women and state authorities acted on a shared set of perceptions, based largely in fantasy, about the relationship between gender and political violence. The perceptions greatly exaggerated the threat that the women posed to social order and thus justified dramatic excesses in security and sentencing the women received.

Over the next several years, I published several articles about this paradox including, and receiving most attention, "Mothering on the Lam: Politics, Gender Fantasies and Maternal Thinking in Women Associated with Armed, Clandestine Organizations in the United States" (1994). Simultaneously, I was engaged in a battle with state authorities, challenging the New York State Department of Corrections' decision to deny my "special" visits with Judy while she was in solitary. With assistance from the NYU Civil Law Clinic, the interviews resumed six months later.

The undiscovered self

When I returned, Judy's political convictions were unchanged. She repeated many of the same things she'd said in court, referring to the robbery as "financial expropriation" and herself as a "combatant" while justifying the murders as "self-defense." But, I have to say, the freedom fighter seemed weary. Her isolation in the box—removed from the chaos and distractions in general population—had made her more introspective. Also, my battle with prison authorities to continue the interviews during her confinement had deepened the connection between us.

As she became more trusting, I became more provocative. I challenged many of the things she said, and did not hide my revulsion at the actions that had brought her to prison. Her responses to my questions about her political life as well as her personal life were at times convoluted, at times tentative but surprisingly non-defensive. As her stock rhetoric wore thin, Judy dug deeper into herself for answers. She began to recognize her need for approval from her comrades was a key force driving her to participate in actions that had jeopardized her physical safety and ultimately her freedom.

For our sixth and supposedly our last interview in July 1986, I planned to focus on her decision to have a child. In earlier discussions about loss of contact with her daughter, Judy consoled herself by likening her situation to that of women guerrilla fighters in the Third World who were torn from loved ones for the sake of a revolution: she felt the sacrifice as hers alone. But as she began to address the emotional issues fueling her political commitment, she realized it was not just herself she had sacrificed. Like the bombshell dropped in the final moments of a therapy session, during this interview, Judy expressed profound uncertainty about her state of mind prior to Brinks. Her composure completely disintegrated. "I can live with taking responsibility for all this for myself, but how did I do this to my kid?"[2]

Despite her clandestine political activities, Judy had maintained a close but volatile relationship with her parents for most of her life, and more so after her daughter was born. After her arrest, she assigned primary care of the infant to a political friend who, at Judy's insistence, facilitated visits between the Clarks and their grandchild. However, in 1983, the guardian was herself arrested and charged with criminal contempt for refusing to cooperate with a federal investigation of a series of bombings connected to the armed underground Puerto Rican nationalist group, FALN, and was sentenced to three years in prison. At that point the child's care became a "collective" responsibility within Judy's political circle. Watching the child bounced around from comrade to comrade, each of whom seemed at risk of a jail sentence, had appalled Judy's parents. After a weekend visit with the child at their vacation home in Massachusetts, the Clarks "disappeared" and filed a custody suit against Judy.

In court, the Clarks characterized their daughter just as had the government—that is, a dangerous and deceitful terrorist, and someone whose friends were just the same. The court ruled the child could not have contact with any of the adults who had been raising her. Judy stopped speaking to her parents. Nonetheless, each evening, Judy made a collect call to their apartment to say good night to her daughter. And, every week, Judy's father brought the child to the prison to visit her mother.

"He brings her in and sits over there," Judy pointed to a rocking chair in the far corner of the children's center. "He reads the New York Times or naps while we color or play games or wrestle. But she senses the tension and keeps asking why I'm so mad." The tears were still pouring.

By then, I was familiar with Judy's background. Her family's involvement in radical politics dated back three generations to the mobilization of Jewish workers against the Tsar in Russia, into the world of Jewish socialism in New York City at the turn of the century, and through the rise and decline of the American Communist Party. Her father, Joseph Clark, had devoted twenty-five years of his life to building a left-wing movement in the US. However, after an extended stay in Russia in the early 1950s where he learned of the atrocities committed by Stalin against "enemies of the revolution," Clark blew the whistle. With others, he demanded that American Communist leaders sever ties with the Soviet Union and rebuild an indigenous, democratic socialist movement. When his efforts to reform the Party failed, he quit. The image of the now 71-year-old Joe Clark—someone who would not ultimately sacrifice his reason or his humanity "for the revolution"—taking his young grandchild into a maximum security prison to see her mother, a freedom-fighter in the Black Liberation Army, rendered Judy's story more than just a political drama. It was an inter-generational family tragedy.

I offered to return the next week as I felt responsible for triggering her distress and worried about her returning to solitary confinement in this vulnerable state. Frankly, I was also curious whether Judy would "hold on" to all the doubts and despair she had expressed even for a week.

On my end, I was a bit overwhelmed but intrigued by this turn. After all, hadn't I pursued Judy with this very scenario in mind? I discussed what occurred with a few trusted colleagues, and gave considerable thought to what my alternative responses to her might be. Certainly, more in-depth interviews with Judy would be to the advantage of anything I wrote. Ironically, the lawyers at the NYU Civil Law Clinic who had represented me in the fight to regain access to Judy in solitary had, in their zealousness, forced the prison to lift all restrictions on the number of interviews I could do. Theoretically, I could visit Judy every day, all day, for the next seventy-five years.

Mainly, though, it was the human and existential dimensions of the situation that compelled me. Judy was in prison for life: she was not quite at the halfway mark in her two-year sentence in solitary confinement, and she was disarming. Moreover, she was a mother whose child's future and mental stability would be determined, in part, by how well Judy could help her understand what had happened.

When I returned the following week, Judy was completely focused on her experience during the last visit. She reported having felt exhausted but unburdened and relieved. She was explicit about anxiety at the prospect of losing contact with me. I proposed a deal—a "phase two" of interviewing—entailing in-depth life history void of ideology and rhetoric. The inquiry would focus on what in-depth life histories do best, namely, analyze the meaning she gave to her experiences, give voice to ambivalence and doubt, explore the roads not taken, and consider alternatives for an identity other than that of armed revolutionary. On a practical level, the interviews would provide a safe place where Judy could discuss that one part of her identity she cherished most—her relationship with her daughter. She would use this time to explore the possibilities and accept the limitations of mothering from prison. She would try to re-establish her relationship with her family.

However, Judy understood that discussions could not be limited to mothering. To confront the impact of her actions on her own child would make her vulnerable to confronting the impact of her actions on the victims. While Judy was haunted by the image of her daughter waiting fruitlessly for her to return home on the night of the robbery, what about the children of the Brinks guard and the police officers? Peter Paige, Edward O'Grady, and Waverly Brown would have to become real people, husbands, sons and all of them, fathers. I will never forget Judy's face at the moment she said their names for the first time. She was staring at me, her upper lip twitching uncontrollably. It was really the most pathetic expression I had ever seen on anyone.

For my part, I knew well I was making more than a time commitment. I knew it would not be simple to keep my bearings and my boundaries among the myriad roles I was assuming: author, researcher, friend, and shrink. Nor were the potential dangers of the endeavor lost on Judy. "I assume you have seen the movie *Persona*," she warned, raising a devil's eyebrow.[3]

Directed by Ingmar Bergman, *Persona* is about the relationship between two women: a famous stage actress recovering from a nervous breakdown and the nurse who has come to care for her. Soon the relationship between the two grows so intense that they eventually merge into each other's persona. In so doing, their bond devolves into hate: the nurse's disdain for her patient is overt, expressed both verbally and in petty sadistic acts, but the actress's assault on her caretaker is far subtler and more devastating. The actress works her way into the nurse's blood-stream like a slow acting poison and, in the end, the nurse perishes in flames.

Amplifying the image was an eerie coincidence I had not discussed with Judy: both the psychologist Jeanne Knutson, author of the study of the Croatian terrorist, and Ellen Frankfurt, the author of a biography of Kathy Boudin, had recently committed suicide. Was God trying to tell me something?

In August 1986, I began bi-weekly visits to the prison, staying three hours each time. Judy wrote to me almost day, reporting on her tribulations in "the box" and following up on things that were said, or left unsaid during the visits. I did my best to keep up with the pace of her correspondence (Hollway and Jefferson, 2000). Fortunately, my tenure at the university was already secure because when colleagues would ask what I was working on, all I could honestly say was "Judy Clark."

No facile renunciations or swift conversions occurred during this period. Judy entered phase two of our relationship as an experiment: she would suspend her insurgent identity to examine the fixed ideas on which that identity had been built. She would limit her communication with former comrades to personal matters and take a "sabbatical" from political discussions.

Releasing herself from her obligations as a revolutionary allowed Judy to make some behavioral changes almost immediately. She became less adversarial in her relations with the prison staff. She developed a close relationship with the prison chaplain, a Catholic Sister, who was also in charge of the Children's Center at the prison. Sensing the change in Judy, the cleric advocated on Judy's behalf to restore normal visiting conditions with her child despite her designation in SHU.

Changes appeared on the family front as well. She began to hug her father when he arrived and thanked him for coming and bringing her daughter. Eventually, the three sat together. During these hours, the child's favorite talk game was to ask Grandpa, in front of Judy, what mommy was like when she was a little girl. Joe would recount loving and funny stories about Judy as a child. Soon Judy followed suit, asking her father what he was like as a little boy and a young man. For the first time in her life, she listened carefully to his reminiscences.

Sensing a new calm between father and daughter, the child soon began asking the more difficult questions: why Judy was in jail and why, unlike most other prisoners, she was never getting out. Judy asked her parents for permission and time to explain it herself. She read Coles' and Kohlberg's theories on the moral development of children as well as Fraiberg's *The Magic Years*, taking excruciating care to craft an explanation for the robbery—a narrative that validated Judy's political history and commitments yet acknowledged, in a neutral way, that most people thought the deed was wrong.

By the next summer, signs of internal change were evident: Judy was calmer and more self-possessed; she listened to others more carefully; and she took time to answer questions about herself, attentive to signs of disingenuousness or defensiveness in her own responses. Most significantly, Judy was looking forward to leaving solitary and her exit plan did not involve an escape. She was eager to return to school and finish her associate degree, and to continue on to major in Psychology. She planned to help organize a program for women inmates with AIDS. She wanted to find a girlfriend and try to have a personal life . . . "You understand," Judy said, quick to point out the absurdity of seeking out "corrective experiences" in prison, "I'm going to have to find someone who is here for first degree murder if I'm going to make a long-term commitment."

Although most prisoners in solitary are given time off for good behavior, Judy was required to serve her sentence to the last minute. On the day she was scheduled for release, I lay awake all night. At 6:30 am, the phone rang: "I'm out! I'm in general population! I have my own cell!

I'm meeting with my counselor to make out a work schedule!" I felt like a mother whose kid had just arrived safely at summer camp. I also felt the tug of separation.

Pulling apart would not be easy. I was not going to disappear—I didn't ever plan on disappearing—but Judy had to develop a life on her own and have a chance, in her own way, to absorb changes she made in the last year. In October 1987, I made my final visit of phase two. When I arrived, Judy entered the room with a big gift-wrapped box the guards had allowed her to carry in: it was a beautiful hand-knitted sweater and a card. On the front of the card, Judy had painted a picture of her stripped cell in solitary and the inscription read: "You can take the woman out of the box, but you can't take the box out of the woman."

Analysis terminable and interminable

Our separation lasted less than four months. One morning in late December, I received word that, at 5 am, Federal Marshals had arrived at Bedford Hills and ordered Judy to pack up her cell. They had placed her in cuffs and shackles, and raced her off to an airport in Otisville. The following morning, Judy called.

"I'm in Alabama. I only have three minutes. I have no idea where I'm going." Judy sounded apprehensive but calm. "I'll call again as soon as I can."

Judy was in transit on the Federal Bureau of Prisons' Inmate Airlift and had spent the night in the Montgomery County Jail. All the doubts I had before beginning "phase two" came flooding back. At Bedford, Judy's changes had been acknowledged and they were allowing her to stabilize as a long-termer in general population. But now Judy was in federal custody. That Judy Clark was majoring in Psychology was not likely to impress Ronald Reagan.

FCI Tucson is a medium security men's prison in Arizona. It maintains a small unit for female detainees. Judy was deposited there and told to unpack. I decided to initiate contact with Judy's parents. I knew that Judy had spoken to them about me, although I had no idea how she characterized our relationship.

"Joe! Joe!!," Ruth Clark yelled at her hard-of-hearing husband when I introduced myself over the phone. "It's . . . it's . . . it's that person, Joe! It's Judy's person."

The Clarks were frantic. Whatever their conflicts with Judy, concern for her safety was primary. Moreover, Joe Clark had been deeply moved by the rekindling of closeness with Judy: he wanted his daughter back.

The Clarks contacted someone at *The New York Times* who agreed to write a story about Judy's transfer focused on the close relationship Judy had established with her child and how dependent the child was on the visits. The next day, the *Times* published an editorial entitled "Punish the Mother, Not the Child," urging Judy's return to Bedford Hills for the child's sake (Johnson, 1987a, 1987b).

Due to the media attention, the New York State Department of Corrections was forced to reveal their intentions. Evidently, when Judy was sentenced, Bedford Hills was given the mandate to upgrade security. Construction of a new watchtower, gatehouse, and the replacement of barbed wire with razor wire would now begin. The directive ordered that Judy be removed during the construction and not returned to Bedford until the construction was completed.

Judy had only been out of the box three months and was now facing at least a year in another version of isolation. We spoke on the phone several times a week during her first month there. I heard a lethargic, teary voice totally unfamiliar to me. I got to Tucson as soon as I could. Judy was clinically depressed: she wasn't sleeping and had already gained a noticeable amount of weight. I tried to be reassuring. It would only be a year. Both parents were planning to visit. They would bring her daughter. I would visit monthly. She would go back. She had survived two years in the box. She would survive this. In prison, there is an old saying, "you can either do the time or let the time do you."

"How do you want to do the time, Judy?" It was quite ironic that in that moment, I longed to see even a hint of the old bravado.

"I want a psychiatrist. And I want a subscription to *The New York Times.*"[4]

In which direction Judy's life was going to head from here was unknowable. But the wind had changed course, and was blowing far away from the Weathermen.

The prison kept to their word. Judy was flown back to New York State on a commercial airliner. She was seated in the last row, in handcuffs between two marshals, but there was none of the security hype that had previously surrounded her transfers. At Bedford Hills, she was placed directly in general population. The process of our separation resumed. It was a timely break because now my own mother was declining physically and confined to a bed in a medical facility, no longer with the stamina to sit up or hold a book. Reading, especially biographies, had always provided the grist for her fantasy mill. Near death, she still wanted to hear stories about "interesting people." She totally perked up when our visits included a reading of excerpts from my early interviews with Judy.

"You go a lot easier on her than you do on me," she growled.

Conjuring the image of Judy's 8-year-old daughter—adorable, smart, and growing more assertive by the day, I replied. "Don't worry, Ma. In Judy's life, I'm just the warm-up act."

Into rehab

Through these years, I continued to publish. In 1992, while writing "Mothering on the Lam," I presented a draft of the paper in a pro-seminar at the New School for Social Research: the session was directed by Charles Tilly, the premier gate-keeper of social movement studies. Tilly complimented the richness of detail and the critical but nuanced tone of the piece. He was amused by (as in laughed at) my focus on fantasy, especially those I attributed to state authorities. But as Tilly assessed the project, its impact on the sociological discipline was bound to be negligible. Analysis of the material through the "dreamy lens of psychoanalysis" (his words) diverted attention away from the aspects of political violence that concerned sociologists studying social movements—that is, political processes defining the transition from activism to terrorism for the New Left as a whole, and the provocative role of the state in this transition. The latter required more data, different kinds of data, and the use of vocabulary shared by social movement scholars.

In the late 1970s Tilly, with others, had led a theoretical revolution in social movement research (Tilly, 1978). Previously, emotions were seen as key for understanding political protests and movements developing outside mainstream institutions. Informed by structural functionalist assumptions that saw danger in rapid and radical social change, such extra-institutional forms of political action were interpreted as affective and irrational expressions of social discontent. In this "classical" model, activists were considered deviant individuals who, in psychoanalytic terms, could not manage the "normal" balance between id and ego required by modern, secular democratic institutions. Instead of engaging in conventional politics, the "agitator" seeks to abandon the self by participating in relatively unregulated sphere of protest.

By contrast, the later political process model developed by Tilly and others including John McCarthy, Mayer Zald, Doug McAdam, and Sidney Tarrow shifted attention from the psychological characteristics of individual to the rational, strategic, and structural aspects of social movements. By examining large—and largely successful—movements, the model highlighted continuities between institutionalized politics and protest politics, and emphasized processes by which movements mobilize, strategize, negotiate with political elites, and often achieve significant reforms (McAdam et al., 1988).

While crucial for advancing research on 1960s and 1970s social movements, the correction bequeathed a new set of biases. In trying to counter the discipline's prior emphasis on social movements' emotional volatility, the new paradigm now focused on rationality rather than emotionality—and almost exclusively on peaceful and popular elements activism. Research on violent groups, underground organizations, failed movements was virtually non-existent.

"That," declared Tilly, "is your job!" "By demonstrating that the theoretical tools social movement scholars were using to analyze successful (and largely peaceful) mobilizations were also applicable to studying small, clandestine, and violent groups," he instructed, "you would be placing these violent activists (the 'lambs' as he jokingly called the women I interviewed) in the context of a movement identity and your study would be placed on the research map in the field." But I was in serious need of rehabilitation. Tilly outlined the program and described the accommodations. "You will become a 'research associate' at the New School; you will have an office and it will be lined with book shelves filled with the current scholarship in social movements; you will spend your time reading and writing papers in dialogue with this literature; and you will attend the pro-seminar weekly." Tilly even appointed himself as my "sponsor," a role that entailed reading and commenting on umpteen revisions of my work and writing letters of recommendation for grants and fellowships, all aimed at increasing the distance between my analysis of the armed underground and Sigmund Freud.

The study size expanded from fourteen to forty. I interviewed some of the men in these movements; I interviewed their political supporters and attorneys as well as militants who left the movement at different points on the path toward violence. Consistent with the political process frame, I began to examine violence as an outcome of dynamics in the broader cycle of protest. I asked questions relevant to social movement scholars' research: when and where in the cycle of protest did the violence appear? What were the points of contact between the armed underground groups and non-violent social movement organizations? Why did the violence persist even after the non-violent movement dissolved? What role did the government's responses to non-violent protest play in both the transition to and persistence of political violence?

As the inquiry into broader dynamics of protest cycles progressed, references to emotion, splitting and fantasy faded; individual activists' experiences were now only interesting insofar as illuminating structural dynamics leading to and sustaining violence. Eventually, I spent more time in library archives than in the prison visiting room as I scoured primary movement documents, intelligence reports, trial transcripts, and media coverage of specific events.

In 1997, the study went global. I began collaborating with two colleagues, Donatella della Porta and Patricia Steinhoff, who were conducting similar studies on armed underground movements in Western Europe and Japan (Zwerman et al., 2000; Zwerman and Steinhoff, 2005). Pooling our data, we traced patterns of radicalization and state-dissident conflict that not only transcended individual experiences but also merged organizations, suppressed racial and gender differences, leveled cultural distinctions, and even crossed the borders between nations. The vivid anecdotes that once animated my writing were eliminated as they, according to peer reviewers and other gatekeepers of academic sociology, "distracted the reader with sensational material" and thus drew attention away from the "scientific" findings of the study. Extensive first-person quotations and thick description were replaced with tables, time lines, flow charts, and diagrams.

At present, the study shows no sign of the dependency I once had on Freud, feminism, or the Frankfurt School. And, as Tilly predicted, research on small, violent, and clandestine groups has become a small but integral part of the canon in social movement research. When Charles Tilly died in 2009, I regretted never telling him about Judy and hearing what would undoubtedly be his cutting, wry response to learning that the entire study was really all about my relationship with my mother.

Punish and discipline

A quarter of a century later, Judy Clark is a profoundly changed woman. Over these years, she completed a BA and an MA in Psychology as well as certification as a Clinical Chaplain. In the late 1980s, she co-founded the ACE project in order to address the impact of the AIDS epidemic at Bedford Hills. The organization was so effective it has been replicated at prisons all across the country. Judy also helped to rebuild a college program for which public funding for higher education in prison was eliminated in the 1990s. For the past fifteen years, she has served as a staff member of the Nursery Program where she teaches pre-natal parenting classes for pregnant women; she mentors mothers who live with babies on a special unit in the prison. Judy also lives in a special volunteer unit with inmates who train puppies to become guide dogs for the blind, as well as training explosive detection dogs for law enforcement agencies and service dogs for disabled people (primarily veterans). She remains an intensely attentive, loving, and influential mother to an extraordinary 32-year-old daughter (Robbins, 2012).

As for us, I never did set myself on fire. Our selves never merged. But as Judy occasionally reminds me, "I am the longest relationship with a woman you have ever had."

And it's true: while sociology and psychoanalysis got "divorced," Judy and I have stayed "married." Almost thirty years have gone by without a rupture or a dishonest word passing between us. I continue to visit Judy several times a year and we speak on the phone regularly. I never leave town without making certain that Judy knows where I am and how to get a hold of me "just in case." However in the case of "just in case," Judy now has many others to whom she can turn. Over the years, her circle has widened. Teachers, civilian volunteers at the prison, politicians, religious leaders, former inmates, even officials in the NYS Correctional system itself, including the former Superintendent of Bedford Hills, have befriended Judy and become her advocates. A coterie of high-profile civil law attorneys have worked—and continue to work—tirelessly on efforts to get Judy released. But I am—and will always remain—"Judy's person." No sociological theory, no big structure or political process model or comparative analysis could have uncovered the knowledge our relationship produced about political consciousness and unconsciousness or the human capacity for self-transformation.

Social movement actors are not always rational, nor strategic, nor successful in achieving social change. They can lose their way, their capacity for critical thinking, and even their morality. The consequences and casualties of persisting—acting out a fantasy of revolution as did Judy and her compatriots—by splitting and hiding and bombing and robbing banks—were nothing short of horrific. But beginning in 1986, in a period of eighteen months, inside of a "box," Judy Clark began to mobilize what might go down as the smallest demonstration in the history of the American left—a demonstration of one.

While most of the former armed activists of the 60s era have done "good time" in prison and continue to do good work on their release— in fact, the recidivism rate is zero—to my knowledge, no one has put themselves through such a thorough process of self-examination, taken the degree of personal responsibility, or expressed remorse so publicly as has Judy Clark. Every step that Judy has taken toward change, every relationship she has forged, every achievement she has earned and contribution to the prison community she has made has been encased in sorrow and mindful of the responsibility she has to men who lost their lives in the robbery and to their families who have lived their lives without fathers and husbands and sons.[5]

Yet Judy Clark is still a radical. Her courage, tenacity, and intense desire to "make it better" are fueled by the same ideals and commitments that brought her to activism in the first place. The real person is all there. The persona has become superfluous.

Notes

1. Interview with Judy Clark, Bedford Hills Correctional Facility, October 9, 1985.
2. Interview with Judy Clark, Bedford Hills Correctional Facility, July 1986.
3. Interview with Judy Clark, Bedford Hills Correctional Facility, August 1986.
4. Interview with Judy Clark, FCI-Tucson, March 1988.
5. Zwerman, G. "Letter to Governor Paterson", March 2010.

References

Chernin, K. (1983) *In My Mother's House* (Massachusetts: Houghton Mifflin).

Frankfurt, E. (1983) *Kathy Boudin and the Dance of Death* (New York: Stein and Day).

Freud, S. (1938) "Splitting of the Ego in the Defensive Process," in J. Strachey (ed.) *The Standard Edition Of the Complete Psychological Works of Sigmund Freud*, Vol. 5 (London: Hogarth Press).

Hanley, R. (1983) "3 in Brinks Case Given Long Terms," *New York Times*, 10 July 1983.

Harding, J. (2006) "Questioning the Subjective in Biographical Interviewing," *Social Research*, 11 (3), online.

Holloway, W. and T. Jefferson (2000) *Doing Qualitative Research Differently* (New York: Sage).

Johnson, K. (1987a) "Brinks Figure is Transferred to U.S. Prison," *New York Times*, December 29, 1987.

Johnson, K. (1987b) "Punish the Mother, Not the Daughter," *New York Times*, January 22, 1987.

Knutson, J. (1981) "Social and Psychodynamic Pressures Toward a Negative Identity," in Y. Alexander and J. M. Gleason (eds) *Behavioral and Quantitative Perspectives on Terrorism* (New York: Pergamon).

McAdam, D, J. McCarthy, and M. Zald (1988) "Social Movements" in *Handbook of sociology* (Thousand Oaks: Sage Publications).

Robbins, T. (2012) "Judith Clark's Radical Transformation," *New York Times Magazine*, January 15, 2012. See also www.JudithClark.org

Tilly, C. (1978) *From Mobilization to Revolution* (Reading: Addison-Wesley).

UPI (1985) "Escape Plot Laid to Brink's Convict," *New York Times*, November 9, 1985.

Zwerman, G. (1988) "Special Incapacitation: The Emergence of a New Correctional Facility for Women Political Prisoners," *Social Justice*, 15 (2), 31–63.

Zwerman, G. (1989) "Domestic Counterterrorism: U.S. Government Responses to Political Violence on the Left in the Reagan Era," *Social Justice*, 16 (2), 31–47.

Zwerman, G. (1994) "Mothering on the Lam: Politics, Gender Conflict and Maternal Thinking in Women Associated With Armed, Clandestine Organizations in the U.S.," *Feminist Review*, 47, 33–56.

Zwerman, G., P. Steinhoff, and D. della Porta (2000) "Disappearing Social Movements: An Examination of Clandestinity in the Cycle of New Left Protest in the United States, Japan, Germany and Italy," *Mobilization*, 5 (1), 85–104.

Zwerman, G. and Steinhoff, P. (2005) "When Activists Ask for Trouble: State-Dissident Interaction and the New Left Cycle of Protest in the United States and Japan," in C. Davenport, C. Mueller, and H. Johnston (eds) *Repression and Mobilization* (Minnesota: University of Minnesota Press).

B. Applying Freud's Ideas to Contemporary Culture

12
Foreclosure from Freud to Fannie Mae

John Andrews

One of the events that inaugurated the Great Recession was the countless home foreclosures in 2008, culminating in the credit crisis in fall of that year and subsequent government bank bailout. Between 2007 and 2008, the number of home foreclosures grew anywhere from 20 per cent to 30 per cent, and continued to grow throughout 2009. A fundamental cause of the crisis was the proliferation of subprime loans, mortgages sold to borrowers who represented a high risk of default. These loans were then used as a guarantee to securities sold by the lending bank, effectively passing along the risk to other investors. Karl Marx used the term "fictitious capital" to refer to any kind of capital—money, credit, financing—with no material basis in commodities.[1] For Marx, fictitious capital is "the fountainhead of all manner of insane forms" of capital; yet at the same time, it becomes indispensable for the production of surplus value and capital accumulation, manipulating the *time* of production by trading in the future. In the case of subprime loans, we see an exponential abstraction of capital from any commodity, what Swiss economist Christian Marazzi (2010) calls "the production of surplus-value *by* accumulation" (Marazzi, 2010, p. 63), which supports the insight from historical sociology that capital expands in *systemic cycles* (see Arrighi, 1994).

There is of course a commodity here—the houses themselves—which in the case of foreclosure are typically reclaimed by the bank, and then sold at auction or sometimes left to sit. While banks might expect some loss or decrease in value, a strange phenomenon has accompanied the explosion in home foreclosures: the former owners are trashing and vandalizing the property to the extent that it significantly decreases its value. More than minor wear and tear, these houses exhibit signs of major *intentional* damage. Common occurrences include stripped out appliances, graffiti on the walls, broken windows, and buckets of paint smeared into carpet. In other instances, it appears that a crowbar has been used to rip out moldings, tear holes in the wall, and smash light fixtures and thermostats. In one Las Vegas house, a ferret was left behind by the residents to wreak havoc—including scratched up floors, gnawed plaster, and leaving feces in the carpet; this particular house sold for an estimated 35 per cent less than it could have (Phillips, 2008). In fact, "foreclosure pets"—cats and dogs left behind by their owners upon vacating—became a growing problem, which in some cases attracted other abandoned animals in the neighborhood, like in one Cleveland-area home where more than ninety feral cats were found after it had been foreclosed (Miller, 2009). According to one survey by a Washington D.C. marketing research firm, real-estate agents estimate that about half of foreclosed properties nationwide have "substantial" damage (Griffin and Fitzpatrick, 2009).

Michael Phillips of the Wall Street Journal called these instances of home destruction "buyers' revenge" (Phillips, 2008), but I argue that they reflect a kind of *rage* unique to the present financial crisis. Imagine the resentment or hate, the bodily strength, the single-minded purpose it would take to destroy houses to this extent. Indeed, many instances of foreclosed home damage have been so well planned out that professional contractors were hired to inflict irreparable damage to expensive, custom-made features of the house. In all of these instances the house itself appears to be the object of rage given the extent of damage inflicted onto the physical structure. However, I argue that this rage be seen as abstract, unattached, generalized, and even politically productive—an *emotional situation*[2] concomitant not just with home foreclosures but also with new configurations among the psyche, personal life, and the economy born of the Great Recession.

An immediate conceptual question arises: how do we account for psychic phenomenon at the level of the social? (Or reciprocally, social phenomenon as iterations of psychic processes?) Rage, for example, is a rather difficult affect to pinpoint and assess: one may be "blinded" by rage in an instant, animated by passion or some exceptional circumstance. Alternately, one may be prone to frequent rages—suggesting a personality characteristic or neurotic symptom. Perhaps one's rage relates specifically to work or a relationship; or perhaps it is a more generalized outlook on the world. A leading theorist of affect and emotion, Sianne Ngai (2004) uses the term "ugly feelings" to describe certain negative affects that have surfaced culturally and in relation to the aesthetics of late capital. Ugly feelings like envy or irritation vary in duration, lack a subjective/objective distinction, and are non-cathartic. Anger, for example, usually has an object, duration, and resolution. Rage on the other hand is more akin to Ngai's ugly feelings in that its objects and duration are ambiguous. Yet, rage is violently dramatic and often transformative while Ngai's ugly feelings are "minor," muted, and ambient.

Psychoanalytic theory has also had relatively little to say about rage or affects in general. For Sigmund Freud, affects are expressions of repressed instincts and memories. Affects themselves are not repressed but are rather outward expressions attached to repressed ideas or drives. Affects vary qualitatively but are quantitatively proportionate to the corresponding instinctual energy involved, suggesting an *economy* of accumulation in which affect takes form as a particular expression as psychic energies become amplified or muted.[3] Jacques Lacan builds on Freud's rich but fragmented thought on affect, claiming that Freud viewed affects "not as signifiers but as signals" which explains their "displaceable significance" qualitatively. This insight prompted Lacan to theorize affect—he uses anger as his example—as "the failure of an expected correlation between the symbolic order and the response of the real" (Lacan, 1986, p. 103). Even while affect is under-theorized within the Freudian tradition, psychoanalysis's silence with regard to rage is still somewhat surprising: after all, as clinician Michael Eigen (2002) points out, Oedipus killed his father in an instance of road rage! For Eigen, rage consistently appears in his own clinical practice—taking numerous forms from the life-affirming to the life-obliterating. Importantly though: "Rage can lead to change. It can force others to hear that something is wrong, call attention to oneself or one's cause, stimulate the need to help. Rageful cries of pain sometimes have social value. Noise attracts notice and makes aspects of one's state visible to others" (Eigen, 2002, p. 10).

In effort to interpret homeowner rage in terms of affect, I turn to the psychoanalytic concept of *foreclosure*. Ostensibly very different, both the financial and psychoanalytic usages of the term foreclosure suggest a cutting off or establishment of boundaries: on the one hand between an individual and a bank, on the other between the psyche and the (symbolizable) outside world. Both Freud and Lacan used the term 'foreclosure' to indicate a special problem that reality poses for the subject. Foreclosure is unique in psychoanalytic theory in that it structures subjectivity without (necessarily) structuring the psyche, at least not directly. For Freud, foreclosure is the repudiation or breaking off from the ego of some unacceptable idea connected to reality, and thus a kind of breaking off from reality itself.[4] Lacan developed the term more fully to describe a domain of symbols that cannot enter the subject's unconscious: the domain of the Real. Foreclosure—the barring of certain signifiers or self-aspects—is foundational for subject formation. In other words the "I" involves some sort of constitutive loss, the separation of the Real from the Symbolic. Foreclosed feelings or ideas are not repressed—they do not return—but are rather *desired*. The "subject" of foreclosure then is an intensive site of production—the production of desire vis-a-vis the outside world.[5] Unlike repression, the concept of foreclosure assumes a very broad sociality in subject-formation. In other words, foreclosure is a psychical process that constitutes an inside and outside, but one in which the outside functions to produce desire for the Other. As a concept, foreclosure presents a vital link between psychoanalysis which typically privileges *depth* (as in a dynamic unconscious) and affect theory which tends to emphasize situational, embodied but ultimately surface exchanges among multiple—indeed infinite—actors. The notion of foreclosure acknowledges the unconscious, but (somewhat paradoxically) the power and efficacy of foreclosure as a psychical process stems from the barring of those unthinkable aspects of reality from entering the unconscious. Foreclosure establishes a boundary that places unconscious processes and the outside world in a tenuous relationship – one of proximity and distance, safety and danger. The boundaries entailed by foreclosure produce in the subject a vexed desire—vexed because the object of desire is unclear, unknown, or not yet present. Judith Butler observes: "As foreclosure, the sanction works not to prohibit existing desire but to *produce certain kinds of objects* and to bar others from the field of social production" (Butler, 1997, p. 25, emphasis mine). Foreclosure produces objects of desire but ones that are still in-formation.

The mobilization of the term *foreclosure* here as a simultaneously financial and psychic phenomenon demands an expansive understanding of their respective fields (in Bourdieu's usage), where the subject of foreclosure might involve an individual, a social class, or an "at-risk" population, and the object an amalgam of sexual, ideological, material, or national desires. In the context of this chapter, the object of desire is the house, but one that is necessarily situated within particular histories, institutions, and knowledges.[6] In the US, home ownership has long been synonymous with the American Dream and its range of positive significations (upward mobility, hard work rewarded, prestige, assimilation) alongside more ugly histories (genocide, Jim Crow segregation, anti-immigrationism). Jan Cohn (1979) has traced the long history of the American house as a cultural symbol imbued with contradictory national values. Cohn shows that unlike in Europe, the American house is uniquely emblematic of its larger *community*.[7] In the colonial period, the house stood as a visible indicator of a community's success—and as such should not be ostentatious or excessive, nor should it be too shabby. With the establishment of the American state and a burgeoning national consciousness, the question of how houses should reflect American-ness aesthetically came to occupy the minds of politicians, architects, writers, and everyday people alike. Nonetheless, houses in the nineteenth century became a key index of national and individual progress, regardless of style. As homeownership expanded in the twentieth century, the style of home became increasingly important—as a mode of individual self-expression, but also as a way of distinguishing oneself from racialized and "alien" populations. For Cohn, the contradictions of mass homeownership in the twentieth century are embodied in the ideas and work of Frank Lloyd Wright. For him, the American house was an emblem of freedom and democracy, "the answer to the dilemma of modern life [and] the salvation of the democratic system and even the source for the alleviation of the woes of the world" (p. 111). Alternately, Wright worried that mass homeownership would result in aesthetically bland, mediocre houses built to be resalable.

In the latter half of the twentieth century, the home became the privileged site of the expanding, standardized consumption associated with Fordism—the house itself now available to an increasingly affluent working class but also the cars, televisions, appliances, and furniture that filled it. In this sense, home ownership might be viewed as one of Fordism's key regulatory mechanisms by providing a focal point for consumption and investment. Ideally, the house would help to establish and maintain discrete subjectivities (citizen-subject, consumer-subject, laboring-subject) by stabilizing a boundary between inside and outside, private and public. Thus, the house serves too as reference point for conceiving our individual selves—for memories and how we remember, for childhood and family, for emotions like joy, love, pain and trauma. To own a home—to be a homeowner—is to own too that symbolism and history: to be *subject* to it. Moreover, this history of mass home ownership belies a contradiction within Fordist accumulation strategies in that *personal life* enters the commodification process on a much larger scale. The Federal Housing Administration was established as part of Franklin Roosevelt's New Deal to "encourage improvement in housing standards and conditions, to facilitate sound home financing on reasonable terms, and to exert a stabilizing influence on the mortgage market" (National Housing Act, 1934). The scope of the FHA was greatly expanded by the Servicemen's Readjustment Act of 1944. The GI Bill as it is more popularly known was devised as an antidote to what was considered the most pressing national problem of the time: the question of how to re-integrate the 16 million veterans returning from war. The GI Bill provided numerous benefits to veterans such as education, health care, and importantly government-guaranteed home loans. While the Bill was ostensibly motivated by concern around the national economy, it was also meant, as Roosevelt announced himself, to "teach [our youth] to live useful and happy lives."[8] The GI Bill was implicitly designed to address the psychological tolls of war—trauma, loss, stress—along with its more explicit public agenda of providing soldiers the economic means for private life.

The commodification of personal life and regulation of sexuality attendant in the promotion of mass home ownership intensified with the introduction of Freudianism. The popularization and medicalization of psychoanalytic thought became a vital if unacknowledged propeller for the American economy in the twentieth century. As Eli Zaretsky argues, the Fordist model of mass-production and its concomitant rationalization of work and consumption paradoxically turned "personal life into a mass phenomenon" (2005, p. 138). He writes: "The result was a fatal convergence between Fordism and Freudianism . . . and a new focus on psychology. In the workplace, managers were urged to find out 'what the employee thinks . . . what are the worker's satisfactions and aspirations.' In the marketplace, concerted efforts to entice consumers spawned such new enterprises as advertising, film, and survery research" (pp. 138–139). While much of this human relations and management psychology came from without psychoanalytic theory proper, Zaretsky argues that "Freudianism fueled the overall drive toward psychological thinking and provided the dominant, if implicit, conception of the mind" (p. 140).

One explanation for this was the particular version of psychoanalysis that came to prevail in the US. In order to avoid the marginalization that troubled the field in Europe, American psychoanalysts sought to make the field more "scientific" which would secure closer ties to universities and established medical institutions. Thus, those who dominated the field—physicians and other professionals (researchers, clinicians, human resources specialists)—were pressured to deliver pragmatic, *measurable* results (see Turkle, 1992). A consequence of this was a theoretical emphasis on fostering the defenses of the ego rather than tackling the obscure dynamics of the unconscious. The triumph of ego psychology—what Jacques Lacan sardonically but also very tellingly called "the New Deal of psychoanalysis" (2006) —proliferated a narrow, instrumental version of psychoanalysis, not just clinically but also in the work place, advertising, self-help culture, and eventually everyday parlance. The concept of foreclosure can be re-fashioned here to consider how we interpret the development of knowledge, including psychoanalytic knowledge: that what is excluded (discredited, overlooked, etc.) often plays an operative role in shaping its objects. Indeed, one lesson from the sociology of knowledge is that knowledge is deeply contingent on its institutional and historical conditions of production, and thus never exhaustive of possibilities. American ego psychology *foreclosed* the more radical and liberatory strains of psychoanalytic theory.

We see then that mass home ownership and ego psychology were part of the same post-war apparatus of governance. State-guaranteed housing loans provided financial security not only to lending banks but especially to middle-class families as a site of lifetime investment. Home ownership was a way of interiorizing individuals' labor and wealth from the uncertainties of market ups and downs. Mass home ownership also expanded a vast financial "language" into everyday life: a language for assessing property value, for "rating" the credit and earning potential of individual workers, and most importantly for binding value and credit into the very life and future of populations. As with mass homeownership, the therapeutic culture born of ego psychology simultaneously bracketed and commodified personal life by creating proper domains through which inner life (from war trauma to sexual "normalcy" to depression) could be defined, diagnosed, and treated. Together, homeownership and therapeutic culture produced entangled spheres where personal life could be interiorized into psyches (at the doctor's office) and homes (with government guaranteed mortgages). The effect was to produce standardized languages of (optimal) psychic and financial outcomes. Centered on intervention and optimization, these standardized languages are also easily translatable. On what is good credit predicated if not a sound mind?

By 1972, 62 per cent of all American families lived in their own (owned) home. And although this translated into effective de-vestment of cities in favor of government subsidized suburbs, it is important to recognize how home ownership intertwined not just with national identity but also with the national *economy*. Statistics from the Department of Commerce show that "housing services" (which includes house construction, remodeling, and brokers' fees) constituted anywhere from 15 per cent to 20 per cent of GDP since the 1970s.[9] More than just material production, the housing industry stimulated the very idea of a national economy in public imaginations. Home ownership interiorized the economy as a simultaneous personal and national concern; it brings the abstraction of a unified economic whole into the personal life of individuals and future generations—a concern that intensified during the economic crises of the 1970s. While the economy might be volatile and jobs may come and go, it was believed that the house would be permanent and worthwhile above all else.

The increasing number of subprime loans throughout the 2000s demonstrates how *desire* for homeownership—even when financially unviable—was put to work. For lending banks, the expansion of the real estate market was grounded in the extension of loans to risky borrowers in hopes of "banking" on the short-term profit of securities issued against these loans. This type of capital accumulation also meant that for *low-risk* borrowers (in other words, those who had a substantial down payment, a salaried job, and a good credit rating), home ownership became tethered to the *future failure* of *high-risk* borrowers as a calculated risk on the part of banks. There is a strange blurring or entanglement emergent here—an entanglement not so much between a person and a bank but between some people's credit ratings and others' rage; between some people's desire and others' loss. When we consider the desire for a home, as in the housing market of the last decade, fore-closure—in the financial sense—is required for that market *as a whole* to expand. More simply, home ownership for 'good' borrowers means others will invest but necessarily fail. Christian Marazzi writes, "The expansion of subprime loans shows that, in order to raise and make profits, finance needs to involve the poor, in addition to the middle class. In order to function, this capitalism must invest in the bare life of people who cannot provide any guarantee, who offer nothing apart from themselves" (Marazzi, 2008, p. 40). Thus that home owning citizen-subject, consumer-subject, and laboring-subject of the Fordist regime today becomes a quasi-subject intimately tied to the future well-being or loss of other quasi-subjects, a type of biopolitical production where fictitious capital increasingly permeates the world of people's homes and everyday life as much as its more familiar territory of banking.

The mortgage crisis also underscores how financialization generates unique modes of racialization—unique not necessarily in form but in speed, intensity, and anonymity. Since its inception, the Federal Housing Administration linked race to house and property value explicitly in its *Underwriting Manual*, stipulating racial "covenants" in the house deed that disallowed persons of African descent to occupy the property except in a service capacity. Even after such covenants were deemed illegal in 1948 (*Shelley v. Kraemer*[10]), the FHA devised methods for indirectly coding race into property value: Residential Security Maps, neighborhood rating schematics, and insurance underwriting all took race into account in order enforce existing segregation but also to invest in all-white suburbs (Jackson, 1985, pp. 203–218). While these techniques served to promote racial exclusions, the proliferation of subprime loans in the 2000s advanced a kind of *inclusion* at the substrate of financial data. The practices of rating credit and assessing house values dissociate racial discrimination from humans and re-articulate it in the "neutral" language of finance. Indeed the recipients of subprime loans have been disproportionately black and Latino borrowers. More troubling is the predatory nature of these loans: not only were they disproportionately marketed to black and Latino borrowers, they were purposely devised not to be efficacious as home loans but as mortgage-backed securities.

Of course, the permeation of market logics and activities into any aspect of life is one of the cornerstones of post-Fordist production. Randy Martin (2002), for example, has shown how financialization has become so integrated into daily life that every *life* decision ends up being a *financial* decision. Financialization attaches us to the market in so far as everyone cooperates, markets do well, and there are returns in terms of 401k's, savings and investments, or employment. (Or alternately, when fear or lack of confidence slow down market activity.) In the last decade scholars and critics have paid increasing attention to immaterial and affective labor and to how value is extracted from the *general intellect*—a term Marx used in the *Grundrisse* and has since been elaborated by Italian autonomist theorists. Extending this thought, affect itself has also become a source of value, even the destructiveness of rage. Returning to psychoanalytic theory, foreclosure of certain desires or feelings can be considered a sort of pre-condition for affects. Affects are never unconscious (as affects); rather they *happen*—sometimes as expressions of unconscious ideas and memories, or here, from the repetition of foreclosure, that is unending, modulating desire. We could consider foreclosed homes then to be desire foreclosed. For the owners who destroy their own homes, desire is transformed into affect, into rage. Paulo Virno (2004) has pointed out that negative sentiments such as fear and cynicism in the post-Fordist milieu often become de-politicized and even made to work for capital. Here rage does something similar: wrangling fictitious capital—a toxic financial abstraction—back into a tangible but also toxic commodity. And, while the damage to the homes significantly decreases their prices, in many cases these homes are actually *more likely* to sell precisely because the price is so low. Rage has become marketable.

Foreclosure as potential

It should be clear at this point that I have intentionally blurred the psychoanalytic understanding of foreclosure with the financial one to highlight two things: (1) the historical entanglement of national economy with personal life and the psyche; (2) that psychoanalytic theory presents conceptual tools for understanding this historical entanglement—and necessarily so because psychoanalytic theory itself is implicated in that history. More fundamentally, psychoanalysis acknowledges that its most basic site of concern—the unconscious—cannot be known directly but rather appears through process and exchange, transference, and countertransference. In a sense, the unconscious is *produced* in these exchanges. Given this, foreclosure might seem a negative, unproductive concept—barring desires, enforcing boundaries and identities, and dislocating people from their houses. It bears repeating however that foreclosure in psychoanalytic theory references objects that are not-yet here. If financial foreclosure thwarts one desire (as in homeownership and its attendant histories), it also creates new desires.

Consider the following: The 2012 documentary *The Queen of Versailles* by Lauren Greenfield depicts a wealthy family's stress and malaise after their dream mansion falls into foreclosure. Greenfield's initial goal for the project was to document the building of "the largest home in America" which was to be loosely modeled after Versailles and to reflect its grand excess. Yet the Siegel family's lives take a turn after the financial collapse in 2008. Eventually, the Siegels are no longer able to afford their Versailles even though they have already spent millions on the partially completed mansion. (Several scenes feature matriarch Jackie Siegel walking through the property and describing what might have been—imported marble, decorative fountains, grand staircases.) More than a depiction of foreclosure finally affecting the rich, the film presents a deep irony for the Siegels in that their own fortune was built in large part on the speculative real estate boom—specifically by selling vacation time shares on credit to people who cannot really afford them. In one of the documentary's scenes, we follow a Siegel salesman in Las Vegas touring an African-American couple through the property's various amenities, and then finally selling them the timeshare even after they expressed concern about paying for it.

The Queen of Versailles depicts the lives of several people (both before and after the financial collapse), including the Siegel's seven children, the family's Filipino nanny (who lives in what is essentially a giant dog house), the cranky and despicable father David Siegel, and of course the story's titular figure: Jackie Siegel, the McNugget-loving ex-pageant queen mom whose shallowness and casual callousness provide much fodder for audience contempt. Jackie's vapid lack of self-awareness or irony (especially given her own rags to riches past) elicits a kind of *Schadenfreude* for viewers. Yet the representation of the Siegel's demise in *The Queen of Versailles* points to a much more complex set of emotions and political positions than mere smug self-satisfaction—ones that suggest how ugly feelings present possibilities for social and political transformation.

In his provocative analysis of the psychic, philosophical, and religious histories of rage, Peter Sloterdijk (2010) argues that psychoanalysis has been relatively silent with regard to rage because psychoanalytic theory neglects to account for a third basic drive: the thymotic. While eros accounts for the desire for objects we lack and thanatos for (self-)destructive instincts, thymos refers to a fundamental drive for respect, dignity, pride, and above all recognition.[11] Thinkers such as Wilhelm Reich and Herbert Marcuse have shown how the psychic dimension—erotic desire and destructive impulses, for example—profoundly inform social relations from the politics of authority to the extraction of surplus value. For Sloterdijk, all social formations must also be seen as "the interplay of thymotic centers of tension" in which the thymotic impulses of individuals shape and sustain the thymotic affects of political collectives. Simply put, the need for dignity, self-assertion, and recognition sustains multiple publics (including political, racial/ethnic, sexual, cultural, and class-based publics) and thus propels social transformation and conflict among groups.

Sloterdijk thesis has important implications. The suppression of thymotic impulses *culturally* leads to what he calls a "darkening" of the thymotic dimension and provoking collective emotions such as indignation, over-zealous ambition, and rage. Sloterdijk locates this thymotic suppression as due in large part to the capitalist emphasis on consumption and greed over self-respect and recognition. The resulting rage can emerge in a sudden explosion or can simmer as a "chronic presentiment"; nonetheless, rage circulates and accumulates like capital, it becomes an *asset*. Sloterdijk writes: "If one admits the banking and saving functions of rage assets are real and efficacious, one also understands how it is possible for rage to develop from its diffused initial stage to higher levels of organization. By passing through this progression, rage travels the road from local and intimate emotion to public and political program" (pp. 59–60). Sloterdijk eschews much of the insight and nuance of psychoanalytic theory (especially the unconscious) in order to describe a very specific circulation and exchange of affect. Nonetheless, his work acknowledges *desire* as an operative force in social recognition, and that rage is one way that foreclosed (thymotic) desire takes form.

For examples of how rage can morph from the individual to the social and political, we need only to look at recent history. The Tea Party movement congealed in part from shared rage: whether it was outrage over the 2008 bank bailout or indignation over the election of an African-American president or rage around "illegal" immigrants, rage seemed to be a unifying element around which disparate political constituencies could rally and organize. Or consider the outrage following the "random" shootings in a movie theatre in Aurora, CO, at a Sikh temple in Oak Park, WI, and at an elementary school in Sandyhook, CT. Rage surrounding these incidents has energized progressive campaigns for greater gun control, religious tolerance, and expanded mental health services. We could thus think of rage as assembling different kinds of "publics," even ones that are fleeting. Building on the work of Michel Foucault and Gabriel Tarde, Tiziana Terranova (2007) argues that publics are multiple: they come and go, and they co-exist with other publics. For her, publics result from some kind of affective capture, from some shared event, object, or feeling. Rage then is not an identity but the precondition for particular kinds of publics that need thymotic expression.

In the case of home foreclosures, individual homeowners expressed their rage by destroying and trashing their homes upon foreclosure. I argue that this rage has transformed over time into a political project, creating a *public* concerned with housing justice, homelessness, and a range of related issues. Occupy Our Homes (occupyourhomes.org), an offshoot of the Occupy Wall Street movement, organized in Fall 2012 to protest evictions, interrupt auctions, and even take over vacant houses. Occupy activists have devised many creative tactics for realizing the groups' goals. In East New York, activists took over a foreclosed two-story home and moved in a homeless family (Devereau, 2011). In Atlanta, protestors went to local county courthouses to disrupt foreclosure auctions (Christie, 2011). In Los Angles, artist Olga Koumoundouros transformed a vacant foreclosed house into an art piece entitled "Notorious Possession" in which she painted the house gold and built sculptural installations. Indeed, art has been a powerful means of directing foreclosure rage into a politicized aesthetic project, as in a group art show in May 2012 in New York City entitled "Foreclosed: Between Crisis and Possibility" curated by Jennifer Burris, Sofia Olascoaga, and Gaia Tedone, and sponsored by the Whitney Museum of American Art. Since the National Day of Action to Occupy Our Homes on December 6, 2012, the movement has taken hold in cities around the country and aligned itself with other activist organizations.

The Occupy Our Homes movement exemplifies how rage and other negative affects can be transformed into political potentials. It points to the necessity for developing cultural and political outlets for thymotic expression. Following Sloterdijk, we see above all that the economy—any economy—can and must be understood in terms of rage. He writes:

> Just like the monetary economy, the rage economy passes a critical marker once rage has advanced from local accumulation and selective explosion to the level of systematic investment and cyclic increase. In the case of money, one calls this difference the transition from treasure hoarding to capital. For rage, the corresponding transformation is reached once the vengeful infliction of pain is transformed from revenge to revolution. Revolution cannot be a matter of resentment of an isolated private person, although such affects are also instantiated in its decisive moment. Revolution rather implies the creation of a bank of rage whose investments should be considered in as precise detail as any operation before a final battle, or actions of a multinational corporation before being taken over by a hostile competitor. (2006, p. 64)

Although still a nascent effort, Occupy Our Homes represents how individual rage is invested and transformed into affective capital, presenting the possibility for "untraveled paths for collective rage" (p. 25). Critics of the various Occupy movements (including Occupy Our Homes) are swift to dismiss these possibilities: for the Right, Occupy lacks a clear agenda much less clear demands; for the Left, Occupy's reluctance to align itself with a party or to enter the political process formally (e.g. lobbying for legislative reform) signals a certain kind of impotency, one that resurfaces in current academic discussion of the movement. Nonetheless it is desire itself, desire foreclosed that is the precondition for creating new ideas and new alliances around objectives not-yet-formed. This is one reason why foreclosure is such a fecund concept: Even as it describes a tenuous boundary separating the thinkable and unthinkable, reality and psychic life, it also suggests how desire—be it individual or collective—might reconfigure that boundary and indeed our collective futures.

Notes

1. Quoted in Harvey (2006, p. 70); originally in Marx's *Capital*, Volume 3.
2. Virno, 2004 uses the term "emotional situation" to describe an affective atmosphere that structures social and cultural life in post-Fordist capitalism.
3. American psychologist Sylvan Tompkins developed this thesis in a much more complex, nuanced manner. See Sedgwick and Frank (1995).
4. The reference point here is Freud's analysis of Dr. Schreber. See Freud (1996) *Three Case Histories*.
5. Another way to say this is that foreclosure is a process through which one kind of "subject" and one kind of "outside world" are mutually constituted, but always with a remainder or excess. Desire is the necessary counterpoint to foreclosure—desire for the subjects/outside posed by the excess of fore-closure but not yet realizable psychically, institutionally, financially, or any number of ways.
6. Thus far I have not distinguished between *home* and *house*. I think it's fair to say that *house* designates the physical structure of a space of private, domes-tic life whereas *home* designates the specific and general meanings, ideolo-gies, memories, expectations, and experiences attached to *house*. I use the terms interchangeably here but only within my argument that houses were physical and financial modes of interiorizing larger historical phenomena.
7. Cohn's point is that the house, estate, manor, etc. in Europe are "grounded" in feudal social relationships whereas Americans were confronted with the need to cultivate original meanings. Missing from Cohn's account however is an account of the necessity of houses and community-building within the larger project of settler colonialism. An elaboration of this facet of "the American house" might elucidate why houses needed a special meaning both locally and nationally. I would contend that the American house was— from its first brick—a structure in search of meaning.
8. Reprinted from Jackson (1985).
9. As reported by the National Association of Home Builders, www.nahb.org
10. *Shelley v. Kramer*, 334 U.S. 1 (1948).
11. Of course, Jacques Lacan (following Kojeve and Hegel) introduced recogni-tion as a fundamental aspect of psychoanalytic theory. Yet for him, the need for recognition ultimately originates in *lack* of the signifying aim.

References

Arrighi, G. (1994) *The Long Twentieth Century: Money, Power and Origins of Our Times* (New York: Verso).

Butler, J. (1997) *The Psychic Life of Power* (Stanford: Stanford University Press).

Christie, L. (2011) "Occupy Protestors Take Over Foreclosed Homes," *CNN Money*, December 6, 2011.

Cohn, J. (1979) *The Palace or the Poorhouse: The American House as Cultural Symbol* (East Lansing: Michigan State University Press).

Deverau, R. (2011) "Occupy Our Homes: Protestors Bid to Move Families into Foreclosed Houses," *The Guardian*, December 7, 2011.

Eigen, M. (2002) *Rage* (Middletown: Wesleyan University Press).

Freud, S. (1996) *Three Case Histories* (New York: Touchstone).

Greenfield, L. (dir.) (2012) *The Queen of Versaille* (Documentary) (Evergreen Pictures).

Griffin, D. and D. Fitzpatrick (2009) "Experts: Some Foreclosed Homes too Damaged to Sell," *CNN*, http://www.cnn.com/2009/US/04/16/damaged.fore-closures/ (Online Article).

Harvey, D. (2006) *Limits to Capital* (New York: Verso).

Jackson, K. (1985) *Crabgrass Frontier: The Suburbanization of the United States* (New York: Oxford University Press).

Lacan, J. (2006) "Response to Jean Hyppolite's Commentary on Freud's 'Verneinung'," B. Fink (trans.) *Ecrits* (New York: W.W. Norton and Co).

Lacan, J. [1986] (1992) *The Ethics of Psychoanalysis: Lectures 1959–1960*, D. Porter (trans.) (New York: W. W. Norton & Company).

Marazzi, C. (2008) *Capital and Language*, G. Conti (trans.) (Los Angeles: Semiotext(e)).

Marazzi, C. (2010) *The Violence of Financial Capitalism*, K. Lebedeva (trans.) (Los Angeles: Semiotext(e)).

Martin, R. (2002) *The Financialization of Daily Life* (Philadelphia: Temple University Press).

Marx, K. (1993a) *Grundrisse Foundations of the Critique of Political Economy*, M. Nicolaus (trans.) (London: Penguin Books).

Marx, K. (1993b) *Capital Volume 3*, D. Fernbach (trans.) (New York: Penguin Classics).

Miller, D. (2009) "Rescuers Still Trying to Catch Cats in Foreclosed Lakemore Home," *Cleveland Plain Dealer*, July 19, 2009.

Ngai, S. (2004) *Ugly Feelings* (Cambridge: Harvard University Press).

Phillips, M. (2008) "Buyer's Revenge: Trash the House after Foreclosure. Banks Pay People Off to Deter Home Rage; Loose Pets; Paint Spills," *The Wall Street Journal*, March 28, 2008.

Sedgwick, E. K. and A. Frank (eds) (1995) *Shame and Its Sisters: A Silvan Tomkins Reader* (Durham: Duke University Press).

Sloterdijk, P. (2010) *Rage and Time: A Psychopolitical Investigation*, M. Wenning (trans.) (New York: Columbia University Press).

Terranova, T. (2007) "Futurepublic: On Information Warfare, Bio-racism and Hegemony as Noopolitics," *Theory, Culture, and Society*, 24, 125–145.

Turkle, S. (1992) *Psychoanalytic Politics* (New York: The Guilford Press).

Virno, P. (2004) *A Grammar for the Multitude*, I. Bertoletti, J. Cascaito, and A. Casson (trans.) (Los Angeles: Semiotext(e)).

Zaretsky, E. (2005) *Secrets of the Soul* (New York: Vintage).

13
Melancholia and the Racial Order: A Psychosocial Analysis of America's Enduring Racism

Jeffrey Prager

Introduction: The American racialized order and recursive inequality

A distinctive feature of the US, since its inception, is a remarkably steady and persistent division between *whites* and *blacks*. This distinction was based on the premise of a natural, real and durable *racial* difference between Africans and Europeans. Still today, the *black/white* binary sustains systematic inequality between the two groups through a set of largely unconscious institutional practices, rules, values, mores, emotions, and beliefs systematically producing for each unequal opportunities, discrepant life-chances, and distinctive social outcomes. This pattern of inequality has sustained itself over time, remaining in place post-slavery, post-Jim Crow, post-desegregation, post-Civil Rights reforms, and post-Obama.

And yet, while this inequality is treated by social scientists as a discrete social problem requiring various institutional responses to correct it, the constancy of the division over time suggests something quite different. The racialized division is not, in the first instance, a "social problem" amenable to repair. It is more intractable, describing, I argue, a key organizing principle of American society there from the start: a legitimated social hierarchy through *racial* division. Lying mostly beneath conscious awareness and despite profound challenges to them over the past two centuries, racialized categories remain a key determinant, of the American stratification system. It is characterized here as the *American racialized order*. The questions posed in this paper are (1) what *function* does racialized inequality serve, and (2) through what mechanisms is it maintained and reproduced over time? Why and how has *racial* demarcation, in other words, remained a constant feature of American history, despite periodic moments challenging the depth and nature of inequality (though never the category of race itself). I conclude, not with a set of prescriptions for inequality's overcoming. Rather, based upon this new understanding of the nature of the problem, informed by psychoanalytic ideas, I pose a new set of questions to think how best to overcome America's traumatic history of racially defined domination.

Blacks and *whites* for Americans serve, then and now, as a critical *raison d'être*, a satisfactory explanation for the presence of inequality *naturalized* through the lens of racial category. These particular categories, designated to specific individuals and groups, have no counterpart outside American society. As the sociologist Michael Banton writes, "The USA is exceptional in the extent to which *race* is a basis for social categorization" (2013, p. 1003). As I will argue, it is "a product of domination" and reproduced, as Pierre Bourdieu might describe it, through an "immense symbolic machine." "When their (the dominated's) thoughts and perceptions are structured in accordance with the very structures of the relation of domination that is imposed on them," Bourdieu writes, "[the dominator's] their acts of *cognition* are, inevitably, acts of *recognition*, submission" (2001, p. 13).

Americans, throughout their history, have continually discussed the following questions: to what extent has the condition of *blacks* improved over time, in what ways and where has the gap between *whites* and *blacks* narrowed, and what factors account for the continuing inequality between these two *racial* groups? These, however, do not illuminate the role that *race* plays as a **category** shaping American perception of the world they inhabit. Further, these questions detract from exploring racism's purpose, the *task* that racial inequality *accomplishes* in American society.[1] The question, the obverse of the conventional ones usually asked, is the more relevant: why, in America, through the course of its history, has *race* continually served an important role as regulator or stabilizer of inequality? Racialized categories originally designed to secure domination for Europeans continue to serve this first function, *viz., the exclusion of a sector of the population from power, authority, wealth and control.* Continued inequality by race—*whites* over *blacks*—documents the pattern and persistence of an American hierarchy of domination thoroughly naturalized through categorical distinction. This inequality has been more or less continuous over time even though *real*, that is, actual, material, *racial* differences play no role in its reproduction. The questions that presume the possibility of gradual improvements between *blacks* and *whites*, or predict the eventual *overcoming* of racial inequality, what might be called the *humanistic fallacy* of inequality's elimination, distracts attention away from the built-in and possibly permanent relation of racialized inequality to America's unique system of stratification and hierarchy.

Independent of cultural construction, *racial* groups as discrete entities do not exist.[2] Paradoxically, they exert a powerful effect, decisively shaping political, economic and social outcomes, i.e. *whites* as the beneficiaries, *blacks* as the deprived, *thereby* reinforcing the perception of American racial reality. In fact, the presence of racial groups promotes an important sense of a solidaristic, inclusive society comprised of the *racially* dominant, revealed through the constant presence of an unequal *racial* and subordinate other.

Three features of contemporary American racialized reality, as a result of having asked the *wrong* questions, have been hidden from view. First, *black* and *white* is a **civil** designation indicating one's participation (and one's place) in American "civil society." The categories, in fact, possess no reality independent of civil society,[3] and carry with them no *essential* or irrefutable information of a person's ancestral past, past personal history, nor of personal capacities, propensities, values, and so forth, of the person identifying or being identified as *white* or *black*.[4]

As designations generated within civil society and denoting difference, however the categories possess powerful assumptions and projections toward the of their *essential* features and traits of the individual other. Simply put, one symbolically serves as the *anti-representation* of the other. Perceiving individuals *through* racial category, as Americans do, simultaneously locates the perceiver and the perceived in a temporal trajectory uniquely American. A contemporary encounter with a *racial other* necessarily includes the memory, inscribed in the physical appearance of the person, of a distinctive and unequal past history. Each racialized interaction between individuals, in other words, is inescapably fraught with a uniquely American historical memory to be denied, acknowledged, refuted, ignored and so forth but, nonetheless, in some interpersonal sense always to be responded to.

Each American expresses a history that he or she cannot entirely possess (Caruth, 2002), a racially identifiable visage, always a possible trigger for a traumatic reminder that no one can fully contain. This *excess* possession interferes with *mutual recognition* of one human being to another, promoting instead an interaction between one (historically) dominant person and one (historically) subordinate one. It is a relationship, in the context of the story of America, to be presently negotiated against the backdrop of a thick, meaningful and racialized history.

The result is a structure of interaction reinforcing "symbolic domination" and "symbolic force" (Bourdieu, 2001, pp. 37–38) and, in fact, continues to produce for the aggregate group of African-Americans *and* all those designated as *blacks* profoundly detrimental effects economically, politically, educationally and in many other respects.[5] As these various forms of inequalities are reproduced, these racialized differences in outcome endure and generate the real, material conditions for racist thought to persist and even thrive. The category generates its own confirmation in reality.

Second, *blacks* and *whites* participate in the same civil society and more or less share the racist conviction of the real and taken for granted differences that exist between the two groups. Those who identify themselves either as among the dominant or the subordinate typically understand differently the sources of those differences. Some may locate the source of difference more squarely on the shoulders of social factors, while others on natural differences to account for one's own position in the hierarchy. Nevertheless, the entire civic population is involved in the reproduction of durable difference and subject to the same system of meaning and significance implied by it.[6] As I describe later, the potency of this binary **civil** designation of *white* and *black* in America closely parallels the binary of being male or female. Yet gender identity, unlike racial identity, is forged first largely in the crucible of **private**, family life and not in the public sphere.

What has gone largely unnoticed, at any given point in time, is the significant alteration of demographic composition of those perceived as *white* or *black*, despite the presumption of its unchanging and natural character, simply a "mirror of reality." Racialized differences and their treatment as natural generate a perception by all at any point in time of the permanence (as trans-historical and trans-social) of the categories, and who among the social members are included, and where.

Thus, this third important feature of the American racialized reality: while the composition of those included as *white* and *black* has changed over the course of American history, the pattern of inequality expressed through the perception of racial difference remains constant. "Mere perceiving," Erving Goffman writes, "is a much more active penetration of the world than at first might be thought . . . Observers actively project their frames of reference into the world immediately around them, and one fails to see their doing so only because events ordinarily confirm these projections, causing the assumptions to disappear into the smooth flow of activity." (Goffman, 1986, pp. 38–39). Social scientists, policy makers, and the general public do not notice that the principles by which ethnic or cultural groups are included has shifted. Through scientific and natural observation, the reality of racial difference is *found* as an objective fact despite its social construction.

Oddly enough, those included in this racialized binary corresponds only in the most imprecise way to actual phenotypical differences possessed by various American ethnic groups. In the first place, the terms *white* and *black* belie the fact that no one, in terms of complexion, in actuality is either white or black. Skin tones, while wide-ranging with respect to pigmentation, do not extend to either of these extremes. Nonetheless, Americans perceive individuals categorically, and, unless made aware of it, believe they are "seeing" white and black people. The perception of whiteness implies, I suggest, an understanding of the group members place among the dominant group while blackness, in contrast, reflects membership among the subordinate. A notable feature of the United States is that Americans feel seemingly compelled, if there is any uncertainty, to ask a person to self-identify his or racial membership; once it is established that an individual possesses a *black* lineage, even the lightest complexioned African-American, for example, is seen to be *black* and suitably located as possessing a history of ancestry belonging to the subordinate group. As Goffman suggests, the perception of whiteness and blackness implies "an active penetration of the world" and, for those in American civil society, "naturally" need to locate individuals with respect to the hierarchical frame of race relevant to the US.

Three instances demonstrate the fluidity of membership: (i) Once considered as dangerous foreigners, dark-skinned and explicitly barred from equal participation among the dominant, Jews, Catholics, Irish, and Italians now identify themselves and are perceived by others as *white*.[7] Over time, new immigrants, following the trajectory of earlier immigrants, mark successful assimilation to American society by similarly succeeding in "becoming white." (Roediger, 1991, 2005; Thandeka, 1999; Loveman and Muniz, 2006).

(ii) Those immigrants, seemingly corresponding with those, like Filipinos and Mexican and Central American immigrants, who possess fewer financial resources and arrive in the US with less human capital have found "becoming white" far more challenging. Those with fewer cultural and economic resources find it more difficult to be perceived as "white." In each of the social institutions in which these immigrants come into contact, they tend to encounter more hostility and greater barriers to assimilation. The police, criminal justice system, health care services, and schools become site of considerable conflict, often generating a strong oppositional culture. High gang-related participation by the young, social withdrawal and indigenous political critique, sometimes inflected through the lexicon of race, historically more closely parallels the African-American experience and becomes responded to similarly. *La Raza* and Aztlan—assertions of racial difference—emerged as reactions to inequality and exclusion reflecting a strong identification with "black" inequality. As Edward Telles and Vilma Ortiz argue, the increased "racialization" of Mexican and Central American populations has been occurring (2008).

(iii) In similar fashion, eighteenth and nineteenth century America consisted of individuals possessing graduated "racial composition." Distinctions were made and acted upon between full-blooded Africans, mulattoes, octoroons, high yellow, quadroons and so forth. These categories of distinction have long since given way to what is now colloquially referred to as the one-drop rule. Evidence of any blood connection to an African past necessarily denotes "being black." The *black* side of the racial binary over the years, in sum, has become more inclusive, including any individual, or group of individuals, deemed *non-white*. Barack Obama, no less, is designated as *black* or *non-white*. This parallels the process by which those deemed to be *non-black* have increasingly become included as part of the *white* side. Inclusion and exclusion is a *negotiated* feature of the American racial order, increasingly dualistic, and the rules of who goes where has changed over time.

Fourth, the American racial order has had many challenges to the treatment accorded and opportunities afforded to *blacks;* yet none of these campaigns have challenged the *reality* of racial difference upon which racism is built. There have been times in American history when the rights of the subordinate have been significantly renegotiated and specific features of the hierarchical relationship between *blacks* and *whites* altered. Most dramatically, the passage of the 13th, 14th and 15th Amendments to the US Constitution following the end of the Civil War; the *Brown v. Board of Education* decision by the Supreme Court in 1954 declaring segregation by race unconstitutional in public schools; and the passage of the Civil and Voting Rights Acts in response to the Civil Rights movement of the 1960s marking the end of Jim Crow legislation and mitigating against its continued practices. To be sure, these changes marked significant improvements for the lives of African-Americans and other *blacks* in America. Each of the political movements that propelled these changes were motivated to respond to racialized inequities and to challenge inequality by racial category in America. Still, the stability, cohesiveness and distinctiveness of these "two separate societies—one white, one black" (US Government, 1968) remains impressive, and secure.

The *capacity* of the racialized binary to organize, shape and effect social relations in the US is demonstrated in a number of ways. Nearly every indicator of inequality in America demonstrates of this phenomenon. I offer only a sample of available evidence documenting the persistence over time of inequality by racialized inequality. The ratio of black to white unemployment, for example, over the last 50 years has remained remarkably stable: in 1963, black unemployment was 2.2 times greater than white unemployment; in 2012, it was 2.1 times greater.[8] According to the Pew Research Center, over the past 50 years, the rate of blacks living below the poverty line declined close to fourteen per cent (and rising), while the rate of whites living below the poverty line declined to five per cent (and rising more slowly). The rate for Hispanics closely parallels the black rate both in absolute numbers and in change. Said differently, since 1963, the percentage of the black population living below the poverty line was on average about twenty per cent higher than whites. At best, the difference between groups narrowed (about thirteen per cent) the most in the year 2000, but now the gap appears to be widening once more, as a steeper climb of blacks living below the poverty line is occurring compared to the total population of blacks than it is for whites.[9] Similar striking parallels are provided with respect to average family wealth over the past 50 years, and real median household income.[10] The *rate* of inequality on all these measures, despite variation in absolute numbers, remains remarkably constant. It indicates no dramatic decline in the degree of inequality between whites and blacks. Finally, as another indicator of the stability of the racialized binary, incarceration rates for both black men and black women are dramatically increasing with respect to the percentage of the black population over the last 50 years and the ratio of black to white incarceration is significantly larger now than it was in 1960.[11]

Several times in recent history the nation has been confronted with events or a series of events demonstrating the power of the *black/white* binary to be decisive for shaping individuals' perception. In both the case in which O. J. Simpson was tried for murder and in the George Zimmerman trial over the killing of Trayvon Martin (Hunt, 1999), the radicalized context through which information was processed reveals the variance in opinion between *blacks* and *whites* toward both Simpson and Zimmerman. In an ABC News/Washington

Post poll, eighty-six per cent of blacks disapproved of the verdict exonerating Zimmerman from murder, compared to thirty-one per cent of whites. Similarly, thirty-three per cent of whites believed the shooting death of Martin to be unjustified compared to eighty-seven per cent of blacks.[12] For those whose perception is shaped by their subordination in America, the country continually violates the *social contract* that it putatively honors. Civic identity as *white*, in contrast, implies fundamental trust in the institutions of social control to uphold fairness and justice as foundational to the American rule of law.

As these various examples demonstrate, racializing American inequality is as American as apple pie. It is also uniquely American. The invocation of racial difference *as if it is real* has long served in the US as a principal mechanism of social, political, economic and cultural exclusion for those determined to be *racially other*. Based upon the assertion that these *categories of classification* reproduce the reality imagined by the distinction drawn, the conclusion is a bold one: Americans' *perception* of racial difference—seeing persons as *white* and *black*—**follows** rather than **precedes** these socially structured and collectively imposed distinctions of dominance and subordination. The appearance, the taken-for-granted, is that the history of racial difference in America, a legacy of the institution of slavery, continues to *explain* American inequality. In fact, *the belief* in racial difference, first enabling the institution of slavery restricted to Africans and remaining more-or-less unchanging since, serves as justification and acquiescence to the on-going pattern of inequality by racial category.

American melancholia: Acquiescence, misrecognition, and collective devitalization

A further remarkable feature of American civil society is its long-standing *tolerance* for racialized inequality. This is a corollary to recognizing its persistence throughout the course of American history. Even as inequality has been strongly challenged and increasingly overcome for other subject classes in America—women, in particular, but also religious minorities, gays and lesbians, those from non-European national and linguistic backgrounds, members of American society, for all intents and purposes, have been more-or-less reconciled to these racialized patterns of difference. The stability of inequality by racial category in nearly all institutional spheres is one demonstration of this national acquiescence, the routinization of *de facto* different treatments accorded *whites* and *blacks*, especially by various institutions of social control. The relative quiescence of active challenges to the racialized *status quo* by subject members (and their advocates) is further demonstration of this form of acceptance. Racially-encoded myths are almost universally accepted *as if* they are true, what Foucault might call ironically as a *"true* discourse of power and domination" (Foucault, [1978] 1900, p. 69, my emphasis). Inequality is so long-standing and accepted as taken-for-granted, rather than promoting outrage, the racialized order itself is reinforced. The inequalities generated by the categorical distinction serve as evidence for the *real* differences existing between *whites* and *blacks*. The stability of the racialized order both contributes to the stability of American culture and society **and** promotes acquiescence to the way things are.

Melancholia, as Freud defined it, is a psychological condition when individuals suffer from an oftentimes vague, ill-defined sense of loss that lingers over time (Freud, [1917] 1954). Here, I identify American civil society as beset with *racialized melancholia*, a result of the universally held conviction of the reality of racialized difference and wide-spread belief in the inequalities generated. Unlike societies in which the past is mourned, American society, I argue, has been a collectivity largely unable to either identify or mourn its loss and, as a result, possesses melancholic relation to it. It is constituted by an (largely) unconscious conviction that racialized division, inherited from the past, constitutes a permanent feature of American life.

Melancholia, as it is used here, describes, first, the subjective experience of those who live within the American racial order. It describes a particular psychic structure common to nearly all those socialized as participants in the nation. Racialized melancholia is especially resistant to change because of its insistence that common membership in the social order is *naturally* split by racial difference. Thus, the reification of the category assumes the form of a personal characteristic "possessed" by the observable person, persons who act and are acted upon as if racial difference is real. Indeed, sometimes when that characteristic cannot be easily discerned, one feels compelled to establish it through a direct question: *what* are you? The need to establish race is almost as compelling as it is to establish, as first order of business, the gender of an infant boy or girl. In that sense, American society creates an unhealthy, or pathological, psyche, one that is convinced of the reality of its own collectively generated perception. As a result, it is a reality on extremely difficult to undo. Melancholic racial orders are those where the promise of assimilation, to quote Martin Luther King, Jr. in which individuals will be judged "not by the color of their skin but by the content of their character," has failed significantly and systematically.

What will be described is the uniqueness of melancholic subjectivity in America, a product largely of a society that simultaneously asserts the equality of all humankind while insisting, as well, on the truthfulness of its categorization of its own members by race. Gunnar Myrdal, in 1944, describes the "American Dilemma" as the conflict between American liberal ideals and the actual plight of African-Americans. In contrast, the American dilemma here is defined through the concept of *racial melancholia*: In the US, melancholy powerfully captures the subjective, or feeling state, both of *whites* (whose "Dilemma" Myrdal was **only** addressing) **and** *blacks*, especially in their institutional and interpersonal interactions between one another. *Blacks* and *whites* have an intertwined history, where existence and identification of each marks a **common** American past and, therefore, who are inextricably linked culturally and affectively. It has generated nearly impossible relationships, or painfully self-conscious ones, between those who identify themselves or are identified as dominant and those who see themselves or are seen by others as subordinate. Typically covert and *de facto*, racism continues to structure interpersonal and institutional relationships. What, in fact, is nothing more than a broadly-cast civil category imposed on one's own sense of self, nonetheless easily overwhelms the capacity of two individuals to interact independently of the inherent domination and subordination implied by the category. The "American dilemma" might be reformulated as a cognitive conflict between liberal ideals and the commonly held conviction by *all* social members that racial difference and inequality in America expresses real, or essential, differences between peoples.

Racial melancholia also can be described from the perspective of an American political structure built upon two essential racialized features: a) **an institutional denial** of the past and **a forgetting** of the history of slavery of Africans as foundational to the construction of American society and b) **a suppression** of the fact that this history of oppression was legitimated through a narrative of the sub-human characteristics of Africans as well as Native Americans. This particular defensive relation to the country's past, its racialized form of denying, forgetting and suppressing, forecloses the possibility of a future where relations between *whites* and *blacks* can be anything significantly different than they are now: America is premised upon the permanent and uneasy encounter between dominant *whites* and the *black* other, while *blacks* remain ever-alert to being singled out as other. The result is a social system in which both institutional and interpersonal mechanisms are in place to promote American life as lived *eternally in the present*. In contrast with an acknowledgement of the contribution played by the past in the present, history now is either romanticized or demonized—or romanticized by some and demonized by others. But either way, it serves to reinforce the categories of melancholic resignation in the present: Racialized inequality is simply a feature of the US. Described here is a social and political system, from its beginning, organized defensively through denial and suppression.

In *Melancholy and Society*, the sociologist Wolf Lepeneis describes certain societies as melancholic when political energy and will is strategically employed restrictively in order for a particular past not to overwhelm its functioning in the present. He describes this as a "**surplus of order**" (Lepeneis, 1992). In the American case, the restrictive use of the past might be seen to be a case of a "**surplus of racialized order.**" Both as subjective experience and as socio-political structure, racialized melancholia and the surplus of racialized order generate what will be characterized as a defensive and protective stance toward other Americans who, as a result live eternally in the present. In the present, it insures a societal incapacity to recognize the "other." Misrecognition, and defensive forms of self-protection from the harm induced by "not being seen" define the nature of American racism. In its self-protectiveness and self-absorption, it detracts from richer, more robust imaginings of the future for the nation as a whole and ways enthusiastically to imagine ones place in it.[13]

Melancholia for the individual suffering it, as Freud describes, generates a poorer and emptier "ego" (Freud, [1917] 1954). Unable to detach affect (for Freud, libido) from an ill-defined lost object, the melancholic does not feel the freedom to move freely and affectively in the present. Instead, unable to be rid of his or her emotional attachment to *a something that cannot be clearly identified*, he or she lives nostalgically. Features of a melancholic society parallel Freud's description of the suffering individual. Unable to emotionally detach itself from the past—because of denial, suppression, and forgetting—the entire society structures itself, institutionally and interpersonally, to continue to relive its past, or, said differently, to live *in the past* **as if** it were the present. Because these categories of perception are generated collectively, they are products of American civil society. Melancholia is a product of the collectivity. Though racism is carried by those individuals who have become part of American society, its elimination depends on a change of collective perception. It requires a **civil remembering** of its exploitative past, an acknowledgment of the damages that resulted and continues to result for all those who participated. Only as a result of collective remembering and acknowledgement, I argue, will the pattern of domination instituted through racialized demarcation cease to be reproduced. Only then will the compulsive repetition of the pattern be broken.[14]

The American child and the racialized traumatic rupture: The transmission of racism across generations

As Freud describes in his wonderfully rich essay "Mourning and Melancholia," the melancholic never binds his or her sense of loss, it remains an open wound though it is a loss so deep it oftentimes cannot be specified because it always remains unconscious. "The distinguishing mental features of melancholia are . . . in some way related to an object-loss which is withdrawn from consciousness, in contradistinction to mourning, in which there is nothing about the loss that is unconscious." (Freud, [1917] 1954, pp. 244–245). The idealized lost object is introjected, that is, it becomes part of one's self, and serves, in its perfected and internalized guise, as an agent of self-criticism and harsh judgment. In mourning, Freud suggests, loss is eventually internalized into one's self, as ego, and therefore does not stand in super-ego judgment over ego. "In mourning, it is the world which has become poor and empty," Freud writes, "in melancholia it is the ego itself" (p. 246). The unconscious lost union becomes forever a shadow over the self that promotes, in individuals who suffer it, an incapacity to be fully and presently alive.

Freud, later in his writings, as well as many psychoanalysts and social theorists today, move away from his original assertion that melancholia is necessarily pathological. Rather he and others, recognize this as part of the human condition. Judith Butler, for example, writing in *Melancholy Gender/Refused Identification*, suggests that heterosexuality, because of the cultural potency of homosexual prohibition, "requires" the foreswearing of overt sexualized love for the same-sex parent. This loss of love cannot be overcome, Butler asserts. It generates instead a diffuse, unconscious, melancholic attachment to a connection now "necessarily" broken, though unconsciously preserved (Butler, 1997). This follows upon Freud's (*The Ego and the Id*) own later revision in which he suggests that the lost wholeness once felt, in the effort to preserve it, generates *identification* with that object. Butler describes this process as a "melancholic identification" with the lost object. This identification, a boy with his mother, for example, inscribes on the boy a "gendered character," in which he "melancholically" incorporates his mother as part of himself; he preserves his connection to her by taking her inside of him. Dangerous to his "masculinity," these "feminine" features need to be repudiated. As Butler writes, "the desire for the feminine is marked by that repudiation: he wants the woman he would never be. He wouldn't be caught dead being her: therefore he wants her" (p. 137). Desire, both for Freud and Butler, expresses this melancholic rupture, the brokenness of the world, and the desire for reunion. Men, for women, typically make their world whole; women, for men, theirs. They are each "primary others" for one another, and help repair each other's world.

For both Freud and for Butler, the family serves as the interpersonal crucible through which heterosexual identity occurs. It requires the suppression of sexual ambivalences, and the re-directed striving for wholeness fundamental to one's core sense-of-being. But other challenges productive of self-formation happen too outside the family context, within various settings in civil society. Identification and identity acquisition continue to be driven by other kinds of tears in the experience of wholeness, as children experience the loss (sometimes traumatically) of the sense of security and one-ness or wholeness they had once felt in their relationship to mother and father. Perhaps less fundamental than sexual and gender identity but nonetheless required for a person to operate meaningfully in this world, these largely unconscious psychic acquisitions are navigated outside of the family, in civil society, and in the context of the broader social and cultural institutional life. These identities influence a person's positioning and participation in the larger society and culture.

The novelist Michael Chabon poignantly captures the universal experience of a child coming-to-terms with his or her (the) imperfect world. He writes, "the world is so big, so complicated, so replete with marvels and surprises that it takes years for most people to begin to notice that it is, also, irretrievably broken. We call this period of research 'childhood.'"

(2013, p. 23). But brokenness, as in the discovery of human mortality, is a condition every human being must reckon with. He continues:

> There follows a program of renewed inquiry, often involuntary, into the nature and effects of mortality, entropy, heartbreak, violence, failure, cowardice, duplicity, cruelty, and grief; the researcher learns their histories, and their bitter lessons, by heart. Along the way, he or she discovers that the world has been broken for as long as anyone can remember, and struggles to reconcile this fact with the ache of cosmic nostalgia that arises, from time to time, in the researcher's heart: an intimation of vanished glory, of lost wholeness, a memory of the world unbroken. We call the moment at which this ache arises 'adolescence.' The feeling haunts people all their lives. (p. 23)

American children—once they are exposed to the media, to school, to religious institutions, and to other voluntary or secondary associations—find themselves confronted with the reality of *blacks* and *whites*, a socio-cultural construction enhanced and made real by the elaboration of unique histories for each group, epic tales of triumph and tragedy discrete for each, and separate social experiences currently distinguishing one people from the other. It is the necessary stuff of identity-formation. Racial difference in America is civil society's counterpart to sexual difference as discovered and navigated in the family. Because race in America has always been so affectively fraught (replete with feelings of fear, guilt, anger, danger, etc.), a child's encounter with it likely is the first traumatic encounter outside the family with brokenness.[15] There are many different motivations by adults to teach their children about racial difference that include a humanitarian one (describing the evils of slavery and the achievement of civil rights for all), a protective one (to prepare the child for the reality of discrimination and danger because of the *perception* of difference and individuals willingness to act on it), or a racist one (to demarcate good people from bad ones). Nonetheless, the imposition of racial difference on children's perception typically precedes a Natural awarness of phenotypical differences. It constitutes for the children a traumatic rupture in their world of wholeness. From then on, race serves a continual and irreparable trigger for the brokenness of the world: a source of fear, danger and distinction. This is the reason why encounters between *whites* and *blacks* can often be so emotionally fraught, full of affective excess. Racial difference, for all who subscribe to it, is a remainder of the world's imperfection.

Racism, the conviction of the immutable difference between people who vary (at best) only phenotypically, serves as a first line of defense against the trauma of loss—a loss defended against by the reassuring presence of a non-incorporable other. *Grief* over the loss of wholeness transposes itself to *grievance*.[16] Just as the boy defends against knowing his internalized mother through various expressions of hypermasculinity and desire for the girl, racial otherness is its civil counterpart. It is a defense against the wish for unbrokenness, the wish that "the affliction had never existed." (Abraham and Torok, 1994, p. 134).

The incontrovertible American belief in two kinds of people—*whites* and *blacks*—is a way **not to know**. It constitutes a grievance that may express itself in many different ways, sometimes dependent on one's place in the racialized American hierarchy. It operates so individuals might not re-experience the pain of early separation and loss, life's imperfection, and the longing to return. Typically invoked first in the social world beyond the family, racism fends off the childish wish for wholeness. The American belief in the reality of racialized difference and one's identification with one **or** the other *race* is necessarily melancholic, as Freud defines it. Individual differentiation—autonomy, activity, and private pleasures as an adult—are pursued while simultaneously (unconsciously) yearning, "aching," for reunion, for a reconnection with a once simpler, safer, and singular world.

In the US, the racialized other also becomes an important receptacle of projection, a splitting of those undesirable traits or attributes now both physically and materially located *in* someone else.[17] "They" serve as the site of projections of elements seeking suppression within oneself. Jessica Benjamin in her book *The Bonds of Love* characterizes differences putatively possessed by men and women in patriarchal society. She refers to Simone de Beauvoir's insight: "that woman functions as man's primary other, his opposite—playing nature to his reason, immanence to his transcendence, primordial oneness to his individuated separateness, and object to his subject" (1988, p. 7).[18] In the US, a similar bifurcated distinction operates with respect to racialized difference, a civil counterpart that, like gender, has been challenged through political critique and institutional reform but, nonetheless, persists as a central organizing principle distinguishing one from the other, as all members—men and women, *blacks* and *whites*—in various degrees seek to rid themselves of the coercive features inherent in these categorical distinctions. Splits between mind and body, reason and passion, self-sacrifice and indulgence, individualized transcendence and collective immanence, masculinity and femininity, at various times throughout

American history have been viewed through this distinctive racialized prism. In every case, *blacks* have been cast, like women, as carriers for those qualities that the aspiring man came to believe dangerous in his striving to be masculine, self-confident, and successful (see Prager, 1995). It is how Winthrop Jordan described the inner world of *white* racists of a much earlier period of American history as "anxious aggressors" (Winthrop, 1968). *Blacks*, like women, are hardly immune from internalizing the symbolic representations imposed by the system of domination and, over the years to a greater or lesser degree, have tended to succumb to or to only self-consciously resist the collective stereotypes. They may resist their typification, attempt to counteract it, challenge it. But, nonetheless, the meanings behind the category (more-or-less) remain.

And the racialized counterpart to the boy's "desire for the girl?" For American racism, the unconscious impulse becomes expressed, on the one hand, through an affectively laden desire (as American history has documented) to exclude, to partition, to separate, to not see, to castrate, to defile, to lynch, to protect, to repress. On the other hand and more commonly now especially among those attempting to combat racism, a countervailing impulse has grown to promote inclusion, to celebrate diversity, to romanticize, and to establish interpersonal contact by *race*. Still, in either form, the racialized category is preserved and the sense of otherness maintained. This characterization is not intended to diminish the efficacy of substantial challenges to a racialized order made over the course of American history, and the "declining significance of race" in spheres of American social and cultural life (Wilson, 1978). But racialized domination nonetheless prevails as a structural and structuring feature of the nation. Otherwise, various efforts to account for racialized difference would not remain such a prominent feature of early childhood socialization. Said differently, the brokenness of the world prevails and appears as an omnipresent feature of life today. The melancholic is unable to mourn, as Freud argues, to ever overcome his or her reminiscences. Therefore, the memory of the painful past is never disabled. Racism and racialized inequality is preserved as a reminder of (and defense against) the world's brokenness.

A case example

Over the past few years, the New York City police and criminal justice system have confronted their own racialized conundrum, seeking to develop a policy of police practice to reduce crime rates in the city. In April 2012, a New York Times columnist, Michael Powell, wrote a column entitled "Former Skeptic Now Embraces Divisive Tactic" (2012). It was about New York's police chief who was once a strong critic of a police practice of stopping and frisking thousands of men. Yet upon returning as New York's police commissioner himself, he resumed the same tactics he had once criticized. When out of the office he had been encouraging what he had called "community policing" where uniformed police fostered a program in which local communities policed themselves, yet now he reverted back to a policy in which police were far more intrusive in specific neighborhoods. In 2011, the columnist reports, his officers stopped nearly 685,000 New Yorkers, nearly a sevenfold increase from when he took office. Eighty-eight per cent of them were completely innocent of any wrongdoing. A vast majority of those stopped, it comes as no surprise, were *black* or Latino young men.

Powell discusses the hidden injuries of race as a result of public policy—though arguably effective in cutting the crime rate down in New York City—whose targets are breathtakingly imprecise. Less than two per cent of the stops led to the recovery of a weapon and, the columnist writes, "The unbridled use of stops leaves a deep bruise of unfairness, particularly around the issue of race." When Powell polls his two *white* sons, nineteen and twenty-four years of age, who had spent their adolescent years traveling to various corners of New York City, they report never having been stopped by the police. But he also interviews eight *black* male students enrolled in a local community college. All together, he reports, they had been stopped ninety-two times and, he notes, each "spoke with surprisingly little rancor." One 19-year-old, who wants a career in theater arts, was forced to take off his sneakers in the subway, commenting how he never saw whites being asked to do the same. Another 18-year-old, the son of a police detective and a doctor, was forced out of his parents' SUV one afternoon and forced to take a Breathalyzer followed by both he and his car being searched. A third, a 19-year-old, described by the columnist as "sweet and soft-spoken with a neat goatee" told of a van driving up on the sidewalk, a man jumped out yelling "I'm a cop, get down on the sidewalk." When the young man feared that he might be being robbed and asked to see the cop's badge, the officer responded by putting his shoe to his face and pressing it to the pavement. While not angry in recounting the story, he speaks mainly of his humiliation at lying on the sidewalk where white young people stood and gawked.

In this same column, Powell provided a description of the police-chief's encounter with a City Councilwoman who nearly pleaded with him to adopt a less hostile approach to policing. "There needs to be prevention and deeper community-based tactics and strategy," she said. The police chief's eyes narrowed, "yeah," he shot back at her, "what is that?" The columnist concludes by writing: "a particular melancholy attends to the public official who can imagine nothing better than the flawed present." Since then, these New York City police practices were challenged in court and the "stop and frisk" policy deemed improper because of "racial profiling."

The columnist is right to refer to the accompanying emotional affect to be a melancholic one. It serves as an emotionally rich description of this racialized stand-off when all of the participants seemingly embody a hopelessness toward a better future, a resignation—much like the feelings held by the young men interviewed at the community college—that little basis exists to imagine anything, at least concerning one's place in the racialized order—different than that which exists today. Typically, indignation is only a response for the uninitiated, and careful instructions in the family, in schools, and in the media are provided on how best to learn to best accommodate to racialized domination. Or, indignation might assume the role of a sentimental humanism insufficiently woven into the fabric of interpersonal and institutional life. It is always possible for expressions of anger and rage to break-through, or for moments of intensive anti-racist impulses to occur. Those moments have been well documented in American history. American society has been witness to both forms of resistance at the institutional (macro) and interpersonal (micro) level of social engagement. But in racialized melancholic societies, indignation mostly gives way to a more passive acceptance of a racist society-in-action.

For these young African-American and Latino men, police harassment may more likely unconsciously evoke a reminder of the safe, secure, and whole world of their early childhood lost now and replaced by misrecognition and suspicion. For the likely more jaded police officers with more life experience under their belts, the stop-and-frisk encounter perhaps unconsciously captures the tarnished and dangerous world of a now that will always be. For the former, rage and indignation threatens to burst forth, and for the latter, guilt may be in more jeopardy of breaking through.

In other words, the brokenness of the world is likely to be experienced differently by those being threatened by or victimized by racism as compared to those who resort to racist practices in the everyday world in which they operate. The difference in social location, of course, contributes decisively to distinctively different renderings of the social reality to which both sides are exposed. *Blacks* and *whites*, as a result, draw profoundly different conclusions about how the world works, the amount of good-will that operates on the other side, the degree to which the subjugated population has made gains over the years, the likelihood of continued advances in the decline of social inequalities, and so forth. But for both sides, the fractured world of self and other constitutes the dominant experience that requires a potent, and humanly numbing defense. Is it possible for the police ever to imagine these young men as their sons? Similarly, is it imaginable that these men might ever imagine the police as possibly their fathers? Racialized difference makes both next to impossible. And so it goes.

Melancholy, while evoking stillness and resignation in the present, as the columnist implies, references the past and extends into the future. It expresses more than stasis, more than eternal recurrence. It is a *presentist* sentiment that effectively closes off a vital connection both to one's own and to a collective past—the experience of loss—as well as to future possibility and a desired reunion. The presence of racialized others serves as a painful reminder, an unconscious trigger, of the trauma of distinction from a once undifferentiated past. In America, a result of the experience of racialized difference, it is a past prematurely shattered. The past, instead of being mourned and integrated within oneself, becomes repressed and nearly impossible to access. This helps account for the emotional intensity accompanying the danger or anxiety often felt when experiencing the racialized other.

In sum, racial melancholia is subjectively devitalizing. In the interest of warding off past trauma, it promotes a hyper-individualism or self-concern that effectively stunts the drive for loving, erotic attachment to the world beyond the self. The twentieth-century French philosopher Georges Bataille writes, human beings by nature struggle with the experience of discontinuity: "we are discontinuous beings, individuals who perish in isolation in the midst of an incomprehensible adventure, but we yearn for our lost continuity." (Bataille, 1986, p. 15). Eroticism, Bataille argues, is a natural, omnipresent response to the difficulty with which it is to bear our own (fractured) individuality.[19] The desire for erotic attachment, whether directly through love relationships or indirectly in sublimated form, constitutes the quest to undo, or reverse the sense of isolation. From this vantage point, social life constitutes the quest to undo, or dissolve, separateness. But melancholia inhibits the quest. It places (certain) others off-limits. Racial melancholia consolidates this inhibition around the constant reminder of the presence of the other, with whom one is unable to dissolve. As Kristeva writes, melancholia or depression expresses the power of one's defense "against the anguish prompted by the erotic object." (p. 20).

Melancholia does not only distort one's relation to the past and perceptions in the present. It interferes with a capacity to imagine and act toward a future different than now. Preoccupied in this racialist society with protecting oneself from identification with the other or experiencing guilt for harboring hostile, rageful, aggressive feelings to negate identification, it is impossible to imagine a different humane future world for ourselves defined by full participation with all others in the same world of which we are a part. Warding off the results of a traumatized past, the present comes to be seen as forever the way things are.

In a non-melancholic world, individuals are guided by hopes and expectations for the future, the American psychoanalyst Hans Loewald writes, imagining the recapturing of a lost past. Personal behavior typically is unconsciously guided by this goal in mind. As he writes, "to be at one with one's environment and to be guided by ethical, evaluative judgments about one's own behavior (our superego) are different expressions of the same phenomenon . . . we can say that the future state of perfection, which is the viewpoint of the superego by which we measure, love and hate, judge ourselves and deal with ourselves recaptures the past state of perfection that we are said to remember dimly or carry in us as our heritage and of which we think we see signs and traces in the child's innocence when he is at one with himself and his environment." (Loewald, [1962] 2000, p. 50). Yet in racialized America, people are not "one with their environment." The defense against identification with the other generates a kind of hunker-down mentality by all participants—to isolate, to retreat, to disengage from the larger social collectivity.

Racial melancholia is the discomforting experience of an eternally divided world, one in which no alternative can be imagined except for our separateness, or estrangement, from others. It is a society necessarily preoccupied with eternally living in the now. Racial melancholia is synonymous with a common and constricted psyche: it defines an intersubjective universe in which, for all parties involved, individuals live **with resignation** more or less exclusively in a psychic present. The traumatic moment of difference is relived over and over *as if* it was happening now.

The surplus racialized order: Is psychic change possible?

Jean-Paul Sartre in a famous short book entitled *Anti-Semitism and Jew* makes the startling (and controversial) assertion: the Jew did not create anti-Semitism but the anti-Semite created the Jew (1965). "If the Jew did not exist, the anti-Semite would invent him." (p. 13).[20] This work, published in French in 1946 just following the end of World War II, heralded an entirely new direction to understanding the nature and function of racialized discourse. First, it identified the inextricable relationship between Jew and anti-Semite—the continuous connection between them that results, by virtue of their co-existence, in their co-creation. The divisions between them effectively become passed from one generation to the next, and anti-Semitism continues to thrive. Second, Sartre's work shifted the focus of anti-Semitism away from a set of feelings or opinions, lodged in an individual to a focus instead on the relationship between these two groups. Anti-Semitism is a social production and not an expression of individualized preferences or aversions. Sartre's work is part of a whole corpus of brilliant work authored in France around the same time that shifted the question of race and racism away from descriptions of either its *natural* occurrence in human beings or from what Freud referred to as "the narcissism of minor differences." (Freud, [1929] 1965, p. 114). In this new formulation, racism is societally created, a ubiquitous feature of certain social systems, constructed within a given social matrix and organized as a result of racialized thinking. It is not inherent to human beings, either as a human proclivity to discriminate by race or as a presumption of inherent differences between racial groups. Moreover, Sartre's essay expresses his insistence that each individual is forced to choose how best to live in a racially unequal society.

Anti-Semite and Jew was written only shortly before one of Sartre's students, Albert Memmi, wrote his remarkable *The Colonizer and Colonized*. A Tunisian Jew, writing in the same kind of simple, direct language as Sartre's, Memmi described the seemingly inextricable and destructive relations between the various social actors in a colonized society: the colonized, the colonizer who accepts, and the colonizer who refuses. His point is that in colonial society there is no place to stand where one can feel non-complicit in the system or morally non-culpable. At least compared to Sartre, Memmi presented a far bleaker picture of the possibilities of breaking through to create systemic change because in a colonial society, Memmi argued, everyone was either a colonizer or colonized ([1957] 1965). And Frantz Fanon, a West-Indian, French-trained psychoanalyst, also deeply influenced by Sartre published *The Wretched of the Earth, Black Skin, White Masks,* and other writings that emphasized the psychological damage inflicted on the colonized as a result of colonial domination ([1952] 1967; [1961] 1968). Sartre wrote the Preface to *The Wretched of the Earth* and restates a central thesis of

Fanon's; namely, colonial rule dehumanizes individuals subjected to it (Sartre, [1961] 1968). For Fanon, violent acts to overthrow colonialism were not only politically necessary for political independence but also required for the colonized to regain his or her humanity. Psychological emancipation can only occur, Fanon argues, through cathartic violent purging. Psychic wholeness can only be restored through violent acts.

Sartre, Memmi and Fanon recognize that social analysis cannot be distinguished from the psychological, and that race has no reality except as an intersubjective phenomenon. For Fanon, for example, the colonized's embrace of violence is a prerequisite for political acts of liberation because the necessary counter-reaction by oppressors enlarges the pool of colonized now prepared to engage in violence. Locked into a system of dehumanizers and dehumanized, restoration of one's humanity is only possible by the dehumanized engaging in efforts to destroy the dehumanizers.

Racialized melancholic social orders are not colonial societies, as Tunisia and Algeria once were, and the conclusions drawn by Fanon and others concerning the role of violence in political liberation and psychic emancipation are not wholesale applicable in the US. Nonetheless, the form of psychosocial analysis done by Fanon and Sartre apply no less to the US. It is impossible to identify structures of social domination without simultaneously describing the psychic life of those who live within them. The racist mind expresses the order. Moreover, Fanon especially emphasizes the irreducible relationship between social and psychic change: failure to transform racialized structures of perception, the racist mind, means an inability to upend this social structure of domination. In the racially melancholic American society, the misrecognition of the racial other means, too, a defensive denial of the attributes of the other in oneself. Domination is carried forward, at the same time, institutionally *and* psychically.

Different from colonized societies, a racially melancholic one generates its own specific obstacles to psychic change for overcoming racialized domination. Thinking of the possibilities for psychic change, the following three questions concerning civil policies and practices present themselves. First, what strategies might be engaged to disable the symbolic and narrative identifications of Americans as **either** *white* or as *black*. This is a special challenge because these two groups understand their origins as distinctively different: one group as historically linked to the story of the dominant first-immigrant Europeans while the other to the subordinate slave-African. Second, what actions or strategies might be possible to lift from the racialized self the shadow of the internalized object of loss—the racialized other—now powerfully constricting thought, imagination, and behavior of Americans? How to remove the powerful defenses erected to deny the humanity of the racialized other? Third, how to activate a sense of erotic potentiality, of disarming defensive energy promoting insularity from the other and direct it instead to pursue the utopian possibility of the ideal of reunion—a naturalized, post-racialized (though **not** a culturally uniform, post-ethnicized) world? Stated differently, how to liberate the collective psyche from compulsive repetition, and to disturb the impulse to reproduce the past in the present?

Overcoming the racialized binary, letting the past go, making new friends

Analyzing the American psyche

In psychoanalytic treatment, "solutions" to individual problems are indistinguishable from the work of making the unconscious conscious, or making explicit certain bedrock assumptions implicitly guiding one's life despite the fact that they have not stood the test of time, that is, they have caused trouble. The analyst does not suggest steps or solutions to overcome the internal conflicts that have produced various unwanted symptoms. Only the analysand can do that as a result of these conflicts emerging in clearer and deeper self-understanding through the analytic relationship. The analysand (with the analyst) overcomes conflicts by better seeing their ongoing function in thought and action in the present, though their origin usually derives from past efforts as a child to overcome anxieties, insecurities, and unfulfilled needs and desires. In the same spirit of "cure," here, I, provide no set of practices or policies to overcome racialized difference and inequality in America. Yet by summarizing the insights offered thus far and by posing the further questions they raise, inspired by psychoanalysis, racial melancholy is properly named and its mechanisms for repetition better understood. The description of the phenomenon points the way toward its overcoming.

No different than the patient's challenge when seeking treatment, the undoing of more than 200 years of America's implicit patterns of relatedness based upon the delusion of race difference is no small task. Psychic change takes time and energy; an effort largely devoted to reversing inscribed and embodied ways of being and thinking. Similarly, the US' negation and undoing of deeply structured and embedded racist patterns of thought and action is a *process* not an event. In the first place, the nature of the problem needs to be properly identified. Racial melancholia, as has been argued, confuses the present for the past and resigns itself to it. In racially melancholic societies, the present, in fact, is being lived *as if* it were the past. Loss of a sense of one's wholeness and discontinuity with others both in the past and presently weigh upon its members without resolution. *Whites* see themselves as the unencumbered inheritors of America's past great achievements, enabling them to freely embrace the American dream and act putatively *freely* in today's world: they *are* the world. *Black* presence, however, for whites, serves as a contemporary impediment to the full realization of their dream, as freedom's inhibition. *Blacks*, in contrast, necessarily tie themselves to America's past and understand their linkage to an exploitative history still yet to be overcome. For them, *white* disregard still represents the principal culprit in *black* underachievement and *grievance* as the vehicle best designed to combat it. Significantly, neither group understands their relationship to the racialized category, no different than in earlier American history, as a powerful contributor to its perpetuation and to racialized patterns of domination.

Adherence to the meaningfulness of the racialized category, in America serves as a (perverse) social resource. Racism becomes a comforting defense, shared by *whites* and *blacks* alike, to the experience of the brokenness, fragility, and precariousness generated in American society, and its attendant anxieties, insecurities, unfulfilled needs, and desires. It enables social members to project onto racialized others an elaborate set of assumptions, connected to a historical narrative that is some combination of imposed and chosen. One's own relation to that narrative reinforces, perhaps justifies, the experience of discontinuity. Both the narrative and the framing of the experience of the other as a result of the narrative become critical ways for individuals to locate themselves in every social interaction, organized around hierarchy/ deference, inside/outside, etc. in the contemporary racialized order.

This bedrock conviction of the reality of racial difference is accounted for from another vantage point as well. Racialized difference represents a denial and repudiation of a **common** historical past of American destructiveness, violence, appropriation, and usurpation, enabling misrecognition that the legacy for **all** Americans today is premised on this history. Naming the perpetrators as *white* and the victims as *black*, while in one sense obviously true, also promotes denial of a *universal* contemporary complicity in the spoils of America's exploitative past. Denial, thereby, reinforces the impulse to continue to racialize, and therefore depersonalize and objectify American history. All Americans, today, in some sense, are the beneficiaries of the nation's history of accumulation, exploitation, and appropriation (including, of course, toward the Native American); the nation is richer and more providing to all as a result. In fact, while many Americans may be able to trace their ancestry back to a slave past, or a master past, many more only symbolically identify with one side or the other. Presumptions or fantasies of the racial other, and the binary division, express a particular, socially legitimated, mechanism by which to deal with a desire so intense that it might otherwise break the order. This is the human desire for reunion, or wholeness, what Michael Chabon calls "cosmic nostalgia" (Chabon, 2013, p. 23). It is the converse of brokenness. The presence of the racial other makes desire more "orderly," more contained and, from the perspective of the social system itself, more containable. The nation is resigned to the non-occurrence of even the desire for wholeness' return. The persistent presence of the racial other serves to suppress desire for reunion; it makes impossible any wish to become whole, to be victorious, to achieve it all. By dividing the world racially, desire is suppressed and only unconsciously realized in the other. The "symptom" is melancholia, the unnamed, unconscious longing for a non-specific lost object (wholeness, innocence) continuing to haunt the present, is shared by nearly all members of the nation.

The perdurance and resilience of the American surplus racialized order remains. At least since the end of the Jim Crow period, culminating in the 1954 *Brown v. Board of Education* Supreme Court decision declaring a policy of "separate but unequal" an unacceptable national standard, substantial sectors of the population have articulated the goal of eliminating racial difference entirely, implementing instead a "color-blind" approach to law and policy. Nonetheless, melancholic resignation, acquiescence to a conviction of racial difference and largely accepting an eternal present, describes the American steady-state, and the often returned-to racialized equilibrium. The "pathological" feature of these attempts at conflict resolution reveals itself as flawed along three different axes.

First, the defensive strategy of forgetting the exploitative past has not succeeded. Domination is preserved in place and its continued radioactivity insured. Thus the following question: how might one live in the **present** as present, relegating the **past** to its proper place, acknowledging it as the site upon which our lives have been built but no more? Stated differently, how might one "disable forgetting" so it does not determine one's lived-experience in the present and, thereby, foreclose imaginary possibilities for the future? Within this framework, issues of apology, forgiveness, reconciliation and reparations require reopening for debate and discussion (see Brooks, 1999, 2004). How significant is it that the US Government refuses to apologize for the institution of slavery? How do we explain the presence of a Holocaust Museum on the Capitol Mall, and not a museum to the history of American slavery?

Second, how might one's **ancestors** be honored and respected, while, at the same time, insuring that one remains unencumbered by a guilty conscience because of his or her own "modern" or contemporary search for freedom? This issue especially bedevils (though not exclusively) those who powerfully identify with their ancestors. Then, new opportunities and pathways available today may be resisted as acts of betrayal to those who came before. Yet an over-identification with parents, grandparents, and great-grandparents can easily generate a transformation of ancestors into **ghosts**, haunting decisions and actions in today's world (Loewald, [1962] 2000). In other words, how to overcome feelings that one is the carrier of one's predecessors' desires, overwhelming one's own life and the nation's challenge to determine what rightfully are one's own present-day desires? How to lift the shadow of the internalized object? To what useful or productive end is the discourse to young African-Americans, often championed by other young African-Americans, of promoting "acting Black"; how stifling the imposition of informal sanctions against "forgetting one's community" as a challenge to the American racialized order?

This third set of psychoanalytically inspired questions, perhaps, is the most challenging. Melancholic resignation, while describing large blocs of historical time in America, does not always dominate. Various intense and productive challenges to the racialized order have occurred, and important adjustments have been made. Nonetheless, each of those historical moments has given way to a renewed stasis. Racialized domination and subjugation remains. Melancholia ultimately triumphs, and the structure of racial inequality prevails.

Why have these efforts not yielded the elimination of a racialized order, only its amelioration? How to avoid **repeating compulsively** the struggle for racial emancipation by employing strategies of transformation that ultimately fail? How to prevent a politics of change that does not repeat past dead-ends? As I have suggested, doesn't organizing around the racialized categories themselves serve to reproduce the divisions in spite of whatever ameliorative measures might be achieved? Might new categories of association and affiliation help undermine the reality of racialized differences and patterns of subordination?

The question is mistrust not race difference. The answer is new and stronger friendship circles

This article has focused on the invidious nature of racial distinction and the defensive purposes that racial categorization continue to serve in a melancholic society. In fact, the human anxiety generated because of loss, disappointment, and discontinuity with others and the racialized defenses against knowing it might also be described as a crisis of trust: racial categorization as a defensive palliative to the anxieties of profound mistrust. The experience of basic mistrust between one another and the brokenness of the world describe in different language the same experience. Differentiation, separation, and loss are profound human emotions. In an ideal social world we might expect that, at each stage in a person's development, necessary resources are provided by various social institutions to reassure the person that the painful process of individuation from one's past and from one's ancestors is recognized and accommodated. Provisions are provided in early schools to reassure children upon their first separations from home that they are safe and their caregivers will return. Even in the first job, provision is typically made to the un-ease of a new worker at being able to perform competently from the beginning. A safety net for catastrophic events, when possible, are provided should it be needed—though, here, certain modern societies are much more providing than others. Empathic understanding, in short, of the experience of the other is typically employed in various social settings. Provisions are available to ease the burden of psychic challenges faced by others. But in those societies where there is a surplus of racial order, racism and melancholia represent not the providing of appropriate reassurance but rather an internalized defensive response brutally denying the anxiety of separation and individuation. The shameful national response to the New Orleans *black* poor in the aftermath of Hurricane Katrina constitutes, I believe, a real and also symbolic expression of the capacity of the civil society to treat the racial other as profoundly different, less worthy of compassion and empathy.

In an important book by Danielle Allen, entitled *Talking to Strangers, Anxieties of Citizenship since Brown v. Board of Education*, the author notes that, at least in most modern societies, one of the first lessons taught to children is "don't talk to strangers" (2004). Don't trust the world, in other words, because it is a dangerous place. To be by yourself has built-in dangers located in the world outside of you. Using a different vocabulary and a different frame of reference than employed here, Allen is describing the same melancholic world, what she calls a world with "insufficient citizenly practices." Feeling the unsafety of the world leads to retreat and resignation, Allen argues that since the *Brown decision*, political obligation to others, a feature of democratic politics, has emerged as central to contemporary understanding of politics. It implies a democratic responsibility to *not* be resigned and not to retreat into one's private world. Yet the institutional and ideological frameworks still are not in place to fully implement this more assertive conception of the good citizen.

"Don't talk to strangers," remains a directive firmly lodged in the American psyche, despite the 1954 Supreme Court ruling that instructs citizens to play a more active and empathic role in the polity. Allen insists that citizenship requires the ongoing work of political friendship: a sense of obligation and responsibility to fellow citizens, not unlike those we feel toward personal friends. Importantly, she insists, this new directive includes obligation to understand why some might not trust others; just as one might try to imagine why a friend might be mad or harbor a grudge toward oneself at any given time. To feel oneself safe to talk to strangers in the public sphere, at least metaphorically, implies a community of trust, of citizenly trust, and of mutual understanding. It means the possibility of feeling oneself more complete in the presence of others. The answer that the question of racial melancholia poses is to describe and implement the social conditions—the necessary societal provisions—that enable political friendships—erotized others—to develop across lines that historically have not been crossed.

Acknowledgements

I would like to thank the editors of this volume, Lynn Chancer and John Andrews, for their support, forbearance, and editorial suggestions to an earlier version of this paper. I appreciate especially their hard work in creating this volume of essays, demonstrating the gains to be derived in sociological research when psychoanalytic and depth psychological ideas are interwoven into the analysis. In addition, thanks to the Working Group on Race and Ethnicity in the Department of Sociology at UCLA and to members of my Study Group on Intersubjectivity supported by the New Center for Psychoanalysis for their comments on an earlier draft. Ravaris Moore has been helpful in the preparation of the graphs and tables and Matthew Nesvit for comments on an earlier draft. I would like to thank especially Aaron Crawford who listened and commented thoughtfully as I talked through many of the ideas now included in the paper, and many more not included. Also, thanks to my colleagues at UCLA Darnell Hunt and Robert Hill for their comments, suggestions and encouragement.

Notes

1. On the economic features describing the durability of racial inequality, see Brown, 2013.
2. The constructed and situational character of racial category is firmly established in the sociological literature, principally a result of the influence of Michael Omi and Howard Winant's book *Racial Formation in the United States, From the 1960s to the 1990s*. See also HoSang et al., 2012.
3. It is true, of course, that these categories are often potent sources of identification, pride, love, hate and other strong personal, "private" emotions. They are affectively charged, reflecting powerful psychic density. Still, the origin of the distinctions by race originates not in the private sphere of family but in the public sphere where these distinctions are made to matter. Racial difference is a project of the American public sphere.
4. The American racialized order I describe is *not* coincident with what Americans otherwise refer to as the US' "minority groups" or "ethnic groups." Ethnic groups are understood as possessing shared cultural characteristics, typically located with a specific national homeland, and a common language. Racial groups are defined as sharing common biological characteristics.
5. The intersubjective character of racial identity made here was anticipated in an important article published in 1958 by Herbert Blumer, one of the founders of symbolic interactionism. Blumer writes, "To fail to see that racial prejudice is a matter (a) of the racial identification made of oneself and of others, and (b) of the way in which the identified groups are conceived in relation to each other, is to miss what is logically and actually basic." The insights of Blumer's article, especially concerning intersubjectivity and the intergroup dynamics of racial identity, have largely been lost to social scientific studies of ethnic and race Relations. For two notable exceptions, see Bobo, 1999, and Bobo and Hutchings, 1996. For another intersubjective perspective, both building upon the work of Pierre Bourdieu, are Wacquant, 1997, and Brubaker, 2006, especially Chapter 2, pp. 28–63. Wacquant, for example, says of the category race, the "continual barter between folk and analytical notions, the uncontrolled conflation of social and sociological understandings of 'race' is "intrinsic to the category. From its inception, the collective fiction labeled 'race' . . . has always mixed science with common sense and traded on the complicity between them." (pp. 222–223).
6. A recent study measured empathy toward individuals experiencing pain. The researcher, Silverstein, 2013, describes a "racial empathy gap," summarizing findings demonstrating that blacks are believed to possess a higher tolerance for pain than whites. Especially significant, black respondents shared with whites the view that blacks had a higher threshold for pain than whites. All respondents, in short, concurred that there was a difference between the two groups with respect to the experience of something as human as pain. This framework of expectations and expected orientations toward the world, penetrating to the most basic of human qualities and understood through the lens of racial difference, describes the racial categories' coercive and defining power for all Americans. For further evidence on the distinction between the *white* body and the *black*, see also Pollock, 2012, Metzl, 2009, Feldman, 2010, Koenig, 2010.

7. See, for example, Brodkin, 1998; also Fields, 2001; Ignatiev, 1995; Jacobson, 1998.
8. Economic Policy Institute, "Ratio of Black to White Unemployment Rate, 1963–2012"
9. Pew Research Center, "Poverty Race by Race and Ethnicity, Percent below the Poverty Line, 1963–2011."
10. Pew Research Center, "Average Family Wealth by Race and Ethnicity, 1983–2010"; Pew Research Center, "Real Median Household Income by Race and Hispanic Origin: 1967 to 2010".
11. Pew Research Center, "Incarceration Rates, 1960–2010, Inmates per 100,000 Residents" 2011.
12. ABC/Washington Post Poll, "Reaction to the Zimmerman Verdict," "Views of Trayvon Martin's Shooting," 2013.
13. See, Gilroy, 2006, who makes a similar argument concerning the failure of the British to acknowledge their exercise of colonial violence against various subject peoples around the world.
14. These themes will be returned to in the conclusion.
15. It is possible to understand racism's persistence as a result of the transmission of traumatic encounters with racialized others onto the next generation. See, my Prager, 2003.
16. See Cheng, 2001, p. 3, who writes, "The transformation from grief to grievance, from suffering injury to speaking out against that injury, has always provoked profound questions about the meaning of hurt and its impact." Grievance, as it is being used here, is the active, egocentric form of protest, a defensive and agentic way-of-being and speaking intended to deny or overcome brokenness.
17. See Cheng's (2001, p. 108) discussion of the opening scene of Ralph Ellison's *The Invisible Man* for the potent role that projection plays and how, in one interaction, different projections may operate at the same time.
18. See Riley, 2003, for a comparable analysis of the role the category of women in creating a reified conception of difference.
19. Kristeva, 1992, captures it most powerfully, and even more dramatically, from a Freudian vantage point when she writes, "The child king becomes irredeemably sad before uttering his first words; this is because he has been irrevocably, desperately separated from the mother, a loss that causes him to try to find her again, along with other objects of love, first in the imagination, then in words."
20. On the anti-Semite, "he has chosen to find his being entirely outside himself, never to look within, to be nothing save the fear he inspires in others. What he flees even more than Reason is his intimate awareness of himself." (p. 21).

References

Abraham, N. and Torok, M. (1994) *The Shell and the Kernel, Volume I* (Chicago: University of Chicago Press).
Allen, D. (2004) *Talking to Strangers, Anxieties of Citizenship since Brown v. Board of Education* (Chicago: University of Chicago Press).

Banton, M. (2013) "In Defense of Mainstream Sociology," *Ethnic and Racial Studies*, 36, 1000–1004.

Bataille, G. (1986) *Erotism: Death and Sensuality* (San Francisco: City Lights Books).

Benjamin, J. (1988) *The Bonds of Love, Psychoanalysis, Feminism, and the Problem of Domination* (New York: Pantheon Press).

Bobo, L. (1999) "Prejudice as Group Position: Microfoundations of a Sociological Approach to Racism and Race Relations," *Journal of Social Issues*, 55 (1999), 445–472.

Bobo, L. and V. Hutchings (1996) "Perceptions of Racial Group Competition to a Multiracial Social Context," *American Sociological Review*, 61 (1996), 951–972.

Bourdieu, P. (2001) *Masculine Domination* (Stanford: Stanford University Press).

Brodkin, K. (1998) *How Jews became White Folks & What That Says about Race in America* (New Jersey: Rutgers University Press).

Brooks, R. L. (2004) *Atonement and Forgiveness, A New Model for Black Reparations* (California: University of California Press).

Brooks, R. L. (ed.) (1999) *When Sorry Isn't Enough, The Controversy over Apologies and Reparations for Human Injustice* (New York: New York University Press).

Brown, M. K. (2013) "Divergent Fates: The Foundations of Durable Racial Inequality, 1940–2013," www.demos.org, Rockefeller Foundation.

Brubakar, R. (2006) *Ethnicity without Groups* (Cambridge, MA: Harvard University Press).

Butler, J. (1997) "Melancholy Gender/Refused Identification," in J. Butler (ed.) *The Psychic Life of Power, Theories in Subjection* (Stanford: Stanford University Press).

Caruth, C. (2002) "Introduction," *American Imago*, 59 (3).

Chabon, M. (2013) "The Film Worlds of Wes Anderson," *New York Review of Books*, March 7, 2013.

Cheng, A. A. (2001) *The Melancholy of Race: Psychoanalysis, Assimilation, and Hidden Grief* (Oxford: Oxford University Press).

Fanon, F. ([1952] 1967) *Black Skin White Masks* (New York: Grove Press).

Fanon, F. ([1961] 1968) *The Wretched of the Earth* (New York: Grove Press).

Feldman, M. (2010) "The Biology of Ancestry, DNA, Genomic Variation and Race," in H. Markus and P. Moya (eds) *Doing Race, 21 Essays for the 21st Century* (New York: Norton Press).

Fields, B. (2001) "Whiteness, Racism and Identity," *International Labor and Working Class History*, 60 (2001), 48–56.

Foucault, M. ([1978] 1990) *The History of Sexuality, An Introduction, Volume I* (New York: Harper Vintage).

Freud, S. ([1917] 1954) "Mourning and Melancholia," *The Standard Edition of the Complete Psychological Works*, Vol. 14 (London: Hogarth Press).

Gilroy, Paul (2006) *Post-Colonial Melancholia* (New York: Columbia University Press).

Goffman, E. (1986) *Frame Analysis: An Essay on the Organization of Experience* (Northeastern University Press).

HoSang, D., O. LaBennett, and L. Pulido (ed.) (2012) *Racial Formation in the Twenty-first Century* (Berkeley and Los Angeles: University of California Press).

Hunt, D. (1999) *O. J. Simpson, Facts and Fictions, News Rituals in the Construction of Reality* (Cambridge: Cambridge University Press).

Ignatiev, N. (1995) *How the Irish became White* (London: Routledge).

Jacobson, M. F. (1998) *Whiteness of a Different Color: European Immigrants and the Alchemy of Race* (Cambridge: Harvard University Press).

Koenig, B. (2010) "Which Differences Make a Difference? Race, DNA and Health," in H. Markus and P. Moya (eds) *Doing Race, 21 Essays for the 21st Century* (New York: Norton Press).

Kristeva, J. (1992) *Black Sun, Depression and Melancholia* (New York: Columbia University Press).

Lepeneis, W. (1992) *Melancholy and Society* (Cambridge: Harvard University Press).

Loewald, Hans ([1962] 2000) "Superego and Time," in H. W. Loewald and N. Quist (eds) *The Essential Loewald, Collected Papers and Monographs* (Hagerstown: University Publishing Group).

Loveman, M. and J. Muniz (2006) "How Puerto Rico Became White, Boundary Dynamics and Inter-Census Reclassification," *American Sociological Review*, 72 (6), 915–939.

Memmi, A. ([1957] 1965) *The Colonizer and the Colonized* (Boston: Beacon Press).

Metzl, J. (2009) *The Protest Psychosis, How Schizophrenia became a Black Disease* (Boston: Beacon Press.

Myrdal, G. (1944) *An American Dilemma: The Negro Problem and Modern Democracy* (New York: Harper and Bros).

Omi, M. and Winant, H. (1986) *Racial Formation in the United States, From the 1960's to the 1990's* (London: Routledge).

Pollock, Anne (2012) *Medicating Race: Heart Disease and Durable Preoccupations with Difference* (Durham and London: Duke University Press).

Powell, M. (2012) "Former Skeptic Now Embraces Divisive Tactic," *New York Times*, April 10, 2012.

Prager, J. (1995) "Self Reflection(s): Subjectivity and Racial Subordination in the Contemporary African-American Writer," *Social Identities*, 1 (1995), 355–371.

Prager, J. (2003) "Lost Childhood, Lost Generations: The Intergenerational Transmission of Trauma," *Journal of Human Rights*, 2 (2003), 173–181.

Riley, D. (2003) *Am I that Name? Feminism and the Category of 'Women' in History* (St. Paul: University of Minnesota Press).

Roediger, D. (1991) *The Wages of Whiteness: Race and the Making of the American Working Class* (London and New York: Verso).

Roediger, D. (2005) *Working toward Whiteness, How America's Immigrants Became White, The Strange Journey from Ellis Islands to the Suburbs* (Cambridge: Basic Books).

Sartre, J. ([1961] 1968) "Preface," in F. Fanon (ed.) *The Wretched of the Earth* (New York: Grove Press).

Sartre, J. (1965) *Anti-Semite and Jew* (Boston: Beacon Books).

Sigmund Freud, (1961/1929) *Civilization and its Discontents*, Vol. XXI, *The Standard Edition of the Complete Psychological Works*, Hogarth Press, pp. 59–145; p. 114.

Silverstein, J. (2013) "I Don't Feel Your Pain," *The Slate*, June, 2013. www/slate.com/articles/health_science/science/2013/06/racial_empathy_gap_people_don_t_perceive_pain_in_other_races.2.html

Telles, E. and V. Ortiz (2008) *Generations of Exclusions: Racial Assimilation and Mexican Americans* (New York: Russell Sage Foundation).

Thandeka (1999) *Learning to be White, Money, Race and God in America* (New York: Continuum Books).

US Government (1968) *Report of the National Advisory Committee on Civil Discord* (Kerner Commission Report).

Wacquant, L. (1997) "For an Analytic of Racial Domination," *Political Power and Social Theory*, 11, 221–134, and Brubaker, R. (2004) *Ethnicity without Groups* (Cambridge: Harvard University Press).

Wilson, W. J. (1978) *The Declining Significance of Race* (Cambridge: Harvard University Press).

Winthrop, J. (1968) *White over Black, American Attitudes toward the Negro 1550–1812* (New York: Penguin Books.

14
On the Melancholia of New Individualism

Anthony Elliott

This essay builds on the theory of "new individualism" to explore its psychosocial ramifications (Elliott and Lemert, 2006, 2009b; Elliott, 2008, 2009, 2010; Elliott and Urry, 2010). I have argued elsewhere that the conditions and consequences of new individualism are especially evident in the new economy of high finance, media and technology industries. "New individualism" penetrates the very core of culture and institutional life, and represents a kind of shorthand for describing various and disparate modalities that shape, and are shaped by, global social transformations. The key institutional drivers of new individualism are (a) continual reinvention, (b) instant change, (c) speed, and (d) short-termism or episodicity. I elaborate this theoretical work by examining the psychic and emotional contours of a life lived in the new individualist fast lane. In so doing I draw on psychoanalysis—in a necessarily partial and restricted way—to focus on the melancholic elements of new individualism.

The new individualist thesis: The sociological backcloth

As originally formulated, the theory of the new individualism comprises four core dimensions: a relentless emphasis on *self-reinvention*; an endless hunger for *instant change*; a fascination with *social acceleration, speed* and *dynamism*; and a preoccupation with *short-termism* and *episodicity* (Elliott and Lemert, 2009a; Elliott and Urry, 2010; Elliott, 2013). The argument is that a new individualism can be deciphered from the culture in which people live their lives today—especially (but not only) for those living in the polished, expensive cities of the West. Corporate networking, short-term project work, organizational downsizing, self-help manuals, compulsive consumerism, cybersex, instant identity makeovers and therapy culture: these are just some of the core features of global individualist culture, and immersion in such an individualist world carries profound emotional consequences for individuals' private and public lives.

The thesis of new individualism rests on the claim that individualism, the moral and social ideal, has undergone, in our times, still another transformation. "Individualism," the concept, was coined in the 1830s by Alexis de Tocqueville to describe the bourgeois gentlemen he observed in America who, having acquired means and manners, lived as if to cut themselves off from the masses. Thereafter, the individualism Tocqueville associated with the brash inventions of the still adolescent American culture of the nineteenth century became united with the older ideals of the European bourgeoisie. In the 1920s and 1930s, however, all this began to change as European critical theorists challenged the liberal ideal of the cutoff individual freed from the fetters of common life. The global wars and holocausts of the twentieth century required the concept to adjust to the evidences that individuals were subject to terrible manipulations of political ideologies, social forces, capitalist economies, and the like. Hence the emergence of "manipulated individualism" in the discourse of critical social theory.

Following the wars of the first half of the twentieth century, another vision of individualism arose. In the affluent superabundance of postwar America, individualism appeared neither heroically arrogant (as Tocqueville had it) nor tragically threatened (as the German critical theorists thought) but now tragically *isolated*. David Riesman, in *The Lonely Crowd* (Riesman, Glazer, and Denny, 2001), put forth the idea of a mature modern individualism in which the productive force of the entrepreneur had fallen into a sad sort of conformism. The theory as it turned out was ironic. As individualism lapsed into conformism, so the individual became increasingly isolated, cutoff; hence *isolated individualism*. Then, as the earlier revisions were responses to perturbations of the tragic 1920s and the conformist 1950s, in the 1990s still another new individualism was called forth by the then (and still) strange effects of globalization. What has been termed *reflexive individualism* is a way of underscoring that globalization, whatever its benefits, entails risks and risks require individuals to reflect coherently on their changing circumstances—and thus to revise their interior and exterior agendas to risks and costs of the new global order.

In order to better grasp the confluence of interior and exterior changes in peoples' lives I developed. At the core of this new individualist orientation lies a cultural fascination for, and institutional pressure towards, self-reinvention. This cultural tendency toward reinvention carries profound consequences for reorganizing the relations between self and society. In sociological terms, "new individualism" cuts both externally and internally. The triumph of globalization is that it not only operates on a horizontal axis, universalizing the operations of multinational capital and new digital technologies across the globe; it operates also on a vertical axis, reorganizing identities and pressing the ethos of new individualism into its service. In current social circumstances, it is not the particular individuality of an individual that is most important so much as how individuals re-create identities, the cultural forms through which people symbolize individual expression and desire, and the speed with which identities can be reinvented and transformed. This stress on instant transformation—in particular the fears and anxieties it is designed to displace or lessen—distinguishes the theory of the new individualism from notions such as "reflexive individualization" and "technologies of the self."

Key institutional drivers of the new individualism

Ours is the era of a new individualism: our current fascination for the instant making, reinvention, and transformation of selves is integral to contemporary social life. The new individualism requires individuals to be capable of designing and directing their own biographies, of defining identities in terms of self-actualization and of deploying social goods and cultural symbols to represent individual expression and personality. The following part of this essay reviews and reiterates the core sociological ideas comprising the thesis of the new individualism. There are four major points to consider:

1. The new individualism is marked by a relentless emphasis on *self-reinvention*. The twenty-first century craze to constantly reinvent identities is fast becoming integral to contemporary living, and oftentimes involves a "tipping point" into addictions, obsessions, and compulsions. Contemporary consumerism pressures us to constantly "transform" and "improve" every aspect of ourselves: not just our homes and gardens but our careers, our food, our clothes, our sex lives, our faces, minds, and bodies.

More than just personal or cultural stresses on self-reinvention, it is increasingly evident that the of reinvention is also operational on an organizational or institutional level. Ceaseless corporate reinvention, organizational downsizings, and institutional remodellings have become commonplace in the global economy. Faith in the powers of plasticity and plurality is evidenced by the huge numbers of multinational corporations undertaking endless reinventions of their organizational cultures, markets, and products. The Finnish communications multinational Nokia has become a classic instance of such organizational re-fashioning (Merriden, 2001; Haikio, 2002). Manufacturing mobile devices for the convergent communications and Internet industries, Nokia employs staff in 120 countries with global annual revenues of over fifty billion euros and sales in more than 150 countries. Yet this telecommunications giant actually began as a paper manufacturer, subsequently expanding into rubber works and the manufacture of galoshes; it was not until the 1960s that the company moved into electronics and then in the 1970s into telecommunications. In the early years of the twenty-first century, the reinvention continues as Nokia refashions itself away from mobile phones and towards mobile devices.

While some corporate reinvention is geared to product and market refashioning, some companies extend the remodelling principle to the fabric of organizational structure. This is true of Cisco Systems, one of America's leading technology giants. In early 2000, Cisco enjoyed a market capitalization of $US550 billion—making it the world's most valuable company. Twelve months later, following the tech-wreck, its stock-market value crashed to $US100 billion. Ever since, the company has aggressively sought to move beyond its core business of Internet guiding data into new diversifications, such as Internet telephony and optical networks. In a world that has fetishized outsourcing and just-in-time deliveries, Cisco has been a corporate leader. Manufacturing has been outsourced at Cisco for some years, and so too has research and development. Such corporate remodellings extend to the very core of Cisco's institutional structure. Under CEO John Chamber, Cisco has established a complex set of committees comprising managers from different sections of the company—engineering, manufacturing, marketing and the like. Under Chamber's reinvention plan, Cisco has set up "Boards" charged with identifying new markets that might reach $US1 billion. Then there are "Councils," charged with identifying new markets that could reach $US10 billion ("Reshaping Cisco", 2009). Both committees are serviced by "working groups." Cisco are unable to calculate how many working groups exist throughout the company, such is the fast assembly and even faster disassembly of these structures in the context of new global markets. Nonetheless, a growing faith in dismantling, destabilizing, and deconstructing existing organizational structures and institutional processes is echoed throughout corporate life more generally, and evidenced in the rise of short-term contracts, fast-paced networking, and multiple working identities. This chapter now considers how cultural demands for reinvention unleash other fundamental social changes in organizational forms, technologies, and lifestyles.

2. New individualism is driven by an endless hunger for *instant change*. This trend is discernible throughout contemporary social life, from the rise of plastic surgery and the instant identity makeovers of reality TV to compulsive consumerism, speed dating, and therapy culture. Desire for immediate results and instant gratification has never been as pervasive or acute. We have become accustomed to emailing others across the planet in seconds, buying flashy consumer goods with the click of a mouse, and drifting in and out of relations with others without long-term commitments. Is it any wonder we now have different expectations about life's possibilities and the potential for change? There are various market-directed solutions that offer the promise of instant transformation—ones reduced to a purchase mentality. As individualism becomes increasingly on a par with shopping, consumerism promotes a fantasy of the self's infinite plasticity. The message from the makeover industry is that there's nothing to stop you reinventing yourself however you choose. But your redesigned sense of individualism is unlikely to make you happy for long. For identity enhancements are only fashioned with the short-term in mind. They are until "next time." This relentless emphasis on self-reinvention thus equates to a culture of "next-ness" (Elliott and Urry, 2010).

Zygmunt Bauman describes consumerism as an "economics of deception" (2005). The consumer's world consists of frustrated desires, dashed hopes; deceit—the broken promises of producers—is the *sine qua non* of consumerism and its ever-expanding terrain of new needs, wants, and desires. For Bauman, the consumer industry deploys two key strategies in keeping people orientated to its markets. The first consists in the *devaluation* of consumer products soon after, and increasingly as they near, market saturation point. Yesterday's DVD player is today outperformed by digital recording; the mobile phone purchased recently from the high street is already supplanted by new features of the latest stock. Such degradation of product durability, says Bauman, goes hand in hand with stimulation of new elements, designer markets, and products. Although the degradation of durability is nothing new, the timeframe in which consumer products remain of lasting value is dissolving. What previously lasted five years may now last several months; such is the spread of *transience* throughout consumer culture. In the global intermeshing of human affairs, particularly in the service and technology sectors of the new economy, deciding whether a purchased product is still relevant or desirable to today's lifestyle of accelerated consumption is no easy matter. The consuming self confronts not simply some exterior set of guidelines regarding product or service durability, but those guidelines "internalized" in the course of preparing oneself for new consumer offerings, now looming over individuals as a benchmark measuring the adequacy of the self. In today's society of consumers, the main task is

> to develop new desires made to the measure of new, previously unheard-of and unexpected allurements, to 'get in' more than before, not to allow the established needs to render new sensations redundant or to restrain the capacity to absorb and experience them. (Bauman, 2005, p. 77)

The second strategy developed by the consumer industry to stimulate consumers' desires, according to Bauman, is more subtle yet effective. This consists in "the method of satisfying every need/desire/want in such a fashion that it cannot but give birth to new needs/desires/wants" (2005, p. 73). Such exploitation of consumerist attitudes involves the continual cross-referencing of products, labels, brands, and services. Consumer marketing now works (and overtime) to ensure that the product on offer does not result in the *closure* of the consumer's consumption of goods. It does this by *linking* products and services with other consumer options. The consumer of skincare moisturizer, for example, may wish to re-energize their skin. However, in shopping for the desired product they are likely to be cross-referred to endless related products—UV protection, pure ginseng extract creams, vitamin E and C products—all sold with the marketing hype of "how to look radiant." The capacity to keep all consumer options open, the embrace of the fluidity and cross-currents of market-supplied services and substances: these are the key traits of contemporary consumption. "Desire," writes Bauman, "becomes its own purpose, and the sole uncontested and unquestionable purpose" (2005, p. 73). Such desire feeds spontaneity in shopping: the desire not simply to consume more, but to consume the endless possibilities offered by the consumer industries for the reconstruction and reinvention of the self. As Bauman reflects: "The code in which our 'life policy' is scripted is derived from the pragmatics of shopping" (2005, p. 74).

While the deep drivers of self-reinvention are essentially culturalist, the institutional parameters underpinning instant change are corporate. Consider the recent global expansion of cosmetic surgical industries. Although precise figures on levels of investment and returns across cosmetic surgical industries are difficult to specify, we are clearly dealing with a multi-billion dollar industry (Elliott, 2008). In the US alone, the cosmetic surgical industry generates in excess of $20 billion a year. Whilst this may fall short of the $25 billion-a-year cosmetics industry and the more than $30 billion-a-year diet industry, cosmetic plastic surgery is the fastest growing makeover corporate concern in the world. And in all products—from Botox and collagen fillers to liposuction and mini-facelifts—the message from the industry is one of instant change. This corporate message communicates that the self can be changed however the individual so desires: literally, there are no limits.

Various factors, in conditions of advanced globalization, prompt individuals to demand instant change, and specifically, to contemplate undergoing the plastic surgeon's knife in order to obtain a perceived personal and professional edge over others. The "new economy" has ushered in changes of enormous magnitude, in which people are under intense pressure to keep pace with the sheer speed of social transformations. Seemingly secure jobs are wiped out literally overnight. Technology becomes obsolete almost as soon as it is released. Multinational corporations move their operations from country to country in search of the best profit margin. Women and men clamber frenetically to obtain new skills or be discarded on the scrapheap. Simultaneously, these objective social transformations are mirrored at the level of everyday life. The demand for instant change, in other words, is widely perceived to demonstrate an appetite for—a willingness to embrace—change, flexibility, and adaptability.

3. The new individualism is constituted through a fascination with *speed*. The novelist Milan Kundera, in his book *Slowness* (1995), suggests that contemporary societies have become intoxicated with "pure speed." Kundera writes:

> Speed is the form of ecstasy the technical revolution has bestowed on man. As opposed to a motorcyclist, the runner is always present in his body, forever required to think about his blisters, his

exhaustion; when he runs he feels his weight, his age, more conscious than ever of himself and of his time of life. This all changes when man delegates the faculty of speed to a machine: from then on, his own body is outside the process, and he gives over to a speed that is noncorporeal, nonmaterial, pure speed, speed itself, ecstasy speed. (1995, p. 2)

For Kundera, the contemporary epoch has raised speed to the second power.

A huge social science literature documents the rise of social acceleration, speed, dynamism, and accelerated change in conditions of advanced globalization (Eriksen, 2001). "We now live," writes Paul Virilio, "in an era with no delays" (1986). With the acceleration of speed, according to Virilio, space is compressed. Speed compresses distance, global telecommunications transcend state boundaries, and our experiences of self and world become squeezed, rushed, hurried and harried. Scheuerman nicely captures this social acceleration: "Everywhere we turn—from the 15-second 'sound bites' of television news, our high-speed capitalist workplace, to our culture's eroticization of fast automobiles and fascination with high-speed sports—contemporary society exhibits an obsession with speed" (2005, p. 453). This obsession with speed flows is, in turn, linked to massive changes in social processes. As German social theorist Hartmut Rosa (2003) has argued, our individual experiences of living life faster, busier and speedier is tied to fundamental technological transformations—especially high-speed digital technologies, communication networks, and just-in-time global production processes. Objective technological and temporal speed-up, in other words, results in the experience of life in the fast lane.

From the vantage point of the new individualism, our fascination with speed is perhaps nowhere more apparent than in demands for, and dramas of, consumerism. In high-speed flows of cosmopolitan culture, consumption emerges as the most sublime phenomenon, attempting to reconcile the apparently contradictory forces of desire and disappointment, beauty and terror. If consumerism mesmerizes it is not only because it trades in extravagant expectations of pure speed but because it discards and deceives as well as seduces. Promising scintillating satisfaction and yet frustrating fulfilment, consumerism inhabits a terrain of lethal ecstasy—each repeated frustration of desire helping to unleash, in turn, new wants and fresh appetites. These wants and appetites, needless to say, emerge faster and faster—and the demand is for instantaneous response. A realm of deception, there is something always *excessive* about consumerism, in that it represents both cultural continuity and anti-social rupture. In one sense, consumerism is enthralling, overwhelming, transgressive and traumatic—it promises to lift one beyond the known world to a power of pure speed and instantaneous pleasure. In another sense, these fearful powers of the consumer society are brought low, rendered dazzlingly empty, by the frustration of fulfilment. Consumerism thus oscillates between the utopic immensity of its promises and the non-satisfaction rendered by its products. The speed of consumerism is addiction incarnate. Like watching a computer screen downloading software with the latest updates, the want-now consumerism of contemporary women and men indicates a fascination with speed, acceleration, and rapidity. The message issuing from the global consumer economy, in effect, is: *"Have you had your latest identity update today? New individualism 4.2.1."* The rapid-fire speed of everyday life in turn correlates with developments in the global electronic economy, leading to my final point.

4. The new individualism is shaped in and through a preoccupation with *short-termism* and *episodicity*. Here, there are important links between the advent of the global electronic economy and socio-economic logics of intensive globalism on the one hand, and the popular explosion of interest in reinvention or makeover industries and short-term identity reconstruction on the other. The root of the problem is largely cultural, driven by a corporate ethos that flexible and ceaseless reinvention is the only adequate response to globalization. Globalization is evidently a world of transformations, affecting every aspect of what we do and what we think about our lives. For better or worse, globalization has given rise to the 24/7 society in which continual self-actualization and dramatic self-reinvention has become the rage.

Globalization is also a key buzzword of our times—and our lives in these times (Giddens, 2003). Arguments about the consequences of globalization need to be carefully assessed, as "globalization" has many different meanings, not all of them coherent, few reconcilable. For many critics globalization describes advanced capitalism in its broadest sense, and by implication the term has come to revolve around Americanization. This is the view that globalization is a central driver in the export of American commerce and culture, of the vast apparatus of mass consumerism, of the unleashing of US-controlled turbo-capitalism. Others view globalization through the lens of a much longer historical perspective, beginning with the age of discovery and the migrations from the Old to the New World.

A full discussion of the many facets of globalization goes beyond the scope of this essay. But I do want to stay with the theme of our globalizing world to suggest there are important new links between the dynamism of intensive globalization and the popular explosion in the makeover industries and cosmetic surgical culture. In this connection, the impact of communications media and new information technologies is perhaps most important for grasping what is truly new about globalization. Political theorist David Held captures this point well:

> What is new about the modern global system is the chronic intensification of patterns of interconnectedness mediated by such phenomena as the modern communications industry and new information technology and the spread of globalization in and through new dimensions of interconnectedness: technological, organizational, administrative and legal, among others, each with their own logic and dynamic of change. (1991, p. 145; see also Held et al., 1999)

Transformations in the organizational and corporate dimensions of global interconnectedness, to anticipate my argument, are creating the conditions in which instant self-reinvention occurs.

The ability of multinational corporations to export industrial production to low-wage spots around the globe and to restructure investment in the West away from manufacture to the finance, service and communications sectors has spelt major changes in the ways people live their lives, how they approach work, as well as how they position themselves within the employment marketplace. A key institutional fact redefining the contemporary condition is the rapid decline of lifetime employment. The end of a job-for-life, or of a career developed within a single organization, has been interpreted by some critics as heralding the arrival of a "new economy"—flexible, mobile, networked. Global financier and philanthropist George Soros (1998) argues that "transactions" now substitute for "relationships" in the modern economy.

Recent sociological studies emphasize such global trends towards short-termism and episodicity—in personal relationships, family dynamics, social networks, employment, and work. American sociologist Richard Sennett (1998) writes of the rise of "short-term, contract and episodic labor." Yesteryear's job-for-life, he argues, is replaced today by short-term contract work leading to an erosion of loyalty and trust that employees previously vested in their workplaces. Authors like Sennett see the worker flexibility demanded by multinational corporations as demonstrating the reality of globalization, promoting a dominant conception of individuals as dispensable and disposable. Against this sociological backdrop he cites statistics indicating the average American college student graduating today can expect to hold twelve positions or jobs in their lifetime, plus, they will be required to change their skills base at least three times. In *The Culture of the New Capitalism*, Sennett examines the deeper emotional consequences of such big organizational changes thus: "people fear being displaced, sidelined, or underused. The institutional model of the future does not furnish them a life narrative at work, or the promise of much security in the public realm" (2005, p. 132). Further, "work identities get used up, they become exhausted, when institutions themselves are continually reinvented" (2005, p. 141).

Likewise in their research on global economic outsourcing, Gene Grossman and Esteban Rosi-Hansberg (2006) find that "at-risk" workers are not just in unskilled or semi-skilled jobs but also in skilled and highly skilled ones (such as those working in finance, legal, medical, and hi-tech sectors). The outsourcing of industrial production over recent decades, they say, finds its counterpart today in the outsourcing of knowledge-intensive jobs. Electronic offshoring, for Grossman and Rosi-Hansberg, is more than the rise of call centres in countries such as India. After all, any service job can be electronically outsourced if it involves substantial reliance upon information technology and involves little face-to-face interaction. Incredibly, they estimate that somewhere between *30 and 40 million* service jobs in the US will become open to electronic offshoring in the near future.

The fast, short-term, techy culture of globalization is unleashing a new paradigm of self-making where the capacity to change and reinvent oneself is fundamental. A faith in flexibility, plasticity, and incessant reinvention means we are no longer judged on what we have done and achieved but on our flexibility and readiness for instant makeover. The culture of short-termism promoted by globalization pressures people to "improve," "transform," and "reinvent" themselves. Driven by both desire and fear of such metamorphosis, individuals desperately attempt to "refashion" themselves as more efficient, faster, leaner, inventive, and self-actualizing than they were previously. Day-in day-out, society in the era of the new individualism is fundamentally shaped by this fear of disposability.

The psychodynamics of disposability: Some psychoanalytic reflections

This chapter now broadens this account to suggest that new individualism and its cultural props—driven largely by fear of disposability in our age of intensive globalization—work as a *screen* onto which people project their discontent. People increasingly turn to reinvention when socioeconomic circumstances link deeply with *melancholic* aspects of identity. Melancholia, as Freud uncovered, is a form of intense sadness over nothing in particular. It is a free-floating grief that attaches to various persons, objects, and events—from the death of a loved one to the assassination of a political leader to the break-up of a pop group. A feature of melancholic experience is that it locks the self into a restricted relation to others and the wider world; this involves emotional fixation and the closing down of human complexity. The discontented husband who refuses to admit the desirability of his wife because she is now "middle-aged"; the older woman who buys endless trend fashions she will never wear for fear of looking foolish in a youth-obsessed culture; the ageing executive who resorts to cosmetic practices or surgery as a means of competing with his younger and energetic colleagues. All are melancholic identities.

Psychoanalysis gives useful leads on what is going on here. The preoccupation with loss in various versions of psychoanalysis concerns both the *fear and pain of loss*. From Freud through Melanie Klein to Julia Kristeva, the individual forges a relation to itself and other people through loss: the loss of loved ones, the loss of selves, the loss of pasts. From a psychoanalytic point of view, it is necessary to stress therefore that people create themselves through forgetting and remembering their losses. In what follows, this essay looks toward psychoanalytic theory in considering how loss operates within the broader contours of new individualism.

From his earliest writings, Freud argued that self-experience begins with the experience of loss. For Freud the mother (or primary caretaker) is the child's first and most significant loss. Through her absence, the infant comes to recognize that the mother is different to itself. It is only through the mother's absence, says Freud, that the infant comes to desire her presence. This founding moment of separation is both frightening and exciting, and to cope, the infant creates fantasies about the mother as a compensation for her painful absence. Said otherwise, the infant reacts to the absence of the mother in reality by imagining her present in fantasy. In its capacity for imagination, writes Freud, the infant has "created an object out of the mother" (1926, p. 170).[1]

It is worth considering what the denial of loss might mean at the level of the inner world, given the emphasis on repression in psychoanalysis. In his 1915 essay, "Mourning and Melancholia," Freud reconstructs the connections between love and loss on the one hand, and the limits of identification and identity on the other. "The loss of a love object," writes Freud, "is an excellent opportunity for the ambivalence in love-relationships to make itself effective and come into the open" (1915, p. 251).[2] The loss of a loved person, he suggests, brings into play ambivalence and aggression. Under such circumstances, both one's passion and anger for lost love comes to the fore. Since the other person is loved, the self incorporates some aspect of the loved other into itself in order to maintain the emotional tie. However, because the other person is also hated, this incorporated aspect of the other now becomes something despised within the self.

On this basis, Freud distinguishes between "normal mourning" and the "complex of melancholia." Freud considers mourning a normal response to the loss of a loved person in which the self incorporates aspects of the other person and then gradually detaches itself from the lost love. By acknowledging the pain of absence, the mourner emotionally draws from the lost love; he or she borrows, as it were, personality traits and feelings associated with the loved person, and in so doing, is able to work through these feelings of loss. In the "complex of melancholia," the individual fails to break from the lost love, keeping hold of the object through identification. Unable to mourn, the melancholic cannot express love and hate directly towards the lost love, and instead denigrates its own ego. Freud describes this melancholic process as an "open wound": the melancholic is caught in a spiralling of identifications in which hatred rounds back upon the self, "emptying the ego until it is totally impoverished." Whereas the mourner gradually accepts that the lost love no longer exists, the melancholic engages in denial in order to protect the self from loss.

Put differently, selfhood is drafted against the backdrop of our willingness or unwillingness to mourn loss. If the pain of loss can be tolerated, the individual subject can relinquish primary involvements. If the pain of loss cannot be tolerated, there is a grafting of sadness on to the lost object itself, transforming mourning into melancholia.[3] Language plays a central role here as words fill in for what has been lost. Words are a stopgap, helping to close up the pain of lost love.[4] Julia Kristeva writes:

> The child becomes irredeemably sad before uttering his first words: this is because he has been irrevocably, desperately separated from

the mother, a loss that causes him to try to find her again, along with other objects of love, first in the imagination, then in words. (1989, p. 6)

This essay invokes psychoanalytic theory to consider the complexities of the relation between self, loss and melancholia, and so raises fresh questions concerning how we might think about how new individualism and its culture of reinvention contains and represses grief. In doing so, this essay focuses on a tendency discussed within the debate over individualism and the cult of reinvention that is perhaps not very familiar: the emerging *global economy of grief* in these early days of the twenty-first century.

The idea that the endless reinventions of new individualism contain and repress melancholic grief raises the following questions. In what ways does loss manifest itself in identities dedicated to ceaseless reinvention? How does an unconscious refusal to work through loss—the hallmark of melancholia—attach itself to the lures of identity revision enhancement or body augmentation? If the short-termism of reinvention solutions is now a culturally sanctioned means of displacing the power of loss in our lives, what are the longer-term consequences of such human decisions?

The first way new individualism and its culture of reinvention calls grief into play is through the relentless stress placed upon youth in modern societies. Of course this is not entirely new: youth, as interwoven with representations of sex and beauty, has long formed part of the cultural obsessions and ideals of the West. Currently, however, we witness a far denser media and informational system of diffusing images, signs, and symbols pertaining to youth. This cultural worship of youth at once renders young bodies as desirable and older bodies as not. A certain self-awareness about and understanding of bodies has thus been increasingly generalized in a startlingly new way. Among populations of the pricey cities of the West, the body is now an immensely fashionable concern—and certainly the youthful, sleek body is preferred.

This is where the reinvention culture of new individualism comes into its own. By drawing attention to the visible signs of ageing, from blotchy patches to crow's feet, the makeover industries attempt to "sell youth" to an ageist culture. From the skin tightening of mini-facelifts to the enhancements of collagen, cosmetic surgeons and the makeover industries seek to sell their "products" through associations with youth. But what is considered youthful appears to be getting ever younger. As Shelley Gare writes, cosmetic surgeons now proudly say there have been so many improvements and breakthroughs in their procedures, women can start having rejuvenation treatments in their 30s. We may be trying to believe 50 is the new 30, but with such emphasis on looks, lines and reinvention, 30 is in danger of eventually looking like the new 100. (2007, p. 16)

It is not difficult to see in all this the influence of grief, the hungering for lost youth, coupled with the attempt to outflank the pain of loss through cosmetic procedures and surgical interventions.

A second sign of the imprint of grief in new individualism and reinvention culture lies in its attempted *freezing of time*. In the epoch of advanced globalization, the cult of reinvention now stands for the annihilation of time. As such, new individualism is anti-linear; it warps traditional assumptions that one starts to look older as one ages. The makeover industries thus claim to provide a glimpse of "forever," the promise to arrest our biologically ageing bodies—which is to say that it is not hard to detect a good deal of wish-fulfilment operating here. But if the ideology of new individualism confers on its subjects a pseudo-halt to time and ageing, it also strikes the world traumatically empty of movement, development, progression. Margaret Gibson writes:

> The economic and symbolic value of youthful bodies creates a false but nevertheless seductive fantasy of bodies as static and unchanging. Frozen in time through the image, the youthful and beautiful are idealized as eternal forms appearing to defy, or, alternatively, not appearing to embody, temporal mortal existence. (2006, p. 55)

But if this alleged arresting of time in new individualism has a soothing, compensatory dimension, it also has a more intimidating one. This contradiction is not accidental, since it must resort to invocations of shock, trauma, and horror in order to provide the fleeting moments of imaged escape offered through the "rewind" of age. In *Powers of Horror* (1982), Julia Kristeva describes such horror as the realm of "abjection." Abjection is an imagined disintegration of the body in the wider frame of relations with others, which Kristeva associates with the ultimate imprint of the death drive, a primordial anguish or fear of a horrifying void. From this angle, the promised "rewind" to youth offered by cosmetic surgical culture represents a fantasy compensation to the horror of the void or blank that constitutes death for the unconscious. Yet this compensation remains illusory, fantasmatic. At the deeper level of the unconscious the forces of life and death remain intricately entangled. No amount of collagen, liposuction, or Botox can erase the deathly constituent of all human existence. The individual self, said Freud, is constituted by a primary masochism, the imprint of the death drive incarnate; this deathly form of self-destruction is what leads people to symbolically attack their lives, to annihilate the self—of which reinvention culture is arguably a fast-emerging twenty-first century strategy of turning this instinct outwards. However much people attempt self-reinvention or instant makeovers the pain of loss reappears whenever a spacing or hiatus of meaning announces itself in the psyche. This may come in the form of noticing a new ageing line, or simply less energy. In this emotional realm, there lies pain, fear, anguish.

The third sign of the containment and repression of grief in new individualism lies in the negation of death. Nothing more powerfully reveals the ultimate uncontrollability of our lives than death—one reason why countless millions have responded to the terrors of non-being by trying to organize their lives around firm blueprints, fixed meanings, and secure projects. "To give death a certain kind of purity," wrote Maurice Blanchot, "was always the task of culture: to render it authentic, personal, proper."[5] The job of culture, in other words, is to help rescue us from the terrors of death. Culture both structures social practices and rituals relating to mortality and suppresses our awareness of the frail character of such meaning. But as with individual psychopathology, so too cultures can develop neurotic styles of handling impending death and non-being. One key way cultural attitudes to death become bent out of shape or neurotic is through a process that sociologists call "sequestration" (see Giddens, 1991). The sequestration of death involves the squeezing of non-being to the sidelines of social experience. This is death displaced, denied, and disowned. At present, one of the most graphic illustrations of this sequestration of death occurs through the transformation of dying from a community affair into a medical process. In *A Social History of Dying* (2006), Allan Kellehear argues that we witness throughout the West "the disintegration of dying." From people dying of AIDS or poverty to those in concentration camps, death is "removed" from the wider social radar and circumscribed to a narrow institutional definition involving end-of-line medical supervision. This is perhaps nowhere more obvious than in nursing homes, where dying has become increasingly unconnected from its biological, psychological, and interpersonal roots. "Large proportions of our dying," writes Kellehear, "are now commonly hidden away from our communities. We do not easily witness the massive number of dying in nursing homes, in developing countries, or in totalitarian moments of our recent history" (2006).

Another contemporary Western strategy, by contrast, involves a morbid fascination with death itself. From mangled bodies to mediated mass killings, from the medicalization of dying to the "snuff" movies of hard-core porn, death obsesses the contemporary imagination. This may sound paradoxical, and in a certain sense it is. On the one hand, Western culture seeks to render death invisible through sequestrating it from daily life and, on the other hand, it morbidly immerses itself in images and media representations of destruction, dying, and death. From another angle, this contradiction is not what it appears once it is borne in mind that those caught up in such a neurotic fix are, in fact, attempting to outflank death by deftly incorporating non-being into the very tissue of life itself. Arguably, it is to this end that the Freudian death drive exerts its sway. As Terry Eagleton reflects on current Western attitudes to death:

We have to find a way of living with non-being without being in love with it, since being in love with it is the duplicitous work of the death drive. It is the death drive which cajoles us into tearing ourselves apart in order to achieve the absolute security of nothingness. Non-being is the ultimate purity. It has the unblemishedness of all negation, the perfection of a blank page. (2003, p. 213)

What might such morbid attempts to outwit death have to do with new individualism? My argument, following Eagleton, is that the culture of reinvention today promises precisely the "perfection of a blank page." Both the culture of reinvention and makeover are in their different ways denials of death. In Western culture, which actively devalues older people and especially older women's bodies, this denial manifests as an imagined rewind to the splendours of youth. In rejecting mortality and the ultimate non-being of death, new individualism contains our aggression—the force of the death drive—only by turning it against our selves and bodies. What we find in new individualism is the corollary of a new global economy of grief. It marks the historical point in which death avoidance is raised to the second power. The reinvention culture of new individualism represents, in Eagleton's terms, "tearing ourselves apart in order to achieve the absolute security of nothingness."

Conclusion

New individualism hinges on the emergence of a cultural imperative to reinvent. This imperative, advanced by business leaders, politicians, personal trainers, and therapy gurus, emphasizes flexible and ceaseless reinvention as the only adequate personal response to life in a globalizing world. It is a paradigm that pervades the mission statement of countless makeover service providers: personal trainers, spas, gyms, weight-loss and detox centers, cosmetic dentists and plastic surgeons, all chasing the money people will spend to realize their reinvention ideal. While new individualist practices are not wholly shaped or determined by recent changes in the global economy, it is important to recognize how the new economy has ushered into existence changes of enormous magnitude—ones that place people under intense pressure to keep pace with the sheer speed of change. Job insecurity, planned obsolescence, outsourcing, skills extinction, short-term contracts, endless downsizing—all are reasons for new individualist self-reinvention and makeover that might demonstrate one's personal readiness for change, flexibility and adaptability.

The reinvention paradigm extends beyond the core of the self to the body, that distracting reminder of mortality in a world where disposability is elevated over durability, plasticity over permanence. The culture of speed and short-termism promoted by the global electronic economy introduces fundamental anxieties and insecurities that are increasingly resolved by individuals at the level of the body. Bodies today are pumped, pummeled, plucked, suctioned, stitched, shrunk, and surgically augmented at an astonishing rate. Of course, previous ages have been plagued by anxiety too, and insecurities pertaining to employment and career prospects are hardly new (Giddens, 1991). But the method of coping with, and reacting to, anxieties is quite different to previous times. In contrast to the factory-conditioned certainties and bureaucratic rigidities of yesterday's work world, in which personal insecurities "locked in" tightly with the organizational settings of economic life, today's new corporatism is a world in which individuals are increasingly left to their own devices as regards their working life and its future prospects. This is a societal change that creates considerable scope for personal opportunities, but it is also one of severe stresses and emotional costs. The faith in flexibility, plasticity, and incessant reinvention throughout the corporate world means that employees are judged less and less on previous achievements and ever more on their willingness to embrace change, their adaptability for personal make-over. In such circumstances, anxiety becomes free floating, *detached* from organizational life. Consequently, anxiety rounds back upon the self and many feel an increased pressure to improve, transform, alter, and reinvent themselves. Today's makeover culture arises in this social space, in response to such ambient fears.

Just as flexible capitalism engages in ceaseless organizational restruc-turings, so now do people—employees, employers, consumers, parents, and children. Don DeLillo argues that global capitalism generates trans-formations at "the speed of light," not only in terms of the sudden move-ment of factories, the mass migration of workers, and the instant shifts of liquid capital but in "everything from architecture to leisure time to the way people eat and sleep and dream" (1998, p. 786). In thinking about the complex ways in which our emotional lives are altered by the socio-economic changes wrought by globalization, this essay adds to the wealth of transformations mentioned by DeLillo by focusing on people's changing experiences of their identities, emotions, affects, and bodies as a result of new individualist social practices. The argument is that global forces, in transforming economic and technological structures, penetrate to the very tissue of our personal and emotional lives.

Notes

1. The infant, it seems, relies on the mother in a profoundly imaginary way: through the medium of fantasy, constructions of self and other, sameness and difference become possible. The forging of some preliminary sense of identity, Freud argues, arises through an imagined incorporation of the mother into the self. In effect, Freud argues that what is on the outside (the body of the mother) can be taken inside (psychic space), internalized and devoured. Our primary experiences with the mother become part of the emotional structure of subjectivity.
2. For a discussion of the centrality of mourning to psychoanalysis see Sprengnether (1995). See also Homans (1989).
3. The shift from the process of mourning to that of melancholia involves acute narcissistic depression. Projective identification and incorpora-tion, as Melanie Klein has shown, give the fantasized dimensions of this idealization and valorization of self/other merging. Klein describes the object relation as structured by a paranoid, schizoid position. This is a schizoid splitting that underpins the integration of the subject (the divi-sion between the "good" and "bad" mother), but it is also linked to a logic of fragmentation in which the subject imagines itself disintegrating into pieces see Klein (1935, 1940).

4. In the psychoanalytic frame of reference, loss lies at the foundation of personal and social life. The Freudian Oedipus complex, as the French psychoanalyst Jacques Lacan has emphasized, accounts for the dissolution of the child's narcissistic omnipotence, and of his or her insertion into the law-governed world of language and symbols. After Oedipus, the individual lives out a symbolic relationship to loss in and through an object world of introjects and identifications. But the negotiation of loss depends on the ability to mourn, an ability that is profoundly disrupted and disturbed with the advent of melancholia. See Lacan (1977, ch. 5). For a critical appraisal of Lacan's return to Freud, see Elliott (1992, ch. 4).
5. Reprinted in Bauman, 1992, p. 6.

References

Bauman, Z. (2005) *Liquid Life* (Cambridge: Polity).

DeLillo, D. (1998) *Underworld* (London: Picador).

Eagleton, T. (2003) *After Theory* (London: Allen Lane).

Elliott, A. M. (1992) *Social Theory and Psychoanalysis in Transition* (Oxford: Blackwell).

Elliott, A. M. (2008) *Making the Cut: How Cosmetic Surgery is Transforming Our Lives* (Chicago: University of Chicago Press).

Elliott, A. M. (2009) *Contemporary Social Theory* (London: Routledge).

Elliott, A. M. (2010) "The New Individualism after the Great Global Clash," *Journal of Studies in Contemporary Sociological Theory*, 4, 55–66.

Elliott, A. M. and C. Lemert (2006) *The New Individualism: The Emotional Costs of Globalization*, Revised Edition (London and New York: Routledge).

Elliott, A. M. and C. Lemert (2009a) "The Global New Individualist Debate: Three Theories of Individualism and Beyond" in A. Elliott and P. du Gay (eds) *Identity in Question* (London: Sage).

Elliott, A. M. and C. Lemert (2009b) *The New Individualism: The Emotional Costs of Globalization*, 2nd edn. (London: Routledge).

Elliott, A. M. (2013) *Reinvention* (London: Routledge).

Elliott, A. M. and J. Urry (2010) *Mobile Lives* (Oxford: Routledge).

Eriksen, T. (2001) *Tyranny of the Moment* (London: Pluto Press).

Freud, S. (1915) "Mourning and Melancholia," in J. Strachey (ed.) *The Standard Edition of the Complete Psychological Works of Sigmund Freud*, Vol. 14 (New York: Basic Books).

Freud, S. (1926) *Inhibitions, Symptoms and Anxiety*, Vol. 20, in J. Strachey (ed.) *The Standard Edition of the Complete Psychological Works of Sigmund Freud* (New York: Basic Books).

Gare, S. (2007) "Do You Think I'm Sixty?," *The Australian Weekend Magazine*, 7–8 April, p. 16.

Gibson, M. (2006) "Bodies without Histories," *Australian Feminist Studies*, 21 (49), 51–63.

Giddens, A. (1991) *Modernity and Self-Identity: Self and Society in the Late Modern Age* (Cambridge: Polity).

Giddens, A. (2003) *Runaway World: How Globalisation is Reshaping our Lives* (New York: Routledge).

Grossman, G. and Rosi-Hansberg, E. (2006) "The Rise of Off-Shoring: It's Not Wine or Cloth Anymore." A paper presented at The New Economic Geography: Effects and Policy Implications, 2006, Jackson Hole Symposium, Kansas City, MO, July 2006.

Haikio, M. (2002) *Nokia: The Inside Story* (Boston: Prentice Hall).

Held, D. (1991) "Democracy, the Nation-State and the Global System," *Economy and Society*, 20 (2), 138–172.

Held, D., McGrew, A., Perraton, J., and Goldblatt, D. (1999) *Global Transformations* (Cambridge: Polity).

Homans, P. (1989) *The Ability to Mourn* (Chicago: Chicago University Press).

Kellehear, A. (2006) *A Social History of Dying* (Cambridge: Cambridge University Press).

Klein, M. (1935) "A Contribution to the Psychogenesis of Manic-Depressive States," *The International Journal of Psychoanalysis*, 16, 145–174.

Klein, M. (1940) "Mourning and Its Relation to Manic-Depressive States," *The International Journal of Psychoanalysis*, 21, 125–153.

Kristeva, J. (1982) *Powers of Horror* (New York: Columbia University Press).

Kristeva, J. (1989) *Black Sun: Depression and Melancholia* (New York: Columbia University Press).

Kundera, M. (1995) *Slowness* (New York: HarperCollins).

Lacan, J. (1977) "The Agency of the Letter in the Unconscious of Reason since Freud" in J. Lacan (ed.) *Ecrits* (London: Tavistock).

Merriden, T. (2001) *Business the Nokia Way: Secrets of the World's Fastest Moving Company* (Oxford: Capstone).

"Reshaping Cisco: The World According to Chambers" (2009) *The Economist*, 27 August.

Riesman, D., Glazer, N., and Denny, R. (2001) *The Lonely Crowd: A Study of the Changing American Character*, revised edn. (New Haven: Yale University Press).

Rosa, H. (2003) "Social Acceleration: Ethical and Political Consequences of a Desynchronized High-Speed Society," *Constellations*, 10 (1), 3–33.

Scheuerman, W. E. (2005) "Busyness and Citizenship," *Social Research*, 72 (2), 447–470.

Sennett, R. (1998) *The Corrosion of Character* (New York: Norton).

Sennett, R. (2005) *The Culture of the New Capital* (New Haven: Yale University Press).

Soros, G. (1998) *The Crisis of Global Capitalism: Open Society Endangered* (New York: Public Affairs).

Sprengnether, M. (1995) "Mourning Freud" in A. Elliott and S. Frosh (eds) *Psychoanalysis in Contexts: Paths between Theory and Modern Culture* (London: Routledge).

Virilio, P. (1986) *Speed and Politics* (New York: Semiotext(e)).

15
The Shame of Survival: Rethinking Trauma's Aftermath

Arlene Stein

Some 140,000 Jewish refugees from war-devastated Europe arrived on American shores after the defeat of the Nazis. Generally between the ages of 15 and 35, they spent years in concentration camps, hiding in forests, passing as gentiles in Warsaw or Berlin, or exiled in Russia. Many were the sole survivors of their families, or nearly so (Dinnerstein, 1982). They spoke a variety of different languages—Russian, Polish, German, Greek, Yiddish, and more—and had as many different conceptions of what it meant to be a Jew. What they shared was the experience of destruction, of having their once-familiar worlds ripped apart, and the challenge of reconstituting their lives.

Today the remaining survivors garner large, attentive audiences when they speak in high school auditoriums and public libraries across the US. The survivor/witness has emerged as a very visible and public narrator of Holocaust memories, particularly in North America. But this was not always the case. For at least two decades after the end of World War II, there was little unified understanding of who the Jewish survivors of Nazism were or what they had endured, or consciousness of the "Holocaust" as a singular entity spanning years and locations, encompassing different nations, forms of expulsion, displacement, and extermination. Those who settled in the US after the war were known as "refugees," "displaced persons," "greenhorns," individuals who hailed from a particular town or nation or survivors of Buchenwald, Dachau, and other concentration camps. Few spoke openly about their experiences to their families, much less in public, having been convinced, sometimes for very good reasons, that others did not want to hear. The vast majority of survivors limited their public revelations to those they believed understood them best: other survivors. They faced difficulties integrating their traumatic pasts into their everyday lives and did not, for the most part, see their personal distress as something in which others would be interested. And while they joined together with others like themselves for social and commemorative activities, they rarely saw themselves as a collective identity transcending national origins or having a political purpose.

In fact, if talk of the Holocaust was in the air in the 1970s while I was growing up, I was barely aware of it even in New York City, home to a large Jewish population of which a good number were survivors. We did not learn about it in school; there were no public memorials or museums. There was barely a category of experience called "The Holocaust," and the genocide of European Jewry was generally subsumed under the rubric of "the war." A patchwork memorial culture was emerging in Jewish communities: religious leaders worked to incorporate the Holocaust into Jewish liturgy, synagogues constructed small-scale shrines, *landsman-shaftn* (local and regional Jewish associations) erected makeshift memorials at numerous cemeteries, and summer camps lit candles to remember the dead. But it was somber, locally based and small-scale, barely visible in American Jewish culture, and generally not seen as relevant to non-Jewish Americans.

Today, in contrast, the destruction of European Jewry is the subject of documentaries and Hollywood films and widely recognized as a moral touchstone. Washington D.C.'s Holocaust Memorial Museum draws twice as many visitors as the White House, and numerous states mandate Holocaust education. This foregrounding of the Holocaust in popular consciousness since the 1970s, symbolized by memorials, museums, films, and the proliferation of survivor testimonies, is part of a broader preoccupation, especially in North America, with traumatic memories and catastrophic histories. Survivors of rape and incest are encouraged to transform their private memories into public speech; families and friends who have lost loved ones in the AIDS epidemic and the Vietnam War erect memorials and bear witness to their loss; the descendants of African slaves invoke their history of the Middle Passage.

How can we account for this extraordinary shift, this rise of social consciousness regarding the Holocaust, and collective trauma more generally? What we know is that the processing of traumatic events requires a listening space and that this space is not granted automatically: it has to be fought for. For example, while slavery was certainly traumatic for those who experienced it, it only became a resonant historical trauma for African Americans many years after it had ended, when black leaders and intellectuals framed slavery as a symbol of oppression (Eyerman, 2004, p. 61). Similarly the sexual abuse of children, once believed to be a private family matter and rarely discussed publicly, became widely known as traumatizing when feminists named it as such and mobilized to change the way we think about relationships between parents and children, and the nature of power in the family (Whittier, 2009). And so it was with the genocide of European Jewry: it took the collective efforts of survivors, their families, and others to push Holocaust stories into the public sphere.

Some observers say that for at least two or three decades after the war, the genocide of European Jewry was not widely discussed because as a group struggling for integration into the mainstream, American Jews did not wish to see themselves as victims and could see few benefits in embracing Holocaust memory. That began to change in the 1960s as the Adolf Eichmann trial and then the Israeli Six Day War re-sensitized American Jews to existential threats posed to the Jewish people, and the publication of Eli Wiesel's *Night* helped bring the term "Holocaust" into public discourse. At that moment, according to one historian, "a series of choices by Jewish leaders, tacitly ratified by their constituents, transformed the genocide into the signal event of modern Jewish history" (Novick, 1999, pp. 10, 280).[1]

But even before a broad public understanding of the ongoing effects of the genocide emerged, before the Holocaust was widely discussed and commemorated in this country, survivors worked through the past individually and collectively. "History affects people psychologically no less than it does physically and materially," writes Nancy Chodorow, "and this psychological impact is registered emotionally and unconsciously as well as consciously and cognitively" (Chodorow, 2002, p. 298). Indeed, during the first three decades after the end of World War II, survivors grappled with their experiences in varied ways, individually and collectively, but had few opportunities to openly narrate their experiences of traumatic loss. There was not yet a "memory milieu," a culture of remembrance, into which they could fit their traumatic experiences, or communicate them to others.[2] While individuals are surely not reducible to the groups of which they are members, survivors shared many common experiences, including witnessing death and destruction during the war, struggling to create new lives afterwards, and facing challenges in making themselves understood to others, which led to common ways of knowing, and common kinds of collective feelings.

Becoming "survivors"

As I use the term, the "Holocaust survivor" is any Jew who lived under Nazi occupation during World War II and was thus threatened by Nazi policies but who stayed alive–including those who were confined to a ghetto, forced labor in work camp, and/or incarceration in a concentration camp, in hiding or living under false identities, refugees who left their families behind, those who fought with the partisans, those who were sent away in the "kindertransport," and others. While my focus is on Jewish survivors, I certainly recognize that non-Jewish Roma, leftists, homosexuals, and members of other groups also suffered.[3] Those who settled in the US after World War II came from far flung parts of the Europe, from small villages and big cities, and were religious and highly secular.

In the decades after World War II, expert observers faced challenges in accounting for the diverse experiences of Jewish survivors. The dominant account pictured survivors as individuals who were busily rebuilding their lives and searching for normality (Bar-on, 2005). This account emphasized survivors' great flexibility and resilience when confronting the challenge of rebuilding their lives after the war. Despite their extraordinary experiences having been rescued from death by American troops and offered a second chance, the story went, survivors could take their place among other immigrants to the US, thrive in their adopted home, and focus upon the promise of future rather than the horrors of the past. And, indeed, the oral histories of survivors recount that neighbors, family members, social workers, and others counseled them to leave the past behind in order to create new lives (Cohen, 2007, p. 117).

During the first decade and a half after the war, most psychiatrists believed that even survivors of concentration camps, if given schooling, work, and a place to live, could integrate and carry on in the grand tradition of other American immigrants, and become part of the American tapestry (p. 137). A minority of the survivors, psychologists believed, endured ongoing psychic damage from their experiences. Although social service agencies charged with the resettlement of survivors found significant evidence to the contrary, social workers, physicians, and psychiatrists treated the survivors as they would any other immigrants, and focused upon locating housing and employment as key to reintegration. They tended little to survivors' numerous somatic complaints, refusing to delve too deeply into the sources of their clients' pain.

In the classical psychoanalytic model dominant during that period, trauma was considered to be a temporary malady after which one would return to "normal" (see Bergmann and Jucovy, 1982, p. 8). Dwelling on past problems was considered counterproductive and self-reliance was seen as the best medicine. There was not yet an understanding of the "post-traumatic stress" that would pose ongoing problems for those who had undergone displacement and witnessed death firsthand, and survivors were typically counseled to live as if the past no longer existed. Self-revelation was discouraged.

But in the early 1960s "trauma," defined in relation to the tragic event and its traces, began to make its way into psychiatric accounts of survivors (Niederland, 1968). Psychiatric journals began to publish articles that documented survivors' ongoing personal problems, suggesting that trauma might be a permanent injury that could reshape personal identities–identities previously assumed to be continuous, static, or impervious to the experience of war. An American psychoanalyst and refugee from Nazi Germany, William Niederland, coined the term "survivor syndrome" in 1961 to describe the long-term effects of having been subjected to persecution.

Niederland suggested that survivors of concentration camps represented "traumatization of such magnitude, severity, and duration" as to produce a "recognizable clinical entity" that differed from other forms of psychopathology. Having clinically observed about 800 survivors of Nazi persecution, he described the syndrome as manifesting in the "persistence of multiple symptoms among which chronic depressive and anxiety reactions, insomnia, nightmares, personality changes, and far-reaching somatization prevail." He suggested that survivors' psychological profile included chronic and severe depressions coupled with apathy, emotional withdrawal and disturbances in memory and cognition; feelings of guilt (about their own survival while others died) marked by anxiety, fear, agitation, hallucinations, and sleep disturbances; and syndromes of pain, muscle tension, headaches, psychological disease, and occasional personality changes.

Survivors' overwhelmingly intense feelings of guilt became the central focus of this new psychological approach. In this account, survivors of genocide felt that their lives came at the costs of others' deaths, and that they might have done more to help or to resist. As they turn these feelings inward, "survivor guilt" they feel emotionally unworthy of the memory of those who perished; some believed their own lives had been saved by the deaths of innumerable others, and that only those who suffered the most extreme forms of victimization had the right to be heard (see also Bettleheim, 1979). The internal conversation was that "If I had done this or that, perhaps he or she would have lived today." This emphasis on survivors' guilt was derived mainly from clinical samples which skewed toward the experience of those who had sought out psychological help.

On the one hand, then, we have accounts of survivors' integration and upward mobility, of individuals who were focused on the future; on the other, we see individuals who are stuck in the past and somehow feel responsible for the deaths of their loved ones. Neither of these approaches grappled simultaneously with the enduring impact of massive psychic trauma on so many individuals who endured war and genocide, and the specific social contexts into which survivors were thrust after the war. In countries like the US, survivors of the genocide were often received grudgingly at a time of persistent anti-Semitism; they constituted a relatively small group in relation to other immigrant populations. Moreover, at a time of rebuilding, when the US was poised toward the future, there was generalized apprehension about confronting survivors' wartime experiences. We need an account of survivors' postwar experiences that is simultaneously attuned to the psychological and social impacts of trauma—to the ways survivors experienced the world, and the ways they were received by others.

When we consider the experience of Holocaust survivors through a psychosocial lens, it is *shame* rather than guilt which emerges as the most salient and telling concern. In his essay, "Shame," in *The Drowned and the Saved*, Primo Levi describes the feelings of those who were liberated from Auschwitz, the sense that "each one of us . . . has usurped his neighbor's place and lived in his stead" (Levi, 1989, pp. 81–82). What is most striking here is the portrait he paints of a landscape filled with betrayal and destruction, one in which humanity turned its back on its own. He describes survivors' feelings of shame. Guilt can lead to individual self-questioning but the world evoked by Levi in his numerous writings—a world of terror and loss—is one entirely lacking in meaning and compassion. It is a world that denies the individuality of the persecuted, and, even in the aftermath of the war, refuses to listen to their stories.

While guilt can be mainly individual, involving feelings of internalized remorse for something one has done, shame is a much more social, deeply intersubjective emotion. Though it plays a typically unmarked and invisible role in social interactions, some scholars suggest that shame is the "master emotion" of social life, arising in situations where social bonds are under threat. Unlike guilt, which can fester quietly inside you, shame "requires an audience" (Leys, 2007, p. 127). It connotes a denial of recognition which, Jessica Benjamin argues, is the core of selfhood (Scheff and Retzinger, 2000). We wish to know ourselves, and we want those closest to us to know us. Our very individuality depends on the willingness and capacity of others to recognize us.

Whereas recognition is a basic human need, shame occurs when "one['s] wishes to look at or commune with another person," in Sylvan Tomkins' words, but where one "suddenly cannot because he is strange . . . or unfamiliar" (Sedgwick, 2009, p. 49).[4]

Indeed, in interviews collected by the US Holocaust Memorial Museum in the 1990s, when survivors were in the latter part of their lives, it is the experience of shame they tend to recall.[5] By virtue of the fact that they survived the Nazi onslaught and made their lives in America, survivors were faced with many challenges, including figuring out how to communicate their experiences to others. Though the war years had come to define them, talking about those experiences was very difficult, and they felt that others could and would not understand them. Their inability to communicate frequently led to feelings of shame. I will illustrate this through the life histories of survivors.

The shame of survival

Harry Alexander was captured by the Gestapo in Nice and sent to a camp outside of Algiers. In the camp he and other prisoners worked ten hours a day building train tracks through the desert. They worked in 110-degree heat with only two cups of water a day, and at night had no blankets, despite bitter cold weather. Upon release from the camp, a British officer told Alexander, "in England you will start a whole new life. The war is over." But it was not as simple as this, Alexander acknowledged. "How do you start with no family, no home, no country, no money, no trade, no skill, no education?" As he recounted this exchange, his anger was palpable. "How do you start a new life? They had taken all this away from me and they haven't given me, any of them back. How do you start a new life?"

Like many other survivors, particularly those who had experienced the war years in isolation, Alexander lost his trust in the world. The postwar years seemed like a double betrayal. As he recalled: "I didn't have a place, any place to go, I had nobody to talk to. At least in the army, you have some people, some friends. Here I had no one. I was all on my own, all alone in a strange land. A land that didn't even want me. Let's face it. If you don't speak English like the English do, you're an outsider. They don't like you and they show it. I had no other place to go, what could I do? I got into a lot of fistfights. I was bitter. I was disappointed. I was hurt. Inexperienced to stand on my own two feet. For a year, I wandered around. Did odd jobs. And then I decided I'd go to America." He emigrated in 1948.

In the US, things were not much better. Alexander described the ways Americans distanced themselves from the survivors and their experiences. "They will make a joke or forget about it," he said. During his first years in the US, he never spoke about his experiences with anyone. He chose not to, he said, because he "just wanted to keep busy." Dwelling on the past was too painful. It reminded him of his overwhelming losses. So he deliberately drove his difficult memories inward, keeping them to himself: "I suppressed these feelings and these memories," he said, "and this hurt and this pain for so long, for so many years."

He describes living a quiet life after the war, of being devoted to his family and having little to do with organized social activities, Jewish or otherwise: "My mother was Jewish, [we had a] kosher house, my father, what did it get them?" he scoffed. "I said to the Rabbi, he came to my house, he said, come to *shul* (synagogue), and I said when you give me the answer to my question, to my satisfaction. Give me one good reason why I should go to *shul*. To empty my consciousness of guilt? I have done nothing wrong in my life that I have to ask forgiveness. God has nothing to forgive me for, but I have plenty to forgive Him for. Straighten that out and I'll come to *shul*. Convince me that there is a God and I'll go. The only thing I believe in is me. That's the only thing. If I don't keep myself alive, nobody will. If I don't work and make a living, nobody will pay my bills. I'll be in the street. That's all I know."

As this story suggests, Alexander's sense of estrangement was primed by his experiences of dehumanization during the war years. But what was so disturbing, as he described it half a century later, were his feelings of betrayal upon arriving in his adopted nation, when he interacted with others and encountered reluctant audiences. As he and others described, survivors wanted to be known by others; they wanted to tell their stories, at least in limited ways. By telling one's story we develop bonds of mutual recognition. But after the war, many of those closest to them refused to listen, averting their eyes. They felt widely misunderstood, unrecognized, and at times stigmatized.[6]

Eva Edmands's story illustrates these dynamics as well. After the German annexation of Austria in March 1938, Edmands' family left Vienna for Paris, and were trapped in Nazi-occupied France. Attempting to find refuge in Switzerland, they were caught by French police, and survived the war under a priest's protection. After the liberation of France in August 1944, Eva and her parents returned to Paris. In 1946, they emigrated to the US. Having believed that "we left all of that behind," Edmands was shocked by her encounters with anti-Semitism in the US. Even in New York City, she recalled, some landlords refused to rent to Jews and certain hotels were off-limits. Although anti-Jewish attitudes were fading in the postwar era, anti-immigrant sentiment, fused with anticommunist fervor, led to the imposition of immigration quotas on peoples arriving from Communist countries. Frequently, many Jewish survivors who hailed from countries of the Soviet bloc became suspect as enemy aliens and potentially subversive to American national interests (Dinnerstein, 1982).

In response to these attitudes, Edmands said, she began to revert to her wartime practice of covering her identity—emphasizing less stigmatized identities such as her French origin rather than her Polish-Jewish one. "A strange thing happened at this point, I was really almost ashamed of having a Jewish background and so I didn't tell anybody," said Edmands. "I told them I was French but I didn't tell them about my background of being a survivor or anything like. I just determined I wasn't going to tell people. I told them I was French but I didn't tell them about my background of being a survivor or anything like that because the Germans had done such a good job of propagandizing and making you feel like you were the scum of that earth, that so, it is so insidious that after a while, you're being told, you know, over these years, you're scum, you're scum, you wind up believing. I said, well maybe I am inferior, maybe I'm not good as anybody else. And so I just determined I wasn't going to tell people."

Here we can see how feelings of stigma and inferiority may have begun years before, during the war itself. When they arrived in the US, survivors brought with them a sense of diminished trust in others. As Primo Levi and others have described so eloquently, the world had seemed to turn its back on them. Indeed, their sense of betrayal was reinforced by encounters in their newly adopted nations. Few Americans had a way of understanding who the survivors were or what they had endured, much less their experience of social exclusion in the US. Psychiatrists and social workers were similarly baffled; these refugees did not fit into conventional treatment frameworks or understandings. Author Eva Hoffman, the daughter of survivors who grew up in Poland and England, writes: "Survivors did not think their status was going to be enhanced by radical vulnerability. Aside from shame, there was the fear—and the reality—of stigma. The survivors may have spoken of what they had endured among themselves. But among strangers who had not lived through similar things and might not credit those who had, among those who, even if they did credit the stories, might misunderstand or were almost certain to do so, the survivors kept silent. They passed for normal" (Hoffman, 2004, p. 46).

In my reading of survivor narratives, feelings of shame—a powerful signal of social exclusion—are much more prominent than those of guilt.[7] In shame, one feels unrecognized, misunderstood, strange, and unfamiliar. While guilt attaches to what one does, shame attaches to and sharpens the sense of who one *is*. Guilt describes acts individuals have committed for which they may be remorseful; shame attaches to the person, and signifies a failure of recognition, a social breakdown. In shame, the individual feels invisible and unseen. While many survivors were undoubtedly stricken with feelings of guilt after their wartime experiences, the extent of their feelings of shame has been understated, perhaps because recognizing such feelings would implicate the host societies. The primary exceptions to this pattern were those who were active in the wartime resistance; feted in American Jewish communities and venerated by other survivors, this group alone managed to elude a sense of shame.

We can be heroes

Lisa Derman was born in 1926 in Raczki, Poland, and fled with her family to a forest, where she witnessed the massacre of Jews, including her mother. Lisa was sheltered by Christians and returned to the ghetto to find her father and brother who had survived the massacre. There she met a man, Aron, who was involved in the underground movement. Together they became partisans during the war, living in the woods under the command of the Soviets, and fighting against the Nazis. After war's end, they immigrated to the US.

Lisa recalls that when they arrived in the US, everyone did their best to make them feel comfortable and welcome. Lisa and Aron stayed with her relatives: two uncles and an aunt. Her relatives inquired about who had survived among their immediate kin, and little by little, Lisa recalls, "we revealed some of it, but they didn't press." She admits that she and her husband "weren't so anxious to tell them all the details." There was, in other words, an implicit compact between the two sides, a compact borne of the desire to protect one another from knowing too much. Her relatives did not inquire, and Lisa and Aron "only told them as much as they asked. But we did not tell them in detail."

Lisa believed her American relatives wanted to protect them: "They were afraid for our feelings. They thought we had suffered so much, why remind them? They kept on saying: this is America, things will be different here, things will be good." Their relatives threw them a shower, took them on drives to Coney Island, and tried to show them a good time. Lisa recalls that she and her husband "were taken over by the greatness of the city," and every night they were hosted and "treated royally everywhere we went." Friends and distant relatives imagined they had endured a series of events too horrible to discuss, and steered conversations to less unsettling matters. The Dermans never encountered stigma, they said: "Everywhere we went, we were the elite of survivors—because we resisted."

The cult of the hero was pervasive in Europe, the US, and Israel. Those who actively defended the nation or combated fascism, including ghetto fighters and partisans, were framed as warriors and heroes (Chaumont, 1997). They were accorded status for "doing something"— for their ability to act. And indeed, some of the first and most influential survivor organizations formed to commemorate moments of resistance, transforming survivors' tragic stories into "restitution" narratives that emphasized survival and overcoming.

Founded in 1962, the Warsaw ghetto resistance organization honored the 1943 insurgency in which several hundred young Jews held off their Nazi attackers for several months, and was among the most public survivor organizations, sponsoring an annual commemorative program in New York City. Each year, its public program began with a cantor singing the national anthem, and continued with a Hebrew prayer, and the singing of ghetto songs. A host of dignitaries—senators, Israeli representatives to the United Nations, governors, mayors, and rabbis— spoke and lit six memorial candles, chanted the *kaddish*, the memorial prayer, and recited the last words of the commander of the ghetto uprising. Finally, at the end of the event, the crowd sang the Partisan Hymn, written by a young poet and partisan in the Vilna Ghetto upon hearing about the Warsaw Ghetto Uprising. "This song was written with our blood and not with lead," it proclaimed. "This is no song of free birds flying overhead. But a people amid crumbling walls did stand. They stood and sang this song with rifles held in hand."[8]

By commemorating the ghetto uprising, survivors affirmed those who stood up to the Nazis—rather than the vast majority, who escaped by going into hiding, or survived by sheer luck, or even by selling out those around them. Such commemorations elevated resisters to the status of heroes, framing them as soldiers who exercised valor and agency. Since all but a few resisters were eventually killed, this focus was bittersweet. While affirming pride in the bravery of others, this "restitution narrative" distanced itself from the full extent of the tragedy, playing into many survivors' sense of powerlessness. Why, many asked themselves, were they not able to resist? The focus on resisters may also have inadvertently intensified the sense of guilt survivors felt about having survived while other family members, friends, and neighbors, did not, contributing to their public silence. As few survivors had the capacity to resist, the preoccupation with resisters during the first two decades after the war failed to give those who fell outside of this category a position from which to speak and bear witness.

Ludwik Szliferstejn was neither a resistance fighter nor a concentration camp internee. He had spent the war years in Russian-occupied Poland and later in Russia, having fled Warsaw immediately after the Nazi invasion on September 1, 1939. During the war, he hid, working as a teacher, and was eventually sent to a Soviet labor camp in Siberia, and then to fight for the Red Army at the Romanian front. In 1945, at war's end, he was among 180,000 Jews who were repatriated from the Soviet Union. When he returned to Poland to look for surviving relatives, with the exception of a cousin who had also hid in Russia, he found no one. After war's end, Ludwik was in limbo, sitting in deportation camps, wandering from country to country, barred by restrictive immigration policies from entering the US. He spent five years in transit: first in Sweden, and then in Cuba awaiting permission to enter the US, and was finally granted entry. His family, or at least what was left of it, consisted of his uncle Joe and his wife Tola. Joe had left Poland, immigrated to America on the eve of the war. His uncle arranged for him to obtain an American visa.

In 1951, when he landed in New York, Ludwik rented a room in the apartment of a Polish refugee couple whom he had met in Cuba. The Washington Heights neighborhood in upper Manhattan, which had earlier been dubbed "Little Berlin" because of its large German-Jewish population, became a home to yet another wave of Jewish immigrants in the 1940s and -50s' survivors. There were so many survivors in fact, that Poles, Germans and other groupings constituted small subcultures with their own religious and communal institutions. Because Ludwik spent the war years outside of Nazi-occupied territory, rather than in the ghettos and concentration camps, he occupied a liminal position among survivors. His experience suggests an additional set of explanations for why it was difficult, if not impossible, for many victims of Nazi persecution to speak on their own behalf: they did not conform to normative understandings of who was a "survivor." Ludwik's experience was not officially recognized by the agencies entrusted with distributing reparations to Jewish victims of Nazi policy, or even by Jewish organizations that sought to represent the survivor community in the postwar period. Within the survivor population, the distinctions among concentration camp internees, those who were trapped in the ghettos of Warsaw, Lodz, and other cities, and those who lived outside of Nazi occupation, were blurrier.

Was he a survivor? If we use an expansive definition, he certainly was. Presently, the US Holocaust Memorial Museum defines survivors as: "any persons, Jewish or non-Jewish, who were displaced, persecuted, or discriminated against due to the racial, religious, ethnic, social, and political policies of the Nazis and their collaborators between 1933 and 1945. In addition to former inmates of concentration camps, ghettos, and prisons, this definition includes, among others, people who were refugees or were in hiding."[9] Included in this broad definition are those who were confined to a ghetto, forced to labor in work camps, who were incarcerated in a concentration camps, who lived out the war years in hiding, often under false identities, refugees who left their families behind, those who fought with the partisans, and those who were sent away in the *kindertransport*, among others.

But in the immediate aftermath of the war, survivors were often defined by official agencies as those who had been held in ghettos and interned in concentration camps and in lands under Nazi occupation, categories that excluded people like Ludwik (Henry, 2007). Like many others, he had lost his family, his home, his nation—everything but his life. But as he was on the run for most of the war, and in the Soviet Union, where he was eventually imprisoned in a labor camp, his story did not fit into emerging restitution narratives that emphasized heroism.

The only formal survivors' organization he ever participated in was the annual Warsaw Ghetto Uprising commemoration in New York. By attending an annual rite focused on redemption, resistance, and martyrdom, he linked himself to a heroic moment in the history of the war, a moment in which he himself could not rightly claim a role, but with which he nonetheless deeply identified. Stripped of power during the war, and of having no recognized heroic role after the war, he attended this commemoration alone, and never with friends or family. As he saw it, he was neither a victim (the "true" victims were all dead), nor a survivor (if that term signified the experience of being directly persecuted by the Nazis), nor a resister (in the sense of taking up arms against the Nazis, as symbolized by the Warsaw Ghetto Uprising organization and other associations of resistance fighters).

However, he never spoke of himself as a "victim." During the first two decades after the war, the term "victim" was used almost exclusively to refer to those who had perished during World War II. Those who survived did not refer to themselves as victims—in homage to the dead, because they wished to distance themselves from the "real" victims, or because they identified with them. As few survivors had the capacity to resist, the preoccupation with resisters during the first two decades after the war failed to give those who fell outside of this category a position from which to speak and bear witness. While the focus on heroism helped to temper the horror of the events, elevating the status of some, it aggravated others' feelings of shame.[10]

Between victims and heroes

"Immediately after the war, we were 'liberated prisoners'; in subsequent years, we were included in the term 'DPs,' or 'displaced persons.' Eventually, we became 'emigrants' or 'immigrants,' as well as 'refugees'; in the US we were sometimes generously called 'new Americans.'" So wrote Werner Weinberg, who was imprisoned in Bergen-Belsen. Weinberg noted that "for a long time the fact of liberation and migration were not reflected in a name assigned to us, and there was a good chance that we, as a group, might go nameless." But one day, he said, "I noticed that I had been reclassified as a 'survivor'" (Weinberg, 1985, p. 150)[11]

One might ask: why should we concern ourselves with the lives of this population today, seven decades after the end of the war, when many other populations have come to endure war and dislocation, and at a time when most Holocaust survivors are gone? I do so in part because without an understanding of the early prewar period, and the emotional lives of survivors and those around them, it is difficult to fully understand the significance of what came afterward: the growing public role of survivors as witnesses to the Holocaust, amid the growing social recognition accorded victimhood more generally. As I have suggested, visibility was not something that emerged easily or without tremendous effort; survivors' capacity to speak, and to act as witnesses on behalf of those who perished, had to be actively won in a culture that was reluctant to listen to them. Shame permeated interactions between survivors and those they encountered when they first arrived, and came to inhabit the families they made, and shape their very being. It coexisted with what Geoffrey Hartman calls "anti-memory"—a stance toward the Holocaust that "tries to ward off the resurgence of deeply unsettling, intolerable memory and replace it with reconciliation, forgiveness, and closure" (Hartman, 1998). Anti-memory seeks premature closure on the past, and comfort rather than confrontation.

During the past few decades in the US, an unprecedented focus on mourning and memory has converged with concepts of healing and closure that suggest "one can always heal, move on, and place the past in its proper context, and do so quickly" (Sturken, 2007; see also Berns, 2011). We are told to "get on with our lives" and resume expectations of productivity and forward trajectories. Those who would display ongoing grief long after the typical period of mourning concludes are often chastised. And in fact, some would argue that the very figure of the "survivor," which in a post-Holocaust world has become widely generalized to include victims of traumatic events of all sorts, has become synonymous with transcending feelings of despair (Orgad, 2009, p. 152).

In this context, the formation of Holocaust collective memory, and the growing recognition of survivors as witnesses, was an ethical accomplishment that afforded survivors a sense of recognition that had before eluded them. If shame is a social emotion, related to the breakdown of recognition, alleviating shame is a social act, one that requires the repair of social bonds, and the rebuilding of interpersonal bridges.[12] As psychologist Judith Herman suggested, this work of reconstruction "transforms the traumatic memory, so that it can be integrated into the survivor's life story" and by insisting that the "goal of recounting the trauma story is integration, not exorcism" (Herman, 1992, p. 175). If an earlier notion of "survivor syndrome" cast the survivor as deeply wounded and lacking the capacity to speak, an emergent notion of trauma, and what was coming to be called "post-traumatic stress," suggested that the positive regeneration of the self is contingent upon the ability to articulate and integrate the harm done to it. This requires a psychological as well as social response—and a recognition of the corrosive effects of shame.

"It is easier for us to accommodate the guilty survivor," psychologist Henry Greenspan, who has worked extensively with survivors writes, "than the utterly abandoned survivor or the rageful, indictful survivor" (Greenspan, 1998, p. 33). The guilty survivor directs pain inward. Their guilt remains *their* problem, not ours. By focusing on guilt we recast the "outward, moral horror into a somehow more bearable and re-tellable form" (p. 32). Guilt locates the problem in the individual; shame is simultaneously individual and cultural: it is a psychosocial emotion. The shift from guilt to shame in the conceptualization of survivors carries implications for understanding trauma more generally. Narrowly psychological understandings of trauma understate the ways that events such as wars, disasters, mass disruptions of all sorts, where people's lives are disrupted, families are separated, and they witness death and destruction, become meaningful in relation to others (see Erikson, 1995). The responses individuals receive from others are vital in how they experience traumatic events. The lasting harm of being traumatized arises not simply from the events themselves but also from social isolation and conflict afterward.

For example, researchers studying former child soldiers in Nepal followed the fates of Nepalese children who returned to their villages after serving with the Maoist rebels during their country's 1996–2006 civil war. While they experienced violence and other events considered traumatic, their postwar mental health depended not on their exposure to war but on how their families and villages received them, according to the study's findings. In villages where the children were stigmatized or ostracized, they suffered high, persistent levels of post-traumatic stress disorder. But in villages that readily and happily reintegrated them (through rituals, for example), they experienced no more mental distress than did peers who had never gone to war (Dobbs, 2012). This finding is echoed in studies of American soldiers returning home: PTSD runs higher among veterans who cannot reconnect with supportive people and new opportunities. The traumatic event is more than just the event itself, but perhaps the event plus some crucial aspect of the social environment that has the potential to either dull or amplify its effects.

More recently, others have documented the experiences of the children of American servicemen and Korean prostitutes, products of the strange alliances that are often born of war—in this case the Korean War. "An unspeakable trauma does not die out with the person who first experienced it," writes Grace M. Cho. "Rather it takes on a life of its own, emerging from the spaces where secrets are concealed" (Cho, 2008, p. 6). Although Korean "comfort women" tried to maintain silence about their sexual enslavement, their secrets were already being transmitted to the next generations, and would come to haunt the diaspora.

What this suggests is that trauma is a psychic as well as a cultural phenomenon. It impacts individuals as well as the groups they are part of. How others receive the traumatized shapes their future lives as well as the lives of their descendants. Creating a culture, a memory milieu, in which losses are remembered and narrated can alleviate traumatic shame. While collectively, North Americans are much more receptive to such discussions today than they were six decades ago when Holocaust survivors first arrived on these shores, collectively we remain ambivalent about confronting and acknowledging traumatic loss, particularly the losses of distant others.

Notes

1. For similar temporalizations, see Arthur Hertzberg, "The First Encounter: Survivors and Americans in the Late 1940s" (Washington, DC: United States Holocaust Memorial Museum, 1996); Alvin H. Rosenfeld, "The Americanization of the Holocaust," *Commentary* 6 (June 1995). (1995); Annette Wieviorka, *The Era of the Witness* (Ithaca, NY: Cornell University Press, 2006). For a dissenting view, which focuses on continuities in memorialization, see Hasia Diner, *We Remember With Reverence and Love: American Jews and the Myth of Silence After the Holocaust, 1945–1962* (New York: New York University Press, 2009).
2. On the "memory milieu" concept, see Jeffrey Prager, this volume.
3. I focus on the Jewish Holocaust not to privilege Jewish suffering, but because that is where my personal and intellectual investments begin, and because the scope of the Jewish genocide overshadowed the mass murders of other groups during the Nazi period. I am mindful, however, of the ways that a focus on Jewish loss may at times inadvertently obscure other groups' (such as Roma) search for memory and recognition today.
4. On shame in the context of sexuality, see my *Shameless: Sexual Dissidence in American Culture* (New York: NYU Press), 2007.
5. I made use of the Oral History collection of the United States Holocaust Memorial Museum in Washington D.C. In the 1990s, the museum conducted oral histories with 520 survivors, broadly defining them as persons who were victims of Nazi policy 1933–1945, including those who had escaped the war years in the Soviet Union. Of these, museum staff members and local journalists interviewed 105 individuals about their postwar lives. At the time of my research, the museum's collection was among the most extensive archive of interviews focusing on survivors' postwar lives, and particularly on the dynamics of the families they created. These oral histories were structured as a conversation between the survivor and the interviewer in which the interviewer tried to engage people in telling their story. While interviews were originally conducted on video, some subjects were chosen for audio interviews as well. The museum transcribed the interviews, and these transcripts average 80 typewritten pages each; from these I randomly selected 25 interviews to analyze. From these interviews, we can gain considerable insight into the survivors' impressions of how family members, social workers, and others greeted them upon arrival in the US, how they saw themselves in relation to these groups over time, and how they devised strategies of self-presentation in daily life, including with their children.
6. See for example, Aaron Haas, *In the Shadow of the Holocaust* (Ithaca: Cornell University, 1990), as mentioned in Henry Greenspan, *On Listening to Holocaust Survivors* (Westport: Prager, 1998).
7. Translated into English by Elliot Palevsky, the hymn is widely known by its Yiddish title, *Zog Nit Keyn Mol!*
8. US Holocaust Memorial Museum website, http://www.ushmm.org/remembrance/registry/
9. As psychologist Bruno Bettleheim, himself a survivor, suggested: "the depiction of survivors as active agents responsible for their survival is a completely misleading distortion." He and others challenged efforts to link survivors

with resistance, action, or heroism. It was essentially passivity and lack of agency, he believed, that enabled survival. Most survivors including himself "survived because the Gestapo chose to set them free, and for no other reason." See Bettleheim, *Surviving and Other Essays*, 288.
10. Thanks to Krista Hegburg for bringing this to my attention.
11. Leys, R. (2007) *From Guilt to Shame: Auschwitz and After* (Princeton: Princeton University Press), 130.

References

Bar-On, D. (2005) "Legacy of Silence in Nazi Perpetrators' and Holocaust Survivors' Families," A paper presented at Henry Schwartzman Faculty Seminar, Rutgers University, September 2005.

Bergmann, M. S. and M. E. Jucovy (eds) (1982) *Generations of the Holocaust* (New York: Basic Books).

Berns, N. (2011) *Closure: The Rush to End Grief and What It Costs Us* (Philadelphia: Temple University Press).

Bettleheim, B. (1979) *Surviving and Other Essays* (New York: Knopf).

Chaumont, J. M. (1997) *The Competition of Victims: Genocide, Identity, Recognition* (Paris: La Decouverte and Syros).

Cho, G. M. (2008) *Haunting the Korean Diaspora: Shame, Secrecy, and the Forgotten War* (Minneapolis: University of Minnesota).

Chodorow, N. (2002) "Born into a World at War: Listening for Affect and Personal Meaning," *American Imago*, 59 (3), 297–315.

Cohen, B. (2007) *Case Closed: Holocaust Survivors in Postwar America* (New Brunswick: Rutgers University Press).

Dinnerstein, L. (1982) *America and the Survivors of the Holocaust* (New York: Columbia University Press).

Dobbs, D. (2012) "A New Focus on the 'Post' in Post-Traumatic Stress," *New York Times*, December 24, 2012, date accessed March 13, 2013, http://www.nytimes.com/2012/12/25/science/understanding-the-effects-of-social-environment-on-trauma-victims.html

Erikson, K. (1995) "Notes on Trauma and Community" in C. Caruth (ed.) *Trauma: Explorations in Memory* (Baltimore: The Johns Hopkins University Press).

Eyerman, R. (2004) "Cultural Trauma: Slavery and the Formation of African American Identity" in J. C. Alexander et al. (eds) Cultural *Trauma and Collective Identity* (Berkeley: University of California Press).

Greenspan, H. (1998) *Listening to Holocaust Survivors* (St. Paul: Paragon Books).

Hartman, G. (1998) "The Vicarious Witness: Belated Memory and Authorial Presence in Recent Holocaust Literature," *History and Memory*, 10 (2), 5–42.

Henry, M. (2007) *Confronting the Perpetrators: A History of the Claims Conference* (London and Portland: Vallentine Mitchell).

Herman, J. (1992) *Trauma and Recovery* (New York: Basic Books).

Hoffman, E. (2004) *After Such Knowledge: Memory, History, and the Legacy of the Holocaust* (Cambridge: Perseus Books).

Kosofsky Sedgwick, E. (2009) "Shame, Theatricality, and Queer Performativity: Henry James' *The Art of the Novel*" in D. M. Halperin and V. Traub (eds) *Gay Shame* (Chicago: University of Chicago Press).

Levi, P. (1989) "Shame" in *The Drowned and the Saved* (New York: Vintage Books).

Leys, R. (2007) *From Guilt to Shame: Auschwitz and After* (Princeton: Princeton University Press).

Niederland, W.G. (1968) "Clinical Observations on the 'Survivor Syndrome'," *International Journal of Psycho-Analysis*, 49 (2), 313–315.

Novick, P. (1999) *The Holocaust in American Life* (New York: Houghton Mifflin).

Orgad, S. (2009) "The Survivor in Contemporary Culture and Public Discourse: A Genealogy," *The Communication Review*, 12 (2), 132–161.

Scheff, T. and S. Retzinger (2000) "Shame as the Master Emotion of Everyday Life," *Journal of Mundane Behavior*, 1 (3) http://www.mundanebehavior.org/issues/v1n3/scheff-retzinger.html

Sturken, M. (2007) *Tourists of History: Memory, Kitsch, and Consumerism from Oklahoma City to Ground Zero* (Durham: Duke University Press).

Weinberg, W. (1985) *Self-Portrait of a Holocaust Survivor* (Jefferson: McFarland).

Whittier, N. (2009) *The Politics of Sexual Abuse: Emotion, Social Movements, and the State* (New York: Oxford University Press).

C. Integrating Sociological Subfields and Psycho/analytic Frameworks

16
Racial Hatred and Racial Prejudice: A Difference that Makes a Difference[1]

Tony Jefferson

When is calling someone a "fucking black cunt" racially abusive behavior and when is it just "handbags" (grown men trading insults like schoolboys)? Given the acquittal of millionaire premiership footballer John Terry, who admitted using the words in a spat with fellow professional Anton Ferdinand but denied any racist intent, one could be forgiven for thinking that it depends on one's ability to pay for an expensive legal team.[2] Certainly racist tweets addressed to black footballers by ordinary male students have been responded to much less tolerantly, in one case resulting in a prison sentence. But to focus on this aspect of the case is to miss a more difficult question: what is racism and how can we know it?

John Terry was prepared to admit he had said "fucking black cunt" (and other abusive but non-criminal phrases like "fucking knobhead") but claimed he was merely sarcastically echoing Ferdinand's comments to him with no racist intent. The lack of other evidence to the contrary, and the support of his teammates who all said he was not a racist, left sufficient doubt about the intent to ensure his acquittal after a five-day trial (Conn, 2012a).[3] Even Ferdinand did not think the remarks were serious enough to warrant legal involvement, which only entered the arena after the complaint of an off-duty policeman who had lip-read the offending words on television. So when do racist words signify racism? And what is the connection between racially prejudiced words and the sort of racial hatred that can lead to racist murder? The mother of Stephen Lawrence, the black teenager murdered by white racists that led, eventually, to the biggest shake up in the policing of race relations in a generation, must have seen one since she sat beside Ferdinand's parents throughout the trial. But, even supposing John Terry is more racist than he imagines[4] and had been found guilty of a racially aggravated public order offence, are a racially prejudiced diatribe and a murder motivated by racial hatred necessarily kindred events? They are both race-related incidents, but how exactly?

These are the questions motivating this chapter. Specifically, I wish to argue that the current debate about racism is horribly confused about the relationship between racial prejudice and racial hatred. Especially since the Stephen Lawrence murder and the subsequent Macpherson Report (1999), the political, legal, and policing responses all seem to proceed on the assumption that there is a simple continuum linking racial prejudice and racial hatred and thus that a tough line on racist talk and attitudes (racial prejudice) is needed to pre-empt a resurgence of racist violence (racial hatred). Although racially prejudiced words can be both offensive and hurtful and should be taken seriously (although not without attention to context and motive), to confuse prejudiced words with racially motivated violence is a conceptual error which can produce bad law, poor policy and, in consequence, injustice for individuals. The origins of this confusion can be found in the theoretical literature on the social psychology of racism. This has found its way into contemporary politics and policy and reveals itself in the stories of individuals charged with racially aggravated offences. My intention in what follows is to demonstrate how this happened: how poor theory led to bad politics, and the effect of both on a piece of contemporary research. But first we need a preliminary definition of racism.

What is "racism"?

As is by now a commonplace, at least in academic circles, the idea of race as a marker of difference between peoples is a fiction, albeit a powerful one. As Dalal (2002, p. 27) concisely puts it, "although there are no races, there is racism." This distinction provides the basis for his working definition of racism as "anything—thought, feeling or action—that uses the notion of race as an activating or organizing principle" (p. 27). Should this denude racism of any emotion, he adds the proposition that "racism is a form of hatred of one group for another" (p. 28). However, Dalal is also quick to note that the "mechanisms" driving both propositions will "not necessarily" be the same. Later still he adds aversive and institutional racism to his umbrella definition, now citing four "very different types of things . . . habits of thought . . . explicit expressions of hatred and violence . . . conscious or unconscious feelings of aversion . . . the invisible and impersonal racism structured into institutions"

(p. 203). The contemporary confusion of these four "very different types of things" is now thoroughly embedded. The theoretical overview that follows will show how this came about.

Anticipating the broad structure of what follows, two unfortunate disciplinary rifts have developed: one, between psychology and psychoanalysis, which left the dominant cognitive and (later) discursive psychologists of racism ill-equipped to understand feelings of racial hatred or "aversion"; the other, between sociology and psychology, which left social psychologists of racism ill-equipped to understand structural or institutional racism and sociologists of racism ignorant of the literature on racism's social psychology (and thus ill-equipped to understand individuals motivated by racial hatred or prejudice). Yet all presented theoretical explanations of "racism." It was not always like this. In post-World War II studies of Nazi antisemitism, conceivably the starting point of contemporary efforts to understand racism, scholars tried to integrate psychology, psychoanalysis, and sociology and thus offer a multi-leveled explanation linking the individual, family structure, and the social structure of fascism.

The theoretical story

Social psychology and personality-based theories

Both Fromm's *Fear of Freedom* ([1942] 2002) and Adorno and colleagues' *The Authoritarian Personality* (1950) attempted to understand antisemitism using theories that argued that prevailing socio-economic conditions promoted particular character or personality structures. Both tried to link a Marxist understanding of the social with a Freudian understanding of the psyche. Both produced a picture of the "authoritarian personality"—rigidly conventional in values with a submissive, uncritical and often over-idealized attitude towards authority combined with highly aggressive, punitive tendencies towards those who deviate from conventional morality. For Adorno et al, such personalities were the product of harsh, unpredictable, and oppressive parenting styles (which left parts of the self "split off" and parents' attitudes towards the self redirected towards weaker groups). But in both theorizations character structure originates in the social realm. In Fromm's words, "[T]he concept of social character is a key concept for the understanding of the social process. Character in the dynamic sense of analytic psychology is the specific form in which human energy is shaped by the dynamic adaptation of human needs to the particular mode of existence of a given society" (2002, p. 239).

Although there are no index entries for "hate" or "hatred" in *Fear of Freedom*, he deploys the cognate terms "death instinct" (which he finds unable to account for historical differences in levels of human destructiveness) and "destructiveness" instead. For Fromm, human destructiveness is rooted in the degree and constancy of anxiety precipitated by feelings of powerlessness and how much life's "sensuous, emotional and intellectual potentialities" are "thwarted"; hence, "[D]estructiveness is the outcome of unlived life" (pp. 156–158). Specifically, the new, individualistic "freedoms" of capitalism were anxiety-invoking (hence the book's title, *Fear of Freedom*). To escape these freedoms, and the resulting anxieties, new dependencies (like those on authoritarianism) were established.

Social character thus suggests a rather fixed response to situations ("character in its turn determines the thinking, feeling, and acting of individuals," p. 239), rather than specific situations calling forth a variety of contingent responses. To be fair, Fromm does note that "there will be always 'deviants' with a totally different character structure" since the "accidental factors of birth and life experience . . . differ from one individual to another." However, the effects of such differences and the deviants they produce are not theorized since they are not seen as having any social significance; they are helpful only "if we want to understand one individual more fully" (p. 239). Thus, for all their sophistication and openness to psychological and psychoanalytic concepts, these early studies, in the end, are overly social; ultimately, they reduce the unique, psychic level of an individual to the level of the social, thus denying the influence of the former on the latter.

While the idea of character structure has fallen out of favor overall, a more recent echo appears in Joel Kovel's *White Racism* ([1970] 1988, pp. 55–57). Kovel attempts to link the "logic" of "political and economic interests," "an irrational social order," and "the structure of unconscious phantasy." "Put simply," he summarizes, "we must derive the symbolism and fantasies underlying racism, and study their historical emergence and transformations, simultaneously" (Kovel, 1988, p. 6). He called the result "psychohistory." According to Kovel, the authoritarian personality corresponds with a type of racism he called "dominative." This involves acting out bigoted beliefs and, historically, was basically the racism of the American south. Kovel contrasted this with "aversive" racism. This involves believing in white superiority without acting on it; historically, the racism associated with the American north. This distinction is similar to the one I am proposing between hatred (dominative racism) and prejudice (aversive racism). However, while initially prioritizing the unconscious over culture, Kovel later reversed the order of priority to again over-emphasize the social, thereby presenting a "congruence" between personality and culture that could have come straight from the pages of Fromm's *Fear of Freedom*.

Prejudice and the cognitive turn

Like personality-based theories, and prior to social psychologists abandoning interest in psychoanalysis, Gordon Allport's *The Nature of Prejudice* ([1954] 1979) viewed prejudice from a psychosocial perspective. His work is simultaneously social, psychoanalytic, and cognitive. Allport recognizes that prejudice encompasses positive as well as negative biases towards others. He distinguishes between "anger" (a temporary "emotion" directed toward an individual) and "hatred" (a more enduring and aggressive "sentiment" felt "toward a person or class of persons" (p. 363)). He argues that hatred cannot exist unless some kind of love relationship is interrupted ("love is a precondition of hate" (p. 364)). Prejudice, he argues, is for some an incidental matter ("merely conformative, mildly ethnocentric, and essentially unrelated to the personality as a whole" (p. 395)). However, for the "prejudiced personality," "it is organic, inseparable from the life process" (p. 395) and rooted in "underlying insecurity" (p. 396); such "bigoted personalities," he writes, tend to display "a sharp cleavage between conscious and unconscious layers," normal on the surface but "underneath" showing evidence of "intense anxiety . . . buried hatred towards parents, destructive and cruel impulses" (p. 397).

Having emphasized emotions and anxieties, it is somewhat surprising that Allport is largely remembered as the first cognitive theorist of racism. But Allport also defined "ethnic prejudice" as "an antipathy based upon a faulty and inflexible generalization" (p. 9), thereby introducing two cognitive elements: the tendency of the mind to generalize/categorize/simplify (or "prejudge") in order to process experiences, and to favor in-groups over out-groups (a preference for the familiar over the strange and to attack that which threatens our primary attachments). While he does not neglect, as do later social psychologists, larger issues of history and culture as well as situational contingencies, he gives most attention to personality (a la Adorno et al, on whose work he draws unselfconsciously), and social learning issues involving identification with loved ones.

This tendency of the mind to prejudge, and our preference for in-groups over out-groups, was taken up by subsequent social psychologists: a "cognitive turn" that moved away from Alllport's multi-causal (albeit eclectic) explanation of racism. In the work of Allport's one-time student Henri Tajfel (1969), the cognitive orientation took a decisive turn away from psychoanalysis. Probably the most influential of subsequent cognitive theorists of racism (especially his later work with John Turner on inter-group conflict and social identity theory (Tajfel and Turner, 1979)), Tajfel used experimental research with groups as a basis for theorizing and narrowing the notion of the social to the group. Since Tajfel strove to comprehend the Holocaust—perhaps the ultimate example of racial hatred—it is ironic that his hostility to psychoanalysis ensured that his work, and its legacy, became ever more narrowly cognitive and thus only capable of illuminating less deeply rooted prejudice. Here, then, seems the original site of the current confusion between racial prejudice and racial hatred: Tajfel's experimental work with small groups was actually designed to measure the former while purporting to shed light on the latter (namely, the Holocaust).

Lest there be any misunderstanding, let me clarify the prejudice/hatred distinction I am proposing. When Allport differentiates the "mildly ethnocentric" from the "bigoted personality," he uses the term "prejudice" to cover both, but hatred is only implicated in the latter case. To understand the hatred of the bigoted personality we will need, as Allport says, access to "unconscious layers" of an individual and thus psychoanalytic ideas. Thus, although Allport talks only of different types of "prejudice," his understanding broadly corresponds with my prejudice/hatred distinction, where psychoanalysis is necessary to understand the latter but not necessarily the former. In terms of a continuum linking prejudice and hatred, this suggests that while social and cultural differences produce a ready supply of target groups for the negative "prejudgments" of everyday prejudice, Allport's "mildly ethnocentric" prejudice, whether individuals are susceptible to developing intense hatred towards such groups and to act on such prejudices (Allport's bigoted personalities), depends on their unique psychic backgrounds: their underlying insecurities and anxieties. Since the origins of mild prejudice and deep-rooted hatred are different, the former need never develop into the latter.

Another way of thinking about this distinction is through the idea of "acting out." In psychoanalytic terms, this occurs when something is too painful or emotionally distressing to contemplate or verbalize. Putting your fist through a window, throwing something across a room, or banging your head against a wall might all be simple examples of reactive anger. They become examples of hateful "acting out" if they constitute a patterned, generalized response to frustration. In other words hatred, as opposed to mild prejudice, will tend to find a violent behavioral outlet rather than simply a linguistic one, even if this may sometimes take on self- rather than other-destructive forms.

The discursive turn

This confusion between hatred and prejudice was not rectified by the turn to discourse, a term that references anything—events, processes, objects, as well as language—that produces meaning (Barrett, 1991, p. 76). Whereas both personality-based and cognitive theorists presume a knowable "inner" world—of character in the former case, of the classifying mind in the latter—discursive psychologists insist that "inner" worlds cannot be known; rather, all that can be known are the meanings through which inner worlds become manifest. Researchers in this tradition are thus interested in racist talk and its connection with wider social discourses and ideologies, thereby placing the cognitive individual in a wider social world than small groups, but they fail to address the emotional appeal of racist discourses (why only some are drawn to them). They are thus exclusively about prejudice with nothing to say about hatred (even though, as already noted, those guilty of racially prejudiced talk may also be full of racial hatred).

Wetherell and Potter's (1992) analysis of how the discourse of Pakeha (white) New Zealanders legitimates their racial superiority and Billig's (1995) insightful look at how nationalism is sustained in mundane, everyday talk are both excellent examples of work within this genre. Billig's discussion of *"banal nationalism,"* defined as "the ideological habits which enable the established nations of the West to be reproduced" (Billig, 1995, p. 6, emphasis in original), broadly exemplifies what I would call (nationalistic) prejudice. Although "banal does not imply benign" (p. 6), nor is it harmless, nationalistic prejudices can be understood without recourse to psychoanalytic insights because sociocultural ideologies, not hatred with its roots in the unconscious, are its object. But, because both analyses are offered as contributions to explaining "racism," they have also contributed to the confusion surrounding prejudice and hatred.

Sociological understandings of racism

A potted history of British race and ethnic relations of the past fifty years reads as follows: early [culturalist] race-relations studies were critiqued by [structuralist] class-based anti-racist analyses, which in turn are now being criticized by a new [post-structuralist] politics of cultural difference position. (Mac an Ghaill, 1999, p. 5)

What is revealing about this "potted history" is what it leaves out, namely, the entire social psychology of racism literature from Fromm onwards just outlined. This is a "potted history" of the *sociology* of "British race and ethnic relations," although it does not say so, thus neatly demonstrating the complete divorce between the disciplines on this topic.

Culturalist approaches

Sociological culturalist approaches regard racism as a product of *cultural differences* between racial or ethnic groups. As Mac an Ghaill (1999, pp. 5–6) again summarizes:

[T]he primary focus of race relations studies was on inter-ethnic relations between minority and majority communities in such institutions as employment, housing and education (Patterson, 1963; Banton, 1977; see also Barth, 1969). They examined minority communities' distinctive cultural attributes, suggesting that social behavior was to be understood primarily in terms of culture . . . Although the culturalist perspective received much theoretical criticism from other sociological approaches, it was nevertheless a significant "common-sense" explanation of minority communities' experience of British society.

Structuralist approaches

By comparison, structuralist approaches characterize racism as the product of the *structural inequalities* underlying cultural differences that operate to disadvantage particular racial or ethnic groups. It is thus systematic and is sustained by the use of various ideologies that serve to justify (or naturalize) such unequal treatment. Although Marxist, class-based approaches came to dominate this approach (Castles and Kosack, 1973; Miles, 1982), a Weberian version, based on racially based status distinctions providing the "structural" basis underpinning racial inequality, is associated especially with the work of John Rex (Rex and Moore, 1967; Rex, 1970).

Post-structuralist approaches

Finally, reacting to the demise of Marxism and against emphases on structure, post-structuralist approaches variously explore racism as complexly and contingently related to notions of *identity and difference*. Such work includes minority ethnic feminist work (e.g. Bhavnani and Phoenix, 1994; Brah, 1996), post-colonial theorizing (Bhabha, 1990; Gilroy, 1993), and some work on discourse analysis (where the approach overlaps with that of discursive psychologists).

Whatever their differences, all three approaches are thoroughly sociological and, as such, are only interested in racism as a social phenomenon creating and legitimating unequal relations between races, not in understanding individual racist subjects. This makes understanding racial hatred, with its roots, as we have seen, in the unconscious insecurities of individuals, all but impossible. Yet, by offering themselves as understandings of racism, they too contribute to the confusion, another unfortunate by-product of the unhappy divorces between sociology, psychology, and psychoanalysis.

The political story

Racial prejudice and racial hatred have always been a problem for Britain's black communities. Black youths have been routinely over-policed, their communities under-protected. When reported to the police, racial attacks have been dealt with reluctantly if at all, even after an official report exposed the extent of the problem (Home Office, 1981). In 1993, though, one particular racially motivated hate crime, the killing of black teenager Stephen Lawrence by a gang of white youths in South London, became a watershed moment. The diffident police response prompted tireless campaigning by Stephen's parents leading, eventually, to the incoming Labour government of 1997 establishing an Inquiry. The resulting Macpherson Report (1999) found the police guilty of institutional racism (a conclusion hardly surprising to many), and led to the introduction of a raft of police reforms, including new Codes of Practice and Guidance notes and specially trained Community Safety Units.

However, if New Labour policy in relation to hate crimes was executed in the interests of equality of opportunity, it was also motivated by being seen to take all crime (and immigration) seriously in the interests of pre-empting a populist Tory challenge: "tough on hate" to appeal to the liberal middle classes and minority ethnic groups; "tough on crime" to appeal to the "silent majority." In practice this produced "tougher" legislation in the shape of the Crime and Disorder Act of 1998, with Sections 29-32 allowing higher penalties for certain basic offences—assault, criminal damage, harassment, and public order—where "racial aggravation" could be demonstrated.

Crucial to this whole enterprise would be the meaning of "racial." The Macpherson Report's definition of "a racist incident" as "[A]ny incident which is perceived to be racist by the victim or any other person" (1999, p. 328) settled matters, and reversed earlier official thinking on the topic that "ideally" the offender would be "the only reliable source of information on racial motivation" (Home Office, 1981, p. 7). This new subjectivist definition now came to underpin all related initiatives, and was quickly adopted by police forces across the country. Following the David Copeland nail-bombing campaign in London,[5] dedicated hate crime units were established within the Metropolitan Police and elsewhere. In the post-Macpherson era, these developments have helped the police take hate crimes seriously. Whatever the merits or demerits of this new hate crime politics (see, for example, *Theoretical Criminology* 6 (4), 2002), of importance here is that it institutionalized a subjectivist and thus vague definition of "racist incident." This makes it useless for understanding racist motivation, or for distinguishing between mildly prejudicial and hate-motivated behavior. Thus, politics came to echo the confusion just traced through the theoretical literature. Had the situation been conceptually clearer, perhaps Macpherson could have produced a better and more helpful definition for police, probation, and the courts.

Arming the police with tougher undefined powers was a recipe for unintended consequences. One was quite predictable. Given that police "crackdowns" invariably target the already marginalized and disadvantaged, some of these would end up acquiring, somewhat arbitrarily, the label "racist" in addition to that of "criminal". Since minority ethnic groups are also over-represented in the ranks of the marginalized and disadvantaged, these were also "at risk" of acquiring the label racist. Both consequences were evident in our research story, as I demonstrate below. Macpherson's subjectivist definition also informed the Probation Service's treatment programs for racially motivated offenders: "Boards should ensure that . . . the importance of the Macpherson definition of a racist incident is reaffirmed" (HM Inspectorate of Probation, 2005, p. 7). This meant that any denial of racist motivation was seen as symptomatic of the problem and needed to be countered:

> In many cases we inspected we found that staff had left unchallenged the racially aggravated/motivated dimension and had colluded with offenders' minimization.
> (HM Inspectorate of Probation, 2005, p. 15)

What this approach does not allow for is the possibility that offenders' "minimization" might spring from a strong conviction that, whatever happened in the incident, it was not about race. Once again, our research story has examples of this.

The research story

Between 2004 and 2006, I was part of a team of Keele University researchers investigating racial harassment in North Staffordshire (Gadd, Dixon, and Jefferson, 2005). Our aim was "to study the social contexts in which racial harassment takes place and the motivations of those responsible for committing it" (p. 1).[6] This involved in-depth free association narrative interviews (Hollway and Jefferson, [2000] 2013; Hollway and Jefferson, 2004) with fifteen people to explore the issue of motivation, and focus group discussions with over 100 from a variety of local groups, to shed light on the social context. Broadly speaking, the interviews with individuals were regarded as our perpetrator sample, although not all had convictions and many, even amongst those convicted, denied being racist. Specifically, seven of our twelve individual interviewees recruited through the local Probation Service had been charged with, or convicted of, racially aggravated offences; the other three had far right connections. The interviewer asked participants to tell him the story of their lives. This was then followed up, echoing their ordering and phrasing, by inviting further stories to expand or clarify particular points. If their racially aggravated offence (or alleged offence) was not addressed in their life story, the interviewee would be asked directly to tell the story leading to the charge or conviction. What these free association narrative interviews enable, which conventional semi-structured interviews do not, is some access to the emotional pathways fuelling "freely associated" stories that interviewees told about their lives, and thus to unconscious (or not fully conscious) motivations beyond the apparent meaning of the accounts. Using emotional rather than rational "logic" allows interviewees' stories to be interrogated critically: to be read symptomatically rather than simply taken at face value. In this way we hoped to shed light on the not fully conscious dynamics of racial hatred. Given the unconscious origins of hatred, an interview method that is designed to get behind discursive rationalizations was necessary.

The focus group discussions were designed to explore how issues of race are thought about and discussed locally: the discursive dimension of racial prejudice. Two core findings are of direct relevance to present concerns: "the attitudes of our sample of perpetrators were very similar to those of our focus group participants" (Gadd, Dixon, and Jefferson, 2005, p. 9); and "few people, including those convicted of racially aggravated crimes, see themselves as 'racists'" (p. 1). The meaning of these findings and their relevance for understanding the difference between racial prejudice and racial hatred will structure the rest of this section.

The widespread nature of prejudice

Across all the research participants, young and old, "thinking and talking in terms of 'us' and 'them', of people who belong and people who do not," was common (p. 9). For "many white people," this went along with feeling "disrespected" and a belief that "they are the main victims of discrimination" (p. 1). Older participants shared familiar responses to industrial decline and social change: a "sense of loss," of "industries, jobs, communities, a whole way of life"; whilst "almost everyone . . . felt that the present was unsettling and the future uncertain" (p. 9). Seeking someone to blame, "almost all of them associated immigration and the descendants of immigrants with everything that was wrong with their lives—from crime to unemployment, inadequate healthcare to substandard housing" (p. 9). This is what racially prejudiced thinking in poor, declining areas with growing immigrant populations sounds like, probably across the country. But, it is different from racial hatred: "the vast majority . . . do not condone racist attacks" (p. 1)[7]

This finding that both perpetrators and ordinary people from the region share racially prejudiced views may not surprise. What may be more difficult to comprehend is how to understand racial hatred when even those convicted of racially aggravated crimes deny a racist motivation. This will need some unpacking, a task to which I now turn.

The denial of racism

In our small sample of apparently racially motivated offenders, our "perpetrators," many were prepared to acknowledge the criminal nature of the offence but they usually denied that the motivation was racial. One such was Marcus, a white 22-year-old Englishman, imprisoned for assaulting some Asian men. His story was that it was he, not the Asian men he fought, that was the victim of racial harassment since they had "told him to stay away from the 'half-Asian' woman his friend was dating" (p. 3). He went on to say that "if they say you are being racist, you can't get out of it" (p. 3), a quote that could serve as a summary of Macpherson's definition. His sense of injustice over his treatment in Court, specifically the refusal to consider his plea in mitigation, transformed his former tolerant attitude to Asians to one of not wanting anything more to do with them; another unintended consequence of a confused "get tough" policy.

This sense of injustice at acquiring the label "racist" was echoed in several of our interviewees from minority ethnic groups. Shahid was a 22-year-old Pakistani Briton who acquired the label for calling a group of white police officers "white bastards" after they had "singled him out for questioning because he was the 'only Asian there'" (pp. 3–4) at an altercation "in which he was not involved" (p. 3). Kamron was a 17-year-old British Bangladeshi who spent eight months remanded in custody for a "racially aggravated" assault on a boy who had daubed racist graffiti on school walls, "even though the boy conceded that Kamron had never said anything racist to him" (p. 3) before the racial aggravation element was dropped. Emma was a 28-year-old mixed race woman who got probation for a racially aggravated assault that had arisen after a slanging match (involving racial and sexual slurs) between her and four Pakistani men (none of whom was charged). Whether or not the legislation was designed for cases such as these, our research was full of them. However, in case these brief examples are insufficiently detailed, I want to end this section with a case study of Alan, in an effort to allow you, the reader, to make up your own mind.

Alan: Portrait of a racist?

Alan was a 39-year-old man, the youngest of ten children, who had lived all his life in and around a mining village near Stoke-on-Trent. The family was staunchly Labour and regular Church-goers. He remembers his dad as "always busy" and often out, his mum as periodically depressed. His early love of football soon turned into a fascination with the surrounding hooliganism and, by his mid-teens, Alan was a committed Stoke City hooligan. This was accompanied by going "off the rails" more generally: truanting followed by leaving school early (despite his evident ability), petty thieving, heavy drinking and related trouble with the police, leaving home, regular arrests for hooliganism, and eventual imprisonment. Getting engaged led to him giving up his hooliganism for a while, but when that relationship broke up depression and attempted suicide followed, and then heavy drinking and a return to hooliganism. This was to become a pattern. A new girl-friend led to marriage and three children, but, despite a good period working as a painter and decorator, the marriage was beset by violence, with her giving as good as she got, apparently, and eventually ended after her affair with a neighbor. This coincided with the death of his father, to whom he had become fully reconciled and a dutiful carer, and precipitated more heavy drinking and a further bout of depression, with psychotic symptoms and suicidal feelings. Still signed off sick at the time of the interview, relations with his ex over access to his children had improved and he now enjoyed watching his sons play football rather than fighting over it. As for his self image, this was vehemently not racist (a view supported by his probation officer): he worked very happily with Asian traders in his time on the markets; two of his fellow hooligans were "colored" and never got racist abuse from his gang; he has Asian taxi driver friends and one of his best mates is a Rastafarian; he supported "rock against racism" in his punk days; and three of his nieces, who he loves "to bits," were fathered by an Asian. So, how did Alan come to acquire his conviction for racially aggravated assault?

Racially aggravated assault?

In response to a request from the interviewer, Dave Gadd, to tell the story that led to his conviction, Alan had this to say:

> It was during me second bout, bout of mental illness . . . Em, now I can't recall nothing at all about the night of when I got arrested. Em, all I know is the background to me case. Er, the night I actually got done all I know is what has been said by the prosecution. [DG: Right] Em, it was, the gentleman involved was a taxi driver. Em and I had him several times. I've used his taxi firm on a number of occasions. And he's picked me up loads of times. And we'd fell out. Not so much fell out, but I'd put him right on a few, on a few things in previous journeys where he'd took me somewhere. I've got to try and explain meself here. As we'd be driving along, I mean I didn't know this taxi driver from Adam, this was the first time I met him, first time he'd ever picked me up. Em and we'd be driving along and a couple of young girls had walked past and he'd say something really horrible you know, 'I wouldn't mind giving it to her up the arse' like. And I'm not into that. That is not, not me at all, you know what I mean. Total respect to women kind of thing. And I pulled him straight away on that first occasion. I says 'Eh mate, no offence meant' I says, 'I'm not like that. I don't enjoy people speaking like that about women, you know'. 'Oh, sorry my friend'. And off we carried on. On another occasion, em when I'd had a few to drink it was and he was bringing me back from somewhere he was 'Where you been, mate, you been fucking?' So I says, 'None of your business, you pervert. No offence mate, but this is twice now where

you've made derogatory offence like remarks about women and now you're asking me if I been shagging and all this. You're nothing but a pervert'.

Right, that's the start of the story. Now the same taxi driver, em, don't get me wrong, I know I was in the wrong and I know, you know, I was mentally ill at the time but he, I was arrested several months after the incident and I couldn't remember anything about it what so ever. But apparently, I'd got into the car and within 5 minutes of the journey I'd started an argument with him. Em, and he says basically that I spat in his face which is, yes, I'm quite prepared to say that is something I could do in the heat, I'm terrible for it. I think it's like the ultimate insult to somebody. We've started arguing and I've spat in his face. He's said then that I've called him a Paki bastard etc. etc. Now that word isn't in my vocabulary. It's not something I'd do. Now I've got 3 nieces, my brother's daughter's children who are fathered by an Asian. And I love them to bits. Em and it's just not a word I'd say. On even him giving his evidence in court, I honestly believe, although I can't because I can't recollect anything, I couldn't defend myself, but I honestly believe that he swapped the word pervert to Paki to make it a racial incident. Where as he could have been a white pervert and I'd a still called him a pervert. I just think he swapped the words. Em, but obviously with having no recollection, I couldn't defend meself. I had to accept it. Em, but I know, no matter how heated the argument, and I have fell out with people em of a different creed and color in the past but I just know I wouldn't have used that word. That's why he came across to me as though he was just covering his back. Or even, I mean, perhaps the police prompted him to say 'Well, if he called you that just swap that word for that and we've got him'. You know it's em I've got a bit of a mistrust of the police anyway. Em, but I swear, whatever it was it was over his attitude of him being a pervert not because of his color. Em I still believe that to this day, but here I am, it's racially aggravated assault. I've been convicted of it and that's that. [DG: Did you plead guilty to that at the time?] I didn't. Em I pleaded guilty to common assault but not guilty to racially aggravated assault but was convicted anyway because I'd got no defense. Em but I swear to this day that I didn't call him what he said. Even though I don't know, I just know it wouldn't be in my make up. Even though I was mentally ill at the time, it still come out as pervert, because that's what I genuinely thought of him. Em it's one of them things. I'm here doing me punishment.

This is a convoluted story of which we only have Alan's version. Moreover, he claims not to remember the actual incident, a lapse that he implies may have been related to his mental illness. There are claims that seem contradictory, like his comment about "total respect to women" in contrast to his earlier admission of domestic violence. On the other hand, he is quite prepared to admit that he could have spat at the driver, for him the "ultimate insult," because it is something he has done before: "I'm terrible for it." He is willing to concede he might have called the driver a "pervert" because "that's what I genuinely thought of him." But "Paki," the offending word that secured the conviction and left him labeled a racist, is not a word he'd use: it "isn't in my vocabulary." In other words, Alan is saying he abused the taxi driver, not because he was a Pakistani but because he was, in Alan's view, a misogynist with an unhealthily "perverted" interest in sex. This is reminiscent of John Terry's defense: the offending words, "fucking black cunt," were meant sarcastically; what he really thought was that Ferdinand was (or was being at that point in time) "a fucking knobhead."[8]

Conclusion: From racism to hate motivated violence?

It is significant that so many charged with racially motivated offences are prepared to admit to the abusive behavior, even to physically violent behavior, but not to the racist intent attributed to their actions. One reason might be that there is a greater penalty if such a motivation can be proved. There is certainly a greater stigma than for common-or-garden assault. But, for those whose lives have been a catalogue of punishment and stigma, such reasoning is not terribly persuasive. More compelling is the notion of fairness, of being convicted for what you have done, not for what you have not. If punishment is to be meted out, it should be for what you have done (spitting, say) but not for what you haven't (uttering the 'P' word); and it should coincide with one's own sense of self, however awful (a violent hooligan with a history of depression and failure), but not be entangled with elements that one doesn't recognize ("racist").

Our sample of "perpetrators" had led troubled and troubling lives. Their stories revealed severe, sometimes extreme, material, and emotional deprivation. Like Alan, they offered stories of offending behavior, domestic violence, mental illness, and of drug and alcohol abuse; of being victims and aggressors. If they hid some things, they revealed much, most of it unflattering. So, when they also said, like Alan, that the incident leading to their conviction wasn't racially motivated, we generally believed them. Alan's story was unique; but, as a tale of misspent youth and its catalogue of disasters, it was not untypical of our sample.

This brings us back to my starting point: confusion, a confusion that I have been arguing permeates the theory and politics of race relations and, not surprisingly, is picked up in research on the topic. Specifically, the move by cognitive psychologists away from psychoanalysis led to ever more refined understandings of prejudice but made it impossible to understand the unconscious dynamics of racial hatred. Sociologists, for whom any kind of subject, racist or otherwise, is seen as the province of psychology, have only ever been interested in understanding racism as a group or societal phenomenon, not individual 0perpetrators and their motivations. Thus, explanations of prejudice began to serve as an explanation for everything from the most banal of its manifestations to behavior motivated by a pathological hatred. This theoretical confusion underpins the political response that proceeds as if there is little to choose between prejudice and hatred: the one is the cognitive underpinning of the other.[9] Dalal's careful definition distinguished at least four different aspects of racism and made the point that the "mechanisms" driving each of these will not necessarily be the same. We need to return to this idea, reunite psychology with psychoanalysis and both with sociology, and, informed by such a psychosocial approach, begin to approach this complex topic with the sophistication it deserves (see Sherwood, 1980; Gadd and Jefferson, 2007; and Gadd and Dixon, 2011, for examples of such an approach).

Earlier I suggested that one clue to the difference between those who hate and the mildly prejudiced might be found in the idea of "acting out." All our perpetrator examples, including Alan with his spitting, could be said to show evidence of "acting out": a tendency to respond violently (hatefully) when feeling upset or threatened. Whilst the precise source of such tendencies were particular to each case, painful and distressing experiences were common to all. If this is part of what separates those who hate from those who are only prejudiced, it also helps explain why our perpetrator group also disavow the racist intent of their admitted violence: their hatred does indeed stem from diverse sources (too painful to acknowledge); but it is not specifically racially focused. It can, of course, become so when racially prejudiced "othering" discourses are readily available and legitimated. This could suggest a continuum: the racially prejudiced at one end (all of us, to some extent), those in the middle (full of hate but not necessarily racial hatred) like our sample, and those like Stephen Lawrence's killers on the other end, who, full of a hatred married to a consciously espoused racial prejudice, can properly be called racially motivated offenders. But, bundling all these together under the label "racist" is clearly unhelpful; however, it may help account for the fear induced by the label.

But, rather than focus on racism, perhaps the focus should be on the underlying hatred that unites writings on homophobia, racial violence, antisemitism, and violence against women? The most ambitious attempt yet to synthesize this now huge literature is Elizabeth Young Bruehl's compendious *The Anatomy of Prejudices* ([1996] 1998). To enable this, she makes a distinction between "ethnocentrisms" and "ideologies of desire." For her, "ethnocentrism" is "a form of prejudice that protects group identity in economic, social and political terms" that is found wherever there are groups and "does not, in and of itself, imply violence or entail legitimation for violence [but] . . . is aversive" (Young-Bruehl, 1998, pp. 27, 188). It "can be approached with comparatively simple psychological assumptions" because it involves "real groups" with their associated "histories . . . social traditions . . . economic habits and contexts . . . political structures," and thus entails, primarily, "elaborate sociological work" (pp. 198–199). "Ideologies of desire" (which, following the Greek word for desirous, she calls "orecticisms"), by contrast, are historically specific prejudices which are "ideologically unlimited," can embrace any "marks of difference," and do not stop short of encouraging and legitimating "the beating, mutilating, and killing of people whose humanity has been disparaged or denied" (pp. 27, 28, 188). Studying such prejudices "initially demands a complex psychological description, which must precede any effort to follow orecticists into public domains and, then, to study what their meeting with the public domain means for them and they for it" (p. 199). Within this framework, antisemitism, racism, sexism, and the homophobias are all examples of prejudices that are "in almost all their modern forms [i.e. post-1870] orecticisms, not ethnocentrisms" (p. 185). It is the focus "on the needs and desires different prejudices fulfill" that explains why her approach must be initially "largely psychological" and "rooted in psychoanalytic theory," but without neglecting the social: "it broadens into a social theory" (p. 27). In my terms, this would be a psychosocial theory. It also anticipates the key distinction, between prejudice (her "ethnocentrisms") and hatred (her "orecticisms" or "ideologies of desire"), that has animated and informed this essay throughout

Notes

1. The phrase, "a difference that makes a difference," is borrowed from the late Stan Cohen.
2. Terry was charged with a racially aggravated public order offence. See note 6 for a fuller explication of the legal issues involved in offences being "racially aggravated."
3. The Football Association disciplinary panel later found him guilty and gave him a four-match ban. But, since they also agreed with the assessment that Terry is not a racist, this verdict did nothing to clarify matters (see Conn, 2012b).
4. For another example taken from the world of football, see the discussion of the Ron Atkinson (erroneously called "Atkins" throughout) affair by Rattansi (2007, pp. 120–121) quoted in Phoenix (2010). Here, the explanation (for calling a black footballer a "fucking lazy black nigger" in what he thought was on off-air comment) was in terms of "contradictory and ambivalent" feelings that make Atkinson both racist and non-racist depending on "the context and circumstances" (ibid) of his interaction with black people. Despite Atkinson's denial that he was a racist, it lost him his job as a television commentator.
5. This was a campaign, motivated by homophobia, which consisted of planting nail bombs in pubs and bars known to be frequented by homosexuals.
6. The legal definition of what we called racial harassment is contained in the Crime and Disorder Act, 1998, which allows the court to impose higher penalties for assaults, criminal damage, harassment, and public disorder offences where these can be proved to have been "racially aggravated." This echoes the similar attempt in the US to punish crimes more severely where "hate" can be proved to be a factor. For a fuller explication of the legislative history in this area, both in the USA and the UK, see Gadd and Dixon (2011, pp. 77–107).
7. Forty years ago, Jeremy Seabrook (1973, p. 57), talking of white working class people's responses to immigration and other dramatic post-war changes to their traditional life and culture, made a substantially similar point, in typically eloquent fashion: "[T]he immigrants act as a perverse legitimation of inexpressible fear and anguish. What is taking place is only secondarily an expression of prejudice. It is first and foremost a therapeutic psychodrama, in which the emotional release of its protagonists takes precedence over what is actually being said . . . It is an expression of their pain and powerlessness confronted by the decay and dereliction, not only of their familiar environment, but of their own lives too—an expression for which our society provides no outlet. Certainly it is something more complex and deep-rooted than what the metropolitan liberal evasively and easily dismisses as prejudice."
8. What may not have escaped the reader's attention is the conjunction, in both the John Terry and Alan cases, of sexuality ("fucking . . . cunt," "knobhead" in the case of Terry; "you're . . . a pervert" in Alan's case) and race. It would take me too far from my present purpose to explore here the relations among hatred, sexually derived disgust and the appearance of issues to do with sexuality in racist discourses. But, for an examination of the case of Alan that has tried to relate questions of sex and race, see Gadd (2009).
9. These confusions are not helped by the tendency, evident in the field of gender and sexuality as well as race and hate crimes generally, to ostracize

those who stray from the "politically correct" fold. Thus, to talk of different kinds of rape is to risk suggesting some are more serious than others and thus undercut the politically correct mantra that "rape is rape." In the area of race, differentiating prejudice and hatred is to risk undercutting the politically correct (but analytically meaningless, as I hope to have demonstrated) notion that "a racist is a racist."

References

Adorno, T. W., Frenkel-Brunswik, E., Levinson, D. J., and Sanford, R. N. (1950) *The Authoritarian Personality* (New York: Harper & Brothers).
Allport, G. W. ([1954] 1979) *The Nature of Prejudice* (Reading: Addison-Wesley).
Banton, M. (1977) *The Idea of Race* (London: Tavistock).
Barrett, M. (1991) *The Politics of Truth* (Cambridge: Polity).
Barth, F. (ed.) (1969) *Ethnic Groups and Boundaries* (London: Allen & Unwin).
Bhabha, H. (1990) "Introduction: Narrating the Nation," in H. Bhabha (ed.) *Nation and Narration* (London: Routledge).
Bhavnani, K. K. and A. Phoenix (1994) "Shifting Identities, Shifting Racisms: An Introduction," *Feminism and Psychology*, 4, 5–18.
Billig, M. (1995) *Banal Nationalism* (London: Sage).
Brah, A. (1996) *Cartographies of Diaspora* (London: Routledge).
Castles, S. and Kosack, G. (1973) *Immigrant Workers and the Class Structure* (Oxford: Oxford University Press/Institute of Race Relations).
Conn, D. (2012a) "Verdict returns ball to FA's court with the clean-up still far from over," *The Guardian*, July 14, 2012.
Conn, D. (2012b) "Verdict is clear but punishment is anything but," *The Guardian Sport*, October 6, 2012.
Dalal, F. (2002) *Race, Colour and the Processes of Racialisation* (Sussex: Brunner-Routledge).
Fromm, E. ([1942] 2002) *Fear of Freedom* (London: Routledge).
Gadd, D. (2009) "Aggravating Racism and Elusive Motivation," *British Journal of Criminology*, 49 (6), 755–771.
Gadd, D., B. Dixon, and T. Jefferson (2005) *Why Do They Do It? Racial Harassment in North Staffordshire: Key Findings* (Keele: Centre for Criminological Research, Keele University).
Gadd, D. and B. Dixon (2011) *Losing the Race: Thinking Psychosocially about Racially Motivated Crime* (London: Karnac).
Gadd, D. and T. Jefferson (2007) *Psychosocial Criminology* (London: Sage).
Gilroy, P. (1993) *The Black Atlantic* (Cambridge: Harvard University Press).
HM Inspectorate of Probation (2005) *An Inspection of National Probation Service Work with Racially Motivated Offenders* (London: Home Office).
Hollway, W. and T. Jefferson ([2000] 2013) *Doing Qualitative Research Differently*, 2nd edn. (London: Sage).
Hollway, W. and T. Jefferson (2004) "Free Association Narrative Interviewing," in M. Lewis-Beck, A. Bryman, and T. Futing Liao (eds) *Encyclopedia of Research Methods for the Social Sciences* (Thousand Oaks: Sage).
Home Office (1981) *Racial Attacks* (London: Home Office).
Kovel, J. ([1970] 1988) *White Racism* (London: Free Association Books).

Mac an Ghaill, M. (1999) *Contemporary Racisms and Ethnicities* (Buckingham: Open University Press).

Macpherson Report (1999) *The Stephen Lawrence Inquiry*. Cmnd 4262-I. (London: Stationery Office).

Miles, R. (1982) *Racism and Labour Migration* (London: Routledge and Kegan Paul).

Patterson, S. (1963) *Dark Strangers* (London: Tavistock).

Phoenix, A. (2010) "Ethnicities" in M. Wetherell and C. T. Mohanty (eds) *The Sage Handbook of Identities* (London: Sage).

Rattansi, A. (2007) *Racism: A Very Short Introduction* (Oxford: Oxford University Press).

Rex, J. (1970) *Race Relations in Sociological Theory* (London: Weidenfeld and Nicolson).

Rex, J. and R. Moore (1967) *Race, Community and Conflict* (Oxford: Oxford University Press/Institute of Race Relations).

Seabrook, J. (1973) *City Close-up* (Harmondsworth: Penguin).

Sherwood, R. (1980) *The Psychodynamics of Race* (Brighton: Harvester).

Tajfel, H. (1969) "Cognitive Aspects of Prejudice," Journal *of Social Issues*, xxv (4), 79–96.

Tajfel, H. and J. C. Turner (1979) "An Integrative Theory of Intergroup Conflict," in W. G. Austin and S. Worchel (eds) *The Social Psychology of Intergroup Relations* (Monterey: Brooks/Cole).

Various authors (2002) "Review Symposium on hate crime," *Theoretical Criminology*, 6 (4), 481–502.

Wetherell, M. and J. Potter (1992) *Mapping the Language of Racism* (Brighton, Sussex: Harvester Wheatsheaf).

Young-Bruehl, E. ([1996] 1998) *The Anatomy of Prejudices* (Cambridge: Harvard University Press).

17
Definitive Exclusions: The Social Fact and the Subjects of Neo-Liberalism

Vikash Singh

Few texts have so centrally defined the institutionalized practice of sociology as Durkheim's *Rules of Sociological Method*. Scrupulously differentiating the subject matter of the discipline from biology and psychology, Durkheim argued that the mandate of sociology was to study "social facts," an objective entity—"a new species and *to them must be exclusively assigned the term social*" (Durkheim, 1982). In the relatively nascent field of nineteenth century social sciences confounded as much by the ideal positivism of the physical sciences as by an assertive capitalism constituting a racialized and colonized global social environment, Durkheim's precepts allowed the institutionalization of sociology into a robust and lasting field of inquiry. And if sociology has developed and expanded varied offshoots over its historical course, it finds itself no less obligated to the promise, the assurance, and the apparent profundity of its paternal origins. The stigma faced by the heretic is a social fact: no *good* can come from violating the father's law.

But one may be familiar with many families, and orphans too. If Durkheim would exclusively reserve the "social" as a property of the family of sociologists, it is precisely the interests of the family—and a political economy, an ethics, an ontology predicated on it—that perhaps one must renounce to approach the present human condition. This essay focuses on the moral and epistemological necessity of disciplinary heresy for the contemporary sociologist by analyzing three different social phenomena: religion, neo-racism (or neo-casteism), and the affects of the electronic media. In so doing, I may be accused of violating the law of the father twice over: first because I approach each of these three cases through the domain of the psychic, from which Durkheim most struggled to break sociology free; and second because, in appealing to psychoanalysis, the following narrative subjects the 'social' to an analytic tradition found to be in breach of the father's law and authority from the outset. The inferences I will draw are general though based on specific evidence, that is, my research on contemporary India. I seek to demonstrate the edge psychoanalytic notions like "repetition," "jouissance," "repression," and "abject"—usually scoffed at by sociologists—nonetheless offer for understanding each of these varied social phenomena.

Religious fundamentalism or the everyday violence of capitalism?

Explaining the global revival of religious practices has been a primary concern of contemporary sociologists of religion. The secularization thesis, as we know, proposed that growing rationalization of social activity and scientific-technological development would increasingly diminish the explanatory power and apparent control bestowed on supernatural Being/beings. Taken aback by new developments often characterized as a "worldwide resurgence of religion," sociologists probed in different directions for explanation. Some galvanized new defenses for a stronger secularization thesis; others substantively qualified it; yet others contended secularization had provoked de-secularization (Bruce, 2002; Yamane, 1997). Notwithstanding these differences, a near consensus aligned with the contours of the normative sociological model soon evolved. As Berger summarizes:

> Modernity, for fully understandable reasons, undermines all the old certainties; uncertainty is a condition that many people find very hard to bear, therefore, any movement (not only a religious one) that promises to provide or to renew certainty has a ready market. (Berger, 1999, p. 7, emphasis added)

If the explanation seems hurried, it is nonetheless widely shared, revitalizing a wide literature that could as easily claim the structuralist corpus of Saussure, Levi-Strauss, and Durkheim as contemporary theories of identity and Anthony Giddens' neo-functionalism. Globalization, it goes, causes social anomie, which in turn pushes people to seek security in the traditional forms of ethnicity, nationality, and/or religion. Thus religious movements come to be seen as reactionary expressions of collective solidarity at a time when long-held beliefs, worldviews, and practices are confronted by the prodigious circulations of our epoch.

To the trained sociologist—and indeed to the social scientist insofar as this methodological consensus is shared—this explanation comes *naturally*. But the surmise is nevertheless ridden with many perils, circumscribed, perpetuated, and patrolled as it is by disciplinary mandates leading to a singularly one-dimensional understanding. One must be cautious, indeed scrupulous, when speaking of contemporary religion, as became clear to me through my research on a religious movement in India.

The Kanwar is an annual event in North India in which participants carry water from the river Ganga to distant Siva temples. The majority of participants are young adult or adolescent males from poor or lower middle-class backgrounds. With participants often walking several hundred miles, the journey follows demanding ritual codes that underscore pain, hardship, and the determination and competence the journey requires. Characterized by the liberal use of marijuana and performed under the aegis of Siva's paradoxical mythology, the Kanwar procession is also a merry, carnivalesque event—its transgressions thereafter often attracting the ire of the middle class and established religious authorities. Every year, for several days during the procession, traffic is diverted, and these religious actors occupy some of North India's key highways. Growing from a few thousand participants less than three decades ago, the Kanwar now attracts more than 10 million people every year (for more on this phenomenon, see Singh, 2013a).

From the contemporary sociological perspective of most scholars of religion and South Asia, the Kanwar is seen as a reactive assertion of ethnic, religious, or national (postcolonial) identity in a modernizing social context. This conclusion is hard to avoid if one adopts the usual sociological language focused on *collectivities*. If it is on the collective defined by solidarity or identity that the sociologist predicates her practice, this is what she will see, that is, religious movements opposed to macro-historical, teleological secularist progress, and civic liberalism. The first challenge my research faced, then, was transgressing these imperatives, even at risk of subjective guilt and disciplinary reproach, so as to reconstruct a theoretical perspective. For analyzing the social form would be a hollow exercise in syllogisms unless I could relate to the actors, the subjects, who were its players. It would be unwise for an ethnographer to disregard the subject, denying her significance, for a vague and poorly conceived impulse toward generalization.[1] And, here, I found myself heeding psychoanalysis, perhaps the only discipline that has given systematic, protracted attention to the profound paradoxes of subjective temporality.

Thus Jacques Lacan's subversion of Hegelian teleology and the capitalist social structure in which its symbolic representations are embedded became one of my primary anchors (Lacan, 2006, 2007). Building on Heidegger, Kierkegaard, Gadamer, and Freud, among others, Lacan advocated an analytical language that prioritized the finite time of the subject. As he puts it, a tongue "that can be understood in all other tongues" and yet be "absolutely particular to the subject" (Lacan, 2006, p. 243). This proposition simultaneously displaces reified Cartesian notions of self, individual, and "rationality" as well as dominant ideological insistence on an ego in conformity with prevalent social practices. These notions of self and individuality informed by the ego-psychology tradition, as we know, are also used to construct theories of "identity," the primary conceptual resource of the contemporary social sciences (see, for example, Giddens, 1991). But a critical psychoanalytic understanding required thoroughly reconsidering sociology's dominant conceptual terrain to include psychoanalytic themes like dream work, the simple economy of the pleasure principle, and repetition compulsion—powerful ideas with gestalt-like effects that make coherent the otherwise complexly coded compositions of religious practices. Instead of closeting these practices into a sub-disciplinary enclosure like "pilgrimage studies" or "sociology of religion"—both institutionally recognized "social facts"—a psychoanalytic orientation called attention to the continuities of religion, morality, economy, social status, and politics, thereby recalling (if ironically) Weber's classical sociology.

My pre-conceptions of "Hindu-ness," "identity," or "nationality" were soon challenged by listening to my respondents, closely considering their life accounts and rituals, and by my observations and participation in the Kanwar. Instead of the chimeras of religious fundamentalism or dogmatic opposition to social change and "modernity," I found young adults and teenagers anxiously preparing to deliver on their social expectations and obligations to loved ones in social conditions as precarious as they were hierarchical. Given that the overwhelming majority of workers are informally employed with few economic, social, and health safeguards, and that prospects of stable and respectable employment are for most people faint and elusive, these are certainly daunting steps. At the margins of the economy, I found that the religious phenomenon provided an open and freely accessible, yet challenging, stage—a definite and alternate field—for participants to practice and prove their talents, resolve, and moral sincerity. The Kanwar also offered a way to contest the symbolic violence and social inequities of a hierarchical society now dominated by a neo-liberal social ethic, as imposing as it is exclusive (Singh, 2011, 2013a, 2013b).

How do psychoanalytic themes apply and assist here? First, they beckon one to disregard the facile if pervasive portrayal of such phenomena as rejections of "social change" (often disguised as a normative imperative about universal, "modern" progress) by drawing attention instead to some of Freud's painstaking observations about repetition, working-through, and mastering (see Freud, 1950[1914]). A precise idiom for the Kanwar thereafter becomes "performance," a term that simultaneously alludes to representation and action. As Freud meticulously describes in "Remembering, Repeating, and Working-Through," the best manner of negotiating repressed impulses is to repeat them in the "definite field" of the analytical setting, "a playground in which . . . [they are] allowed to expand in almost complete freedom" (p. 154).

At this point, though, one must radically if cautiously consider the transferences between psychic and social dimensions of repression. In view of the large-scale, manifestly social nature of the phenomenon we are considering—a social issue not a personal trouble, as Mills would have differentiated—"repression" becomes another word for the lack of satisfactory discursive and moral (self) recognition by the subject, as much as by the social or institutional actors in reference to which she addresses herself. Religious practice here then repeats, performs, expresses the concerns, associations, and anxieties repressed by the dominant collective consciousness. The transference allowed by the religious field "is a piece of real experience, but one which has been made possible by especially favorable conditions" (p. 154). So what kinds of repressions are most salient? To make further critical inroads, perhaps it is best to intermittently invert Freud's psychological motif of "repression" and instead call on "expression" or "performance."

The disembedded market economy increasingly clothed in neo-liberal ideological constructs of human capital, and the finality of market-based discursive constructs, today asserts itself as the dominant idiom governing social relations as much as economic, cultural, and political futures. The market economy imposes itself with near absolute power over the whole gamut of social relations even as *exclusivity* is the primary mechanism of incorporation. One cannot fail to register this experience of economic and thereby social exclusion, and yet just as thoroughly deny it insofar as one must keep working with it (for there is no exit). This constitutes a primary repression here. In the achievements of the Kanwar, despite the pain and hardships, in the common competitive banter and wagers, in the anxious expressions of self-worth, the ethnographer finds a repetition of messages exchanged with a dominating neo-liberal ethos. It is a repetition of the subject of the economy, its expectations and directives, in an alternate and definite field. For adolescent and young adult subjects set to encounter the full might and overbearing structure of the "real field" of the exclusive economy, these are obviously anxiety-ridden steps that call for compulsive practice, for "working through."

To practice and prepare, however, is only one part of Freud's articulation of "repetition." In perhaps the culminating expression of this theme in *Beyond the Pleasure Principle*, Freud pondered repetition in the context of a dialectic of renunciation and desire, rejection and anticipation, which has quiescence or death as its transcendental reference (Freud, 1950). And in yet another profound turn Lacan interpreted the death drive, echoing Sade, as the desire for the *ex nihilo*, the desire to destroy and "begin again" (Lacan, 1992, p. 212). Repetition is thus also a striving to *master*—master with nothing less than death, sovereignty, and absolute renunciation at stake. Not a moment passes where the slave who sets out to prepare and work does not have her masterly mantle by her! The anxious repetitions of the economy, the following-through of its directives and apparently willing subjections to its refusals, exclusions, and excesses are no less attended by an imperative of rejection, destruction, and affirmation of sovereignty.

Siva, the primary organizing figure of the Kanwar is Master of the world yet a pathetic beggar (Doniger, 1981). Addressed adorably as Bhola or the Fool, in identification with the participant (*bhola*), He is a "foolish" renouncer who gifts away everything without keeping anything for himself. At the same time, adorned with bones and skulls, smeared in ash from funeral pyres, drinking opium from skulls with rotting flesh, and in the middle of his forehead the all-consuming, grotesque third eye which burned Kama, the god of desire, to ashes, He is the destructive principle itself. Furthermore, despite his hideous and destructive aspect, He is also Kama or erotic desire itself; Siva is the most desirable among men.

These practices in the religious field thus enable a mastering of oppressive and demanding social conditions; they simultaneously perform to, and perform against, the hegemonic social order. Moreover anticipation and preparation for these conditions is also a rejection of their violence: sovereignty is affirmed both as an expression of the desire to destroy (an attitude where the risk of utter destitution and abjection is registered as absolute renunciation) and a gifting away of everything. For these mostly young men of poor or lower middle-class backgrounds, this also asserts their erotic desirability despite their looming abjectness. Sexualities otherwise conforming to (or, in other words, repressed by) dominant protocols of social status are thus radically expressed.

Nor do these representations entirely exhaust the phenomenon: following the lessons of psychoanalysis, one must heed the act at various levels. For example, in the obsessive anxiety I observed—the overbearing necessity to abide by every scruple, to repetitively ensure the ritual appropriateness of every action, the symmetry of every alignment—one also sees a dread of everyday life (Singh, 2013). The violation of every stricture carried the final threat of disintegration, of the journey and the offering having failed. Insofar as the performances are tied to one's performances in the larger world, such obsessiveness reflects compulsive anxiety to ward off every chance of infringement, every untoward instance, every risk of losing the desired object—which may often amount to wanting life to just keep its regular course! Says Lacan with characteristic precision, "If the obsessional mortifies himself . . . it is because . . . he binds himself to his ego, which bears within itself dispossession and imaginary death" (Lacan, 1988, p. 268). The precarious carrying of the water is also the precarious carrying on of life itself; by extension, its breaking down becomes a sign of impending disaster (see Singh, 2011).

Conventional sociological approaches tend to miss such subtle, nuanced meanings of the phenomenon. This is not only because sociology maintains a principled focus on the "social fact" or "social form" as an objective entity. Formalist dissociation is often important as a diagnostic; it frees knowledge from the "thing" itself, elusive and indeterminate, to proceed instead to a stable, empirically verifiable, and comparable entity. This method is further validated by the illustration of the arbitrariness of the signifier in structural linguistics. The issue, however, is that the conventional sociological approach effectively limits the explanatory variables themselves to "social facts"; the play of the signifier is arrested in a manner that hardly parallels linguistic signs.

Thus, by extension, the sociological explanation of contemporary religion usually limits the play to a single signifier: "religious identity." A strict correspondence is set up between the subject and the identity she apparently secures. Much as language is not constituted by a single sign but involves relations between a whole network of signifiers, the human subject cannot be assumed to be the referent of a single signifier (whether "collective identity" or a stable group of social practices). This suggests that a religious development is important not so much to provide the subject a fixed signifier (or "identity") but rather through how it intervenes to re-negotiate, or reconfigure, an existing system of signifiers—and consequently the subject's social existence. Thus, even from a formalist standpoint, the notable component here is not so much the arbitrariness of the identity to which the subject attaches itself; more worthy of attention are the performances of this "identity" in relation to other social forms—that is, its play within a network of signifiers. In the following, I demonstrate the value of the opening provided by psychoanalysis for another social issue: neo-racism and neo-casteism, continuing to draw on evidence from the Kanwar movement.

Miscegenation, (in)discrimination, and neo-racism

Contemporary US racism presents a rather confounding paradox. One account after another attests that it operates by denial, often cynically disguised in the language of civil rights and resulting in discriminatory consequences precisely by advocating a colorblind framework. As though mirroring these contradictions, sociologists have sometimes argued for "the declining significance of race in the United States"; on the other hand, the case is made for systemic racism as a structural determinant of life chances in the US (Wilson, 1978; Omi and Winant, 1994; Omi and Winant, 2012; Bonilla-Silva, 2001; Feagin and Elias, 2013). So nagging are these issues that a theorist like Howard Winant (2004), one of the pioneers of racial formation theory, admits that "the inadequacy of the range of theoretical approaches to race available at the turn of the twentieth century is striking" (Winant, 2004, p. 161). As with contemporary religion, I suggest that circumscription of racial practices into a manifest, easily identifiable social fact—that is, a statist category, a "social structure" apparently complete and analyzable in its own terms—is part of the problem.

If a global historical and interdisciplinary outlook is instead adopted, the modern notion of "race" appears as the product of a differentiating logic of liberal colonial discourse as it negotiated a new system of stratification within colonizing countries aimed at *exceptional* exploitation of the colonized people and territories (see Foucault, 2008; Clough, 2008; Balibar, 1991). Race here became a *deep difference*, framed simultaneously in mutually defining biological and cultural logics, and allowing economic liberalism absolute mastery and exploitation without jettisoning apparent liberal political values. Economic interests and political domination are thus expressed as differences in culture that are, in turn, circularly defined: in other words, domination comes to be practiced as simultaneously an aesthetic and an ethic which constructs the racialized other as *abject* (Kristeva, 2002). In its primary moment, then, race is the construction of the other as a collective abject, a term that Kristeva defines as a social entity overdetermined as worthless on grounds simultaneously moral, economic, cultural, and political.

Thus racism provides the collective with a shared stigmatized other (disorderly, disagreeable, beastly, poor) from which one must distinguish oneself—by contrast—by identifying with positive traits of being culturally refined/educated, morally upright, economically worthy. The function of the raced group is similar to that of the untouchable in India's caste society. Absolute stigmatization, as signified by the term "un-touchable," is the over-determined effect of a super-imposition of sensory repugnance supported by an ethical system interlocked with economic conditions, all further enforced by political power (see Deliege, 1992). The effect is to separate and cast out; the caste society cannot be conceived without the outcast.

How then of race today? Beyond fetishes of skin tones or "body types," race is likewise a social mechanism of exclusion, over-determined by a combination of economic interests, political domination, and aesthetic and moral certitudes. If in the colonial period, the grounds for such exclusion were best marked as deep differences, now—that is, in a world perceived as increasingly unitary—exclusion must present itself as an encompassing discourse interpolating a common subject. Now race has to be constructed and practiced not through a social logic that focuses on division but in a sweeping discourse that putatively incorporates everyone.

That discourse is currently neo-liberalism, especially of the Chicago school variety, at once an economic doctrine, a political strategy, and a moral and aesthetic horizon. In this hegemonic global discourse, economic logic provides a universal grid of intelligibility for social practices from family and marriage to work, crime, and state justice (Foucault, 2008). The "lesser" race is marked by dubious behavior, poor consumption, and poor presentation of the self. This over-determined combination of power interests with a discourse of morality and aesthetics is as important o contemporary neo-racism as to the production of race in classical liberal discourse. I will explicate using the example of my research on the Kanwar, and in reference to India's caste structure.

But, before doing so, let us return to the work of psychoanalysis—primarily to Kristeva's conception of the "abject." The *abject*, the "not-I," is the referent of a primary repulsion, an exclusion, which is the condition of the formation of the ego as a centripetal agent seeking *objects* and mimicking social relations. The abject is that which defiles and contaminates, morally and aesthetically; insofar as the ego is constituted in reference to the abject, its appropriate functioning in the world requires it to remain on guard repressing the abject that threatens to sunder it. Such repression also largely drives metaphysics within which the abject and its defiling seductions must also be controlled through the categorical segregations of social matter in Samkhya, or through the alternative joys of truth and beauty in Plato, "ethical gymnastics" in Kant, or the socio-historical act in Hegel's transcendental idealism (Kristeva, 2002). Likewise modern political economy, now increasingly formulated via the unscrupulous, one-dimensional discourse of American neo-liberalism, is both driven by and capitalizes on such anxieties of exclusion and the inter-woven lures of the "more or less beautiful image" in which to (ideally, potentially) behold or recognize oneself. The exhaustive nature of American neo-liberalism and its singular emphasis on wealth accumulation also means that its exclusions will be that much more compulsive and the race of its abject that much virulently patrolled.

Returning to the Kanwar, pilgrimages understandably do not usually provoke adverse reactions. Instead they often induce tender feelings: participants' motives are often deep and personal, their faith inspiring, group behavior affable, austerities and labors exacting. In such a harmonious field, the Kanwar comes off as a rare and flagrant discrepancy. Although the phenomenon of course has a passionate following among broad sections, negative observations abound. The participants are very described as "hooligans," "thieves," "unmannered," "disorderly," "disruptive," and so on. Consider, for example, this on-line news report:

> They are a strange mix of tradition and modernity—men wearing Nike shoes and gaudy saffron vests walk or trek and occasionally stop to take rest. The resting places are audible before they are visible, with loud, garish devotional music being played over cheap amplifiers. Number of *Shiv Bhakts* can be seen there squatting or resting on makeshift tables or cots and engorging themselves at the *Bhandaras* sponsored by the local traders. (Dutta, 2007)

At a basic visceral level, the indiscriminate and popular religiosity of the Kanwar participants offends sensibilities. For, again, the Kanwar is carnivalesque; it is an unreserved, spectacular public demonstration of a low-brow popular culture with participants dancing to remixes of loud, raunchy Hindi film songs, frequent references to Siva's conjugal life in the songs and slogans, plays, and dances either performed live or on videos with often lascivious themes, ambiguous transgender dressing by performers with garish make-up, and suggestive bodily gyrations of males performing as females or females as males. Yet this example of ritual miscegenation, this abyssal obscene thing, presents itself as religion, as sublime—thereby shamelessly mixing things.[2] *It is the abject.* As Julia Kristeva describes insightfully:

> I endure it, for I imagine that such is the desire of the other. A massive and sudden emergence of uncanniness which, familiar as it might have been in an opaque and forgotten life, now harries me as radically separate, loathsome. Not me. Not that. But not nothing, either. A 'something' that I do not recognize as a thing. (Kristeva, 2002, p. 230)
>
> [W]hat disturbs identity, system, order. What does not respect borders, positions, rules. The in-between, the ambiguous, the composite. The traitor, the liar, the criminal with a good conscience, the shameless rapist, the killer who claims he is a saviour . . . Immoral, sinister, scheming and shady . . . (p. 232)

The revulsion caused by the Kanwar is an effect of this unusual, unseemly mixing of the sensible; it has as its base an aesthetic distaste, a rejection at once sensuous and ideological. In this case, the aesthetic chasm builds on India's caste heritage—a differentiation between the subtle and the gross, the pure and the abject, which is simultaneously aesthetic and metaphysical. While caste is losing legitimacy as an explicit category in India today, the aesthetic discrimination is deeply embedded. Vulgar taste, poor manners, tendency to excess, over-indulgence, these are simultaneously the marked characteristics of the "low" castes, and the ideological moral ground marking their "inferior" status. In contemporary popular interpretations of the *guna* system proposed in Samkhya philosophy, such qualities are identified with the inferior group, *tamasika*, which has the qualities of both being gross as matter and deluded morally and intellectually (Larson, 1998, p. 198). Aesthetic repulsiveness is merged with moral and intellectual degeneration. Collapsed into a group essence, this combination operates as an enduring ideology of caste discrimination.

As formal caste differences currently wither away, the practice now taps a neo-liberal ideology that likewise combines an aesthetic and moral evaluation with politico-economic domination. In the Kanwar, to the contrary, the otherwise suppressed, inferior, abject habitus of the poor pitches itself as absolute, occupies the highways, and performs its ethic under the full splendour of the public gaze. The repulsiveness it causes is thus related to the relaxed sensory regulation in the Kanwar corresponding with lack of social divisions, and where people irrespective of caste, class, age, and (to a large extent) gender merge in the singular identity of Shiva as *Bhola* (the Fool).

Thus, as demonstrated by the epic endurance of caste discrimination in India, racial ideology and practice combine interests of politico-economic domination with normative morality and aesthetics. An over-determined system articulated in terms at once metaphysical, politico-economic, ethical, and sensory, this has a totalizing effect of subjection comparable to that of the "strong discourse" that Goffman observed in the mental asylum (Goffman, 1961). Even as the system changes over time—much like gender distinctions persistent in the face of historic social changes—the same effects of exclusion and repression continue to be reproduced with surprising endurance. If earlier race and caste practices were produced by the dominant discourses of their age—colonial liberalism and Brahminism, respectively—both neo-racism and neo-casteism now align with the common global hegemony of neo-liberal ideology. Moreover, the rigor of Kristeva's conception of the *abject* points to how psychoanalysis both "explains" contemporary racism by showing its predication on the repression of the abject and opens up discourse and social practice to recognizing the abject. In a single stroke, it invites the ego to radically encounter its misrecognitions, and advances an epistemology, ontology, and social practice that radically harkens the abject it represses. Despite frequent bureaucratic clamor to the contrary, true knowledge, we find, is necessarily engaged in a politics of liberation.

Trauma, television, and politics

A third case study of the value of psychoanalytically informed epistemology for understanding the subject of electronic media draws, as primary reference, on an Indian TV series themes about religion telecast in 1987–1988. Analysts have described the unprecedented growth in popular access to television in the late 1980s along with political machinations that devised this medium as a transformative moment in Indian popular history and politics. Scholars have focused particularly on the Ramayana, a TV series based on the eponymous sub-continental epic telecast through the nation from January 1987 to July 1988 (Rajagopal, 2001; Singh, 2012). The wild popularity of this series paralleled the epic significance of the Ramayana itself within the Indic traditions; at a time when television sets were rare in India, the viewership for a Ramayana episode grew to 80 million within a few months of its inauguration (Rajagopal, 2001, p. 84). Ramayana fever seized the country on Sunday mornings particularly in the north. As Lutgendorf described:

> Visible manifestations of the serial's popularity included [. . .] cancellation of Sunday morning shows in cinema halls for lack of audiences, the delaying of weddings and funerals to allow participants to view the series, and the eerily quiet look of many cities and towns, especially in the North during screenings [. . .]. Bazaars, streets, and wholesale markets became so deserted they appear(ed) to be under curfew [. . .] trains were delayed when passengers refused to leave the platform until a broadcast was over. (Lutgendorf, 1990, pp. 136–137)

Researchers also ascribed political significance to ensuing programs in the same genre such as Mahabharata and Shri Krishna; all were seen as aligning a broad public, increasingly resentful of its marginal status in post-colonial India, with the elite and urban middle classes by imagining a common utopian past in the shared present. The 80s, a time of "liberalization" when the once protective domestic Indian economy was increasingly opened to global capital, coincided with the dominance of neo-liberalism in Thatcher's UK and Reagan's USA as well as with pressures for structural adjustment policies coming from the International Monetary Fund and the World Bank. As in Benedict Anderson's (1991) analysis, televised myths enabled a community imagined as much by identity and similitude across time as by difference and exclusion of other social groups.

Literature in the (Indian) sociology of media thoroughly analysed these series by focusing on reception rather than programming and ownership. These arguments diverged both from the Frankfurt School's critique focused on the dominance of the culture industry and from Habermas' emphasis on the role of media in constructing a democratic public sphere. As Rajagopal (2001) argues, while operating within the capitalist logic of exchange, television does not as such reproduce an exchange rationality; rather it registers as a gift, and offers "respite from the compulsions of actually existing social relations . . . on the other hand, it evokes feelings of closeness and reciprocity to unknown participants who may exist only in imagination" (p. 5).

The epistemological lesson, as Rajagopal summarizes, is not to think of a "public sphere" focused on elite politics or even on "elite and subaltern publics" but of "a split" public internalizing different political languages. The most salient question then becomes *terms of translation* reproducing "a structured set of misunderstandings" (25). Hindu nationalism is thus a clever and incendiary, if fortuitous, feat of translation. This is a bad and manipulative translation, far from evoking a shared beyond of different languages according to Walter Benjamin's test (Benjamin, 1986). Yet this translation almost exclusively occupies Rajagopal and other commentators on the Ramayana. The actual texts or subjects that are translated remain peripheral, only coming forth occasionally to claim their misunderstandings.[3] An important question then becomes why a bad and manipulative translation became the exclusive focus of one study after another focused on these TV series' "reception"? What then of the "original"? Where is it to find its audience, its analyst?

Once again, I believe the tendency for social science to focus on abstract social facts rather than finite, socially embedded subjects has tended to warp observers' inferences. As a result, the subject herself is cast as an effect of power, and power itself prioritized and implicated via its bad faith. Neither this choice of epistemology nor its political consequences are neutral. Let us see again though, and by way of contrast, how a psychoanalytic epistemology with the unreserved primacy it offers the subject—making everything else secondary from the outset, as it were—is illuminating vis-à-vis this third research topic, the phenomenon of the mythico-religious televisual.

What made the Ramayana serial attractive in a vast and diverse country?[4] Indeed this cannot be explained abstractly as another instance of the ubiquitous force of "religion." Rather, the Ramayana's unprecedented popularity arose after the genre of mythological films that dominated the Hindi film industry's output disappeared and this decline was accepted as final by Bombay filmmakers (Rajagopal, 2001, p. 84). From a psychoanalytic perspective, unbridled attachment to this mythico-religious virtual product can be understood through the Lacanian notion of *jouissance*: the promise of an ultimate association, a final identification of the subject with what it perceives as a constitutive, mythic or historical beyond. As in Lacan throughout, *jouissance*—which offers a final, ultimate association of the subject with what she perceives as this mystical, historical beyond—cannot be understood beyond the structure where it is found. Thus, the audience of the Ramayana cannot be the abstract, generalized and pre-existing one of religious myth or performance but an audience actually co-produced in the tele-performance of dialectically animated desires.

To elaborate: in late capitalism, "enjoyment" is not just a character-istic of consumption but defines production in many forms of mass entertainment. Indeed, enjoying the TV series is partially a product of fantasized bonds ruptured by intrusions of a "big other" symbol-izing world power, dominant knowledge, and/or commerce. From a psychosocial perspective, this is well illustrated in *Beyond the Pleasure Principle* (1959), within which Freud describes the game of Fort Da that his grandchild played to deal with his mother's departures. The child repeatedly hid and pulled back a cotton reel held by a thread, banishing the subject with a Fort, and then greeting it with a joyful Da! In this paradox of desire and pathos, Freud saw what comprises a drive through a subject both being with and dividing from the object.

The TV series, divided as much by its programmatic structure as by commercials, performs a similar game of supply and denial but in an inverted form. The sides have changed: no longer is it the subject who captures/jettisons the object of desire but the big Other that, in reverse, supplies/denies the object. If the game is the child's way of generat-ing enjoyment through a dialectic of possessing and dispossessing the object, the TV serial realizes this mechanism of producing surplus enjoyment in the form of a commodity. Like most human potentialities, in this case, the drive becomes a productive factor in capital's exploits.

Moreover, the structure of the social order and its influence on the super ego is affirmed by the structure of the serial as a piece-meal prod-uct divided by commercials. The Ramayana was telecast as a weekly 30-minute show on Sunday mornings with ten minutes of commercial breaks on both ends and other breaks in the middle of the show. Having watched this serial as a teenager on a small black-and-white set, in a neighbor's crowded living room, one of my strongest memories is wait-ing for the show to resume. Fantasy supplied is thereby interspersed with bursts of "reality," and the expanse of everyday life acts like a "super ego" suggesting obligations to the powers who/which made the fantasy possible. Even more importantly for my argument here, the episodic telecast allows the TV series to employ "repetition compulsion" within its productive strategy.

How the cathected bond of the subject with the fantasy breaks and is held in suspension through fixed intervals is part of the structure of the viewer's *jouissance*. In psychoanalytic terms, then, the different epi-sodes of the serial can be conceived as *repetitions* in which the jouissance cannot be achieved—it is always in excess. Thus by way of example Constantin Constantius, the pseudonymous author of Kierkegaard's Repetition concludes when unable to repeat the experience of a first holiday that "the only repetition was the impossibility of repetition" (Pound, 2007; see also Kierkgaard, 1983). The subject keeps re-enacting the action, a step ahead each time, if only to continuously lose what is repeated and throwing himself toward a *jouissance* no longer there. In the case of TV serials, repetition is the pleasure/labor of attempts to retrace the fantastic experience of prior episodes, a process that sets up a concatenation of cathected departures. Since TV serials in any case extend forever, these pleasures or nerve stimulations may be expected to subsist.

In repetition, Freud writes, the subject is driven by "an urge . . . to restore an earlier state of things," a compulsion to repeat, driven by "repressed memory traces of his earliest experiences." The exploits of the god-king Rama, and various fragments and morals of the story, are as much a part of Hindu religious practices and collective consciousness as they are common tales with which most grow up. For the viewing subject, the (tele)vision or *darśana* of the deity and his divine escapades in the TV serial is always an event after the original. It is always a recollection, a re-membering, and thus has an historical dimension. Likewise: the drive in psychoanalysis. Writes Lacan, "This dimension is to be noted in the insistence that characterizes its appearances; it refers back to something memorable because it was remembered. Remembering, 'historicizing', is coextensive with the functioning of the drive in what we call the human psyche" (Lacan, 2007, p. 209). As *jouissance* appears as the beyond of a drive, the elusive end of insistent excess, so the virtual commodity-object (the TV serial) is excessive. In Sagar's Ramayana, the divine gestures—Rama's acts of passive grace—are repeated in endless close-ups, allowing immersion in the grace of the otherwise inaccessible god-head. Yet the paradox of *jouissance* is such that it may only be encountered in its inaccessibility. Accordingly, the immersion in the divine is cut short after definite intervals when the viewer/devotee is thrown back into the world.

Consequently the response of the viewer/devotee of the televisual Ramayana approximates Lacan's understanding of fantasy as a relation between the empty, barred subject, and an object intimately featured in subjective historicity or memory though lost on her. However, the fantasy-object produced as a commodity in a dominant ideological schema is also a subversion of the subject's particular fantasy. The lack that the subject experiences in reality is compensated for as an excess in the virtual that performs repetition via the primal lack in the subject. The excess supplied in the virtual sphere is compensation for the lack in reality while simultaneously a factor in (re)producing late-capitalist reality; the virtual excess is born as the necessary supplement of contemporary reality. Reality intervenes most vividly in the commercials interspersed in the fantasy product, continuing as a subtext and ensuring that both affect the reader together—that is, that they *enframe* each other.

In the Ramayana serial, too, primeval historical traces are deployed toward an economically and politically profitable product. Rajagopal and others rightly infer that the Ramayana series marks a moment of crisis in India's state ideology (see, also, Mankekar, 2002). Put simply, the function of the Ramayana serial was to employ mythico-religious traces in an ideological cause, that is, supplementing the ideological totality with the name of God. At the same time, through television, the serial brought home tantalizing commodity images onto the greater Indian landscape. God thus came to be employed as an intermediary, a space and time allowing a transition from one mode of the economy (and attendant ideology) to another.

The religious surplus is thus constitutive of the project of the new economy. Right-wing religious ideology—religious nationalism, as it is called in India—is this ideology of the surplus that effaces the lack that constitutes it while giving a twist to its engagement with the economic externality. The religious ideology with its repetitive message thus functions as a cover. Its social function, and here one may count the political parties with their vested agendas, is to hide something that may not be countenanced; it is founded on a necessary denial. Yet, in psychoanalytic theory, such distortion or dissimulation is itself treated as "revealing" and "what emerges via distortions of the accurate representation of reality is the Real—the trauma around which social reality is structured" (1994, 26). What, then, is the traumatic core that will only be recognized in the consistency that it gives to this social phenomenon of a sudden religious upsurge and attendant ideology? What does this sudden, insistent attachment to religion, this almost new disposition, signify?

I believe one must look for this traumatic Real in precisely what is new to this moment. As I have shown in my narratives about the Kanwar, this is the entrance of the neo-liberal market paradigm including an extravaganza of the commodity form. The fetish of the commodity—this object that "fascinates the subject, reduces him to a passive gaze impotently gaping at the object"—has a powerful effect that must not be underestimated (see Zizek, 1997, p. 115). Yet commodity fixation is not traumatic by itself. Neither can the trauma be traced to the denial, the inaccessibility of the fantasy object, that is, to the condition of being deprived of the commodity or "being poor." The concentration of the trauma is rather in the inability to face this denial of the object and the multitude of social expectations thereby mobilized; it is the refusal to countenance this denial, the inability to provide it a signifying structure.

From a psychoanalytic perspective, then, the mythico-religious world is closer to the discourse of the hysteric. This discourse is related to the repression of the assault from a rushing in of inaccessible fantasy objects following the neo-liberal opening and the radical social expectations it brings. However, the trauma is a consequence of a discursive treatment, and the traumatic moment is the symptomatic sediment of a discursive lack. In the context of a majority living under dire economic conditions, subjected to a ravishing encounter with an extravaganza of the commodity form yet deprived the visions of a modernist dream and socialist utopia, the TV God worked to sublimate the traumatic moment in the very moment and medium of its inception. Here, no sooner does the hysteric speak than his discourse is reverted into the default form of the master's discourse in the ideology of religious nationalism. Central to the latter is the very symbolic system or knowledge that was excluded in the hysteric's discourse. The ideology of Hindu religious nationalism thus functions, to use a Deleuzian metaphor, as a retrogressive machine that turns the outrageous sequences springing out of the moment of crisis back into the master's fold.

Thus the analysis of this TV series unfolds as a narrative of political capitalization of popular faith, memories, and the traumas that the polity itself partly engenders. In terms of "substantive" import, these inferences may appear quite similar to previous studies conceiving these TV series as a conduit for an emergent politics of religious nationalism. What advantage does one "gain" then, as is a central query here, from introducing a psychoanalytic orientation? I believe the difference (and its politics) is subtle, and difficult to translate in dominant norms of scholarly "findings." Principally, the significance is in overturning an epistemology primarily centered on power politics to one where the subject comes first, without exception. It is a revolution in value, from structures of *exchange* to the pathos of use if one likes. This has notable epistemological consequences. Instead of criticism set in reference to an ideal rationalist utopia, from a psychoanalytic perspective, the desire for the Ramayana simultaneously invokes the ethical and sensuous bounteousness of the Ramayana imaginaries, their contrapositions to the violence of the symbolic order, and the subjective mechanics of their social and political exploitation. One can clearly distinguish the part of political agencies, the social operations of media technology, and capitalism in the act of constituting social relations. A psychoanalytic standpoint allows us to witness the paradoxes of desire, and its multifarious, divergent potentialities more clearly even in a brief analytical project. That this epistemology can articulate the mechanics of how repressive power intervenes (or emerges) in the complex interactions between factors like desire, technology, history, and economy further speak to its moral significance.

Concluding note

Through my work, I found the social fact a useful notion to analyze the subtleties of diverse social phenomena, and the force they command, as exemplified through empirical research on ritual obligations in the Kanwar, neo-racism (and neo-caste), and popular culture in India (especially the popular appeal of the Ramayana and widespread disgust at "low brow" popular culture). Durkheim's concept of the "social fact" communicates the physicality of social affects, and marks the object of empirical research in its specificity. On the other hand, it is constraining if assumed to thoroughly encompass multi-dimensional phenomena like "religion," "pilgrimage," "religious fundamentalism," and "nationalism." Indeed analytic creativity beyond this idea is needed to understand how a study of religion can also be a study of the neo-liberal economy; or how a study of the Ramayana series can point to Freud's grandchild missing his mother and playing with a cotton reel; or a study of contemporary US racism also illuminate studying caste in India. I faced such questions many times in my research, and encountered institutional refusals and reprimands reminiscent of Foucault's famous diagnosis of intimate connections between power and knowledge.

If the work of the scholar includes the charge to search beyond the obvious (and how something is made obvious), though, it cannot afford to be arrested by the given. Rather, for the critical analyst, the value of the social fact is as a point of departure but also as an always suspect and therefore easily suspended reference which can—at its worst—encumber rather than enable how we investigate social objects. Specifically, then, my primary aim in this essay has been to demonstrate the problem of fallacious distinctions between the social and the psychic. This opposition, based in the knowledge formations of nineteenth century Europe, is altogether sublimated in Freudian psychoanalysis that has not surprisingly influenced interdisciplinary thought from cultural studies through critical sociology, poststructuralist philosophy, and feminist theory. While transcending this distinction, psychoanalysis also led to a more humane epistemology. Focused on understanding rather than measuring human experiences, it could not but situate itself on this side of the humanities: it was by violating institutionalized scientistic expectations that psychoanalysis brought enduring epistemological developments. Likewise perhaps only by opening itself to psychoanalysis will sociology be able to turn, once more, to a real politics of liberation.

Notes

1. For an excellent illustration of the limitations of ethnographic practice, see Clough, 1998.
2. In India, these anxieties are further reinforced by the insecurities of a post-colonial identity. Such performances thus come across as an uncanny, recurrent, inexorable return of what one seeks to dissociate from, perhaps a past, an ascribed stigma, a lower part, a behind, sexual or excretive, to identify elsewhere in a national imaginary, a future, an image in the world.
3. For example, although Rajagopal apparently interviewed 169 television viewers, these respondents appear in less than a chapter, about 22 pages, in a book with seven chapters running into over 300 pages.
4. Notes Rajagopal, "Crowds gathered around every wayside television set, though few could have seen much on the small black and white TV sets with so many present. Engine drivers were reported to depart from their schedules, stopping their trains at stations en route if necessary, in order to watch" (2001, p. 84).

References

Balibar, E (1991) "Is There a Neo-racism?" in E. Balibar and E. Wallerstein, *Race, Nation, Class: Ambiguous Identities* (London: Routledge, Chapman and Hall).

Benjamin, W. (1986) "The task of the translator," in H. Arendt (ed.), H. Zohn (trans.) *Illuminations* (New York: Schocken Books).

Bonilla-Silva, E. (2001) *White Supremacy and Racism in the Post-Civil Rights Era* (Lynne Rienner Publishers).

Bruce, S. (2002) *God is Dead: Secularization in the West* (Oxford: Blackwell), 30.Deliege, R. (1992). Replication and Consensus: Untouchability, Caste and Ideology in India. *Man,* 155–173.

Berger, P. (1999) *The Desecularization of the World: Resurgent Religion and World Politics* (Washington, D.C.: Ethics and Public Policy Center).

Clough, P. (1998) *The End(s) of Ethnography: From Realism to Social Criticism* (New York: Peter Lang).

Clough, P. T. (2008) "The Affective Turn: Political Economy and the Biomediated Body," *Theory, Culture & Society,* 25 (1), 1–24.

Deliege, R. (1992) Replication and consensus: Untouchability, caste and ideology in India. *Man,* 155–173.

Dutta, S. (2007) "Kanwaria: The Lumpen on the Pilgrim Trail," *Merinews* (10 August) [http://www.merinews.com/article/kanwaria-the-lumpen-on-the-pilgrim-trail/125905.shtml accessed 27 May 2012].

Durkheim, E. (1982) *The Rules of Sociological Method* (New York: Macmillan Press Ltd).

Doniger, W. (1981) *Śiva, the Erotic Ascetic* (New York: Oxford University Press).

Feagin, J. and S. Elias (2013) "Rethinking Racial Formation Theory: A Systemic Racism Critique," *Ethnic and Racial Studies*, 36 (6), 931–960.

Foucault, M (2008) *The Birth of Biopolitics: Lectures at the College de France, 1978–79* (New York: Palgrave Macmillan).

Freud, S. (1950 [1914]) *The Standard Edition of the Complete Psychological Works of Sigmund Freud*, J. Strachey (ed.), Vol. 5, Vol. 12, and Vol. 18 (London, Hogarth Press).

Giddens, A. (1991) *Modernity and Self-Identity: Self and Identity in the Late Modern Age* (Cambridge: Polity).

Goffman, E. (1961) *Asylums: Essays on the Social Situation of Mental Patients and Other Inmates* (Aldine Transaction).

Kierkegaard, S (1983) Fear and Trembling; Repetition, H. V. Hong and E. H. Hong (eds. and trans.) (Princeton: Princeton University Press).

Kristeva, J. (2002) The Portable Kristeva, L. S. Roudiez (trans.) (New York: Columbia University Press).

Lacan, J. (1988) The Ego in Freud's Theory and in the Technique of Psychoanalysis, 1954–1955, S. Tomaselli (trans.), J. Miller (ed.) (New York: W.W. Norton).

Lacan, J. (1992) *Ethics of Psychoanalysis: Seminar of Jacques Lacan Book VII*, D. Porter (trans), J. Miller (ed.) (New York: Norton).

Lacan, J. (2006) *Écrits: The First Complete Edition in English*, B. Fink (trans.) (New York: W.W. Norton & Co).

Lacan, J. (2007) *The Other Side of Psychoanalysis* (New York: Norton).

Larson, G. J. (1998) *Classical Sāṃkhya: An Interpretation of its History and Meaning* (Delhi: Motilal Banarsidass).

Lutgendorf P. (1990) "Ramayan: The Video", *The Drama Review*, 34 (2), 127–176.

Mankekar, P. (2002). "Epic Contests: Television and Religious Identity in India" in F. D. Ginsburg, L. Abu-Lughod and B. Larkin (eds) *Media worlds: Anthropology on new terrain*, (London: University of California) 134–51.

Omi, M. and H. Winant (1994) *Racial Formation in the United States: From the 1960s to the 1990s* (Los Angeles: Psychology Press).

Omi, M. and H. Winant (2012) "Racial Formation Rules," in D. Martinez Hosang, O. LaBennett and L. Plalido (eds) *Racial Formation in the Twenty-First Century*, (Los Angeles: University of California Press) 302.

Pound, M. (2007) Theology, Psychoanalysis, Trauma (London: SCM Press).

Rajagopal, A. (2001) *Politics after Television: Hindu Nationalism and the Reshaping of the Public in India* (Cambridge: Cambridge University Press).

Singh, V. (2012) "TV Serial Ramayana and the Becoming of an Ideology," *International Journal of Žižek Studies*, 6 (2), 1–17.

Singh, V. (2013a) "Work, Performance, and the Social Ethic of Global Capitalism: Understanding Religious Practice in Contemporary India," *Sociological Forum*, 28 (2), 283–307.

Singh, V. (2013b) "Religious Practice and the Phenomenology of Everyday Violence in Contemporary India," *Ethnography* ifirst, 12 June 2012, doi:10.1177/1466138113490606.

Singh, V. (2011) "Precarious Life and the Ethics of Care: Subjectivity in an Indian Religious Phenomenon," *Culture and Religion*, 12 (4), 419–440.

Wilson, W. J. (1978) "The Declining Significance of Race," *Society*, 15 (5), 11–11.

Winant, H. (2004) *The New Politics of Race: Globalism, Difference, Justice* (Minneapolis: University of Minnesota Press).

Yamane, D. (1997) "Secularization on Trial: In Defense of a Neosecularization Paradigm," *Journal for the scientific study of religion*, 36 (1), 109–122.

Žižek, S (1997) *The Plague of Fantasies* (London: Verso).

18

"One Has to Belong, Somehow": Acts of Belonging at the Intersection of Ethnicity, Sexuality, and Citizenship

Ilgin Yorukoglu

I am in Zeynep's apartment in Shoeneberg, Berlin. A mother of three young boys, Zeynep has not had an easy life: She attempted suicide in her teens and suffered years of domestic violence. In recent years, however, her relationship with her parents has improved. Almost in tears, she says that she forgives her family. She accepts them as they are.[1] Forgiveness appears as a way to claim belonging to her family without discarding her other identifications, as she says "one has to belong . . . somehow."

What Zeynep alludes to—"belonging somehow"—signals the importance of what I call "acts of belonging" for communities with a background of migration. Following what Fiona Allon suggests in another context, I believe that instead of asking "where do these people belong," scholars of migration and citizenship studies should ask "how?"(2000). *How* do those with migrant background belong? How do they claim rights in different contexts and with the various groups and power holders they face in their everyday lives?

In order to be able to understand "how" to belong, I examine what I call "acts of belonging." I benefit here from the wonderful work of Engin Isin and Greg Nielsen who define "acts of citizenship" as the acts transforming the ways of being political by creating new sites and scales of struggle. This area which has unfortunately remained unexplored is in fact the subject of politics! Indeed, as Jacques Rancière once said in an interview, "[politics] means precisely this, that you speak at a time and in a place you're not expected to speak."[2]

Different from Isin and Nielsen's "acts of citizenship," "acts of belonging" refer to acts which are not only directed towards the state or state institutions, but are also formed through and directed toward more "intimate" relations. Acts of belonging might not even claim to be "political" as such. Rather, they refer to those times when the individual "acts" on the need to affirm strongly and emotionally that in spite of the lack of "coherence" or in spite of the conflict between her multiple identifications, the individual "belongs" to the entity in question. Through these acts, individuals can momentarily relieve the existential tension derived from their multiple and conflicting identifications (especially as migrants). However, even when they do not claim to be political and are not acting on fixed political ground, they do present vast political possibilities.

"Belonging" does not refer to a simple membership or attachment; rather, it is that strong feeling beyond a simple membership. Freud, in *Group Psychology*, talks about the feeling of "triumph when something in the ego coincides with the ego ideal." When there is tension between the ego and the ego ideal, a sense of guilt appears ([1922] 1990). The tension or conflict within ourselves is strongly tied to the tension felt with and among others. Therefore, "belonging" is a multi-layered feeling, starting within the individual herself, while this psychic position is simultaneously affected by group membership.

Moreover, I suggest that the act of belonging both reproduces the identification and belonging to the group, and it appears as evidence of the individual's belonging. In other words, I neither agree with, nor reject the idea of, an identification and a subject position which has already been produced before the materialization of this act. The act itself is capable of (re)producing this belonging (to the group, to the identity which is identified with the group and so on). Additionally, what I call "acts of belonging" do not always necessitate a conscious, intentional, rational decision-making, nor do they require an audience to "confirm" the meaning behind the act. Finally, *acts of belonging* refers to a subject who is "reclaimed ... for its being-such, for belonging itself" (Agamben, 2003) In this sense, the subject that acts reminds us of Giorgio Agamben's "whatever being" whose community is mediated "not by any condition of belonging (being red, being Italian, being Communist) nor by the simple absence of conditions . . . but by belonging itself" (p. 85), suggesting an emphasis on belonging, rather than a fixed identity.

At its most essential, citizenship differentiates those who belong to the entity in question (be it a nation-state or, say, the European Union) from those who are not entitled to belong. Discourse around the rules and criteria for "naturalization" (granting of citizenship to those who were not born within the entity's territories) is often challenged and transformed to become more "inclusive" and "human rights" oriented.

However, these debates do not change the core of modern citizenship which makes certain groups strangers and outsiders. What is more, in contrast to the lack of adequate attention in the literature on social psychology and the intersection of gender, race and sexuality, populist political discourse around migration, integration, and citizenship explicitly mobilizes emotions such as fear of "the other."

I suggest, therefore, that scholars of migration and citizenship will benefit from looking at the psychosocial aspects and remembering the importance and the use of emotions in not only expressing but also re-creating identifications. Therefore, focusing on issues of citizenship in the contemporary political context will be misleading without situating citizenship in the wider context of contemporary politics but also with the psychosocial context of feelings of belonging. Based on a broader study of citizenship and belonging, this essay focuses on how "queer" women of Turkish descent in Berlin develop different meanings of citizenship that accommodate multiple kinds of individual identifications.

Before focusing on belonging and the ways individuals establish their belonging, I turn to the question of why do we have this need to belong? Benefiting from readings in psychoanalysis, this essay first discussed *anxiety* at the root of this need. Secondly, I define and introduce what I call "acts of belonging," arguing that these acts ensure intimacy and a basis for identification. At the same time, they reveal ways in which people engage with diversity—ways not always the same as the "us" versus "them" narrative familiar in the literature on migration. In the final section, I provide examples from my fieldwork to assist in better understanding and envisioning these acts.

Why do we need to belong?

"But there is no love," says Zeynep, talking about her first marriage years ago to the father of two of her children. "At the same time I hate sexuality. What should I do, how can I manage to run away from him—this is what I am trying to find. Ah . . . Then I got pregnant. [a long pause] My first boy. I wanted it. I wanted a child." I wonder why a woman would want a child with a man who makes her unhappy. "Why? I don't know." She does know, actually, as she says after another pause:

"I wanted to be loved. I think this was it."

Zeynep is now a woman who is and feels loved, as reflected in the way she talks, in her sense of humor, in her mellow attitude and joyful interactions with others. Indeed, after having talked about her past years of physical and emotional violence, years of ambivalence, hesitance, and fear, Zeynep says: "I have this feeling of. . . . that I have now come home. I have found home." As I leave her house with a certain kind of satisfaction of a happy ending, I reflect on Zeynep's earlier comment that she "wanted to be loved." I wonder to what extent this might be tied to "the need to belong, *somehow*," especially for migrant subjects.

At the root of this "need to belong" lies an anxiety which is both an innate characteristic (something that we carry within us from the moment we are born) and also shaped and exacerbated by our social environment. Transgressing the duality between the "natural" versus "cultural" qualities we embody, this dualistic "being" anxiety also challenges distinctions between psychic and social, between internal and external, between the "I" and the "me."

Erich Fromm places anxiety squarely in a socio-psychological context, noting that "certain factors in the modern industrial system in general and in its monopolistic phase in particular make for the development of a personality which feels powerless and alone, anxious and insecure" (1960, p. 207). In discussing two aspects of freedom—that is, freedom from restraints or authority and freedom for new relatedness—Fromm claims that modern societies have only strived for the former. This limited conception of freedom results in the isolation of the individual as "freedom from" is not supported by a 'freedom for' security and the sense of belonging (May, 1977, p. 193). Furthermore, the increasing individuality and the development of medicine throughout the twentieth century accentuated anxieties associated with death.[3] From 1945 and the birth of the atom bomb, writes Rollo May in 1977, "anxiety shifted from a covert to an overt problem" (p. 3), rendering the twentieth century an "age of overt anxiety," that is, characterized by a feeling of "homelessness" (pp. 4–5). With our futures threatened by ongoing economic insecurity, diminishing social welfare, global warming, and constant "security alerts," one can suggest that "overt anxiety" has persisted into the present century as well. As a matter of fact, according to the National Institute of Mental Health, anxiety disorders affect about 40 million adults in the US in a given year.[4]

On the one hand, Fromm's approach seems to differ from psychoanalytic theories on the matter of anxiety. Sigmund Freud, for example, is among those who emphasize the innate character of anxiety. Freud ties this innate character to the separation from the mother, calling this the birth trauma (May, 1977, p. 140). Accordingly, "[T]he child's having anxiety at the appearance of strange people and its fears of darkness and loneliness . . . have their origin in dread lest the child separated from his[sic.] mother" (p. 141). Following Freud, Otto Rank[5] conceives the individual's life history as an "endless series of experiences of separation" (p. 149), birth being the first and most dramatic experience but followed by the same psychological experience throughout life. Karen Horney places anxiety even prior to the instinctual drives: "What Freud terms instinctual drives, far from being basic, she holds, are themselves a product of anxiety." In other words, "impulses and desires do not become 'drives' except as they are motivated by anxiety" (1945, pp. 12–13 cited in May, 1977, p. 161). In this case, drives are ways of coping with anxiety and their actual aim is not satisfaction, as Freud believed, but *safety.*

Thus, human beings are aware of their existence only with an awareness of temporality, that is, the limit of this existence. This awareness brings anxiety: my existence is full of potentialities, I am consisted of potentialities, and am free to make all these happen; simultaneously, these potentialities are limited, *I* am limited, and there is nothing I can do about this. This existential anxiety recalls Otto Rank's discussion of separation in that finite separates me from life, from my loved ones, as well as from my many potentialities.[6]

Although this psychoanalytic approach seems to differ from that of Fromm's, we can say that the *innate* awareness of our temporality has intensified with modernity. Moreover, it seems as if concern with "belonging" has intensified in times of sharpened exclusions. This is probably because this need to belong, the longing for safety, has been increasingly exploited by the politics of exclusion. As Rey Chow puts it, the terms "for grasping the modern world have to do with estrangement, difference, discontinuity, and distance" (Chow Ibid.: 7). Modern life is full of uncertainties: the more we know about the world, the more we doubt it, and the more threats emerge for which to be cautious. In *Liquid Modernity*, Zygmunt Baumann argues that liquidity characterizes the contemporary world where everything is short-lived, and nothing stands still. It is ironic that while human life expectancy increases, so is anxiety and existential insecurity (Bauman, 2000). We exclude as much as we can from our lives all those who or what might cause threat to our existence, and our "way of life," while at the same time romanticizing ideas such as "the community feeling." Therefore, multiple categories are reinforced as separate entities which cannot "belong" together.

Therefore, belonging, which alleviates anxiety, and exclusion seem to go along with each other. I suggest, however, that there are alternative ways which satisfy our need to belong without necessarily exacerbating exclusions. These coping mechanisms are usually invisible in everyday exchanges. They are temporary disruptions of a normative order which draws populations as categories being excluded from each other. Below I will introduce these coping mechanisms, which I call "acts of belonging."

Acts of belonging: A definition

Scholars differentiate between "normal anxiety" and "neurotic anxiety" where the former

i.   is not disproportionate to the objective threat;
ii.   does not involve repression or other mechanisms of intrapsychic conflict;
iii. does not require neurotic defense mechanisms;
iv.   can be confronted constructively on the level of conscious awareness or can be relieved if the objective situation is altered. (May, 1977, p. 210)

Following Freud's discussion of "objective anxiety," Alfred Adler and Otto Rank demonstrated the importance of "normal anxiety" in everyday life. Due to the ongoing separation throughout individuals' life discussed earlier, this "normal anxiety" does not imply hostility and does not even lead to defense mechanisms. I disagree. First, I argue that it is impossible to name the anxiety an individual feels without looking at the defense mechanism she employs to alleviate this anxiety. Moreover as Rollo May recognizes, "[i]n most persons the two kinds of anxiety are intermingled" (p. 211) and that "if . . . anxiety-creating experiences are negotiated successfully . . . the anxiety in such cases should then be described as 'normal' rather than 'neurotic'" (p. 212). Therefore, what might be differentiated, I suggest, is not the anxiety itself, but the way in which the individual attempts to cope with it.

There might be innumerable ways of reacting to anxiety. What makes *acts of belonging* important for the sake of group maintenance is that they highlight belonging itself as the main force behind attachment. More than just possible causes or factors which keep the individual attached to a particular group, *acts* reveal the importance of belonging itself as the primary factor which affects the identification with the group. This should not be confused with what Erich Fromm calls "automation conformity" which describes times when the individual becomes identical with millions of other individuals and thus need not feel alone and anxious. Acts of belonging do *not* necessarily aim to copy the cultural norms and forms of behavior most commonly found within the close environment. Acts of belonging allow the individual to claim belonging *in spite of* possible differences. The individual does not claim that she is just like the others, nor does she suggest that she is different; often she acts on or through those differences in order to claim belonging. Another way to put it is that not all bodies are affected equally by what Sara Ahmed calls "disorientation" and thus the need to emphasize and/or "prove" one's belonging. Discourses on migration, citizenship, sexualities, religion, integration, and so on frequently politicize identifications as the privileged way that migrant subjects mitigate disorientation. The migrant subjects of this study remind us that disorientations and identifications are unevenly distributed and not uniform.

Therefore, it is not surprising that responses or "coping mechanisms" will be various. In my broader work, I discuss *acts of belonging* in greater detail, developing categories or ideal types to understand the differences and commonalities among these acts. Although acts of belonging are not mutually exclusive—each is always hyphenated with the other—I will discuss one of these categories as an example. In particular, I analyze migrant women's decisions in relation to "coming out" as an act of belonging. This decision is an incredible process which reminds us of the defense of the ego ideal which I mentioned before. In some cases, for example, we see the individual giving excuses as to why she prefers not to talk to her (otherwise very "sensible") families. "Even if my lover was a man" some of my respondents would say for example, "I would still not find it necessary to tell my parents"; or, "I have not yet met anyone whom I would like to introduce to my family anyway." This constant attempt to convince ourselves that this matter in fact does not matter might actually be an important clue showing its importance. If this normalization or legitimization process does not prove the importance of our coming out to our families, it definitely shows that we are aware of the importance of "coming out" for the individual we are communicating with. In other words, if the weight of "coming out" was not felt by the individual, the lack of this process would not require a reasoning or legitimization. I suggest, therefore, that the ego here is trying to coincide with the ego ideal.

I should also note here that this normalization process does not only occur in relation to coming out to families. Similar reasoning is employed regarding the individual's sense of acceptance by the ethnic community or the larger society. For example, Ayben talks about how she used to deal with her feeling like an outsider of the Turkish community and the larger society. Her appearance, the ways in which she talked, used her body language, the ways in which she dressed, or even her piercings, "all these" she says, "I was consciously doing in order to create an image of difference while I also wanted to be accepted by those people [the Turkish communities]. I mean, I was marginalizing myself, so that when I was not accepted I could react by saying 'well, I did this myself anyway'."

I hope the excerpts below, all based on my fieldwork which took place in Berlin between 2009 and 2012, will make the process more clear for the reader.

Coming out (or not) as an act of belonging

Can not-acting be an act in itself? Is not "coming out" an act nonetheless? Can a body communicate what is not said verbally? Is a community's "common language" necessarily verbal? As a term and concept, "coming out" does not exist in Turkish language; in other words, there is no direct translation. Turkish speakers talk about whether one's family "knows or not," whether the person "has told them"; or they sometimes simply use the English terminology "coming out." Moreover, the "telling" of one's sexual orientation is experienced and practiced in different ways among my subjects. This led me to question myself the extent to which I, as a "Westernized" researcher, assume a limited understanding of what it means to "come out." What does "coming out" actually entail, what does it mean and why does it matter, and how does it transform the actors involved?

Zeynep attempted suicide by cutting her wrists when she was only a teenager. She did not talk much about this attempt, nor did her parents. She did do one thing, however, which she remembers very well: "Whenever dad wanted something, like water or anything else, I was giving it to him like this [she stretches her arm out in front of her in a way that her sleeve moves upwards, showing her bare wrists]. I was doing this always, always. And how many times he hit my arm saying 'take this away, go away. . . .' I was always doing that, because [now as if talking to her father] 'look, look at what happened to me.'"

Berrin also has not "come out" her parents. She did, however, discuss her sexual orientation with her aunt who lives back in Turkey. Her aunt, "a sensible individual . . . just 10 years or so older than I am. Elderly people cannot . . . like . . . but . . . my aunt took it natural . . . .."

Some of my respondents seem to make excuses as to why they prefer not to talk to their (otherwise very "sensible") families; or why they prefer they not "know." "Even if my lover was a man" some of my respondents would say, for example, "I would still not find it necessary to tell my parents"; or, "I have not yet met anyone whom I would like to introduce to my family anyway." This constant attempt to convince ourselves that a matter of fact does not matter might actually be an important clue to understanding acts of belonging. This legitimization of not coming out to one's families belies an awareness of the importance of "coming out" for the individual with whom we are communicating. In other words, if the weight of "coming out" was not felt by the individual, the lack of this process would not require a reasoning or legitimization.

For example, Berrin claims that her parents and her aunt actually "have the same mentality, actually." She pauses and seems to be thinking over what she has just said. "Definitely so." Why does she not talk with the parents, then, instead of talking with the aunt?

They shouldn't know in the sense that they will feel like they have to lie to everybody else. They can't tell relatives, it will be too complex. Since they wouldn't want that to happen, they will have to lie to others because of me, they will have to hide. I don't want to put them in that situation . . . they love me unconditionally. But I mean I don't want to put them into that complex situation, it just doesn't make sense.

It is still a relief, however, to have the aunt know. Why is it a relief to talk to the aunt? How is it any different from talking to a friend, for instance?

> Because my aunt is like my family. Not like telling any person whatsoever . . . I just thought she deserved to know. I mean towards her I feel like . . . I have a reason to not tell my mom, but my aunt doesn't have that responsibility, so . . . I said to her "I would like to talk with you about something." I said "I am gay." She said "you can't be gay you are a girl," I said "then I am homosexual." She said "oh okay then." Then she said "Oh, I thought you were going to say 'I became vegetarian'!"—she's a very funny lady. If you become a vegetarian, my family excommunicates you!

The extended family—aunts, cousins, or grandparents—seems to be playing a significant role in these coming out stories. It is sometimes the family members themselves who broach the subject. Ayben, currently in her late 30s, recalls a time from years ago when she visited her grandparents in a small Turkish town, with her then girlfriend. Her grandfather tells her they "need to talk."

> "Yes father?" and so on. "So when it's love between two girls, they call them lesbians, right?" I said yes. Wow the man actually uses the word. "When it is women-to-women are they again called lesbians?" "Yes,

father, they are called lesbians also." "You also make love, right?" "Yes, we do." He said "Hmm" and then started to stare into the abyss in a quite ostentatious way! He said: "This, Ayben, does not go along with our religion, doesn't go along with our culture"—"Yes, father." "But you are our grandchild[7] and we love you." This is how they accepted it. His last word, however, was, he said: "But if your brother comes here with a man, I'd chase him away all the way to hell." "Oh come on father, he's not like that" [she laughs]. This is how he accepted it.

Elvan, a social worker and a university instructor, thinks that more "educated" parents find it harder to "accept" the daughter's "situation" as these parents are "know-it-alls."

> They see it [queerness/homosexuality] as a disease. She is ill, let's do a therapy, let's do something, where did we go wrong . . . I mean they correlate homosexuality with disease, or she has had a psychological challenge, or something happened when she was little. Like we can fix this.

"My family" says Elvan, "they are so simple . . . mom is illiterate, had 9 children, raised them all and so on. . . . Who loves what [moves her hand as if to say it does not matter]. What matters [for her mother, and thus for people like her mother] is that the daughter is happy." Does this mean they would "accept" Elvan with her girlfriend had she visited the family—and if so, how would the reaction be? They would treat the girlfriend "as a friend," Elvan says.

> They wouldn't judge like who is this or what is this. Oh I can't know what it would be like if they had a son, if my feudal family had a gay son. But with women . . . For example I have these friends who're living together, dad is very happy about this. He says to me "you shouldn't live on your own either. Look how they are being comrades to each other." I mean if I tell them today that I'm moving in with another woman, nobody would question me like "do you have a relationship with this woman or not." "Oh, it's good, see, she's not being lonely."

Dervise, on the other hand, claims her right for her sexual orientation to be known by her family. "It is my right for them to know," she says.

> And it is their right also. If I say that I love my mother and my father, and that they love me also, and that I am sure of this, this love has

to pass a few things, you know, if it [the love] lives without weathering any storm, this love is nothing in the end. Some storms must be weathered, some bridges must be built . . . But for this, you have to spend time; nothing happens without labor.

Sometimes, sexuality and sexual orientation-based identifications and terminologies are used in order to "punch them in the face": Ida, my only non-Turkish interviewee, talks about "certain spaces when politics is completely private. So like sometimes I choose [when being asked about her sexual orientation] lesbian." Her "labeling" herself as lesbian, especially in Slovenia, where older "lesbians" accept younger "queers" as not political enough, is doing exactly this: being political, doing politics through and through, as she "knows" that "if an outsider calls me a lesbian . . . I know that they mean it in a bad way."

Her relation with her parents who are "homophobic" affect Ida's relation with her girlfriend who has not experienced a similar difficulty coming from her family. "For me," Ida says, continuing only along with many pauses in between, "my parents . . . they are clearly working class . . . and they never came to something like this . . . it was like a long process . . . ." When at one point her mother "blames" feminism and suggests her relationship with another woman is "like a political relationship, or based on our political fight," Ida uses the S-word: "I said that's partly true, but I also want to have sex with her, it's like desire, I want to have her in my bed."

Her deliberate use of desire and sex is also political, being part of her aim to "get rid of this picture of ignorance." On the other hand, though, Ida presents a somehow altered image of herself: Her sexual desire is actually oriented towards all genders, not specifically and only towards women; but she does not want to create doubt in her parents. By staying silent about her sexual involvement with men, Ida tries to prevent her parents from thinking that she "would change my mind, you know? . . . I'm not going to change my mind because of what you say, even though I am attracted to any gender."

Her lesbian identity, therefore, is political, and is "because of the society . . . when it comes to society I say okay, that's when I do politics."

To conclude

Ilkay is one of many of my respondents who say they are "a Berliner." I ask her, then, to draw a map of "her Berlin"—whatever makes her identify with the city. She explains to me the spots she is marking on the map. "Here is the film . . . the script," she says, "I want to make my film within a year." I want to make sure that I do not misunderstand her:

> Do you mean this is where you work at?
> No, it's not about the place I work at, it's something that I do. And there's the "cinema seed" [a movie screening project she is organizing.][8] And there's another project of mine.

And she continues to explain her ideas and projects she is planning to accomplish in the near future. Even Facebook is marked on the map of "her Berlin." Laughing, she explains that she has more than one Facebook profiles in order to "fight"; that is, do online activism without necessarily being recognized with her "true" identity. "An Austrian fascist page," she claims recently has been closed down thanks to those who joined her fight.

This essay started with the suggestion that the need to belong derives from the feeling of anxiety. This feeling is both universal, that is, individuals embody anxiety from birth, and it is also exacerbated in the "liquid modernity" of our time. The aim here is to convince the reader to start recognizing, acknowledging, and embracing this anxiety and to keep reminding ourselves that belonging is possible in spite of conflict, doubt, and anxiety. It is very crucial not to repress the experience of anxiety or to rationalize it in terms of "fears" and finding "demons." I think that denial of conflict, ambiguity, pain, and anxiety in favor of idealized characteristics such as coherence, wholeness, and consistency in our modern societies has affected not only our sense of being with others but also the sense of our being among others. If, instead of insisting on an imagined coherence within ourselves and with others, we rather accept the possibility of the feeling of belonging in spite of conflict, doubt, and anxiety, both the individual lives and the well-beings of societies will be positively altered.

There is not one way to belong. Not one way to integrate. Our multiple identifications might really be in conflict with one another. And conflict might very well come in destructive forms but not always, not necessarily. What we *do* reveals both this complexity and the very possibility to embrace and accept our conflictual situations while alleviating possible burdens. Real life, daily life, is complex: we constantly try to be "in tune" within ourselves. But we cannot "tune" in ourselves without simultaneously "orienting" ourselves in the everyday life—within and among people who are both similar to and different from us. Therefore we need to "complexify" the theoretical discussions on citizenship and migration also. Doing this will be possible by attaching importance to the psychic component and the "acts" in the everyday.

Notes

1. Engin Isin et. al. also mention "acts of forgiveness" as one type of an act of citizenship and give the example of Greek aristocrats in 594 BCE who "committed an act of forgiveness when they cancelled all debts owed by peasants" (Ibid.: 25).
2. "Our Police Order—What can be Said, Seen, and Done: An Interview with Jacques Rancière," originally published in *Le Monde Diplomatique* (Oslo), November 8, 2006, available at http://anselmocarranco.tripod.com/id58.html access date 7/7/2011.
3. Barry Smart, on Michel Foucault's understanding of the notion of finitude. In Barry Smart, Michel Foucault, London: Routledge, 2002, 31, cited in Rey Chow, The Age of the World Target: Self-Referentiality in War, Theory, and Comparative Work, Duke University Press, 2006, 93, n. 2.
4. National Institute of Mental Health publication on anxiety disorders, available at http://www.nimh.nih.gov/health/publications/anxiety-disorders/introduction.shtml access date 11/29/2011.
5. Rank also criticizes Freud for overemphasizing castration and the "libido problem" with regard to the matter of separation from the mother. See "Otto Rank answers Freud on anxiety," 1926, available at http://www.scribd.com/doc/199683569/Anxiety
6. One is reminded of Jan Paul Sartre who suggests that we are "condemned to be free." See Paul Tillich's views in May 1977: 15. Similarly, Søren Kierkegaard defines freedom as possibility, and talks about "the alarming possibility of being able" (Ibid.: 37 and 40 italics original). Kierkegaard describes anxiety as "not a fear of a specific threat, but a fear of nothingness" (See Voegelin, 2003: 405), http://www.ottorank.com/essays/rank-answers-freud-on-anxiety access date 11/30/2011.
7. Turkish is a gender neutral language. The grandfather uses a gender neutral term ("torun") which can only be translated as "grandchild."
8. A brilliant idea and a very creative name, I remember having thought to myself. Following the "intense seed cracking tradition" Ilkay talked about earlier, the "cinema seed" mostly shows old Turkish films at a well-known bar/club in Kottbusser Tor in Kreuzberg, Berlin.

References

Agamben, G. (2003) *The Coming Community: Theory Out of Bounds (Vol. 1)*, Minneapolis: University of Minnesota Press.

Allon, F. (2000) 'Nostalgia Unbound: Illegibility and the Synthetic Excess of Place', *Continuum: Journal of Media & Cultural Studies*, 14 (3), 275–287.

Bauman, Z. (2000) *Liquid Modernity* (Oxford: Blackwell).

Chow, R. (2006) *The Age of the World Target: Self-Referntiality in War, Theory, and Comparative Work* (Durham: Duke University Press).

Freud, S. (1964) *The Problem of Anxiety*, trans. H. A. Bunker (American ed.) (New York: W.W. Norton & Company).

Freud, S. ([1922] 1990) *Group Psychology and the Analysis of the Ego* (New York and London: W.W. Norton & Company).

Fromm, E. (1960) *Fear of Freedom* (London: Routledge).

Horney, K. (1945) *Our Inner Conflicts* (New York: W.W. Norton & Company).

Isin, E. and G. M. Nielson (2008) *Acts of Citizenship* (London and New York: Zed Books).

May, R. (1977) *The Meaning of Anxiety* (New York: W.W. Norton & Company).

Smart, B. (2002) *Michel Foucault* (London: Routledge).

Voegelin, E. (2003) *The Collected Works of Eric Voegelin*, Vol. 32, The theory of governance and other miscellaneous papers, 1921–1938 (Missouri: University of Missouri Press).

Index

"9-11 Truther" movement, 180–1
Nokia, 320
normal anxiety, 406
normalization process, 407
Notman, M., 133

Obama, B., 178, 179, 289
Obeyesekere, G., 134, 135, 220
objective anxiety, 406
Occupy Our Homes, 280–1
Oedipus complex theory, 26–7
O'Grady, E., 256
Olascoaga, S., 281
orecticism, 376
Oremland, J., 114
other, 57, 60, 66, 68, 151, 272, 294
  generalized, 193
  racial, 286
over-attachment, 30

Paige, P., 256
paranoia, 6, 7, 11, 57
  ideological, 146
  political, 61
paranoid
  anxieties/fears versus paranoid
    thinking, 54
  constructs in psychoanalysis,
    theoretical overview of, 56–8
  -depressive position, 57, 71
  fears, 54, 57, 60, 61
  responses, of early American
    psychologists, 53–72
  thinking, 54, 57, 58, 61
Parson, T., 3–4, 5, 22–3, 41, 46–7, 48,
    55, 66, 68, 103–4, 126, 146,
    161, 164, 196, 222
Parsons' Department of Human
    Relations, 46
participatory democracy, new
    social movement ethic of,
    78, 92
partisanship, 140, 146
Patriot Act, 180
performance, 384
person, 191
Person, E., 133
Persona, 256
personal, sociological as, 190–1

personality
  authoritarian, 40, 62, 164, 180, 183,
    361
  -based theories, 361–3
  bigoted, 364
  formation and public opinion,
    relationship between, 25
  public, 32
  social, 63
  social structure and, 63
  terrorist, 113
personal troubles and public issues,
    distinction between, 151–2,
    190, 191, 199, 200
phallocentric, 208
phallonarcissism, 207, 208
pilgrimage studies, 383
Piven, Frances Fox, 178, 179
Platt, Gerald, 34
political story, of racial harted/
    prejudice, 367–9
political unconscious, 152
politics, 391–9
Porta, D. della, 262
postmodernism-poststructuralism,
    128
poststructuralism, 128
post-structuralist approaches to
    racism, 366–7
post-traumatic stress, 94n7, 342, 352,
    353
Powell, M., 300, 301
power elite
  academic, 197
  sociological, 198
Prager, J., 11, 116–17, 229, 284
preconscious, 152
predictability, 221–2
prejudgment, 363, 364
prejudice
  ethnic, 363
  nature of, 370
  racial, 12, 108, 359–78
    cognitive turn, 363–5
    discursive turn, 365
    personality-based theories of,
      361–3
    political story of, 367–9
    research story of, 369–74

Printed and bound by CPI Group (UK) Ltd, Croydon, CR0 4YY